Does Decentralization Enhance Service Delivery and Poverty Reduction?

STUDIES IN FISCAL FEDERALISM AND STATE–LOCAL FINANCE

Series Editor: Wallace E. Oates, *Professor of Economics, University of Maryland, College Park and University Fellow, Resources for the Future, USA*

This important series is designed to make a significant contribution to the development of the principles and practices of state–local finance. It includes both theoretical and empirical work. International in scope, it addresses issues of current and future concern in both East and West and in developed and developing countries.

The main purpose of the series is to create a forum for the publication of high-quality work and to show how economic analysis can make a contribution to understanding the role of local finance in fiscal federalism in the twenty-first century.

Titles in the series include:

Reforming Intergovernmental Fiscal Relations and the Rebuilding of Indonesia
The 'Big Bang' Program and its Economic Consequences
Edited by James Alm, Jorge Martinez-Vazquez and Sri Mulyani Indrawati

Competition in the Provision of Local Public Goods
Single Function Jurisdictions and Individual Choice
Alexandra Petermann Reifschneider

Decentralization in Asia and Latin America
Towards a Comparative Interdisciplinary Perspective
Edited by Paul Smoke, Eduardo J. Gómez and George E. Peterson

The Politics and Economics of Regional Transfers
Decentralization, Interregional Redistribution and Income Convergence
Fabio Padovano

Fiscal Reform in Spain
Accomplishments and Challenges
Edited by Jorge Martinez-Vazquez and José Félix Sanz-Sanz

Fiscal Federalism and Political Decentralization
Lessons from Spain, Germany and Canada
Edited by Núria Bosch and José M. Durán

The Theory and Practice of Local Government Reform
Edited by Brian E. Dollery and Lorenzo Robotti

The Political Economy of Financing Scottish Government
Considering a New Constitutional Settlement for Scotland
C. Paul Hallwood and Ronald MacDonald

Does Decentralization Enhance Service Delivery and Poverty Reduction?
Edited by Ehtisham Ahmad and Giorgio Brosio

State and Local Fiscal Policy
Thinking Outside the Box?
Edited by Sally Wallace

Does Decentralization Enhance Service Delivery and Poverty Reduction?

Edited by

Ehtisham Ahmad

International Monetary Fund, USA

Giorgio Brosio

University of Turin, Italy

STUDIES IN FISCAL FEDERALISM AND STATE–LOCAL FINANCE

Edward Elgar

Cheltenham, UK • Northampton, MA, USA

Published by
Edward Elgar Publishing Limited
The Lypiatts
15 Lansdown Road
Cheltenham
Glos GL50 2JA
UK

Edward Elgar Publishing, Inc.
William Pratt House
9 Dewey Court
Northampton
Massachusetts 01060
USA

A catalogue record for this book
is available from the British Library

Library of Congress Control Number: 2009936230

Mixed Sources
Product group from well-managed
forests and other controlled sources
www.fsc.org Cert no. SA-COC-1565
© 1996 Forest Stewardship Council
FSC

ISBN 978 1 84844 552 9

Printed and bound by MPG Books Group, UK

Contents

PART III SELECTED NORMATIVE AND POLICY ISSUES

Contributors

Ehtisham Ahmad, International Monetary Fund

Pranab Bardhan, University of California, Berkeley

Regina Birner, International Food Policy Research Institute

Giorgio Brosio, University of Turin

Shantayanan Devarajan, The World Bank

Maria Gonzalez, International Monetary Fund

Gabriela Inchauste, Inter-American Development Bank

Maciej Jakubowski, Warsaw University and CASE (Center for Social and Economic Research), Warsaw

Stuti Khemani, The World Bank

Lili Liu, The World Bank

Ben Lockwood, University of Warwick

Jean-Philippe Platteau, University of Namur

Shekhar Shah, The World Bank

Albert Solé-Ollé, University of Barcelona

Irena Topińska, CASE (Center for Social and Economic Research), Warsaw

Joachim von Braun, International Food Policy Research Institute

Michael Waibel, University of Cambridge and Lauterpacht Centre for International Law

Preface

This volume is a follow-up to the *Handbook of Fiscal Federalism* published by Edward Elgar in 2006. It uses the insights of the *Handbook* to discuss issues of immediate policy relevance – and of interest to governments and international agencies alike. It focuses on a framework for effective service delivery and poverty alleviation at the local level particularly, although not exclusively, in developing countries.

Most of the papers in the volume were commissioned specially for presentation at a seminar on the Effectiveness of Decentralized Strategies and Outcomes organized by the Centro Studi sul Federalismo at the Collegio Carlo Alberto in Moncalieri, Turin, on 3 and 4 September 2007. Authors of the commissioned papers attended the seminar, along with representatives of international and bilateral donor organizations actively involved in the decentralization processes around the world. Some papers were commissioned after the seminar.

The Seminar on the Effectiveness of Decentralized Strategies and Outcomes represents the second stage in the cooperation between the Centro Studi and the editors, following an earlier seminar in August 2005 devoted to the preparation of the *Handbook of Fiscal Federalism*. The support of the Centro Studi sul Federalismo and particularly its Director, Professor Umberto Morelli, and its Secretary, Dr Paolo Caraffini, is gratefully acknowledged. Without their outstanding contribution to the success of the seminar, the completion of this volume would not have been possible.

1. Does decentralization enhance service delivery and poverty reduction?

Ehtisham Ahmad and Giorgio Brosio

1 MOTIVATION

Does decentralization enhance service delivery and poverty reduction? This is a fundamental question facing policy-makers in developing as well as advanced countries. It is equally important for international agencies as well as bilateral donors, seeking to provide resources and advice that effectively support poverty reduction. This volume builds on the insights of the recent developments in the intergovernmental literature, reviewed in the *Handbook of Fiscal Federalism*[1] (hereafter *Handbook*). We also present some new empirical evidence from different parts of the world, which have built on both efficiency and distributional aspects stressed in the *Handbook*.

In this volume, we first present a set of policy-oriented papers that take further the discussion of aspects of the literature on fiscal federalism that have a bearing on the evaluation of the effectiveness of decentralized service delivery. We also present a set of careful empirical evaluations of the decentralization process in different parts of the world. Some, including the United Nations Development Programme-sponsored study of the decentralization of education and health care in Poland, and those on Bolivia and Uganda, were commissioned to focus on the political economy process and the outcomes of the decentralization process, specifically building on the insights from the *Handbook*.

2 THE ISSUES

2.1 Trends in the Practice of Decentralization and Federalism

Most countries have experimented with variants of decentralization reforms in the last three decades, addressing different motivations for decentralization. A few have embarked on ambitious decentralization processes requiring constitutional revisions. The most notable cases have been the federalization of Belgium and of Ethiopia, the regionalization of Spain, Italy, France and the United Kingdom. The post-apartheid constitution of South Africa presents an interesting case of a quasi-federal system. The decentralization processes in natural-resource-rich countries, including Indonesia, Nigeria and more recently in Sudan and Iraq, are clearly driven by considerations to keep the country together. Noticeable decentralization reforms have also been introduced in almost all Latin American countries, notably, in Bolivia, although the process is far from complete. The African continent presents a wide array of decentralization processes, some instigated by donors. In other cases, the emphasis on decentralization grew out of political economy solutions to perceived problems of nationhood or governance. In addition to above-mentioned cases of Ethiopia and South Africa, extensive decentralization reforms have been introduced in Uganda and Nigeria.

Despite these changes, decentralization reforms are still far from complete. Countries such as Italy, Spain and Bolivia are debating how to proceed further down the decentralization path. Others, such as, for example, Nepal, are just initiating the decentralization process. Some countries, such as Denmark and Norway, are experiencing recentralization—for example, by transferring extremely important responsibilities, such as the management of hospitals, from counties to newly created regions.

Important changes in intergovernmental relations are taking place under the surface, such as the increasing popularity of contracting between levels of government, the extensive use of asymmetric arrangements and the proliferation of intergovernmental coordinating bodies. These changes lead to a deep reconsideration of essential parts of federal and fiscal federalism theory. For example, contracts imply that the traditional hierarchical links between levels of government are no longer the (most important) organizing principle of intergovernmental relations, even in traditional unitary systems. These newer institutional forms need to be carefully assessed, as the preconditions for their effective use may not be in place in many countries—responsive legal systems and modern budget frameworks that can identify outcomes.

2.2 The Expansion of the Literature: Normative Versus Positive Focus

The literature on decentralization is rapidly expanding; reflecting with some lags the rapid changes in the real world. The abundance of reviews of the so-called second-generation fiscal federalism (Lockwood in this volume; Oates, 2005 and 2008; Rodden, 2006; Weingast, 2009) is an indicator of this evolution. In fact, if we take a broad and very long-term vision and combine approaches and contributions by economists and political scientists, we should distinguish at least three waves or generations of federalist/decentralization theories.

The first wave is the classical one and relies on the works of Montesquieu and of the authors of the *Federalist Papers*[2] (1787–88), namely Hamilton and Madison. Pre-dating or coexistent with, the creation of the first federal systems these authors had no choice but to be normative. Their main concern was that, to constrain the malevolence of public officials, governments had to be small and separated and that only functions affecting wide areas, such as defense and monetary policy, should be assigned to the central government. This led to the idea of dual federalism with two completely separated spheres of autonomous powers for the federal government and the federated states.

The second wave is the theory of fiscal federalism. It was built on the (opposite) assumption that governments are inspired by the public interest (otherwise, it was implied, there would be no need for government). According to this theory, the benefits of decentralization are similar to those generated by market competition. That is, decentralized government allows a better matching of preferences with policies by bringing governments closer to people and thus increasing efficiency.

The third wave—which is referred to in the literature as the second generation of fiscal federalism—replaces the benevolent government assumption with the more realistic one of self-serving officials and politicians. Thus, institutions are critical in determining the effects of centralized or decentralized government—and it becomes necessary to examine the political, legal-constitutional and economic context, such as the structure of political parties, bicameralism, the allocation of responsibilities between governments and economic disparities between local jurisdictions. The role assigned to institutions accounts for the large number and the variety of contributions to the literature. Most of this literature has a theoretical orientation with relatively few applied papers at this time.

2.3 The Importance of Empirical Studies of Effective Outcomes

Not surprisingly, much of the present empirical literature by economists is devoted to the testing of the hypotheses laid down by the theory of fiscal federalism. The studies can be regrouped into three main groups according to the object of their research: preference matching, allocative efficiency and the impact on growth and convergence (see more below in the review by Ahmad and Brosio in Chapter 6 of this volume). The popularity of empirical tests of the fiscal federalism hypothesis is easily explained, not only by the simplicity of the hypothesis (this does not mean that they are easy to test), but also by their relevance. Even if one recognizes that decentralization is almost always an eminently political process and that political processes are rarely promoted exclusively, or mainly, by purely economic considerations, such as in the case of ethnically driven federalization, it is essential at the end of the day to check if a decentralized system of government is able to effectively provide services, moreover, that these are less expensive, or of a better quality, or closer to citizens' preferences than those provided by a centralized system. This is even more important for developing countries, where particularly donors and international organizations view decentralization as an essential instrument for the alleviation of poverty.

The practical policy considerations explain the attention devoted in this volume to country studies on preference matching and allocative efficiency, as well as distributional and political economy considerations. It is also sustained by methodological and information considerations. As mentioned before, assessing the outcomes of decentralization in terms of preference matching and allocative efficiency requires a considerable amount of detailed information on policies and the delivery of services. Data from household surveys and their merging with data from budget documents are the most promising source of information, as shown also in this volume by the chapter on Poland (Chapter 9) and by the survey of the literature provided by Ahmad and Brosio in Chapter 6. The assessment of outcomes also requires a methodology that allows assigning each level of government its due; that is, to disentangle the impact on outcomes deriving from concurrent policies pursued by different levels of government. Obviously, decentralization does not occur in a vacuum or in abstraction from the policies of the central government. Furthermore, each level of government, particularly the central government, has a built-in interest to influence the outcomes of decentralization that it may have sponsored. In some cases, as in Latin American countries in the 1990s, central government politicians may be genuinely interested in the success of decentralization, because this will increase the legitimacy of the political class, countrywide. In other cases, they may be interested to undermine the viability of lower levels of government by engineering decentralized systems devoid, for example, of taxing powers (Ahmad and Brosio, 2008).

2.4 Political Economy and Institutions

The role of incentives for politicians and the importance of institutional considerations resurface constantly and explain the attention given in this volume to a few selected issues. These are the risk of local capture, partial decentralization and the importance of fiscal institutions, particularly the assignment of functions, the structure of intergovernmental transfers and limits on local debt.

There is a need to stress again the relevance of local capture and corruption in shaping the outcomes of decentralized government. The Madisonian "violence of factions" (*Federalist Papers*, No. X) is nowadays possibly the most quoted reference to the political risks of decentralization. Factions and their capture of governments can work also at the lowest and least institutionalized level of government, such as villages and local communities, and their working is determined largely by the gaps in the inflow of information, as shown in Chapter 2 by Platteau in this volume.

Partial decentralization is both a telling example of the "tragic brilliance mechanism" suggested by Weingast (2008) and of the risk of embarking on decentralization processes without properly designed institutions. It can be depicted as a state of the (decentralized) world where political and fiscal institutions are not able to ensure accountability of local elected politicians and officials. We have partial decentralization when, among other occurrences, local governments lack control over tax instruments at the margin, so that they remain dependent on central government grants and revenue shares and correspondingly are less accountable to their electorates. We also have partial decentralization when weak constraints are introduced on borrowing, thus increasing the chances that local governments will be bailed out by the central government. Another example is poor structure of intergovernmental grants, as exemplified by Ahmad in Chapter 12 of this volume with reference to problems with specific transfers geared to poverty alleviation policies.

2.5 Normative Prescriptions

The social scientist's role is to explain the working of the real world (positive analysis) and assist policy-makers in designing policies. To correctly design the tax system the social scientist and more specifically the economist needs to consider incentives, and to assess also all the possible impacts of the policy recommendations. The policies assignment issue exemplifies the difficulty of the task. The fiscal federalism theory was based on simple and clear criteria, the benefit principle and economies of scale, but turned out to be a poor depiction of the real world and a poor source of policy advice, because it lacked political considerations and underpinning. For example, although defense fulfills all criteria for centralization, it still remains decentralized in the EU (and the United Arab Emirates) and all calls from the fiscal federalism theory for its assignment to the center (Oates, 2002) have received no attention by national politicians. Very few attempts have been made in the literature to clarify the assignment problem (Dafflon in Ahmad and Brosio, 2006, is an exception).

However, the issue is crucial, particularly for developing countries, where the burden on local government is increased by the additional task of implementing poverty alleviation policies, often with very unclear boundaries or accountability. The chapter by Birner and von Braun in this volume (Chapter 11) is an attempt to fill the gap.

3 POSITIVE APPROACHES

3.1 Decentralization and Participatory Developments

The chapter by Platteau (Chapter 2) illustrates perfectly the political-economy focus of this volume, and presents some interesting additional insights on participatory development. At first sight, this topic might appear to be only loosely connected with decentralization issues. This is because the participatory development literature focuses on single non-repeated projects, where stakeholders are involved in a finite game, and where reputation mechanisms cannot be built due to the short time period and, thus, it is harder to ensure adherence to commitments.

With fiscal decentralization, it is possible to characterize stakeholders as operating in multi-period games, where reputation can be built, and consequently it is possible to ensure that commitments are met. Thus, in principle, the results from the participatory development literature should be weaker than those on fiscal decentralization. However, on examination it becomes clear that insights from participatory development assessments provide new perspectives that deepen the understanding of the decentralization processes.

The literature on participatory development usually refers to small communities and service user groups, and generally relates to political and institutional organizations that are typically below formal local governments. Applied studies on participatory development use evidence collected in the field, which is not easily replicable or comparable, but allows a deeper level of analysis. For example, in the context of small communities it is possible to model the working of the political process with a greater level of detail than that of typical decentralized governments that rely on standard decision-making procedures, such as majority voting and party competition. Platteau very interestingly juxtaposes applied studies relating to China and Korea, where local accountability is linked to the introduction of formal specific incentives schemes, with studies of local communities in India, where formal democratic institutions do not ensure accountability.

Field studies may be used to collect information on local preferences and priorities and accurately test the effectiveness of preference matching by decentralized governments. The main message of the chapter is that the advantages typically associated with decentralized, or participatory approaches to development, are not as clear as they appear at first sight and that these approaches are much more complex than is often imagined by donors. The success of participatory projects is highly dependent on social stratification of communities and the consequent distribution of powers. Equally important is the information flows between donors and sponsors as well as with beneficiary communities and formal levels of government.

Platteau cautions that multilateral donors' intentions concerning decentralization can be a major distraction, community preferences may be overwritten by donors, or elites or brokers may be able to divert funds away from intended purposes. The dilemma remains that in the areas where inequalities are the highest and the most entrenched, and where one would most like to implement participatory approaches, are those where these approaches are least likely to succeed

3.2 Accountability

Bardhan's paper in Chapter 3 summarizes approaches to accountability and local capture based on his recent work (Bardhan, 2006; Bardhan and Mookherjee, 2006a, 2006b). This chapter complements the assessment by Platteau in providing a concise illustration of the dilemmas facing decentralized provision of public services at the local level. Local provision, Bardhan maintains, can represent an adequate solution to the dilemma between autonomy and accountability of decision-makers. Autonomy is required to isolate decision-makers from short-term political pressure and ensure their commitment to the public interest. At the same time, isolation may lead to arbitrary governance and abuse. At the lowest local level, such as that of villages and small communities, local provision may ensure commitment of people to long-term projects and vigilance on politicians. This is mostly because at the local level there is more visibility of policies and immediate interest towards them.

However, Bardhan is more than conscious of the risks of local capture and of the need for introducing institutions that can reduce this risk. These include a competitive political process, free flow of information and an expanded network of NGOs and reduction of inequality. The latter is, at the same time, one of the main objectives of the policies whose assignment is under discussion.

Finally, a consistent decentralization strategy is also crucial. If, for example, devolution of tax responsibilities does not follow devolution of expenditure functions, local politicians will not have sufficient incentives to ensure accountability (see also Ambrosiano and Bordignon, 2006), even if they are selected by a proper political process and are constantly monitored by their voters. This leads to possibilities of partial decentralization, explored later in the volume by Devarajan, Khemani and Shah in Chapter 5.

3.3 Political Economy Perspectives

Lockwood in Chapter 4 provides a well-structured survey of some recent and mainly theoretical contributions to the study of fiscal decentralization from a political economy viewpoint that build on his earlier survey (see also Lockwood, 2006). He argues that the standard approach to fiscal federalism, based on the idea of benevolent governments and policy uniformity, cannot provide a rigorous treatment of the preference matching and accountability benefits of decentralization, but the political economy approaches provide a better explanation. When the benevolent government assumption is dropped and political institutions and their impact on the behavior of politicians are introduced, most of the main findings of the traditional literature are modified, or reversed. For example, if there are identical preferences, decentralization welfare-dominates a centralized system, even if there are externalities. However, if preferences differ across regions, centralized systems welfare-dominate decentralization, even when there are no externalities.

Lockwood devotes a great deal of attention to reviewing the impact of citizens' information on accountability in centralized/decentralized arrangements. This makes it possible to focus on the possible extent of capture of the benefits of decentralization by local elites.

A suggestion coming from Lockwood's contribution is that the political economy literature, insofar as it relies on specific but more realistic hypotheses, generates conclusions that are less general than those provided by the traditional theory. However, these tend to be much more useful in terms of guidance to policy-making.

3.4 Partial Decentralization

Devarajan, Khemani and Shah (Chapter 5) deal in depth with the issue of partial decentralization. This is increasingly considered in the literature (including in the chapters by Bardhan and Lockwood in this volume, Chapters 3 and 4) as a major obstacle to successful provision of decentralized public services.

Devarajan, Khemani and Shah show that most problems with decentralization stem from a somewhat under-emphasized aspect of the design, namely that attempts at decentralization have not led to citizens' being able to hold local governments accountable for budgetary allocations and their outcomes. In this situation, defined as partial decentralization, local governments have no discretion to choose among competing uses subject to a budget constraint, and citizens are not conscious of this and have no way of evaluating whether the government's decision was a good one. For instance, we have partial decentralization in education when local government is not responsible for allocating resources between education and other sectors. For all sectors, partial decentralization prevails with central-government-led or earmarked schemes for capital expenditures even when it gives untied grants to local governments for current expenditures.

In many decentralization processes, particularly in countries of Africa and South Asia (but as we see in this volume, this is also widespread in Latin America), local village-level governments, which represent the lowest tier, have limited access to own tax bases, and generally have no ownership over a defined policy space. This is generally because politicians at higher levels of government have designed decentralization to be partial. This may be a vestige from the centralization of the past, distrust of the lower levels, or driven by the allure of "influence peddling". As a result, local agents largely perform functions at the behest of the center/province. When decentralization is thus determined by politicians, it reduces local government incentives to pursue "effectiveness" of spending and policies, and results in the provision of narrowly targeted or "club" goods. In other words, it opens the door to clientelistic policies.

Similarly, donor-driven decentralization can ironically lead to partial decentralization even when the objective is the opposite. This happens when greater resources are provided to local jurisdictions to distribute among small local communities, without proper specification of the role of local preferences as well as hard budget constraints.

According to the authors, partial decentralization may well lead to capture of local resources by the elites. However, even without local capture, partial decentralization dilutes the incentives that citizens have to ensure that officials make effective use of resources. Further, without a full assessment of the tradeoffs across public policy options, with partial decentralization poor individuals may prefer projects that are of short gestation such as public works that provide immediate benefits in terms of wage payments, rather than education that may well have larger personal and social benefits in the longer run.

4 WHAT DO WE KNOW?

4.1 A Cross-country Assessment

Ahmad and Brosio in Chapter 6 survey the existing empirical literature on the impact of decentralization in terms of the effectiveness of service delivery. By considering the main avenues of the present empirical research and by trying to assess its results, the chapter provides a methodological introduction to the country-specific papers that follow.

Decentralization is a process through which the role and importance of subnational governments is expanded. This expansion can take place through three main different avenues. (1) Political decentralization involves devolution of political authority, or of electoral capacities to subnational actors, such as the popular election of governors and mayors. (2) Fiscal decentralization involves a transfer of expenditure responsibilities to lower-level local governments, financed by a combination of own and other sources of revenues, including transfers. And (3) regulatory decentralization places mandates but does not imply an appreciable transfer of financial resources or assignments, although its impact may be considerable for citizens (that is, regulation of car emissions).

All forms of decentralization imply the transfer of some decision-making power over the use of public (fiscal) or private (regulatory) resources from the central to the subnational governments. When this transfer does not take place, there is no decentralization even in the case where numbers show a transfer of revenue and expenditure from higher to lower levels of government.

The empirical literature surveyed in the chapter is arranged in four distinct groups: (1) production efficiency; (2) preference matching; (3) convergence of service delivery and, (4) decentralization and growth. The survey of the theoretical and empirical literature suggests a few conclusions that may have far-reaching policy implications.

There is relatively poor evidence to characterize effective changes over time, using comparable administrative and household data sets—for OECD or developing countries, although this lacuna is now beginning to be addressed. Thus, links between decentralization and growth, convergence, efficiency, and the like are tenuous. Claims for improvements in developing countries may be due to the general development process and growth; linkages with decentralization are often tenuous. What evidence exists weakens even further as countries develop. In other words, the benefits of decentralization seem to be less evident in more advanced developing countries.

4.2 Bolivia

Bolivia is an interesting "laboratory" case study. Since the early 1990s Bolivia has undergone a major restructuring program and decentralization has been seen as one of the principal mechanisms to provide additional resources for the poorer and less developed regions of the country. This policy has also spawned a major strand in the literature extolling the virtues of decentralization (Faguet, 2000). Indeed, Bolivia is one of the few countries in which multilateral and bilateral funds from the enhanced Heavily Indebted Poor Countries (HIPC) initiative (derived from the cancellation of Bolivia's external debts) have been transferred directly to local governments. Conditional grants for health, education and other poverty alleviation policies have been provided. Inchauste's chapter (Chapter 7) focuses on the use made by local governments of the HIPC resources.

Inchauste's paper evaluates the effectiveness of decentralization processes over time, and specifically the use of the HIPC funds, by making use of both fiscal and household survey data. The paper, first, checks whether resources channeled to municipalities have been distributed as intended under the enhanced HIPC initiative, and whether there is any evidence of absorptive capacity constraints, particularly in the poor municipalities. It then investigates whether the resources that actually have been spent have had any impact on the social indicators, such as the illiteracy rate, rate of unattended respiratory diseases and household access to electricity and water.

The detailed analysis performed by Inchauste on the links between additional revenue and improvement of social indicators does not provide convincing evidence of the efficient working of local governments. For example, poorer municipalities show substantial problems in transforming increased resource availability into effective spending. A significant capacity problem exists at the local level. For education, for example, increases in education transfers do not significantly affect the share of children not attending school. When looking at infrastructure indicators, there is still no significant effect of changes in spending or transfers on the share of homes with access to water and electricity.

More generally, there is no evidence of a clear improvement of conditions in the poorest municipalities, or for the poorest segments of the population. This is partly due to the criteria used for the distribution of HIPC resources, which have not been specifically targeted only to the poorest regions. Inchauste's findings do not per se speak against decentralization, or provide arguments in favor of the central government since no contrary evidence exists. However, they cast doubts on the working of Bolivian local governments as an efficient instrument for poverty reduction policies.

Inchauste points to excessive earmarking of funds, which prevents the emergence of local priorities, and to misalignment of responsibilities between the central, regional and local governments. For example, although the central government continues to be responsible for payment of wages and salaries of education and health sector employees, it has weak control over staff, or the effective wage bill. This is because the aggregate wage bill is mostly determined at the local level, on the basis of the workload assigned to teachers and health workers by local committees, in which departments, municipalities and popular participation bodies are represented. In addition, the construction of schools and health premises and their maintenance are municipal responsibilities. Here, decisions are made on the basis of needs, on the availability of finance and on the constraints on the use of resources imposed from above. New construction generates new requests for personnel to run the premises and to provide services, but the separation of responsibilities leads to frequent discrepancies between building and staffing of new premises. As a result, there is evidence that in some municipalities, the availability of HIPC resources has led to the construction of new schools, which are ultimately not staffed and therefore not used due to lack of financing from the center for wages.

4.3 Uganda

Ahmad, Brosio and Gonzalez in Chapter 8 provide a detailed account of the working of decentralization in Uganda. This country is (or at least was until quite recently) considered one of the most successful examples of decentralization in Africa. The observation of effective outcomes and of most recent policy decisions suggests that a more nuanced view is in order.

Uganda has engaged in an ambitious decentralization reform over the last 15 years. Designed as a component of the political process of reconciliation following the civil war, decentralization quickly became enmeshed with the country's poverty-reduction strategy, as advocated by bilateral and some multilateral donors. Both political and expenditure devolution in key social areas took place relatively fast, supported by a rapid process of financial and administrative decentralization. This was not paralleled by an improved revenue generation capacity, or by the ability to make significant resource allocation decisions at the local level. Moreover, the tension between central financing and administrative controls, and the devolution of local responsibility for spending is at the core of the divergent forces that have prevented the full realization of the decentralization process.

Uganda provides additional evidence in favor of the theory of partial decentralization. Many of the new mandates were accompanied by a rigid system of conditional grants, possibly to mitigate the risks from low capacity and weak public financial management, and to ensure the appropriate tracking of pro-poor spending—all important requirements from the donor community that has financed more than half of Uganda's spending over the last ten years. However, the model undermined the generation of local autonomy in decision-making, and the system of horizontal accountability links that are at the root of strengthened performance by policy-makers in decentralized frameworks.

Uganda's decentralization reform appears to have fallen short of its promise in key areas of public service delivery. The assessment of service outcomes in key priority sectors—including education, health and water services—tends to provide only mixed results. The sector that has performed best—water services—received only a minimal share of the overall government expenditure over the last 15 years, but has structural features that favor the creation of grass-roots monitoring mechanisms and horizontal accountability. In addition, by being largely domestically financed, it has escaped from the decision-making restrictions faced by other sectors dealing with a largely rigid and politically sensitive wage component.

The education sector has been at the forefront of Uganda's development priorities since early in the 1990s and has received significantly more resources and scrutiny than other sectors—by the central and local governments, and by Uganda's development partners. To this extent, the improvements observed are not directly linked to the benefits of decentralization, but rather to the central government's efforts to strengthen basic education services, including through a tight monitoring system of the local authorities.

The available data hints at a worsening in health care performance. In fact, countrywide trends suggest that mortality indicators have generally deteriorated over the years. Information on infant and child mortality by regions also shows wide geographical variations, reflecting the structural characteristics of the regions. Going forward, Uganda has the option of providing greater responsibilities in the key sectors to the local authorities. Strengthening devolution and the ability to reallocate resources in line with local priorities and needs will require incentives for a better expenditure management cycle. There needs to be an emphasis on an improved budget process, reflecting local priorities, more careful execution and better and more streamlined reporting, to satisfy the requirements for quality assurance of Uganda's development partners. This process will have to be adequately sequenced to avoid failures in service delivery, especially in the poorer areas.

4.4 Poland

Poland is a veritable laboratory, as the decentralization process took place over the past 15 years and adequate data are available. Jakubowski and Topińska in Chapter 9 combine fiscal, household surveys and, in the case of education outcomes, administrative data to evaluate the results of decentralization of education in Poland. The chapter is an illustration of methods that can be used to evaluate the effects of decentralization—and also emphasizes that a combination of fiscal and household information is needed to carry out a proper evaluation of the process. Comparable pre-decentralization data is not available, but the authors look carefully at the working of the decentralized system in two different years, 1998 and 2003, and assume implicitly that with the passing of time decentralization should become more effective and thus capable of delivering expected results.

However, most of the results of their analysis cast a not very favorable light on the working of decentralization in Poland. For example, in pre-school education, decentralization seems to have decreased accessibility in the rural areas. Poorer, mostly rural, local governments (*gminas*) have closed kindergartens and have lowered their spending, while richer, mostly urban, *gminas* were able to increase participation rates during a period of population decline. For primary education, the analysis shows the opposite trend: local expenditure tends to be more spatially equalized over time. However, in the case of primary education, the central government regulatory and fiscal powers are still quite strong, and centrally provided transfers have a high equalizing content.

The most interesting piece of analysis provided by Jakubowski and Topińska refers to lower secondary education, where the authors check if variation in students' scores between two different years can be ascribed to variations in expenditure for education, after having controlled for most relevant factors relating both to students and local governments. Here fiscal, administrative and personal data from household surveys are fully integrated in the analysis. The results again do not speak much for decentralization. More specifically, the variation in decentralized expenditures is not correlated with the variation in educational outcomes. However, there are different explanations of these findings. Local governments have still to acquire, for example, the skills needed to manage education. In addition, education is still overregulated by the central government, leaving no room for the exercise of local autonomous decision-making power.

The chapter by Jakubowski and Topińska provides evidence on the problems associated with partial decentralization, particularly for primary and secondary education in Poland. Most crucial elements of the expenditures that make up the education function, particularly the wages and contracts for teachers, still remain in the hand of the central government.

4.5 Spain

As it is widely known, Spain constitutes not only an extremely interesting case of the transformation of a previously unitary state into a quasi-federal one, but it also provides through its asymmetric regionalization a unique opportunity for checking the outcomes of decentralization. Asymmetry allows a comparison of the results of policies referring to distinct political jurisdictions—the Autonomous Communities—characterized by different degrees of fiscal and regulatory decentralization. Solé-Ollé's paper in Chapter 10 provides empirical evidence on the outcomes of decentralization in Spain. The chapter summarizes and expands two previous papers authored, or co-authored, by Solé-Ollé. The first paper focuses on educational services and examines the effects of decentralization on the survival rate at the age of 16 (that is, the proportion of students in the last course of compulsory secondary education who gain access to non-compulsory post-secondary education). The methodology is quite accurate and provides reliable results that show that decentralization in Spain has actually improved, although at a relatively modest extent, the educational outcomes. In addition to this Solé-Ollé shows that the improvement is more substantial in rich and financially well managed regions.

The second paper surveyed analyzes the impact of decentralization on the pattern of investment in roads and education premises during 1977–98 in Spain. The paper is well constructed, although it is not *strictly* a test of preference matching, but rather an efficiency test of spending decisions. The main focus of the analysis is, in fact, testing if, after decentralization, investment decisions have been more closely targeted to effective needs, such as more road construction in congested areas and more school construction in areas with higher student population growth and if investment activities have become more cost conscious. The results show that with decentralization the regional allocation of investment in these two sectors has become better adapted to local conditions and needs, thus showing a higher level of efficiency than under the previous centralized regime.

Solé-Ollé concludes that decentralization had positive effects on efficiency: without decentralization the survival rate would have been on average 2 percent lower, and without decentralization, investment would have been allocated between jurisdictions in a manner less responsive to local needs and demands. At the same time, Solé-Ollé makes clear that the Spanish decentralized system is not free from problems. One of the main problems, according to the author is the inequity generated by the transfer system and the lack of consensus on the criteria, which should guide the allocation of grants.

5 NORMATIVE AND POLICY ISSUES

5.1 Decentralization and Poverty Reduction

Birner and von Braun's chapter (Chapter 11) is a contribution to the normative literature on fiscal federalism. Its aim is to set up a grid of criteria that can help policy-makers assign responsibilities to various levels of governments with a view to making service provision an effective tool in combating poverty. The main innovation is the use of the transaction costs approach, à la Williamson. According to this approach, the choice of the appropriate organization structure is based on the minimization of the sum of production costs plus transaction costs. The same principle should govern, according to Birner and von Braun, approaches to the assignment problem. The authors disentangle four different activities that affect transactions costs, namely: planning, production, financing, monitoring and activities needed to have access to service, such as queuing and travel. Furthermore, the grid presented in the chapter includes a number of attributes of policies that affect differentially on their cost of provision at different levels of government. The clearest example is heterogeneity of preferences. The cost-effectiveness approach proposed by Birner and von Braun also includes the consideration of factors, such as political capture and participation mechanisms. In this respect, the paper is differentiated from the traditional literature based on benevolent governments at all levels.

However, as the authors recognize in their conclusions, the analytical framework they construct does not cover the political economy of decentralization reforms. Reforming public services, such as health and education, is often confronted with bureaucratic and political resistance, while mobilization of service users, especially of the rural poor, is also a political process. Efficient assignment requires consideration of both normative/economic and positive/political issues. This volume in fact provides a blend of these considerations.

5.2 Better Design of Specific Grants with Incomplete Information

Ahmad in Chapter 12 examines the ways to enhance the effectiveness of decentralized poverty alleviation by a better design of intergovernmental financial relations, more specifically by a better design of specific grant programs. Designing central programs to reach the poorest individuals may be difficult without local information. This is because the central government, particularly in large countries such as Mexico and China, lacks the ability to precisely define marginal groups or households that may not benefit from more general growth and prosperity. Yet local officials may not share the objectives of the center—and may prefer to divert central funds to meet objectives that are of higher value to them. This policy dilemma illustrates difficulties with "overlapping" responsibilities between different levels of government and in designing effective special purpose programs, financed by the center and implemented by local governments.

The constraints in designing effective centrally determined special purpose programs in developing countries are legendary. In many respects, these are similar to the problems in designing foreign assistance strategies to effectively reach the poorest target groups in the recipient countries. The issue is to design policies that build on local information, yet minimize incentives at the local level to divert resources from the target groups to more "personalized" objectives.

The chapter starts with a detailed illustration of the difficulties of targeting specific poverty reduction programs to local conditions in China and Mexico, where the central government lacks detailed information on the relevant target groups. Then, it provides an analytical framework for addressing the problem—the center could provide resources for the purpose to lower levels of government or try to implement the programs itself.

A typical arrangement would involve a system of transfers for the poorest provided to local governments, along with clearly identified criteria provided by the center for the use of the funds. But for this approach to work, it requires that local governments disclose information accurately on the extent of need, and also not divert central funds to other uses. Thus, central governments face a dilemma. Reaching some of the poorest requires local information for effective identification and targeting. This cannot be obtained without the cooperation of local governments, and the latter are quite likely to have different priorities. Local governments may have the information, but the poorer ones lack the financing to carry out the functions, and in the "game" with the center, may lack incentives to effectively use central transfers. Direct central provision is possible but requires significant administrative capabilities and resources.

All levels of government thus face a typical prisoner dilemma game. Ahmad elaborates a few suggestions to solve it—this involves both spatial and intertemporal competition for the resources. Among the crucial ones is the making of transfers conditional on policy reforms, or past performance. Thus, a multi-year budget framework, including multi-year appropriations, would greatly facilitate the achievement of central government objectives. This opens up the possibility of intertemporal competition across lower-level jurisdictions, involving rewards for good behavior and sanctions.

Second, it would also be helpful to be able to draw up actionable contracts between the center and the local governments. Given that the allocation of inputs is not easily observable, as far as possible the contracts should be able to specify identifiable outputs (even if the outcomes may not be simple to specify or monitor in many developing countries).

5.3 Subnational Borrowing and Accountability

The chapter by Liu and Waibel (Chapter 13) explores the policy issues connected to insolvency at the subnational level. In general, the effectiveness of decentralization depends largely on the design and operation of subnational access to credit. Decentralization has given subnational governments the capacity to incur debt. Second, large local infrastructure projects are increasingly seeking capital market financing, while liquidity and growing mobility of international capital across national borders have lowered the cost of borrowing. Thus, local governments around the world are increasingly incurring debt, raising the risk of insolvency, particularly (although not exclusively as seen with the present financial crisis) in developing countries. The risk with limitless access to credit is that it negates the "incentives" for effective service delivery, as the costs can be transmitted to subsequent generations or other jurisdictions.

Liu and Waibel search for "right" subnational borrowing framework and suggest that ex ante subnational borrowing regulations need to be complemented by ex post insolvency mechanisms. Ex-ante limits on subnational fiscal indicators (such as balanced budget rules, limits on the ratio of debt over gross subnational domestic product (GSDP), and debt service ratios) are not sufficient. In fact, the effectiveness of ex ante regulation is limited without an ex post mechanism for subnational insolvency to deter irresponsible borrowers and imprudent lenders.

Liu and Waibel advance several arguments in favor of ex post subnational insolvency mechanisms. They argue that: (1) insolvent subnational governments should be put back on a sustainable fiscal path to guarantee public service delivery; (2) restoring subnational sustainability serves creditors collectively; (3) protecting creditor rights helps nurture embryonic capital markets; and (4) clarity in default processes improves creditworthiness of subnational entities and may enable subnational entities to re-enter the capital market for financing infrastructure.

The chapter also surveys mechanisms for the resolution of subnational financial insolvency in selected countries, such as Brazil, Bulgaria, Hungary, Romania, South Africa and the United States. It thus provides a cross-country survey that represents a key element in ensuring effective incentives for service delivery. It shows that mere existence of subnational insolvency mechanisms shapes incentives ex ante. More precisely, it encourages lenders and debtors to comply with rules voluntarily. While the full financial implications of default cannot be spelled out ex ante, subnational insolvency procedures go a long way in anchoring restructuring and negotiations. The financial crisis in 2008 in the US has also brought into sharp focus the nexus between borrowing constraints and the levels of public service delivery in most of the states and municipal governments.

Insolvency procedures strengthen the hard budget constraint. Pressures for political ad hoc intervention decreases, as restructuring becomes institutionalized. Enhanced credibility for non-bailout better aligns incentives. Finally, subnational insolvency procedures also serve several macroeconomic goals, allowing better management of financial risk and minimizing systemic risk in the banking sector.

NOTES

1. See Ahmad and Brosio (2006).
2. Available online at http://thomas.loc.gov/home/histdox/fedpapers.html.

REFERENCES

Ahmad, Ehtisham and Giorgio Brosio (2006), *Handbook of Fiscal Federalism*, Cheltenham, UK and Northampton, MA, USA: Edward Elgar.

Ahmad, Ehtisham and Giorgio Brosio (2008), "Political Economy of Multi-level Tax Assignments in Latin American Countries", IMF Working Papers No. 08/71.

Ambrosiano, Flavia and Massimo Bordignon (2006), "Normative Versus Positive Theories of Revenue Assignments in Federations", in Ahmad and Brosio (eds) (2006), *Handbook of Fiscal Federalism*, Cheltenham, UK and Northampton, MA, USA: Edward Elgar, pp. 306–38.

Bardhan, P. (2006), "Decentralization and Development", in Ahmad and Brosio (eds) (2006), *Handbook of Fiscal Federalism*, Cheltenham, UK and Northampton, MA, USA: Edward Elgar, pp. 201–23.

Bardhan, P. and D. Mookherjee (2006a), "Pro-poor Targeting and Accountability of Local Governments in West Bengal", *Journal of Development Economics*, **79** (2).

Bardhan, P. and D. Mookherjee (2006b), *Decentralization and Local Governance in Developing Countries – A Comparative Perspective*, Cambridge, MA and London: MIT Press.

Faguet, Jean-Paul (2000), "Does Decentralization Increase Responsiveness to Local Needs? Evidence from Bolivia", Policy Research Working Paper Series No. 2516, World Bank.
Lockwood, Ben (2006), "The Political Economy of Decentralization", in Ahmad and Brosio (eds) (2006), *Handbook of Fiscal Federalism*, Cheltenham, UK and Northampton, MA, USA: Edward Elgar, pp. 33–60.
Oates, Wallace (2002), "Fiscal Federalism and the European Union", paper presented at the Annual Meeting of the Società Italiana di Economia Pubblica, Pavia.
Oates, Wallace (2005), "Toward a Second-Generation theory of Fiscal Federalism", *International Tax and Public Finance*, **12**(4), 349–73.
Oates, Wallace (2008), "On the Evolution of Fiscal Federalism", *National Tax Journal*, **LXI**(2), 313–34.
Rodden, Jonathan (2006), "The Political Economy of Federalism", in Barry Weingast and Donald Wittman (eds), *Oxford Handbook of Political Economy*, Oxford: Oxford University Press, pp. 357–72.
Weingast, Barry (2009), "Second Generation Fiscal Federalism: The Implications of Fiscal Incentives", *Journal of Urban Economico*, forthcoming.

PART I

Positive approaches

2. Information distortion, elite capture and task complexity in decentralized development

Jean-Philippe Platteau*

1 INTRODUCTION

The main advantages associated with decentralized, participatory development lie in the better knowledge of local conditions and constraints (environmental, social and economic) that communities or user groups possess, as well as the dense network of continuous inter-individual interactions that constitute community life (often labelled "social capital" in the recent literature. As a result of these two features, communities are assumed to be better able than a central government or an external donor not only to set up priorities, identify deserving beneficiaries, design projects, select techniques and inputs, but also to enforce rules, monitor behaviour and verify actions. Furthermore, people's motivation to apply effort and to contribute resources is expected to be stronger when they are let free to choose their objectives and their ways to achieve them rather than being told from above what to do and how to do it (see, for example, Hoddinott et al., 2001; Conning and Kevane, 2002; Bardhan, 2002; Platteau and Abraham, 2002, 2004). In view of all these advantages, participatory development is viewed as an effective mechanism for reducing poverty and empowering the poor, for spreading democracy and accountability and for making progress both inclusive and sustainable.

Given the above diagnosis and following the disappointing performances of development aid when channelled through central governments, it is not surprising that the donor community, bilateral donors and big international organizations alike, have laid stress on participation in the design of their development assistance programmes, and/or to funnel substantial amounts of aid money through international or local non-governmental organizations (NGOs) (Stiles, 2002). For example, the World Bank has made the so-called community-driven development (CDD) approach one of the cornerstones of its Comprehensive Development Framework, as reflected in the *World Development Report 2000/2001* devoted to poverty alleviation (Mansuri and Rao, 2004).

The empirical evidence available, so far as we can judge from recent surveys (Conning and Kevane, 2002; Bardhan, 2002; Mansuri and Rao, 2004), does not unambiguously confirm the view that community-based development projects are more effective than more conventional approaches in terms of efficiency, equity (reaching the poor) and sustainability. NGOs themselves, contrary to a widespread belief, have not produced impressive results, even with respect to alleviation of poverty and promotion of participation (Carroll, 1992; White and Eicher, 1999, p. 33). The same agnostic conclusion emerges from a recent review of empirical studies of decentralized delivery of public services. For Bardhan (2002), indeed, although the studies available suggest generally positive effects of decentralization, "it is hard to draw conclusive lessons" (p. 200). Caution is all the more required as most studies are essentially descriptive and point to correlations rather than carefully tested causal relationships. The same agnosticism emerges from other surveys more specifically devoted to assessing the impact of decentralization on poverty reduction. According to them, indeed, there is no demonstrable impact of decentralization on poverty (Crook and Sverrisson, 2001; von Braun and Grote, 2002; Asthana, 2003; Jutting et al., 2004).

A decentralized or participatory approach to development is much more complex than is often imagined by donors, and the advantages typically associated with it are not as clear as they appear at first sight. Communities exhibit characteristics that make them vulnerable to serious pitfalls, particularly in societies dominated by lineage- or patronage-based relations, or in ethnically fragmented societies. Three problems will receive special attention: information distortion, elite capture and task complexity.

This chapter is composed of two parts. The first one (Sections 2 to 5), by far the most important, examines critically the supposed virtues of participatory development in the context of externally supported aid programmes. These programmes involve strategic interactions between the donor agency and targeted communities or beneficiaries, often mediated by intermediaries who act as representatives of the latter. Situations in which the resources available to communities mainly consist of grants made by the central government are also relevant for a large portion of the analysis conducted in this first stage of the discussion. The second part (Section 6) assesses the extent to which the arguments developed at the outset apply to a context of fiscal decentralization in which resources available to local governments arise mainly from taxes levied by the communities or the municipalities themselves.

Section 2 focuses on the possibility of strategic distortion of local information under different circumstances. Section 3 considers the risk of embezzlement of external resources by local elites. Here, the relationship between fraudulent behaviour and the local power structure is explored and, thereafter, the role of so-called "development brokers" is brought to light. Section 4 addresses the issue of perversion of participation under conditions of donor competition when the information gap between donors and recipients is not the problem. Section 5 argues that the effects of participation on project outcomes are not necessarily positive: besides the fact that they vary with community characteristics, such effects may be conditional upon certain project characteristics. In Section 6, which forms the second part of the analysis, attention is turned to fiscal decentralization programmes, and their respective advantages and disadvantages are underlined. One of the points made there is that the risk of elite capture does not vanish when communities are made responsible for generating their own resources for local development. Section 7 concludes the chapter.

Before embarking upon the analysis, an important caveat is in order – the critical approach in this chapter to participatory development does not imply that the author is opposed to it. Quite the contrary: participatory development is deemed too important to be jeopardized by a precipitous and poorly implemented move that underestimates the complexity of the task and runs the risk of perverting participatory processes. In the light of the available evidence it is important to temper present-day excessive optimism about the short-run prospects of participatory development. What is needed is systematic experimentation with, and continuous evaluation of, participatory mechanisms rather than imposition of a new dogma based on a one-size-fits-all approach.

2 INFORMATION DISTORTION IN STRATEGIC INTERACTIONS BETWEEN FUND PROVIDERS AND TARGETED COMMUNITIES

In the following analysis, three cases of information manipulation by grass-roots communities are examined. We first consider the case of strategic distortion of information when priorities are set by the communities, then proceed to the case of strategic distortion in the presence of diverging objectives and finally move to the most complex and interesting case in which communities are heterogeneous and are represented by their local elites in their dealings with the funding agencies.

2.1 Strategic Distortion of Information when Communities are Homogeneous and Donor Preferences are More or Less Fuzzy

As a first step, consider the simplest, ideal case in which a community is defined as a homogeneous entity which (1) has a clear idea about the way to order its priorities in terms of projects to be implemented, and (2) needs external support to finance, at least partly, its preferred project(s). On the other hand, there are funding agencies, foreign donors or the central government of the country concerned, that want to disburse money to the benefit of the communities and according to the priorities set by them. Under these circumstances, it seems, communities would optimally meet their development concerns while funding agencies, assumed to be altruistic (their objective is to increase the communities' welfare), would best allocate their available resources.

In fact, even under these quite favourable conditions, a problem arises when aid resources are perceived to be scarce (communities believe that some types of projects will not be financed) and when some uncertainty exists regarding the yardsticks or the preference system underlying the funding agency's choice of projects or communities. Confronted with this source of uncertainty, communities are tempted to avoid revealing their true preferences when applying for funds so as to better conform to the perceived preference of the agency. Hence, there is a biased revelation of information by the potential beneficiaries of aid money. The point has been shown formally by Somville (2006) under the reasonable assumptions that: (1) the probability of being financed is lower the larger the distance between the preferred project declared by a community and the project perceived to be preferred by the funding agency and that (2) the utility obtained as a result of the implementation of a project decreases with the distance between the community's declared project preference and its true preference.

Interestingly, the greater the uncertainty about the agency's preference, the smaller the bias in the declared preference of a community. As a matter of fact, an increase in the uncertainty regarding the agency's preferred project has the effect of reducing the marginal benefit from a bias in the declared community preference, since the marginal increase in the probability to be financed when lying a little bit more about one's true preferences is smaller when the agency's objective is more fuzzy. Conversely, when communities are certain about the preference of the agency, they are strongly induced to make a declaration close to that perceived preference and, therefore, to depart from their true order of priorities. Such is apparently the situation that obtained in some communities of Kerala, a southern Indian state that embarked upon an ambitious programme of decentralized development in 1996. There, indeed, some local governments (called *Panchayats*) thought that a project would be more likely to be financed by the central government if it was identical to those previously implemented by the state or to the sort of projects presented as models by the State Planning Board, the office in charge of decentralization (Nair, 2000).

In the polar, yet frequent case in which the agency has a clear and explicit pattern of objectives and priorities that it wants to achieve by disbursing funds to communities ready to fulfil them, we expect the latter to behave opportunistically: they introduce project proposals deemed to conform to the donor's wishes so as to secure access to the available resources. In the words of a village chief from Burkina Faso, "if I give you a hen free, you won't start examining the ass to determine whether it is fat or thin. You just accept it" (Guéneau and Lecomte, 1998, p. 100). The extent of benefits drawn by a community will then depend upon whether the actual use of aid resources can be monitored by the agency: the more effective the monitoring the smaller such benefits. Conversely, if communities are not well disciplined in implementing the type of preferred project that they have declared, they will be tempted to divert the resources obtained into their preferred use and their strategic distortion of information will have no welfare consequence.

There is abundant field evidence to show that, in effect, communities strategically adapt their project proposals to the explicit demands of the donors while pursuing their own agenda in the actual use of aid money. In the words of an anthropologist with a long field experience in Mossi villages of Burkina Faso:

> Confronted with the hegemonic "project" of the donor, the local population, for fear of losing the aid offer, prefer to remain silent about their practices and aspirations. This is because these practices and aspirations are perceived to be so far away from those of the donor that they are better not disclosed. Such is the vicious circle of development cooperation: the fear of avowing the discrepancy between the two views because it could lead to the discontinuation of the aid relationship, has the effect of strengthening the donor's confidence in the validity of its approach. (Laurent, 1998, p. 212 – my translation)

The same conclusion has been reached by other authors. For example, Eversole (2003), on the basis of a participatory development programme in favour of Australian Aborigines, observed the following: "Only limited dissent was voiced during the formal meeting in the presence of the funding body. But, privately and in other community meetings, many individuals expressed strongly negative reactions to the proposed project" (p. 785). Referring to a project intended for improving the welfare of Bhil tribal people of western India, Mosse (2001) noted that choice of priority by local communities, growing eucalyptus for use as timber for housing, was decisively shaped by the villagers' perception of the objectives of the State Forest Department. In his study of NGO interventions in rural Malawi, Tembo (2003) provides us with an elaborate account of the concrete mechanisms of information distortion that can arise in participatory development programmes. His main contention is that people and communities tend to profess the objectives, and adopt the style, methods and language of the NGOs so as to obtain access to their support.[1] Typically, this implies pursuing the objectives of empowerment, capacity-building and sustainability, showing concern for gender and environmental issues, following training courses, abiding by certain rules and procedures (for example, creating committees, holding regular meetings, maintaining a cashbook), and so on. Thus, for instance, training was not viewed by the people as a form of assistance, but as "a facilitating activity attached to the process of receiving some kind of NGO assistance" (ibid., p. 97). In fact, people saw training not only as a condition of access to assistance, but also as a source of direct advantages in the form of training allowances. Revealingly, one of the most contentious issues between fieldworkers and villagers concerns the form in which training allowances should be paid: while, on behalf of the NGOs, the former insist that they are paid in kind as gifts of food, the latter want to receive cash allowances so that they can use them in the way they deem fit (ibid., p. 64). As pointed out by Tembo:

> before the training commenced people demanded that they be provided with training allowances in cash and not food... When the NGO turned to the "take it or leave it" approach, the people agreed and the training session was conducted, but with a lot of grumbling on the part of the community members. Fieldworkers were surprised and angry with the people, arguing that they were already beneficiaries of long-lasting assistance and should not demand payment for their access to the assistance (Tembo, 2003, p. 128)

Other sources of disagreement arise from NGO preference for participatory processes and for collective rather than individual enhancement. Activities involving participation, such as registration exercises and meetings, which NGOs intend to use for the empowerment of the people, were seen by them as serving the purpose of facilitating the inflow of external resources. As a result, when an NGO phased out assistance, the people often stopped participating in the committees and organizations built at the initiative of the fund provider. Hence the observation that village organizations set up to secure external financial support "could disband as soon as NGO assistance was over" (ibid., pp. 121, 146). Villages from

Mayo Kebbi in Chad derisively call "*groupements-minute*" (instant associations) these thousands of groups, committees, associations and the like that suddenly emerge when aid funds are available and quickly vanish from the scene when the opportunity has passed (Guéneau and Lecomte, 1998, p. 64).

Partaking of the same logic of spurious participation is the fact that village organizations and committees set up for the purpose of capturing aid are specific to the intervention of a particular NGO. According to Tembo's account for Malawi, when a new NGO came to a community to provide assistance, people did not mention previous programmes and, therefore, new committees were formed to meet the demand of this new NGO. Change thus tends to be seen in project terms rather than in the context of the people's own construction of their livelihoods (Tembo, 2003, p. 122). Revealingly, the same sort of problems arise in the context of World Bank-supported CBD (community-based development) projects: according to a recent evaluation report, "communities do not appear to have understood that their participation is meant to drive the development process, and see participation in a Bank project primarily as a requirement for them to meet part of the sub-project cost" (World Bank, 2005, p. 50).

In some instances, such as in small-scale irrigation schemes, the requirement that aid beneficiaries are grouped together into collectives is essential because the development project involves the creation and maintenance of a local public good. Nevertheless, when groupings have been quickly formed for the sake of acceding to external assistance, these collective organizations are usually dysfunctional with the result that the public good is under-provided and is not kept in the desired state.

In an extreme case, it is possible that a community has no interest in the activities proposed by an external agency. The utility obtained from external assistance may then consist of the social prestige associated with obtaining a development project in the context of inter-community rivalry, and with enhancing the credibility of existing leadership in such a context. Many village leaders want to have a funded project in their community, just like their neighbouring villages: "In essence, they were open to have any NGO activity in their communities" (Tembo, 2003, p. 93; see also Mosse, 1997, p. 486). Women from the Senegal river valley thus wanted to obtain sewing machines from a foreign NGO because "that is what aid-funded development projects give" and what the neighbouring villages have actually received (Guéneau and Lecomte, 1998, p. 99).

To conclude, conflicts of objectives between aid agencies and communities often emerge because the latter pay much less attention to long-term, strategic considerations (including the building of autonomous organizational capacities), and attach much bigger weight to immediate improvements of life conditions. In addition, they tend to place too much hope in externally provided resources and to demand that the scale of development activities is increased beyond the limit of their own absorptive capacity. More fundamentally, the objectives of systems may differ so widely between donors and target groups that the very concept of development at the heart of the donors' approach may not be understood by these groups (Platteau, 2004). As is evident from the above, the main divergence lies in the lack of spontaneous understanding of the sustainability concept by recipient communities. While aid agencies are concerned that improvements in people's livelihoods are sustainable over the long run, at least when they are not under pressure to show rapid results to their ultimate contributors, project beneficiaries tend to insist on quick benefits regardless of future consequences. This attitude is to be ascribed to their short-term time horizon and to strong uncertainties regarding long-term aid commitments of external donors.

2.2 Strategic Distortion of Information with Heterogeneous Communities: General Considerations

In many cases, communities are not homogeneous. Even in Sub-Saharan Africa, village societies are often strongly differentiated along age and gender lines, seniority of the lineage, and so on. This heterogeneity compounds the problem of information manipulation because funding or aid agencies are typically motivated by the objectives of poverty alleviation and empowerment of deprived sections of the population. This gives rise to serious conflicts of objectives with local elites, which are inclined to promote their own interests and do not have the same idea of eligibility for external assistance. To push their own agenda, these elites do not hesitate to exploit the information gap that exists between rural communities and donors.

In many instances, the opportunistic behaviour of local elites consists of deceptively including the poor and disadvantaged in their project activities so as to access development aid. Several social scientists have thus emphasized the ability of the village wealthy to represent their own interests as community concerns expressed in the light of project deliverables. As a consequence, donors are frequently deluded into thinking that the motivations of these elites are guided by purposes of collective good (see, for example, Ribot, 1996, 2002; Molinas, 1998; Mosse, 2001; Harrison, 2002; Tembo, 2003). Delusion is all the more likely as the demands emanating from the elites are replete with the sort of pleas and vocabulary that strongly appeal to the donors and, in order to create the appearance of participation, they may go as far as spending resources to build community centres, hold rallies, and initiate showcase labour-intensive activities (Conning and Kevane, 2002, p. 383). Thus, commenting on the Indian experience with village-level democracy (*Panchayati Raj*), Ajay Mehta writes:

> Despite significant allocation of resources and the creation of institutions for self-governance, these interventions have not succeeded in either empowering the poor or enhancing their well-being. If anything, they have strengthened the ability of more powerful and more affluent segments of society to control and co-opt the poor to serve their interests. (Mehta, 2000, p. 16)

Donor agencies, including NGOs, run the risk of inadvertently helping the objectives of local elites. This happens when they rely on institutional mechanisms that skip the phase of empowerment of the grass-roots. Typically, they ask the members of the targeted communities to form groups or partner associations and to "elect" leaders to direct them. The risk is then that the most prominent members are selected and given training and control over resources for the community – without any detailed and extended communication with the other members about objectives, rights or duties. As a consequence, the agency has little or no communication with the community except through these leaders. This has the effect of entrenching a privileged minority and discrediting the idea of group action for self-improvement (Esman and Uphoff, 1984, p. 249).

When common people are compliant enough, such as is often observed in hierarchical societies, including them in the associations required by the funding agency and exerting natural authority over them in all discussions regarding the allocation of aid resources is usually tantamount to endorsing the preferences of the elite. This fact is attested by many experiences with the World Bank's Social Funds – a major instrument for the financing of participatory development projects by the bank. The "prime movers" of projects, such as village heads or school teachers, often decide which project to choose and implement before any community meeting ever takes place, and it is only later that they take the step of informing community members of their project choice (De Haan et al., 2002; White, 2002). The powerless assume the images of the powerful and, since all negotiations with the external agency take place through local leaders or intermediaries, people's priorities are presented in a manner acceptable to this agency, but also suiting the interests or objectives of the village elite (Tembo, 2003, p. 95, 145; Nygren, 2005). If the poor are somewhat less passive and not so easily manipulable, the elite may have to resort to some sort of arm-twisting tactic to have their way.

Note that, if the external agency is able to monitor effectively the local use of the resources provided, the elite may be compelled to forsake access to these resources, possibly causing damage to the project itself. The example, reported by Tembo, of a self-help scheme for irrigation in a village of Malawi provides a handy illustration of how divergence of objectives between an NGO and the village elite may undermine a development project. The scheme had been devised by a few people willing to divert water from a river in order to grow rice during the dry season. An NGO then appeared and decided to expand the programme in order to allow most people, especially the poor, to benefit from it. This necessitated the construction of a more permanent main water channel made of cement and using skilled labour, both bought by the NGO. Once construction was completed, people were required to divert small channels into their fields and then organize for maintenance of the main channel. Yet, people did not comply. Instead, the original group of irrigators continued to irrigate their crops using the old channel they had built by themselves. The reason behind the boycott is that this group considered the other farmers to be lazy guys prone to free-riding (they will "eat on other people's sweat") and, therefore, liable to undermine collective actions, such as the maintenance of the new channel. Since it was difficult to reject anybody on the new channel, given that it had been financed by the NGO, the original group opted for returning to the old channel and relying only on trustworthy people (Tembo, 2003, p. 115).

To take another example, in a village of Uttar Pradesh (India) concerned by a water supply scheme, groups made of a few households contributed the entire capital cost portion for one handpump. It was understood that neighbouring households would pay them back their share once the pumps were operational. This did not happen, though, and the handpumps were considered by villagers to be the property of individual households. Some of the "owners" even went so far as to prevent usage when they were not using the pump so as to ensure preferential access (Prokopy, 2005, p. 1815).

Incidentally, the above examples show that heterogeneity of interests and objectives does not necessarily arise from an opposition between the village elite and the common people, but may also be caused by more subtle patterns of social differentiation inside communities. In particular, different ideas of eligibility for external assistance, and different notions of social justice, may prevail because of different diagnoses about the ultimate causes of poverty and destitution. While development agencies tend to attribute poverty to bad initial conditions, or to bad luck and adverse shocks, relatively successful members of a community may place the blame on some behavioural traits of the poor themselves, for example, laziness, drunkenness, indiscipline or opportunistic proclivities. Moreover, individuals may be regarded as untrustworthy because they have broken some local social norm (a man has shown disrespect for his father, or has sold a piece of land to a stranger without the approval of village elders), and will therefore be considered non-eligible for aid relief, whereas the donor agency thinks otherwise on the basis of other criteria or principles of justice (Platteau, 2004, p. 249; see also Mosse, 1997).

Exclusionary tendencies often follow from the fact that rural communities are typically concerned with preserving a sense of social inclusiveness that leads them to exclude certain segments of the population (Conning and Kevane, 2002, p. 386). In particular, immigrants of more or less recent origin, nomadic people, erstwhile slaves in caste societies, or widows may be precluded from benefiting from an external intervention. In a recent study of Southern Sudan, it has been found that local views about who should benefit from famine relief efforts were very much at variance with those of the aid workers, which caused a lot of problems in the implementation of the project (Harragin, 2004). A similar difficulty emerges from another study dealing with a CBD project designed to promote community-organized and funded schools in Kenya (Gugerty and Kremer, 1999). A more optimistic conclusion has, however, been reached in still another study that found a good matching in rural Bangladesh between wealth-ranking judgments arrived at through a rapid rural appraisal technique, on the one hand, and ratings obtained by using standard socioeconomic indicators from a household survey, on the other (Adams et al., 1997).

Before looking at the empirical evidence from the economic literature, there is an important theoretical result obtained by Somville and Platteau (2009) that deserves to be mentioned. What he shows is that in heterogeneous communities in which an elite group and a target group of poor people coexist, and in which they have different preferences regarding development projects, the distance between the project submitted to a donor by the community represented by its elite group and the optimal project corresponding to that favoured by the target group depends in a complex way on the level of severity of the donor. More precisely, the relationship between these two variables is not monotonic but U-shaped. Consequently, the donor who maximizes the utility of the target group and chooses his or her optimal level of severity, should avoid maximum severity and zero tolerance. This is because when the donor is too severe, the elite group does not lose much by submitting a project proposal closer to its own preference and further away from the target group's preference. By doing so, the marginal benefit obtained from having a project closer to its own preference actually outweighs the marginal cost resulting from a fall in the probability of project acceptance. Note that in Somville's model the level of donor's severity is measured by a parameter that sets up a maximum distance between the project submitted and the belief of the donor regarding the best project for the poor – and when the maximum distance is exceeded for any submitted project, the proposal is rejected.

2.3 Strategic Distortion of Information with Heterogeneous Communities: Empirical Evidence from the Economic Literature

Economists have focused most of their attention on the issue of whether poverty reduction can be more effectively achieved through a decentralized allocation of resources (via a local government) or in a participatory manner (via a community organization representing the interests of the beneficiaries themselves) as opposed to a centralized mechanism (see Bardhan and Mookherjee, 2000). The theoretical framework usually assumes the existence of some form of voting process at the local or community level in which the weight of the poor, who have different preferences from the rich, is expected to play an important role. In many cases, the theory is then tested against the facts.

Rosenzweig and Foster (2003) use a two-party (the poor and the non-poor) model representative democracy with probabilistic voting in which local governments choose to allocate public resources among different public goods, for which the preferences of the poor presumably differ from those of the rich. A key prediction of the model is that, in villages with democratic governance, an increase in the population share of the landless should result in outcomes that are, ceteris paribus, more favourable to the poor, that is, greater road construction or improvements (which are relatively labour-intensive) and smaller public irrigation infrastructure (which benefit the landed households especially). The prediction is borne out by the econometrics applied to a 20 panel data set from 250 villages in rural India. As a matter of fact, increases in the population weight of the poor appear to enhance the likelihood of receiving pro-poor projects but only in villages with elected *Panchayats*. When more traditional leadership structures prevail, no such effect is observed, leading to the conclusion that local democracy seems to matter in determining whether decentralization benefits the poor.

On the other hand, evidence from a decentralized food-for-education programme in Bangladesh led Galasso and Ravallion (2005) to the conclusion that the programme was mildly pro-poor, in the sense that a somewhat larger fraction of the poor received benefits than did the non-poor. Yet, the targeting performance turns out to have been worse in more remote communities or in communities where land inequality is greater, which presumably reflects a larger extent of appropriation of benefits by the elite when the poor wield little bargaining power.[2] Hernandez-Trillo and Jarillo-Rabling (2008) have looked at the way federal transfers to municipalities have been distributed in Mexico under the Social Infrastructure Fund (SIF), aimed at reducing destitution through the construction of social infrastructure in poor communities. Their conclusion is that, once in the municipalities' hands, the community-based development funds (CBDFs) do not necessarily reach the communities most in need of potable water, drainage, electricity, urbanization works and rural roads. More precisely, the authors show that funds tend to be allocated to communities that have a larger number of registered voters (the more populated areas), regardless of the coverage level of the public services concerned, thus suggesting that distribution is politically motivated. According to them, the decline in the number of electricity beneficiaries that has been observed since the mid-1990s in Mexico actually coincides with the decentralization of rural electrification, which is one of the public services the SIF is supposed to finance.

A study of the impact of the Peruvian Social Fund – a World Bank-supported mechanism for the delivery of public goods (for example, schools, clinics, roads, water and sanitation facilities) in poor communities – on poverty targeting has led Paxson and Schady (2002) to a different conclusion. In fact, the programme successfully reached the poorest districts, yet did not benefit the poorest households within these districts: better-off households were more likely to benefit from the Fund's investments. From a case study on the Jamaica Social Investment Fund, Rao and Ibanez (2001) concluded that the overall quality of the match between local preferences and project achievements was poor. Only in two of the five communities studied were the project achievements consistent with the preferences of a majority in that community. Furthermore, better educated and better networked people were more likely to obtain projects that matched their preferences. Banerjee and Somanathan (2005) emphasize the presence of serious negative discrimination against certain disadvantaged groups in India, the so-called scheduled castes and scheduled tribes, which together represent almost one-fourth of the Indian population. This discrimination is reflected is their low access to public goods and services.

In short, when social differentiation and power asymmetries are strong, decentralized or participatory development is tantamount to participation by the rich and the powerful at the expense of the poor, who remain voiceless and helpless. It is in this sort of context that an empowerment approach is needed to help the poor, to not only articulate their needs and assert their interests in front of the village elite, but also to monitor the behaviour of the latter, to confront them if needed and to take leadership positions. A few studies seem to suggest that, where reliable empowerment mechanisms exist, poverty can be effectively reduced through decentralized development. Thus, Pande (2003) has shown that, in India, when disadvantaged groups (lower castes, tribal groups and landless people) are able to elect their own representatives at the local level where allocation decisions are made, a larger share of available governmental resources accrue to them. The same result has been obtained by Chattopadhyay and Duflo (2004a, 2004b) in a study focused on the situation of women and the impact of reservations of local government positions for women in two Indian states (Rajasthan and West Bengal). They obtain significant effects on the allocation of expenditures between drinking water, roads and education centres, which are thought to better reflect women's interests.

Besley et al. (2005) have studied the relationship between participation and equity in the functioning of the *Panchayat* system in four southern states of India. One of the responsibilities assigned to these village-level elected bodies is the selection of beneficiaries for the distribution of the BPL (Below Poverty Line) card, which is meant to benefit the most disadvantaged households by entitling them to subsidized food and making them eligible for various welfare schemes. A central aim of the study was to assess whether the quality of targeting has been improved when regular village meetings are held in which people get the opportunity to express their demands and hold the elected officials to account. The authors find that, indeed, the holding of these meetings did have a significantly positive effect on equity in the following sense: members of disadvantaged groups, illiterate and landless people and individuals from the lowly scheduled castes and tribes in particular, were more likely to receive the BPL card in villages that held the meeting compared with their counterparts in villages that did not. Yet, the evidence adduced in this study is not all according to expectations based on the virtues of participation and empowerment, for example, the reservation of local office positions for women has a negative effect on the allocation of BPL cards (see below).

In the same line, Kumar (2008) has recently examined the impact of a community-driven project known as the District Poverty Initiatives Project (DPIP), on the targeting of another government-sponsored scheme, the aforementioned BPL card project. The area of study is another Indian state, Madhya Pradesh. Under DPIP, funds are provided to self-help groups for any approved income-generating activity. The approval process occurs through a village meeting wherein all groups have to put forth their project proposals and the entire village votes. Since these meetings are similar and run parallel to the traditional village council meetings called by the elected *Panchayat*, it can be presumed that the village meetings run under the auspices of the DPIP project help familiarize the villagers with the concept of village council meetings and their benefits. Moreover, if the elected village council bears the responsibility of allocating the BPL cards, the preliminary list of beneficiaries is ratified in the village council meeting. There are thus grounds to believe that DPIP could indirectly lead to improved targeting of services administered by the *Panchayats* by promoting awareness, encouraging attendance and active participation in the village council meetings.

In order to test this hypothesis, Kumar designed a survey that covered 6000 households across 300 villages. She is then able to show that being a DPIP village improves targeting of BPL cards among landless households by 5 per cent, and by 17 per cent among households belonging to lower castes. In other words, DPIP villages appear better able to target BPL cards to the most disadvantaged groups. In addition, households in the project villages are more likely to be active in village affairs and there is greater evidence of collective action. Furthermore, households in DPIP villages have greater information about the timing of village council meetings. On the other hand, belonging to a DPIP village has an ambiguous impact on attendance at these meetings. Yet, those who attend are more likely to actively participate in a project village when there is a DPIP in the village than when there is none.

For rural China, Wang and Yao (2007) present ambiguous results about the impact of elections in which the targeted beneficiaries are allowed to play a significant role. On the one hand, using data for 48 villages located in eight different provinces, Wang and Yao find that, paradoxically, competitive elections may actually hurt local-level performances. In the context of this study, a competitive election means that the village committees are chosen in a democratic voting process rather than being nominated in the course of a government-controlled election. A series of dummy variables are used to capture the degree of competitiveness of local elections: popular (direct) election is considered to be the most competitive form of contest while government appointment is the least democratic. Performances are mainly measured by the share of public expenditures in the local budget (compared with office maintenance, salaries of the members of the village committee and revenue shared with the township government). Since public expenditures include transfers to households and spending on public projects such as local roads, village schools, irrigation systems and healthcare facilities, they are assumed to ubiquitously benefit the majority of the villagers.

A central finding of the study is that compared with a candidate from a government-controlled election the village committee chosen in a popular election significantly reduces the share of public expenditures. Moreover, an election in which candidates are nominated by village representatives has the effect of reducing fiscal sharing with the township significantly compared with a government-controlled election. The latter result is an adverse consequence of democratic elections since many public goods and services, such as schools and roads, either directly depend on the township budget or need coordination among villages. By contrast, a study based on a sample of villages from Jiangsu province (Zhang et al., 2004) found that village elections have increased the share of public investment and had no effect on the amount of fees handed over to the township. Another study (Kennedy et al., 2004), focused on Shaanxi province, and relied on subjective evaluations of village leaders' performance in a restricted field of action (land matters). It came to the conclusion that compared with elections with government-appointed candidates, more competitive elections, in which candidates were nominated by villagers, produced village leaders who were more accountable to villagers in decisions regarding land reallocations.

That such results cannot be generalized is evident from a host of studies dealing with the effects of participation in the form of co-management of local-level natural resources. For example, a survey of more than 50 villages in Andhra Pradesh (India) shows that, despite concerted effort by policy-makers to empower poor and weaker sections of rural population in joint forestry management (JFM) programmes, one of the most comprehensive attempts at decentralization in India, richer and more educated people in the community continue to be significantly more likely to influence the decisions taken (Behera and Engel, 2006). In other words, "minority groups in the communities, although they may be formally given some authority in the JFM process, are still de facto kept out of the decision-making process, which is likely to have serious repercussions on the distribution of benefits from the JFM forests" (p. 30). This finding is important as policies to include poorer, more marginalized groups in forest management committees have been somewhat successful. Clearly, the simple presence of disadvantaged people in a committee is not sufficient to give them a real say in the decision-making process. Another study about the same JFM scheme has concluded that the poor are net losers and likely to remain so over a 40-year time horizon. If they participate in JFM, it is just to "state their loyalty to the village leadership". In behaving in this fashion, "the poor ensure that they can partake of at least some village institutions, and they build up their stocks of social capital" (Kumar, 2002, p. 776).

Social differentiation and power asymmetries are not the only kind of heterogeneity that make participatory schemes liable to produce disappointing results. Thus, Alesina et al. (1999) have attempted to explain the quantity of public goods supplied at local level by the heterogeneity of ethnic preferences in the context of Indian villages. Their estimates show that the share of such public goods as schools, paved roads and telephones is inversely related to ethnic fragmentation, which thus comes out as an important determinant of local public finance decisions. In the same vein, Cutler et al. (1993) stress the difficulties for collective action (the production of local public goods, in particular) that arise from ethnic heterogeneity. According to them, this is due to the fact that people do not feel concerned by the well-being of others unless they belong to the same ethnic group. It is therefore not surprising that, in highly fragmented societies, electoral competition at the local level is often based on considerations of identity, whether ethnic, religious or linguistic (Keefer and Khemani, 2005; see also Chandra, 2004). Here, what are required to overcome the problem are subtle steps to gradually develop cooperative practices between the diverse population sub-groups.

All this being said, caution is called for when interpreting most of the above results in so far as they are based on a comparison of predicted and realized outcomes in the absence of strong direct testing of the underlying assumptions. More precisely, it is assumed that a key mechanism of elite dominance is their influence over the type of expenditure or project to be financed from the externally provided resources. Yet, it is not so easy to identify which types of expenditures or projects benefit the poor more than the wealthy. For example, can we really take for granted that, compared with the rich, the poor benefit more from improved roads than from irrigation infrastructure? Thus, "it is often the case that non poor households corner most of the wage work opportunities within their home village, especially when this work is provided by government agencies at an official wage rate that is two to three times the traditional village rate" (Kumar, 2002, p. 776).

As pointed out by Bardhan and Mookherjee (2006a), evidence derived from surveys of living standards of households or individuals classified by socioeconomic status would be much more reliable for assessing the impact of decentralized development on the poor, than reported perceptions of service delivery or evidence based on the composition of public expenditures at the local level. Reported perceptions are vulnerable to serious biases as are all subjective statements, and evidence based on public expenditures is too indirect to be fully convincing (see above). Fortunately, aside from the aforementioned study by Galasso and Ravallion (2005), studies using household-specific data are becoming increasingly available (see, in particular, Banerjee et al., 2006; Björkman and Svensson, 2007).

Finally, we would obviously like to know more about how village democracy works in actual practice. Indeed, in order to show that democratic governance enables the poor to express their preferences and make them prevail, there is no escape from analysing the concrete process through which they raise their "voice" in the relevant institutions. By relying on formal voting processes and formal rules of electoral competition, political economy models also ignore other, potentially effective local accountability institutions. It is thus revealing that, in non-democratic countries such as China and Korea, ingenious mechanisms exist at local level to develop trust and cooperation within the ambit of incentive-based organizations and bureaucratic procedures, whereas in democratic countries such as India local-level accountability mechanisms are often quite deficient (see, for example, Wade 1985, 1990).

A recent study of the poverty alleviation effects of the Ecuadorian Social Fund (Araujo et al. 2006) is less vulnerable to the aforementioned methodological problem regarding the adequacy between composition of public expenditures and the needs of the poor at the local level. This is because the authors exploit the fact that the menu offered by this fund included two types of projects – local public goods (which are accessible to all although they may be valued differently across individuals) and excludable private goods. By far the most important private good provided, latrines built in land plots belonging to community members with no existing access to toilet facilities, were clearly aimed at the poor. The authors propose a simple model of project choice between public and private goods when local political power is unequally distributed. This model yields the prediction that, controlling for inequality, poorer communities would select latrine projects more often than more wealthy ones. Moreover, controlling for poverty, communities that are more unequal would choose latrine projects less often, because of a concentration of power in the hands of richer people.[3] The study finds that the latter prediction is, indeed, supported by the data, strongly suggesting that the elite capture the programme, to the extent that such a choice reflects differences in power, rather than need.

Bardhan et al. (2008) have assessed the impact of local governance on targeting of programme benefits using a household survey conducted in 89 villages spread throughout 15 districts in West Bengal. They find that if intra-village distribution of benefits is generally pro-poor – that is, within a village, less educated people and people from marginal social groups tend to receive more benefits than other villagers do; the opposite is true of inter-village allocation. Thus, villages with larger shares of landless and marginal people receive fewer benefits. Furthermore, reservations of seats on *Gram Panchayats* (local governments) in favour of women and of scheduled castes and tribes (which were implemented in West Bengal in 1993), and reservations of *Pradhan* (that is, head of the village council) offices to the same population groups (implemented in 1998) appear to have had negative effects on the distribution not only of local public goods but also of a wide range of private goods. In particular, and in a sharp contrast with Chattopadhyay and Duflo (2004a, 2004b), Bardhan et al. (2008) do not observe that women in reserved *Pradhan* positions allocate more benefits to female-headed households. In addition, they find significant negative effects of women reservations on targeting of benefits to the population of scheduled castes and tribes. For example, women seem to be worse at targeting BPL cards and employment benefits to the landless and on allocating housing benefits to female-headed households and households from scheduled castes and tribes. Results regarding the impact of reservations of *Gram Panchayat* seats are also disappointing.

The origin of such a discrepancy between the findings of Chattopadhyay and Duflo, on the one hand, and those of Bardhan et al. (2008), on the other hand, deserves to be elucidated. The latter argue that their study rests on a sounder dataset. First, geographical coverage is wider in the second study, which covers all the major agricultural areas of West Bengal, while the data set of the first study includes only the district of Birbhum. Second, the data used by Bardhan et al. cover a period that includes two elections after the 1998 reform, in contrast with the dataset of Chattopadhyay and Duflo, which covers only one election (over the period 1998–2000). Third, Bardhan et al. use information on benefits reported directly by households, while Chattopadhyay and Duflo use *Gram Panchayats*' activities reported by the *Pradhan* and information provided by villagers on infrastructure investment at the village level. Fourth, and most critically, while Bardhan et al. study includes a wide range of private benefits (such as credit, agricultural minikits, employment, BPL cards, housing and toilets), that of Chattopadhyay and Duflo focuses on public goods such as drinking water, roads, irrigation and education centres.

Another study by Labonne and Chase (2006) deals with a community-driven development programme in the Philippines. It is especially interesting because it uses ex ante data on the preferences of both households and village officials regarding the most pressing development problems faced by their community, as well as data on the project proposals put forward for funding in communities that did not actually receive funds. One of the authors' key findings is that inequality has a negative impact on the way household preferences are aggregated at the community level. In more unequal communities, the village official is more likely to have his or her preferences represented in village proposals with the effect of biasing the proposal selection process in a pro-elite direction.[4]

2.4 Strategic Distortion of Information with Heterogeneous Communities: Empirical Evidence from the Social Science Literature

When it comes to assessing the impact of participatory processes, it is striking that the social science literature appears to be much less optimistic than the economic one. While explaining such a discrepancy, one has to bear in mind that the methodology used by social scientists is quite different from that used by economists. Whereas the former follow a case study approach that implies studying a few communities in a rather in-depth fashion, the latter base their conclusions on data systematically collected in a large sample of communities. The two approaches can be helpfully considered as complementary, but since there is a wide discrepancy in the pictures that emerge from them, a lot of effort needs to be devoted in the future to understanding its possible causes.

At this stage, I just want to illustrate this divergence by referring to works of social scientists dealing with the specific case of India. In an aforementioned study, Nair (2000) has studied two villages of Kerala where he observed the impact of decentralized decision-making. In one village, as many as 78 per cent of the beneficiaries, and in the other village 38 per cent did not at all participate in the local projects destined to benefit them. Participation in the meetings of the village council is disappointingly low in the two locations. Moreover, while attendance is quite large in the meetings during which individual beneficiaries are selected, few people deem it worth the while to participate in meetings aimed at discussing local projects. This finding is confirmed by Vijayalakshmi (2003a), and none among the *Panchayats* that she studied succeeded in meeting the 10 per cent attendance quorum to the council meetings (see also Sethuraman, 1999).

The situation outside of Kerala appears to be worse. Thus, in the neighbouring state of Karnataka, we are told that even when women or representatives from the scheduled castes and tribes (which represent marginal social groups in the context of the caste-based system of India) have a seat in the *Panchayat*, they are generally manipulated by their husbands (for the former) or their local patrons (for the latter), who ultimately decide how they should vote or express their opinions (Blair, 2000). In the northern states of Rajasthan and Madhya Pradesh, participation rates in the meetings and decisions of the village councils are below 10 per cent. Educated people wield a lot of influence and the president has the ultimate say in important matters. Ordinary villagers, women and members of lower caste in particular, feel quite helpless about such power asymmetry, which goes a long way towards explaining why they are not motivated to attend the meetings (Alsop et al., 2000).

3 EMBEZZLEMENT OF EXTERNAL RESOURCES BY LOCAL ELITES

3.1 Fraudulent Behaviour and the Local Power Structure

In the above, we have considered a first form of elite capture whereby, in the presence of heterogeneous preferences, the village elite succeeds in imposing their own interests and objectives while negotiating projects with external funding agencies. Let us now turn to a second form of elite capture under which power-wielders at village level, even assuming that their objectives and preferences are identical to those of the poor, do not hesitate to appropriate an unduly large share of the external resources provided to the community. In other words, a direct embezzlement of these resources occurs. Empirical studies by economists concerning this second and more blatant form of elite capture are simply absent for the obvious reason that embezzlement is extremely difficult to document in any systematic manner. Indeed, being a more blameworthy and less acceptable practice than capture of the first kind, it tends to be subtly concealed at least from external fund providers and, a fortiori, from researchers compelled to use interviews of a rather crude kind owing to severe time and resource constraints (for an exception, see Olken, 2005). Not surprisingly, therefore, evidence of embezzlement by local elites is typically anecdotal, which does not mean that it is insignificant. In fact, cases of embezzlement have been uncovered by many fieldworkers, with a prolonged engagement with rural communities. Because of the piecemeal character of the evidence available, however, it is hard to specify the conditions under which elite embezzlement is more or less likely to occur.

It seems a well-grounded fact that inegalitarian village societies are comparatively prone to resource misappropriation, especially if the authority structure has never been questioned by dissenting individuals or groups on the basis of progressive ideologies, and if deferential attitudes prevail among common people. Hence, perhaps, there is a relatively large incidence of fraudulent behaviour on the part of the chieftaincy in lineage-based societies, for example in Sub-Saharan Africa. There, indeed, a rigid hierarchy of ranks often prevails at the top layer, which includes the chief and the council of elders. This council is typically comprised of aged persons belonging to the dominant lineages, foremost among which the lineage is descending from the man who cleared the bush and founded the village. It is from the founding lineage that the village chief usually originates.

What bears emphasis is that African societies have not yet gone through protracted, nationwide struggles whereby the interests of dominated social classes or groups could be asserted vis-à-vis the ruling elite and state power (Kennedy, 1988). In other words, there is no entrenched tradition of genuine civil society movements, emancipated from the state. This is not surprising in a context where state authorities (including chieftaincies in rural areas) have preempted important channels of potentially lucrative activities in the economy, and where dynamic individuals eager to get rich and/or to exercise their entrepreneurial talents have been absorbed into the regime's rent-generating and collecting patronage networks. What is at work is a logic of "politicized accumulation" narrowly linked to the inclusionary and co-optive strategies of regime consolidation described by Bayart (1986, 1989) and Boone (1992) among others.

As a consequence, the social ideals and other-regarding norms of a generalized kind, without which social struggles are doomed to failure, could not evolve in Africa and in other areas with similar characteristics (for example, Haiti, Bihar state in India, Northwestern Province in Pakistan). This is unfortunate as far as such values and norms are precisely useful to promote the emergence of dedicated leaders who are moved by a progressive ideology rather than their own immediate self-interest. By contrast, in many countries of Asia and Latin America, historically rooted ideals of social commitment are alive that have been transmitted over generations thanks to the education system and civil society movements or associations.

In rural societies dominated by a stratum of chiefs and notables, traditional leaders may choose to oppose any outside intervention that has the effect of threatening their social and economic status, thereby disrupting the local hierarchy of privileges and undermining the local power structure. In fact, there are numerous stories attesting that the village elite frequently claim priority access to the new resources brought under the auspices of a development programme. If their request is not satisfied, they attempt to appropriate the programme's assets by force or by guile and, if such a strategy does not succeed, they do not hesitate to sabotage the external intervention by manipulating community members so as to incite them to boycott it (for vivid illustrations taken from the author's own repertoire of field experiences, see Abraham and Platteau, 2004, pp. 220–21).

Part of poor people's passivity in the presence of embezzlement of aid resources by local leaders may be actually attributed to a ruling system of social norms and values, that tend to legitimate elite capture. As a result, what Western donors would consider as blatant fraud or improper behaviour may not appear as such in the eyes of local people who have internalized customary norms that have evolved to vindicate an asymmetrical social structure. The following story illustrates the nature of these norms and their underlying system of justification. Given its rich content, it deserves to be told in some detail (the story is taken from Platteau and Gaspart, 2003, pp. 1689–90).

In the late years of the twentieth century, a Western European development NGO established a relationship with a village association in a Sahelian country (Burkina Faso). This association, a federation of several peasant unions, had been initiated by a young and dynamic school teacher, the son of a local chief. The NGO decided to follow a gradual participatory approach consisting of strengthening the association institutionally before channelling financial resources to it. After two years during which institutional support was provided in the form of guidance to improve the internal functioning of the partner association and to help define development priorities and the best means to achieve them, funds were provided for different types of investment. Within the limits of the budget set for each prioritized line of investment, the local association was let free to choose the project it deemed most useful, to prepare proposals and to programme the activities involved. Continued external support at different levels (technical, administrative, organizational and methodological) was nevertheless found necessary to help in the effective implementation of the different projects.

In spite of all the efforts to strengthen the partner association institutionally, things turned out badly. Thanks to the collaboration of two active members of the General Assembly (actually two animators) and the local accountant, the foreign NGO discovered serious financial and other malpractices committed by the main leader under the form of over-invoicing and falsifying of accounts. It reacted by calling on the local committee to sanction these manifest violations of the rules, yet to its great surprise no punishment was meted out and the general assembly even re-elected their leader in open defiance of its request. The two dissident animators were blamed for being driven by jealousy and envy, while the accountant was fired. Here is a clear illustration of the support that poor people are inclined to give to an elite member on loyalty grounds and because they consider that they have sufficiently benefited from his leadership efforts. That he appropriated to himself a disproportionate share of the benefits of the aid programme is considered legitimate by most of them. They indeed think that without his efforts their own situation would not have improved at all. In particular, he created the village association that had to be formed in order to be eligible for external assistance.

In a context where the ability to establish contact and to deal with external sources of funding is concentrated in a small elite group, the bargaining strength of the poor is inevitably limited, hence their ready acceptance of highly asymmetric patterns of distribution of programmes' benefits. If the intervention of the elite results in an improvement of the predicament of the poor, however small the improvement, the latter tend to be thankful to their leader(s): the new outcome represents a Pareto improvement over the previous situation and this is what matters after all. Revealingly, the ordinary members of the association defended their leader on the ground that "everybody around him benefited from the project and, if he benefited [much] more than the others, it is understandable because he is the leader and he made the whole project possible". They believe it is highly unfair on the part of the foreign NGO to have withdrawn their support to the existing team and to have "humiliated their leader" by depriving him of all the logistical means (jeep, scooters, and so on) previously put at his disposal.

As for the leader himself, he openly admitted (during a conciliatory meeting organized by the high commissioner of the province) to have used a significant portion of the money entrusted to him for his own personal benefit. Yet, he did not express any regret since it was his perceived right to appropriate a large share of the funds. Did he not devote considerable energies to the setting up of the local organization and the mobilization of the local resources as required by the foreign NGO? By attempting to curb his power to allocate funds in the way he deemed fit, the latter exercised an intolerable measure of neo-colonialist pressure. This criticism was voiced in spite of the fact that the NGO paid him a comfortable salary to reward his organizing efforts. Things were left there and the local radio even echoed the leader's viewpoint. Of course, suing him before a court was not deemed to be a realistic option.

Stories like this are easily multiplied. What must be stressed is that the attitudes involved are typical of rural societies dominated by patron–client or chief–subject relationships, that is, hierarchical, asymmetric and highly personalized relations in which poor people's deference and loyalty to the leader(s) is perceived as the best way of ensuring their day-to-day livelihood. In such a social set-up, enrichment of the elite is not considered reprehensible by the poor as long as they are allowed to derive some gains from the elite's actions and they can have their day-to-day subsistence guaranteed by the well-to-do (see Scott, 1976, 1985; Chabal and Daloz, 1999, p. 42). There is no disputing the power of the local "strong men" and, when the poor sit in a village committee or association, it is essentially because they want to state their loyalty to them (Kumar and Corbridge, 2002).

In highly unequal societies, such as in caste-based systems, elite capture is almost certain to occur in the absence of effective empowerment of weaker groups. Even in a state like Kerala, where social struggles have contributed a lot to emancipating marginal people, malpractices are frequent. For example, selection criteria are often bypassed to favour politically connected individuals. In the rural communities studied by Nair (2000), almost half of the people confessed that they ignored the selection criteria, and one-third were of the opinion that these criteria are flouted for the benefit of individuals with good political connections or with strong ties to the local leadership. According to Isaac and Franke (2002), between 26 and 36 per cent of the *Panchayats* manipulated the lists of beneficiaries of local development programmes for which resources had been obtained from the state. Such percentages may be considered rather low by people accustomed to the unfair practices of rural elites prevailing in other Indian states, particularly Bihar, Madhya Pradesh and Uttar Pradesh. More information about the experience of Kerala will be provided below.

In egalitarian set-ups, by contrast, identification and punishment of fraudulent behaviour tend to be easier. Such conditions are especially likely to obtain when people interact within the framework of a particular social group. Thus, in a Karnataka village, a caste leader who misappropriated funds collected for caste festivities, was severely sanctioned. Not only did he lose his position as leader, but he was also ostracized by his caste group. In order to be readmitted to the latter (without being reinstated in his leadership position), he had to tender a public apology, reimburse the money and give a feast to the caste group (Pur 2007, p. 418).

3.2 The Ominous Rise of Development Brokers

It was mentioned earlier that many international donor agencies tend to require the formation and training of village groups or associations as a precondition for disbursing money in the framework of community-based projects. In countries or areas where community empowerment is low, such a mechanism has the unfortunate effect of encouraging the entry of wealthier and more educated people into leadership positions because of the attractiveness of outside funding (Gugerty and Kremer, 1999; Rao and Ibanez, 2001; Brett, 2003; Agrawal and Gupta 2005).[5]

What must now be added is that traditional or locally-based elites (elders, heads of lineage and village chiefs) are not the only sort of leaders who benefit from external resources conveyed under participatory development approaches.[6] Frequently, urban elites "remember" their geographical origin and reactivate their rural roots when new funds become available, which are funnelled through rural groups or communities, or through local governments or municipalities. For example, in Cameroon, as soon as the decentralized programme of forestry management was launched, a "localism fever" set in: members of the urban elite, consisting mainly of senior civil servants and politicians, began to join in local initiatives by getting co-opted or "elected" in local committees or associations, or by featuring as resource persons for them. They then established "alliances with town-based companies, to whom they have promised their villages' forests" (Oyono, 2004, p. 102), giving rise to accusations of "re-centralization". It is therefore not surprising that committee members have disconnected themselves from the rest of village communities, and that cases of financial misappropriation are widespread – in one documented case, members of the management committee (Oyono, 2005, p. 11) embezzled half of the forestry fees.

The spawning of local (and foreign) NGOs is another recent phenomenon that must be understood in the light of the redirecting of foreign aid flows. Acting as "development brokers", political entrepreneurs have been quick to understand that the creation of an NGO has become one of the best means of procuring funds from the international community (Meyer, 1995; Bebbington, 1997; Bierschenk et al., 2000; Lund, 2006). In many instances, government officials themselves are directly involved in the formation and leadership of local NGOs. They often have two visiting cards, one showing their function and title in a government department and the other presenting them as a chairman or a chairwoman of an NGO. As pointed out by Chabal and Daloz (1999, pp. 22–4), a massive proliferation of NGOs is "less the outcome of the increasing political weight of civil society than the consequence of the very pragmatic realization that resources are now largely channelled through NGOs". As a consequence, "the political economy of foreign aid has not changed significantly . . . the use of NGO resources can today serve the strategic interests of the classical entrepreneurial Big Man just as well as access to state coffers did in the past".

Thus, in the case of Benin, a West African country especially spoiled by the donors, local NGOs and associations, which are often "empty shells established with the sole purpose of capturing aid", have multiplied within a short period to number several thousands. Many others wait to receive the approval of the Ministry of Interior (*Le Monde*, 26 February 2001). In Mali, there were 1467 NGOs registered locally in December 2001 (Coulibaly, 2003, p. 24). In non-African countries also, NGOs often constitute "an opportunistic response of downsized bureaucrats, with no real participation or local empowerment" and, inevitably, programme officers themselves become involved in the creation of community institutions (Conning and Kevane, 2002, pp. 383–4; see also Meyer, 1995; Bebbington, 1997; Gray, 1999).

The Economist's allegorical statement that NGOs "often sprout up, like plants in the sunlight, solely to bathe in this foreign money" (Special Report "Aid to Africa", 2–8 July 2005, p. 26) seems well justified in the light of the above sort of evidence. Yet it singularly contrasts with the contention of a sociologist of the World Bank, according to whom "NGOs insert themselves not as a third and different/independent actor, but as an emanation and representation of the community" (Cernea, 1988, p. 10). What needs to be stressed is that the risk of capture by opportunistic development brokers is high when self-conscious, organized local communities do not actually exist prior to the opening up of new development opportunities by state agencies or international donors (see Li, 2001, for a well-documented illustration of this possibility), while donors simultaneously assume a priori that the beneficiary communities are strong and their leadership accountable (McDermott, 2001).

4 PERVERSION OF PARTICIPATION UNDER DONOR COMPETITION

In a genuine participation process, people should contribute toward the production of the private or public goods and services that external assistance makes possible. Indeed, if these goods and services carry a high value for them, and if they have the wherewithal to finance part but not all of the production expenditures involved (in particular, they can bear expenses in kind, such as supplying the labour required for the construction of some village facility), the beneficiaries should be willing to participate in the investment. Leaving the free-rider problem aside (everyone would like others to carry the burden of cost contribution), one would actually expect people's contributions to signal the intensity of their preference and positive motivations for the project at stake and, hence, to have a positive impact on the aid project outcomes.

The available studies do not, however, lead to unambiguous conclusions in this regard. While some studies show that capital cost contribution (measured, say, by the percentage of households in the village who have contributed) is positively related to the effectiveness of project outcomes, other studies lead to the opposite conclusion, or show no significant impact (see Prokopy, 2005, pp. 1801–6, for a survey of the literature on water supply projects). The ambiguity of these results is perhaps not surprising in so far as cost contribution is typically not voluntary but imposed by many donor agencies as a precondition for releasing aid funds. It is, therefore, possible that beneficiaries contribute only reluctantly so that the presumed favourable effect on project effectiveness does not take place.

But why should they be reluctant to participate? Two possible explanations spring to mind. First, as discussed above, the aid-assisted project may not belong to the people's top priorities (thus violating the assumption above), or it may be a priority objective, but only for the village elite, which has the power to shift the entire burden of the local contribution to the poor. Second, people may think that they could get the (desired) project free. This is likely to happen (1) if they feel that the donor agency is rich enough to provide all the necessary resources instead of insisting on a local contribution, and/or (2) if donor competition is sufficiently stiff to make villagers hopeful that the local contribution requirement can be somehow circumvented or tampered with.

There is suggestive evidence to show that, in contexts where competition between donors is acute, such as is observed in many poor countries with a rather good record of political stability and human rights, local contributions are difficult to extract. Worse, potential beneficiaries are often found to demand from the aid agency extra payments for themselves in the form of per diem or special allowances. Here, again, Tembo's findings regarding Malawi are instructive and, according to my own experience, can be safely extended to a great part of the African continent.

The villagers' image of foreign donors, NGOs in particular, rests on a perception of them as humanitarian agencies that have plentiful resources at their disposal to alleviate poverty and improve the levels of living in economically developing regions of the world. As a consequence, beneficiaries believe that these agencies have enough money to cover what they are asked to pay or to supply on account of local contribution. Naturally enough, they may be easily led into thinking that fieldworkers or agents acting on behalf of the aid organizations pocket local contributions, or their equivalent. As expressed vividly by a villager:

> what we perceive is that these organizations are using our villages to eat their money because when a lion catches a cow it goes hiding far away in the forest. This is what happens with these organization officials. When money comes to assist us in the village they just use it themselves and report to donors that they have assisted such and such areas. (Cited from Tembo, 2003, p. 105)

The suspicions of dishonesty thus aroused are not conducive to effective project implementation.

In the same way that as they cannot imagine that aid agencies ask for local contributions, since they are thought to have plentiful resources at hand, they cannot imagine either that these agencies choose to give loans instead of grants, especially so if loans carry interest. As explained by Tembo, the realization that NGOs give loans instead of grants immediately creates the image of "NGOs making their profits" in the minds of villagers, including traditional leaders, committee members and better-off people (Tembo, 2003, p. 109). When NGOs started demanding repayments from people and did not hesitate to use coercive means, such as confiscation of the defaulter's property, the villagers were shocked and conflicts erupted. Again, the suspicion emerged that fieldworkers or NGO agents must have concocted this stratagem in order to steal money intended for the grass-roots.

The pervasive presence of per diem and other allowances is to be seen in the same perspective of aid organizations perceived as richly endowed agencies driven by humanitarian considerations. Yet, it can be properly understood only in a context of stiff competition between such agencies, as reflected in the actual or potential presence of several donors in the same community.[7] Under these conditions, indeed, the village elite or the leaders of the village "partner" associations feel emboldened to ask for additional advantages from the donors. This demand is typically justified on the grounds that they have to devote time (and resources) to the project, and that this time has a substantial value for which they ought to be compensated. There is an obvious parallel between this way of arguing and the reasons put forward by a local leader to vindicate his fraudulent use of NGO funds in an above-told story (see above). This is forgetting that external assistance is aimed at benefiting local people (including the elite), so that compensation is not justifiable. Hence, the understandable surprise and anger of fieldworkers when they find themselves confronted with the pressing demands of local leaders or beneficiaries for particular advantages, such as personal vehicles, training allowances or per diem for the attendance in committee meetings.

The essential difference between allowances (per diem) and aid embezzlement is, of course, that the former is an official payment whereas the latter is an illegal, hidden practice. Since allowances are official, their level is determined because of a bargaining process between an aid organization and a local leader or village elite. What we then expect is that the stiffer the competition between aid donors the more attractive the exit opportunities for a local leader in the event of failure of the negotiation, and the higher the rent (say, under the form of explicit allowances) he will be able to extract from the donor agency. On the other hand, when analysing aid embezzlement, one has to consider that an information gap exists between the donor and the local leader. The leader's fraud can be detected with a probability that increases with the size of the fraud and, in the event of fraud detection, the leader is punished by the donor (through withdrawal of the subsequent tranches of aid money in a multi-period framework, or through imposition of a fine in a one-period set-up). Under such conditions, it can be shown that the leader will capture a positive share of the aid resources at equilibrium, and his share increases with the extent of donor competition. At least, this is true if the leader attaches more weight to his own well-being than to that of the other community members, or if his accountability to the latter is limited. If local leaders are benevolent – a possibility suggested by Rao and Ibanez (2001) – the problem of elite capture obviously disappears.

5 THE POSITIVE EFFECTS OF COMMUNITY PARTICIPATION ON PROJECT OUTCOMES: A CONDITIONAL RESULT

A central question when dealing with the participatory approach to development is the impact of participation of beneficiaries in project decisions on the effectiveness of outcomes achieved. The common assumption is that greater community participation should promote projects and assets (both private and public) that are more responsive to the needs of the poor, better adapted to local expertise and know-how, and more properly maintained. Community participation is expected to improve the circulation of information, either in the bottom-up case (for example, about the preferences and technical knowledge of local people), or in a top-down manner (for example, about the external opportunities available). It is also expected to enhance the bargaining power of the beneficiaries by getting them involved in project initiatives and decisions at all relevant levels (design, planning, mobilization of resources, and so on). This is the so-called "ownership" aspect of participation.

Serious methodological problems need to be overcome in order to assess correctly the impact of community participation on project outcomes. In addition to measurement problems related both to independent (how to build adequate indicators of participation) and dependent (outcome) variables, tricky endogeneity problems must be confronted. A first source of endogeneity lies in reverse causation – better projects may lead to greater participation at the same time as greater participation may yield better projects. A second source arises from missing variables – project outcomes and participation may be jointly determined by an exogenous factor (Isham and Narayan, 1995). Due to all these difficulties, there are only a few reliable empirical studies to document the effects of participation on project effectiveness (for a recent survey of the whole literature, see Pozzoni and Kumar, 2005).

Among those few studies are those of Isham and Kähkönen (2002a, 2002b) devoted to water supply projects in Indonesia, India and Sri Lanka. The authors reach the conclusion that "design participation" and people's involvement in project decisions are significant predictors of community satisfaction with service design, thus confirming the results obtained by Katz and Sara (1997) on the basis of a broader set of countries.[8] Also, household participation led to different technology choices and levels of service, while project outcomes were positively influenced by user contributions to monitoring activities (for construction as well as operation and maintenance tasks). Contrasting with these findings are those attained by Hoddinott et al. (2001) who studied the effects of participation in public work programmes in the Western Cape Province in South Africa. Their results indicate that participation has no effect whatsoever on any of the (employment) outcome variables that they have considered.

The work of Khwaja (2003, 2004) deserves special mention because it underlines the need to take project characteristics (in addition to community characteristics) into account while assessing the impact of participation on project outcomes. Based on primary data collected for 132 infrastructural projects funded by the Aga Khan Rural Support Programme (AKRSP) in Northern Pakistan, the study uses the current state of project maintenance as the main outcome measure. For participation, the measure chosen is the fraction of five randomly selected respondents in each community who responded that their household had participated in a particular project decision. This information was collected for several key decisions made from the inception of a project to its operation. Clearly, some of these decisions (for example, the decision regarding the type of project to choose, how to use and manage it) require a good deal of local information yet do not involve much technical/engineering input. In contrast, decisions such as selecting a particular site for the project, its scale and design are likely to have the opposite characteristics.

The (econometric) results obtained by Khwaja appear to be quite robust. Whether participation levels are considered separately for each type of decision or are averaged in non-technical and technical decisions, they consistently show that greater community participation in non-technical decisions is associated with higher project outcomes, whereas in technical decisions it actually leads to worse project outcomes. In conclusion, participation may not always be desirable, and it would be wrong to place too large a burden on community participation because its limitations are ignored (Khwaja, 2004, p. 436).

There are actually plenty of examples showing that technical choices favoured by villagers may be mistaken owing to a lack of knowledge about general conditions under which a project takes place. For example, there are common problems with local priorities for network infrastructure services that depend on the reliability of activities further up the chain. A rural community may thus identify as their top priority the rehabilitation of an irrigation canal or an agricultural access road, but if the main irrigation channel that feeds the local canal or the main highway to primary markets is in disrepair (and other actors are responsible for the higher-level service), the community may be building a useless irrigation canal or a road to nowhere. In addition to the knowledge problem, some local services have spillover benefits, and higher-level rules on such services or conditional transfers to meet these needs are perfectly legitimate. To take another example, community participation might identify health services as the top priority, but the replacement of a contaminated water supply that citizens are unaware of (because water is plentiful and it tastes fine) could be a more important factor in promoting improved community health than a new health centre.[9]

Let us return to Khwaja's study in order to consider the impact of community characteristics. His conclusion in this respect is that socially heterogeneous communities have lower project outcomes than more homogeneous ones, at least over a certain range (see also, for example, Molinas, 1998; La Ferrara, 2002; Bardhan and Dayton-Johnson, 2007).[10] The latter finding is not always obtained, however. Thus, from the work of Somanathan et al. (2007) on Indian forestry, we learn that communities that are more heterogeneous in terms of caste composition do not have lower outcomes in matters of pine forest conservation. Mosse (1997), who has studied water tanks in South India, has observed that development projects are not necessarily better managed in traditionally cohesive or rather egalitarian village communities. In some areas, at least, tanks seem to be managed more effectively when there is a strong caste authority that creates order and discipline among users, in particular, when it comes to mobilizing individual and communal labour. Moreover, motives and constraints differ considerably if collective action concerns a public good that carries special meaning in the context of local culture (and even productive physical assets, such as irrigation tanks, can be the repositories of symbolic resources), or if it is a development project based on imported concepts such as equality, democracy and efficiency (see also Laurent, 1998; Platteau and Abraham, 2002).

In some important instances, the relevant meaning of heterogeneity may be the fact, largely overlooked in the economic literature, that an individual forms part of several communities, not all of which have a clear geographical location (Conning and Kevane, 2002, p. 381; Lund, 2006, pp. 693–5). In the presence of multiple communities and multiple, possibly conflicting identities, it is difficult to say a priori whether heterogeneity is a good or a bad thing for local cooperation. The circumstances surrounding participation must be spelled out in detail before one can figure out the plausible effects of heterogeneity. For example, if the leaders of a village community belong to networks of relations outside the village, their position may either strengthen or undermine collective action and (democratic) participation at the level of the residential community depending on the nature of the external networks (for example, do they include "development brokers"?), the manner in which they are mobilized by the leaders for development projects, the extent to which they serve as exit opportunities for them, and so on.

In short, the concept of community must be viewed as contextual and endogenous, rather than as a fixed construct, onto which participation mechanisms can be readily grafted. Furthermore, the influence of heterogeneity on project outcomes cannot be stated in any general manner, because heterogeneity may exist along many different dimensions and its impact is likely to vary according to the historical, social and political environment (Baland and Platteau, 2003; Mansuri and Rao, 2004).

6 FISCAL DECENTRALIZATION

Many of the aforementioned failures of participatory development could be surmounted if communities and their leaders could be drawn into a repeated (infinite) rather than a finite game. Repeated games over an unlimited or indefinite period, so the argument runs, would allow reputation effects and punishment mechanisms to come into play, with the consequence of disciplining rapacious local leaders and intermediaries. The ideal situation here is that of fiscal decentralization under which communities have to generate by themselves a substantial portion of the resources required for locally defined development purposes. An alternative situation would have the central government provide grants to local communities or municipalities, and let them more or less freely decide how to allocate them. Yet, transfers are conditional in the sense that government complies with local requests for new grants only if performance achieved with the help of previously released tranches is deemed satisfactory. The second scheme, however, is fraught with a serious difficulty known as a soft budget constraint: this is the risk that the central government, moved by political considerations, does not abide by a commitment to deny new tranches of funds in the event of bad performance by local agencies. If they anticipate such behaviour, the latter would not feel constrained by the conditional transfer mechanism, and allocation of centrally provided funds is likely to be both inefficient and inequitable.

Compelling communities to raise taxes to finance their own needs, at least at the margin could lead to local hard budget constraints. The idea is that, if local voters are not satisfied with the behaviour of their local representatives and elected councils, they would be able to sanction them by not returning them to power, and/or refusing to pay taxes or supply their contributions (in cash or in kind) in subsequent rounds of the game. In other words, it is hypothesized that under a local democracy, common people would succeed in disciplining their leaders by making them accountable, which implies that they can inspect their actions and punish them whenever they detect significant fraud or blatant misuse of the locally provided resources. As is typical in repeated games, a good equilibrium is expected to prevail – here, an efficient and equitable use of funds – if the future consequences of present decisions are properly taken into account (the discount rate of future benefits is not too high), and if information is available at the local level. The latter assumption, in particular, is believed to be well satisfied in the context of fiscal decentralization. Indeed, problems of information distortion between communities, local leaders and external fund-providing agencies do not arise any more since the latter do not play any major role in supporting community development.

Unfortunately, fiscal decentralization may easily fail to meet the expectations placed in it in the light of the predictions of repeated game theory. In the following, attention will be focused on five problems likely to thwart the success of fiscal decentralization schemes or to reduce their attractiveness. This list is not exhaustive since stress is deliberately put on those problems that bear an obvious relation to the preceding discussion of the pitfalls of participation when resources are externally provided.

The first thing to note is that, when a game is repeated infinitely, we know from the Folk Theorem that the good equilibrium is not certain to be established since there is a multiplicity of possible equilibria. If agents do not devise the sort of strategies that lead to cooperation, say because of adverse norms and beliefs, cooperation will never become an equilibrium outcome. In particular, norms that have evolved under a patron–client system and do not prescribe punishment against leaders as long as they are not guilty of blatant disregard for their clients' predicament (see the discussion above), are evidently not susceptible to producing cooperation in a repeated interaction framework. In these circumstances, it is not surprising to hear that, in Nepal, for example, decentralization has created opportunities for elites to dominate decision-making at the local levels (Bienen et al., 1990, pp.72–3). This again shows that empowerment of the poor is often impossible if they do not learn to emancipate themselves from the tutelage of the rich, and to call traditional ways of thinking into question.

Second, the disciplining logic of the repeated interaction framework is broken if leaders have no long-term interest in their local constituency. In this case, their behaviour resembles that of the so-called development brokers (see discussion above). Unlike community members whose well-being depends very much on local conditions, elected leaders may thus have a small interest in the future of their locality because they have valuable outside options. In these circumstances, the assumption of low discount of future results stands violated, and the efficient equilibrium outcome cannot prevail.

It bears emphasis that the problem may arise not only from fleeing political leaders but also because of corrupt bureaucrats, who are largely not under control of the villagers. In Kerala, much like in Indonesia (Olken, 2005), it has been found that a critical aspect of resource embezzlement lies in the special connections existing between private entrepreneurs, on the one hand, and political leaders and bureaucrats, on the other (Isaac and Franke, 2002; Sharma, 2003; Vijayalakshmi, 2003b). These privileged contacts create a lot of room for malpractices consisting of falsifying invoices and over-reporting costs, cheating on quality standards, and so on. In order to overcome this problem, the government of Kerala provided that the beneficiaries themselves, through special committees, should be responsible for the carrying out and monitoring of public works such as the construction of village roads, schools and dispensaries. However, this system has not worked according to expectations. In one-fourth of the cases examined by Isaac and Franke (2002), the committee was completely manipulated, being actually formed at the initiative of the entrepreneurs with the approval of politicians eager to preserve the corrupt system that benefited them. Around one-half of these committees had simply ceased to operate while others had to work under the strong pressures of entrepreneurs and politicians. This raises a particularly awkward problem, if ordinary villagers or the targeted beneficiaries potentially threaten the vested interests of established entrepreneurs, the latter lobby their political friends to act behind the scenes.

Third, local authorities may be nominated through an electoral process that is dominated by political parties that have a nationwide basis. There is then a high risk that these parties attempt to capture local agencies and councils in the same way as at the national level. Consequently, political competition mainly centres around the question of how to allocate patronage between contending political machines. The Kerala experience with decentralization is especially instructive. The left-coalition government decided in 1996 to allocate 35–40 per cent of its annual budget for new development plans to projects designed by the local bodies (Véron, 2001, p. 606). Yet, the central government (the Planning Commission, more precisely) has remained ultimately responsible for setting the national and regional priorities under which the programme is to operate (for example, establishing priority for productive investments), defining the eligibility criteria, fixing the representation of various population groups or strata in the local decision-making bodies as well as their mode of operation, providing guidelines on what village reports should contain, and so on (Isaac and Harilal, 1997; Isaac, 1998; Véron, 2001). It must also be borne in mind that, following a long period of intense social struggle starting in the 1930s and a widespread literacy and publicity campaign, the weakest sections of the rural population – especially agricultural labourers (always belonging to the lowest castes) and women – learned to articulate and express their aspirations, assert their rights and bargain with local power-holders.

These two factors seemed to provide ideal conditions for an effective operation of decentralized development. Unfortunately, however, such a programme has rapidly become a platform for political favouritism in a country plagued by excessive party politicization down to the local level. When a political party dominates a *Panchayat*, it tends to reward its sympathizers exclusively, with the result that many villagers became disillusioned with the participatory process and begin to absent themselves from meetings in the *Gram Sabhas*[11] (Das, 2000, pp. 4302–3).

Inbanathan and Gopalappa (2002) tell us a similar story about the interference of patronage politics in local governance programmes of the neighbouring state of Karnataka (see also Inbanathan, 1999, 2000). Recent evidence presented in the aforementioned study by Bardhan et al. (2008) also suggests that in West Bengal, programme benefits, at least those of a recurring nature (subsidized credit, employment on public works programmes, distribution of minikits of agricultural inputs) and personalized help by the local government, correlated positively with the likelihood of voting for the Left Front. Dominated by the Communist Party, the Front has won consecutive elections over more than three decades, a unique feature in the history of democracy. In theory, causation can run both ways, from benefits to voting (simple voter gratitude), or from voting to benefits and from benefits to voting (two-way clientelism). Since voters seem to respond more to recurring than to one-time benefits, clientelism is probably stronger in voter behaviour than gratitude or loyalty.

What the above evidence suggests is that participatory development can achieve its objectives and realize its potential, especially in the context of economically differentiated rural societies. The pre-conditions include: (1) if an effective and impartial state, genuinely devoted to the protection of the poor, is available to impose and enforce directions and strictures regarding the modus operandi of the decentralization programme and (2) if real empowerment of the weaker sections of the population takes place that enables them to obtain relevant information, influence policies and monitor the state's instructions at the local level. A genuine dilemma actually arises from these conditions. Indeed, participatory development is deemed especially necessary in countries where the state is inefficient and corrupt and where the civil society is weak (such as numerous countries of Sub-Saharan Africa) that is, in countries where it is the least likely to be successful. The fact of the matter is that participatory development is no ready-made solution to circumvent or overcome the drawbacks resulting from the absence of an effective state and the lack of organization among the poor. If the latter are not present, such an approach is bound to be perverted and to miss at least some its main objectives. The experience of Kerala is again useful here because the poor have been genuinely empowered in this Indian state, with the consequence that they were able to express their dissatisfaction at the way the Communist Party managed the decentralized programme. This party was, indeed, defeated in the subsequent elections and the most blatant abuses of the programme could be amended because of this signal democratically sent by the voters.

This was not the case in Indonesia where the new devolution system has resulted in a situation where the provincial regents:

> exercise their new administrative and financial clout so imperiously that locals refer to them as "little kings". Stories abound of reckless extravagance or outright corruption . . . regents have simply seized companies belonging to the central government, or imposed arbitrary new rules on businesses. Fears of decentralization run amok are beginning to replace fears of Indonesia's disintegration. (*The Economist*, 15–21 February, 2003, pp. 54–5)

In Bangladesh, likewise, we learn that, under Ershad's decentralization reforms, although people were mobilized at the local (*upazila*) subdistrict level, the decisions over allocation of resources continued to be made by elites of politically-based factions that controlled the local governments (Westergaard and Alam, 1995).

Regarding the disciplining role of the central state, a detailed inquiry into the reasons underlying Brazil's success in decentralization of public service from state to municipal government (in the state of Ceara in the northeast) has shown that "it had at its core a strong and new role played by central government" (Tendler, 1997, p. 73). More precisely, the (state) government "kept an iron hand" on some crucial components of the decentralized programmes so as to substantially reduce the opportunities for mayors and local power-holders (especially large landowners) to exercise patronage. Simultaneously, it worked actively (through educational and information-spreading campaigns) to raise the hopes of rural communities about what to expect from their government. The result was a profound change in the dynamics of patronage politics as it related to public service at the local level. The ability of the central government to set directions and strictures regarding how programmes of decentralized development should operate locally can create much-needed constraints on rent-seeking behaviour by local elites (and government workers) is also evident from the experience of Bolivia's Emergency Social Fund (ESF). Here, we are told that "Decentralization worked because centralization worked. The ESF centralized the appropriate things: information, negotiations with international donors, and incentive systems for ESF employees. This in turn enabled it to decentralize the design and construction of rural projects" (Klitgaard, 1997, pp. 1965–7 – quoted from Hoddinott et al., 2001, p. 12; see also Stavis, 1982–83, for Taiwan).

A fourth problem that may plague fiscal decentralization programmes is the sheer administrative complexity of assessing, levying and collecting local taxes. Devolution of property tax, to local governments, for example, involves many intricacies that may prove insurmountable when administrative capacity at local level is low. This gives rise to a new paradox: fiscal decentralization is especially necessary in countries where the administrative capacity of the central state is weak, yet in these countries tax assessment and collection tasks are likely to prove equally hard at the local level.

Finally, by promoting autonomy of local constituencies, fiscal decentralization is almost certain to encourage local identification, including ethnic differentiation, to weaken allegiance to the central government, and to increase inter-regional inequalities. Bear in mind here the aforementioned experience of fiscal decentralization in rural China (Wang and Yao, 2007), which has the effect of reducing fiscal sharing with townships. Lack of fiscal solidarity is problematic not only because it encourages local selfishness, but also because it undermines the financing of valuable public goods in the presence of externalities that extend beyond the area of localities.

7 CONCLUSION

This chapter has been aimed at tempering, not defeating, the enthusiasm of the advocates of participatory development. To encourage participation of the intended beneficiaries of pro-poor development is undoubtedly a commendable objective. What has been argued throughout the discussion is that measurement of the impact of participation on development project outcomes is methodologically complex, and, at this stage, there are still few conclusive statements that can be made about the importance and the modus operandi of this impact. Nonetheless, there is no such thing as a one-size-fits-all approach to participatory development. In fact, a proper participation design needs to be based on detailed knowledge of the characteristics of the targeted communities and the environment in which they live. The discussion has drawn attention to the critical role of heterogeneity, which varies from place to place along several dimensions (social differentiation, political domination, ethnic fragmentation).

When heterogeneity reflects deeply entrenched power hierarchies, there is a considerable risk that the local elite will distort information in a strategic manner and opportunistically capture a substantial portion of the benefits of external assistance. The problem in many poor countries is that inequalities, particularly power asymmetries, are often embedded into strong local patriarchies that are not easily called into question. It is, therefore, not surprising that these countries show considerable proneness to elite capture – whether in the hands of local leaders, or in those of development brokers operating from higher up the patronage network – as well as a great readiness on the part of the commoners to accept and even legitimate the unequal apportioning of externally provided resources. In contrast, participatory projects appear to be comparatively effective in areas where economic development is more advanced and more widespread, and where social movements aimed at countering inequalities and oppression have a rather long history. This indicates that characteristics of the institutional environment matter a lot as a support for decentralized development (Finsterbusch and Van Wincklin, 1989; Bardhan and Mookherjee, 2006a, Chap. 1).

Clearly, therefore, participatory approaches to development, such as the World Bank's community-based or -driven development approaches (CBD and CDD), are no magical medicines susceptible of curing all the ills attributed to the (previously) existing centralized mode of governance. In the end, the following dilemma cannot be avoided: the areas where inequalities are the highest and the most entrenched, and where one would like to implement participatory approaches in order to correct them, are also those where these approaches are least likely to succeed.[12] Other kinds of interventions are then needed to complement and support community-based development. Among those complementary measures, employment-creation schemes directed to the poor should figure prominently since they may be expected not only to increase their incomes but also to enhance their bargaining strength by helping them to wean themselves off the dependence of local patrons. The fact that, so far, top priority has been given to social sector expenditures under most decentralized development initiatives must therefore be a cause of concern. It is particularly worth stressing that in all successful cases of participatory development, such as in Kerala, West Bengal and Brazil, "the ground for effective participation was created by years of social and political activism by progressive political parties aimed at mobilizing the weaker segments of the society in a wider enterprise in social transformation" (Osmani, 2008, p. 35).

Another dilemma that may arise in the context of participatory development projects is the following: greedy village elites may happen to simultaneously capture aid benefits and supply effective leadership for the management of local projects. In this case, the poor may eventually draw benefits from aid interventions even though there is unequal sharing of the externally provided resources. There then exists a trade-off between the objective of poverty alleviation and considerations of equity and social justice to which Western donors typically attach great importance. If priority is given to breaking structural inequalities in social relations and to helping subject people to emancipate themselves from a culture of domination and poverty, mechanisms of collective empowerment (starting with learning to work together, to debate, to make decisions, to keep records and to implement development projects) and individual advancement (say, through self-employment) must receive primary attention.

Lastly, a long-term horizon is absolutely necessary. Impatience with results and poor design of the components of participatory programmes – such as moving too rapidly and confronting upfront those who risk losing power and influence – may be counterproductive. It also overwhelms the capacities of those who gain power – and is likely to produce perverse effects and to cause disillusionment on the part of both the external agencies and the beneficiary groups or communities.

It is true that programmes of fiscal decentralization may bring more discipline on unruly leaders because they create a repeated framework interaction that allows for reputation effects and punishment mechanisms. Information distortion problems are also likely to be less important when local communities rely mainly on their own resources to develop. Nevertheless, such programmes are still plagued by serious problems, among which the risk of elite capture figures prominently. Moreover, local autonomy produces a number of negative side-effects that a state bent on reinforcing national integration may wish to avoid. Finally, the success of such programmes critically hinges on a right distribution of tasks between the central state and decentralized bodies, and on sufficient strength of both agencies. In the absence of strong administrative capacities at local level, in particular, fiscal decentralization programmes are bound to fail.

More generally, effective participation requires the adoption of a multi-faceted strategy involving state, society and the common people. The state must play an important role on several fronts. Not only must the state credibly work toward creating the enabling conditions for civil society and social movements to operate adequately. This involves implementing a whole range of human rights so that weaker segments of the society can participate confidently and independently in the presence of entrenched asymmetries of power; and providing space for civil society and social movements to mobilize and educate common people for participatory enterprises (Osmani, 2008, p. 36). However, the central state must also play a disciplining role so as to substantially reduce the opportunities for mayors and local power-holders (especially large landowners) to exercise patronage.

We are then taken to the logical conclusion that sound participatory governance implies the existence of sound governance at the macro level. In other words, effective participatory governance and macro governance are complementary goods rather than substitutes.[13] In the light of the aforementioned experiences of successful decentralization, it bears emphasis that good macro-governance does not imply that all the attributes associated with good governance in the present donors' agenda ought to be present. Such a condition would present an insurmountable challenge to most if not all developing countries where poverty needs to be reduced. What seems to matter most is the capacity of the state to set clear priorities, provide leadership and tame private vested interests that possibly conflict with the objective of medium- to long-term growth. It is interesting to notice the similarity between this final conclusion and the findings obtained in recent, innovative studies of the relationship between governance and development understood as economic growth sustained over a medium to long period of time (Khan, 2000, 2004; North et al., 2006; Meisel and Aoudia, 2008).

What comes out of these studies, indeed, is that institutional indicators that best differentiate between successful and unsuccessful developing countries are factors relating to the state's capacity to offer a strategic vision of the foreseeable future for its citizens, to provide them with credible forms of coordination and to manage divergent interests in the light of this vision so as to stabilize anticipations and reduce uncertainty. Thus, in the study of Meisel and Aoudia (2008) based on a new dataset elaborated by researchers from the French Ministry of the Economy, Finance and Employment (MINEFE) and the Agence Française de Développement (AFD), the following institutional variables have been found to matter most for economic take-off: the priority put on development objectives by the national elite; its ability to develop a strategic vision; effective coordination efforts to make common interests prevail over particular interests; the country's aptitude for innovation; competence of political authorities; effective coordination between ministries and political authorities; technological environment of non-financial firms. In addition, the quality of public goods and the security of agricultural property rights and contracts also seem to matter. Other factors such as decentralization, trade union freedom, efficiency of administrations, effective control of corruption, transparency of public action, formalization of property rights, regulation of competition, observance of labour laws, security of transactions in the financial system and social mobility appear to play a role only at a later stage, when the challenge is to catch up with developed countries rather than to embark on a path of rapid and sustained economic growth.

NOTES

* Jean-Philippe Platteau is Professor of Economics and Director of the Centre for Research in the Economy of Development (CRED) at the University of Namur, Belgium. Many thanks are due to Martina Bjorkman who provided me with detailed comments and suggestions on a previous version of the chapter.

1. In Tembo's words: "People's preoccupation was to align their requests with what an NGO was providing, in a sense of defending their position for assistance even when the critical problem was something else . . . in most cases, people were co-operative, in terms of giving appropriate answers to fieldworkers, in order to please them and have access to NGO assistance. This assistance was in order to fulfill other purposes they already formed on their minds. They were negotiating with fieldworkers from a broad background of their experience in which they had critical problems to be addressed or cured . . . [therefore], the actual purposes of the people could not be reflected in the project design because the people's primary orientation was to successfully access assistance.

If they had based their negotiations on their genuine uses of assistance, they might not have been able to access NGO assistance . . . they preferred to hide the actual uses as long as they succeeded to access assistance, which they could then use for their own purposes" (Tembo, 2003, pp. 93–4, 125, 131–2).

2. To understand the behaviour that underlies the allocation of resources driving such results, the authors have assumed that a community is maximizing a positively weighted sum of utilities featuring the situation of two population groups, poor and non-poor. Communities are thus able to achieve an efficient allocation of the resources put at their disposal by a central agent (the so-called Project Office), which does not observe how much is going to the poor in each area but takes the behaviour of communities into account while setting the budget allocation between them. The weights on the utilities of the poor and the non-poor are interpreted as "capture coefficients" arising endogenously in a voting model with differences in voter information between the poor and the non-poor. Moreover, the weights are assumed to depend on characteristics of the poor and non-poor, as well as the local political and economic environment, and the programme itself.
3. Note that this kind of theoretical prediction is identical to that obtained by Bardhan and Mookherjee in some of their theoretical papers analysing the determinants of the relative efficiency of decentralization. In one of these papers (1999), for example, they have investigated the determinants of relative capture of local and national governments in the context of a model of (two-party) electoral competition with lobbying by special interest groups (the non-poor are organized in a lobby and can make campaign contributions). The most salient result is that relative capture depends on heterogeneity with respect to levels of local inequality and poverty: decentralization will tend to increase elite capture in high inequality localities (since higher inequality reduces the level of awareness of the poor, decreasing the level of their political participation) and lower it in low inequality ones (see also Bardhan and Mookherjee, 2005, 2006b).
4. Rather unexpectedly, they also find that in more unequal villages the elite is more able to influence inter-village competition such that project resources flow to their villages. The net effect on the poor is therefore not clear.
5. Revealingly, a major problem confronted by the community-based drive attempted during the 1950s by the Ford Foundation and US foreign assistance programmes, and which eventually led to its demise, lay in its inability to effectively counter the vested interests of local elites (Holdcroft, 1984, p. 51).
6. This section is largely based on Platteau (2004).
7. Such a situation gives rise to substantial confusion because donor agencies typically act in an uncoordinated manner (World Bank, 2005, pp. 35–6).
8. On the other hand, Katz and Sara found that in numerous cases little effort was made to involve households in decision mechanisms, and the benefits of water projects were appropriated by local leaders.
9. Thanks are due to Paul Smoke for suggesting these examples.
10. Khwaja also found that community-managed projects are better maintained than projects managed by the local government.
11. A meeting comprising the body of people registered to elect the *Panchayat*.
12. This conclusion is close to that reached by Mansuri and Rao (2004) for whom the formation of homogeneous communities, such as are needed for ensuring effective participation, is much less likely in contexts where mobility is low, making communities more likely to be characterized by deeply entrenched power hierarchies. Unfortunately, this is where poverty programmes are most needed.
13. Clearly, the participatory approach is bound to fail in Baluchistan (Pakistan), for example, because there the tribal chiefs tax their people heavily and rule them autocratically. "It is a singular novelty of Baluch politics" that these chiefs "are always in the forefront of every 'democratic' movement to restore the rights of their people . . . Yet almost every such leader has a jail to put away his poor tribesmen who dare to transgress against his authority, but none has as yet been known to have built a school or

a medical clinic for his people. They are not known to have allowed anyone else to do so either, and frequently those making any such attempt are liable to be kidnapped or at least chased out of the area. They would like to have democracy to the extent that it enhances their own power, but would check any advance by civilization in areas under their control" (Abbas, 2005, p. 80).

REFERENCES

Abbas, H. (2005), *Pakistan's Drift into Extremism – Allah, the Army, and America's War on Terror*, New York and London: M.E. Sharpe.

Abraham, A. and J.-P. Platteau (2004), "Participatory Development: Where Culture Creeps In", in V. Rao and M. Walton (eds), *Culture and Public Action*, Stanford, CA: Stanford University Press, pp. 210–33.

Adams, A.M., T.G. Evans, R. Mohammed and J. Farnsworth (1997), "Socioeconomic Stratification by Wealth Rankings: Is It Valid?", *World Development*, **25** (7), 1165–72.

Agrawal, A. and K. Gupta (2005), "Decentralization and Participation: The Governance of Common Pool Resources in Nepal's Terai", *World Development*, **33** (7), 1101–14.

Alesina, A., R. Baqir and W. Easterly (1999), "Public Goods and Ethnic Divisions", *Quarterly Journal of Economics*, **114** (4), 1243–84.

Alsop, R.J., A. Krishna and D. Sjoblom (2000), "Are Gram Panchayats Inclusive? Report of a Study Conducted in Rajasthan and Madhya Pradesh", Washington, DC: Social Development Unit, World Bank.

Araujo, M.C., F.H.G. Ferreira, P. Lanjouw and B. Ozler (2006), "Local Inequality and Project Choice: Theory and Evidence from Ecuador", Working Paper, Washington, DC: World Bank.

Asthana, A. (2003), "Decentralization and Supply Efficiency: The Case of Rural Water Supply in Central India", *Journal of Development Studies*, **39** (4), 148–59.

Baland, J.M. and J.P. Platteau (2003), "Economics of Common Property Management Regimes", in G. Mähler and J. Vincent (eds), *Handbook of Environmental Economics*, Amsterdam: North-Holland, Chap. 4, pp. 127–90.

Banerjee, A. and R. Somanathan (2005), "The Political Economy of Public Goods: Some Evidence from India", Working Paper, Department of Economics, MIT.

Banerjee, A., R. Banerji, E. Duflo, R. Glennerster and S. Khemani (2006), "Can Information Campaigns Spark Local Participation and Improve Outcomes? – A Study of Primary Education in Uttar Pradesh, India", World Bank Policy Research Working Paper No. 3967, Washington, DC: World Bank.

Bardhan, P. (2002), "Decentralization of Governance and Development", *Journal of Economic Perspectives*, **16** (4), 185–205.

Bardhan, P. and J. Dayton-Johnson (2007), "Inequality and the Governance of Water Resources in Mexico and South India", in J.M. Baland, P. Bardhan and S. Bowles (eds), *Inequality, Collective Action and Environmental Sustainability*, Princeton and New York: Princeton University Press.

Bardhan, P. and D. Mookherjee (1999), "Relative Capture of Local and Central Governments – An Essay in the Political Economy of Decentralization", Working Paper, Boston: Department of Economics, Boston University.

Bardhan, P. and D. Mookherjee (2000), "Capture and Governance at the Local and National Levels", *American Economic Review, AEA Papers and Proceedings*, **90** (2), 135–9.

Bardhan, P. and D. Mookherjee (2005), "Decentralizing Anti-poverty Programme Delivery in Developing Countries", *Journal of Public Economics*, **89** (4), 675–704.

Bardhan, P. and D. Mookherjee (2006a), *Decentralization and Local Governance in Developing Countries – A Comparative Perspective*, Cambridge, MA and London: MIT Press.

Bardhan, P. and D. Mookherjee (2006b), "Decentralization and Accountability in Infrastructure Delivery in Developing Countries", *Economic Journal*, **116** (508), 101–27.

Bardhan, P., S. Mitra, D. Mookherjee and A. Sarkar (2008), "Political Participation, Clientelism and Targeting of Local Government Programs: Analysis of Survey Results from Rural West Bengal, India", Discussion Paper No. 171, Boston: Institute of Economic Development (IED), Department of Economics, Boston University.

Bayart, J.F. (1986), "Civil Society in Africa", in P. Chabal (ed.), *Political Domination in Africa – Reflections on the Limits of Power*, Cambridge: Cambridge University Press, pp. 109–25.

Bayart, J.F. (1989), *L'Etat en Afrique*, Paris: Fayard.

Bebbington, A. (1997), "New States, new NGOs? Crises and Transitions among Rural Development NGOs in the Andean Region", *World Development*, **25** (11), 1755–65.

Behera, B. and S. Engel (2006), "Who Forms Local Institutions? Levels of Household Participation in India's Joint Forestry Management Program", ZEF Discussion Papers on Development Policy, Bonn: Center for Development Research.

Besley, T., R. Pande and V. Rao (2005), "Participatory Democracy in Action: Survey Evidence from South India", *Journal of European Economic Association*, **3** (2–3).

Bienen, H., D. Kapur, J. Parks and J. Riedlinger (1990), "Decentralization in Nepal", *World Development*, **18** (1), 61–75.

Bierschenk, T., J.P.O. de Sardan and J.P. Chauveau (eds) (2000), *Courtiers en Développement – Les Villages Africains en Quête de Projets*, Paris: Karthala.

Björkman, M. and J. Svensson (2007), "Power to the People: Evidence from a Randomized Experiment of a Community-based Monitoring Project in Uganda", CEPR Discussion Paper No. DP6344.

Blair, H. (2000), "Participation and Accountability at the Periphery: Democratic Local Governance in Six Countries", *World Development*, **28** (1), 21–39.

Boone, C. (1992), *Merchant Capital and the Roots of State Power in Senegal 1930–1985*, Cambridge: Cambridge University Press.

Brett, E.A. (2003), "Participation and Accountability in Development Management", *Journal of Development Studies*, **40** (2), 1–29.

Carroll, T. (1992), *Intermediary NGOs: Supporting the Link in Grassroots Development*, West Hartford: Kumarian Press.

Cernea, M.M. (1988), "Non-governmental Organizations and Local Development", World Bank Discussion Paper No. 40, Washington, DC: World Bank.

Chabal, P. and J.P. Daloz (1999), *Africa Works. Disorder as Political Instrument*, Oxford: James Currey.

Chandra, K. (2004), *Why Ethnic Parties Succeed: Patronage and Ethnic Head Counts in India*, Cambridge: Cambridge University Press.
Chattopadhyay, R. and E. Duflo (2004a), "Women as Policy-makers: Evidence from a Randomized Policy Experiment in India", *Econometrica*, **72** (5), 1409–43.
Chattopadhyay, R. and E. Duflo (2004b), "Impact of Reservation in Panchayati Raj: Evidence from a Nationwide Randomized Experiment", *Economic and Political Weekly*, 28 February, 979–86.
Conning, J. and M. Kevane (2002), "Community-based Targeting Mechanisms for Social Safety Nets: A Critical Review", *World Development*, **30** (3), 375–94.
Coulibaly, C. (2003), "Revue de L'État de Mise en Oeuvre des Orientations de Praïa au Mali", Bamako, Mali: Institut de Recherches en Sciences Humaines, Université Mande Bukari (mimeo).
Crook, R.C. and A.S. Sverrisson (2001), "Decentralization and Poverty Alleviation in Developing Countries: A Comparative Analysis or, Is West Bengal Unique?", IDS Working Paper No. 130, Sussex: Institute of Development Studies.
Cutler, D., D.W. Elmendorf and R.J. Zeckhauser (1993), "Demographic Characteristics and the Public Bundle", Working Paper, National Bureau of Economic Research (NBER).
Das, M.K. (2000), "Kerala's Decentralized Planning – Floundering Experiment", *Economic and Political Weekly*, 2 December, 4300–03.
De Haan, A., J. Holland and N. Kanji (2002), "Social Funds: An Effective Instrument to Support Local Actions for Poverty Reduction?", *Journal of International Development*, **14** (5), 643–52.
Esman, M.J. and N.T. Uphoff (1984), *Local Organizations: Intermediaries in Rural Development*, Ithaca, New York: Cornell University Press.
Eversole, R. (2003), "Managing the Pitfalls of Participatory Development: Some Insights from Australia", *World Development*, **31** (5), 781–95.
Finsterbusch, K. and W. Van Wicklin (1989), "Beneficiary Participation in Development Projects: Empirical Tests of Popular Theories", *Economic Development and Cultural Change*, **37** (2), 573–93.
Galasso, E. and M. Ravallion (2005), "Decentralized Targeting of an Anti-poverty Programme", *Journal of Public Economics*, **89** (4), 705–27.
Gray, M.L. (1999), "Creating Civil Society? The Emergence of NGOs in Vietnam", *Development and Change*, **30** (4), 693–713.
Guéneau, M. and B. Lecomte (1998), *Sahel: Les Paysans dan les Marigots de L'Aide*, Paris: Editions L'Harmattan.
Gugerty, M. and M. Kremer (1999), *The Impacts of Development Funding on Social Capital: The Kenya Local Community Action Project*, Washington, DC: The World Bank.
Harragin, S. (2004), "Relief and an Understanding of Local Knowledge: The Case of Southern Sudan", in V. Rao and M. Walton (eds), *Culture and Public Action*, Stanford: Stanford University Press.
Harrison, E. (2002), "The Problem with the Locals: Partnership and Participation in Ethiopia", *Development and Change*, **33** (4), 587–610.
Hernandez-Trillo, F. and B. Jarillo-Rabling (2008), "Is Local Beautiful? Fiscal Decentralization in Mexico", *World Development*, **36** (9), 1547–58.
Hoddinott, J., M. Adato, T. Besley and L. Haddad (2001), "Participation and Poverty Reduction: Issues, Theory, and New Evidence from South Africa", FCND Discussion Paper No. 98, Washington, DC: International Food Policy Research Institute.

Holdcroft, Lane (1984), "The Rise and Fall of Community Development, 1950–65: A Critical Assessment", in Carl Eicher and John M. Staatz (eds), *Agricultural Development in the Third World*, Baltimore: Johns Hopkins University Press.

Inbanathan, A. (1999), "Decentralisation and Affirmative Action: The Case of Panchayats in Karnataka", *Journal of Social and Economic Development*, **2** (2), 269–86.

Inbanathan, A. (2000), "Power, Patronage and Accountability in the Panchayats of Karnataka", Working Paper No. 68, Bangalore (India): Institute for Social and Economic Change.

Inbanathan, A. and D.V. Gopalappa (2002), "Fixers, Patronage, 'Fixing', and Local Governance in Karnataka", Working Paper No. 12, Bangalore (India), Institute for Social and Economic Change.

Isaac, T. (1998), "Decentralization, Democracy and Development: People's Campaign for Decentralized Planning in Kerala", paper presented at the International Conference on Decentralization: Devolution and Participation, Government of West Bengal, Calcutta: State Planning Board.

Isaac, T.M. and R.W. Franke (2002), *Local Democracy and Development: The Kerala People's Campaign for Decentralized Planning*, Lanham, MD: Rowman & Littlefield Publishers.

Isaac, T. and K.N. Harilal (1997), "Planning for Empowerment", *Economic and Political Weekly*, **32** (1–2), 53–8.

Isham, J. and S. Kähkönen (2002a), "How Do Participation and Social Capital Affect Community-based Water Projects? Evidence from Central Java, Indonesia", in C. Grootaert and T. Van Batselaer (eds), *The Role of Social Capital in Development: An Empirical Assessment*, Cambridge: Cambridge University Press.

Isham, J. and S. Kähkönen (2002b), "Institutional Determinants of the Impact of Community-Based Water Services: Evidence from Sri Lanka and India", *Economic Development and Cultural Change*, **50** (3), 667–91.

Isham, J. and D. Narayan (1995), "Does Participation Improve Performance? Establishing Causality with Subjective Data", *The World Bank Economic Review*, **9** (2), 175–200.

Jutting, J., C. Kauffmann, I. McDonnell, H. Osterrieder, N. Pinaud and L. Wenger (2004), "Decentralization and Poverty Reduction in Developing Countries: Exploring the Impact", OECD Development Centre, Working Paper No. 236, Paris: OECD.

Katz, T. and J. Sara (1997), "Making Rural Water Supply Sustainable: Recommendations from a Global Study", UNDP-World Bank Water and Sanitation Program, Washington, DC: World Bank.

Keefer, P. and S. Khemani (2005), "Democracy, Public Expenditures and the Poor", *World Bank Research Observer*, **20** (1), 1–27.

Kennedy, J., S. Rozelle and Y. Shi (2004), "Elected Leaders and Collective Land: Farmers' Evaluation of Village Leaders' Performance in Rural China", *Journal of Chinese Political Science*, **9** (1), 1–22.

Kennedy, P. (1988), *African Capitalism – The Struggle for Ascendency*, Cambridge: Cambridge University Press.

Khan, M.H. (2000), "Rent-Seeking as Process", in M.H. Khan and K.S. Jomo (eds), *Rents, Rent-seeking and Economic Development – Theory and Evidence in Asia*, Cambridge: Cambridge University Press, pp. 70–144.

Khan, M.H. (2004), "State Failure in Developing Countries and Strategies of Institutional Reform", SOAS Working Paper, London: School of Oriental and Asian Studies, University of London.

Khwaja, A.I. (2003), "Can Good Projects Succeed in Bad Communities? The Determinants of Collective Success in Maintaining Local Public Goods", Faculty Research Working Papers Series, Cambridge, MA: John F. Kennedy School of Government, Harvard University.

Khwaja, A.I. (2004), "Is Increasing Community Participation Always a Good Thing?", *Journal of the European Economic Association*, **2** (2), 427–36.

Klitgaard, R. (1997), "Unanticipated Consequences in Anti-poverty Programs", *World Development*, **25** (12), 1963–72.

Kumar, N. (2008), "Pro-poor Targeting and Participatory Governance: Evidence from Central India", Discussion Paper No. 176, Institute of Economic Development (IED), Boston: Department of Economics, Boston University.

Kumar, S. (2002), "Does 'Participation' in Common Pool Resource Management Help the Poor? A Social Cost–Benefit Analysis of Joint Forest Management in Jharkand, India", *World Development*, **30** (5), 763–82.

Kumar, S. and S. Corbridge (2002), "Programmed to Fail? Development Projects and the Politics of Participation?", *Journal of Development Studies*, **39** (2), 73–103.

Labonne, J. and R. Chase (2006), "Who is at the Wheel When Communities Drive Development? The Case of the KALAHI-CIDSS in the Philippines", mimeo, Washington, DC: World Bank.

La Ferrara, E. (2002), "Inequality and Group Participation: Theory and Evidence from Rural Tanzania", *Journal of Public Economics*, **85** (2), 235–73.

Laurent, P.J. (1998), *Une Association de Développement en Pays Mossi – Le Don Comme Ruse*, Paris: Editions Karthala.

Li, Tania Murray (2001), "Boundary Work: Community, Market, and State Reconsidered", in A. Agrawal and C.C. Gibson (eds), *Communities and the Environment – Ethnicity, Gender, and the State in Community-based Conservation*, New Brunswick, NJ and London: Rutgers University Press, pp. 157–79.

Lund, C. (2006), "Twilight Institutions: An Introduction", *Development and Change*, **37** (4), 685–705.

Mansuri, G. and V. Rao (2004), "Community-based and -driven Development: A Critical Review", *World Bank Research Observer*, **19** (1), 1–39.

McDermott, Melanie H. (2001), "Invoking Community – Indigenous People and Ancestral Domain in Palawan, the Philippines", in A. Agrawal and C.C. Gibson (eds), *Communities and the Environment – Ethnicity, Gender, and the State in Community-based Conservation*, New Brunswick, NJ and London: Rutgers University Press, pp. 32–62.

Mehta, A. (2000), "The Micro Politics of Participatory Projects: An Anatomy of Change in Two Villages", in P.E. Peters (ed.), *Development Encounters – Sites of Participation and Knowledge*, Cambridge, MA: Harvard University Press, pp. 15–28.

Meisel, N. and J.O. Aoudia (2008), *Is "Good Governance" a Good Development Strategy?*, Paris: Research Department, Agence Française de Développement.

Meyer, C.A. (1995), "Opportunism and NGOs – Entrepreneurship and Green North–South Transfers", *World Development*, **23** (8), 1277–89.

Molinas, J.R. (1998), "The Impact of Inequality, Gender, External Assistance and Social Capital on Local-level Cooperation", *World Development*, **26** (3), 413–31.

Mosse, D. (1997), "The Symbolic Making of a Common Property Resource: History, Ecology and Locality in a Tank-irrigated Landscape in South India", *Development and Change*, **28** (3), 467–504.
Mosse, D. (2001), "People Knowledge, Participation and Patronage: Operations and Representations in Rural Development", in Bill Cooke and Uma Kothari (eds), *Participation: The New Tyranny?*, London and New York: Zed Books, pp. 16–35.
Nair, G. (2000), "People's Planning in Kerala: A Case Study of Two Village Panchayats", Discussion Paper No. 16, Thiruvananthapuram: KRPLLD.
North, D.C., J.J. Wallis and B.R. Weingast (2006), "A Conceptual Framework for Interpreting Recorded Human History", NBER Working Paper No. 12795.
Nygren, A. (2005), "Community-based Forest Management Within the Context of Institutional Decentralization in Honduras", *World Development*, **33** (4), 639–55.
Olken, B.A. (2005), "Monitoring Corruption: Evidence from a Field Experiment in Indonesia", NBER Working Paper No. W11753.
Osmani, S. (2008), "Participatory Governance: An Overview of Issues and Evidence", in *Participatory Governance and the Millennium Development Goals (MDGs)*, publication based on the Expert Group Meeting on Engaged Governance: Citizen Participation in the Implementation of the Development Goals including the Millennium Development Goals (MDGs), 1–2 November 2006, United Nations, New York, pp. 1–45.
Oyono, P.R. (2004), "One Step Forward, Two Steps Back? Paradoxes of Natural Resources Management Decentralization in Cameroon", *Journal of Modern African Studies*, **42** (1), 91–111.
Oyono, P.R. (2005), "Profiling Local-level Outcomes of Environmental Decentralizations: The Case of Cameroon's Forests in the Congo Basin", *Journal of Environment and Development*, **14** (2), 1–21.
Pande, R. (2003), "Can Mandated Political Representation Increase Political Influence for Disadvantaged Minorities? Theory and Evidence from India", *American Economic Review*, **93** (4), 1132–51.
Paxson, C. and N. Schady (2002), "The Allocation and Impact of Social Funds: Spending on School Infrastructure in Peru", *The World Bank Economic Review*, **16** (2), 297–319.
Platteau, J.-P. (2004), "Community-based Development in the Context of Within Group Heterogeneity", in F. Bourguignon and B. Pleskovic (eds), *Proceedings of the Annual World Bank Conference on Development Economics 2004*, Washington, DC: The World Bank, pp. 241–70.
Platteau, J.-P. and A. Abraham (2002), "Participatory Development in the Presence of Endogenous Community Imperfections", *Journal of Development Studies*, **39** (2), 104–36.
Platteau, J.P. and A. Abraham (2004), "Participatory Development: Where Culture Creeps In", in V. Rao and M. Walton (eds), *Culture and Public Action*, Stanford: Stanford University Press, pp. 210–33.
Platteau, J.P. and F. Gaspart (2003), "The Risk of Resource Misappropriation in Community-based Development Projects", *World Development*, **31** (10), 1687–703.
Pozzoni, B. and N. Kumar (2005), *A Review of the Literature on Participatory Approaches to Local Development*, Operations Evaluation Department (OED), Washington, DC: The World Bank.

Prokopy, L.S. (2005), "The Relationship between Participation and Project Outcomes: Evidence from Rural Water Supply Projects in India", *World Development*, **33** (11), 1801–19.
Pur, K.A. (2007) "Rivalry or Synergy? Formal and Informal Local Governance in Rural India", *Development and Change*, **38** (3), 401–21.
Rao, V. and A.M. Ibanez (2001), "The Social Impact of Social Funds in Jamaica: A Mixed-methods Analysis of Participation, Targeting and Collective Action in Community driven Development", DECRG, Washington, DC: The World Bank.
Ribot, J.C. (1996), "Participation Without Representation: Chiefs, Councils and Forestry Law in the West African Sahel", *Cultural Survival Quarterly*, Fall, 40–44.
Ribot, J.C. (2002), *Democratic Decentralization of Natural Resources – Institutionalizing Popular Participation, Washington*, DC: World Resources Institute.
Rosenzweig, M.R. and A.D. Foster (2003), "Democratization, Decentralization and the Distribution of Local Public Goods in a Poor Rural Economy", BREAD Working Paper No. 10.
Scott, J.C. (1976), *The Moral Economy of the Peasant – Rebellion and Subsistence in Southeast Asia*, New Haven and London: Yale University Press.
Scott, J.C. (1985), *Weapons of the Weak – Everyday Forms of Peasant Resistance*, New Haven and London: Yale University Press.
Sethuraman, K. (1999), "Participation in People's Campaign Programmes: A Case Study of the Participation of Tribal People", MPhil Thesis, Thiruvananthapuram (India): Centre for Development Studies.
Sharma, R. (2003), "Kerala's Decentralization: Idea in Practice", *Economic and Political Weekly*, **38** (36), 3832–50.
Somanathan, E., R. Prabhakar and B.S. Mehta (2007), "Collective Action for Forest Conservation: Does Heterogeneity Matter?", in J.M. Baland, P. Bardhan and S. Bowles (eds), *Inequality, Cooperation and Environmental Sustainability*, Princeton and New York: Princeton University Press.
Somville, V. (2006), "Information Distortion in Community-based Development", Working Paper, Centre for Research on the Economics of Development (CRED), University of Namur (Belgium).
Somville, V. and J.-P. Platteau (2009), "An Analytical Approach to Information Distortion in Participatory Development Programs", Working Paper, Centre for Research on the Economics of Development (CRED), University of Namur (Belgium).
Stavis, B. (1982–83), "Rural Local Governance and Agricultural Development in Taiwan", in N.T. Uphoff (ed.), *Rural Development and Local Organization in Asia*, New Delhi: Macmillan, Vol. II, pp. 166–271.
Stiles, K. (2002), "International Support for NGOs in Bangladesh: Some Unintended Consequences", *World Development*, **30** (5), 835–46.
Tembo, F. (2003), *Participation, Negotiation and Poverty: Encountering the Power of Images*, Aldershot: Ashgate.
Tendler, J. (1997), *Good Government in the Tropics*, Baltimore and London: The Johns Hopkins University Press.
Véron, R. (2001), "The 'New' Kerala Model: Lessons for Sustainable Development", *World Development*, **29** (4), 601–17.
Vijayalakshmi, V. (2003a), "Gender Accountability and Political Representation

in Local Government", Working Paper No. 102, Bangalore (India): Institute for Social and Economic Change.

Vijayalakshmi, V. (2003b), "Accountability and Governance: Local Government in Kerala and Karnataka", Working Paper No. 125, Bangalore (India): Institute for Social and Economic Change.

von Braun, J. and U. Grote, (2002), "Does Decentralization Serve the Poor?", in E. Ahmed and V. Tanzi (eds), *Managing Fiscal Decentralization*, London: Routledge , pp. 68–95.

Wade, R. (1985), "The Market for Public Office: Why the Indian State Is Not Better at Development ?", *World Development*, **13** (4), 467–97.

Wade, R. (1990), "Employment, Water Control and Water Supply Institutions: India and South Korea", in W. Gooneratne and S. Hirashima (eds), *Irrigation and Water Management in Asia*, New Delhi: Sterling Publishers.

Wang, S. and Y. Yao (2007), "Grassroots Democracy and Local Governance: Evidence from Rural China", *World Development*, **35** (10), 1635–49.

Westergaard, K. and M. Alam (1995), "Local Government in Bangladesh: Past Experiences and Yet Another Try", *World Development*, **23** (4), 679–90.

White, H. (2002), "Social Funds: A Review of the Issues", *Journal of International Development*, **14** (5), 627–42.

White, R. and C. Eicher (1999), "NGOs and the African Farmer: A Skeptical Perspective", Staff Paper No. 99-01, East Lansing, Michigan: Department of Agricultural Economics, MSU.

World Bank (2005), *The Effectiveness of World Bank Support for Community-based and -driven Development*, Operations Evaluation Department (OED), Washington, DC.

Zhang, X., S. Fan, L. Zhang and J. Huang (2004), "Local Governance and Public Goods Provision in Rural China", *Journal of Public Economics*, **88** (12), 2857–71.

3. Governance dilemmas in service delivery

Pranab Bardhan

In discussing the governance issues on the question of service delivery in developing countries one inevitably faces several trade-offs, which make the often-recommended exercises in decentralized governance rather ambiguous as a project and the outcomes dependent on how the trade-offs play out in the different socio-economic context of different areas. Policymakers have to be particularly sensitive to these issues. In this chapter I shall focus on delineating the nature of some of these governance dilemmas, looking at them mostly at the analytical level, with occasional examples from some empirical work:

- autonomy versus accountability
- capture versus exit by local elite
- stake in delivery of public versus private goods
- local elections versus local accountability.

1 AUTONOMY VERSUS ACCOUNTABILITY

A central dilemma of governance institutions in a poor country is a trade-off between autonomy (or commitment to an autonomous agency) and accountability. On the one hand, one needs institutions of credible commitment to insulate the system from marauding special interest groups and partisan or faction politics. It is easy to cite many instances of short-sighted political interventions in economic decisions in developing countries. In particular, long-term investment projects or economic policy decisions that have consequences over a prolonged period will not get off the ground without such commitment. (A major example is the lack of political commitment to implement adequate user charges in some developing countries, hurting long-term investment, domestic or foreign, in projects for supply of drinking water or electricity.) Commitment is also difficult when the tenure of top administrative officials at a given job is short and at the mercy of politicians. Even outside the economic sphere, if one thinks of the all-important public service of law and order one needs some degree of commitment that civil servants, judges, and the police are not at the mercy of ruling politicians. (Examples of lack of autonomy may be given from appointments of civil servants as political patronage in Latin America, or even India, where meritocratically appointed civil servants are dependent on politicians for promotion and transfers.) In the macroeconomics literature the credible commitment problem is usually emphasized in the context of central bank independence, but the problem is much wider and deeper, pervading many areas of public service.

On the other hand, too much insulation often means too little accountability. This leads to high-handed arbitrary governance, leading to abuses and waste. Even when the administration is benevolent, large-scale development projects directed from above by an insulated modernizing elite are often inappropriate technologically or environmentally, far removed from or insensitive to local community needs and concerns, and failing to tap the large reservoir of local information, initiative, and ingenuity. These projects often treat poor people as *objects* of the development process, and end up primarily serving as conduits of largesse for intermediaries and contractors, and also encourage widespread parasitism on the state.

In a developing country where much of the economy is in the vast informal sector and dispersed in far-flung villages and small towns, the accountability mechanisms are particularly important at the local community level. In some sense, the dilemma of autonomy versus accountability is also best resolved at the local level. If commitment is necessary for long-term projects, it may be easier to persuade the local people to make sacrifices for projects that are to benefit them in the long run. This is particularly because of more visibility or transparency of benefits at the local level, possibly more trust and peer monitoring among local citizens, and because resisting populist pressures may be easier to coordinate. In contrast, individuals and groups may perceive more uncertainty in the trickle-down from future growth arising out of large-scale centrally administered projects, and they may instead opt for the "bird-in-hand" of current subsidies and short-term benefits.

Accountability is also more direct at the local level, if the local democratic processes work. There is more local vigilance on issues where more local stake is involved ("it's our money you are wasting or stealing"). Electoral sanctions may be more effective at the local level, than at the central level where multi-dimensionality of electoral issues dilutes responsibility.

2 CAPTURE VERSUS EXIT BY LOCAL ELITE

In situations of serious economic or social inequality, there is the ever-present danger of capture of local institutions by the elite, interfering with the delivery of services to the poor and misappropriating and diverting funds to non-target groups. Sometimes collusion is easier to organize at the local level than at the central level. Much, of course, depends on the following:

- The initial levels of inequality (both social and economic) that have a direct bearing on the social power of the elite; here the importance of land reforms and mass educational expansion is clear in making such collusion among a small clique more difficult.
- How lop-sided the nature of political competition is at the local level; examples of political competition in effective service delivery may be given from Tamil Nadu in India, where the electoral agendas of rival political parties have over the years involved items of their respective social welfare programs, and in West Bengal closer elections have been associated with better targeted delivery of benefits at the local level—see Bardhan and Mookherjee (2006).
- How free is the flow of information about the functioning of governments, and about the entitlements and allocations at the local level; here the importance of information campaigns about resources allocated to local governments and how they have been spent, and of a Freedom of Information Act for citizens, cannot be overemphasized.
- How regular and well-functioning are the deliberative processes of local democracy (public hearings, town hall meetings or *Gram Sabhas*[1] in Indian villages), and the monitoring function including provisions of periodic independent audits of accounts.

On the other hand, if the local elite cannot capture the provision of public services, there is sometimes the opposite danger in their seceding from the system, and without their political support the institutional machinery may collapse. This is particularly the case when leadership, organizational resources and expertise are currently provided by the elite in the local institutions. This is the familiar story of the rich turning to private schools and health clinics, and their exit plays havoc with the condition of public schools and health clinics—both in rich and poor countries. It is thus important to organize the following:

- Broad-based lobbies for these public goods or services, so that they can survive the exit of elite members (NGOs can obviously play an important role in this context).

- Leadership training.
- Vouchers may give poor people access to private facilities patronized by the rich; however, there is not much empirical evidence on the efficacy of vouchers in poor countries—a careful study of the operation of school vouchers in Chile by Hsieh and Urquiola (2006) does not show much improvement in average test scores.

In some cases of public goods, allowing exit by one section may undermine the very foundation of the state (for example, in the case of the public good of law and order, if the elite opt out and create their private militia).

3 STAKE IN DELIVERY OF PUBLIC VERSUS PRIVATE GOODS

There are differential degrees of public vigilance over (or effectiveness of) different types of delivery programs, as Bardhan and Mookherjee (2006) found in their study of the nature of leakage from anti-poverty programs in West Bengal villages under the *Panchayat* (village government) administration. In general in our statistical analysis of the panel data for 89 villages spread out over the whole of West Bengal we found that in the government distribution of "private" goods like subsidized credit (under a development program like the Integrated Rural Development Program [IRDP]) or subsidized agricultural 'minikits' of inputs, targeting was on average substantially pro-poor, and the leakages small. But in the use of more "public" fiscal grants there is evidence of significant local elite capture (both in intra-village and inter-village allocations) and some effect of local political competition. There is a similar finding in Ben Olken's (2007) study of road projects in Indonesia. He found in a field study of 600 village road projects that in grass-roots monitoring there is more vigilance on corruption in matters like wage payments for private individuals, than in public procurement of materials for the roads.

Such differential vigilance by local communities on private versus public services may be a special problem in the monitoring of public service delivery. In fact, politicians sometimes prefer delivering private goods to voters, in order to strengthen bonds of a patron–client political system. Even within the general category of public goods, politicians prefer the opportunity of inaugurating a new hospital (where a citizen may get individual medical care) to spending money on public sanitation where benefits are long term and diffuse, and difficult to take credit for (particularly in poor areas where health consciousness of the benefits of preventive measures is low). In this context, social movements raising such consciousness and awareness of poor people of their entitlement to the public services are very important. It is also necessary to organize user groups that can collectively demand public goods (to encourage election promises by politicians of schools rather than private goods like subsidized rice or color TV, a common election promise in southern India).

4 LOCAL ELECTIONS VERSUS LOCAL ACCOUNTABILITY

In situations of what Devarajan et al. (Chapter 5 in this volume) call "partial decentralization" local elections need not ensure accountability of local government officials. If local governments have highly inadequate access to devolution of funds, functions and functionaries—as is usually the case in many developing countries even with regular local elections, local officials can always get away with blaming higher authorities for non-delivery of services or diversion of funds to clientelistic relations. In such cases, local elections need not ensure genuine local accountability, even when the local polity is not captured by the elite, and elections are free and fair. It also depends on the issues that are salient for the local elections; more often than not party politicians above the local level hijack local elections to be fought on supra-local issues and local small-scale grievances about delivery of public services go unaddressed.

The literature on decentralized governance now has to go beyond the standard pros and cons of decentralization and tackle the kinds of dilemmas briefly discussed in this chapter in context-specific and politically sensitive ways.

NOTE

1. A meeting comprising the body of people registered on the electoral role, who elect the local government or *Panchayat*.

REFERENCES

Bardhan, P. and D. Mookherjee (2006), "Pro-poor Targeting and Accountability of Local Governments in West Bengal", *Journal of Development Economics*, **79** (2).

Devarajan, S., S. Khemani and S. Shah (2009), "The Politics of Partial Decentralization", this volume, Chapter 5.

Hsieh, C.T. and M. Urquiola (2006), "The Effects of Generalized School Choice

on Achievement and Stratification: Evidence from Chile's Voucher Program", *Journal of Public Economics*, **90** (8–9).
Olken, B.A. (2007), "Monitoring Corruption: Evidence from a Field Experiment in Indonesia", *Journal of Political Economy*, **115** (2).

4. Political economy approaches to fiscal decentralization

Ben Lockwood

1 INTRODUCTION

This chapter surveys recent contributions to the study of fiscal decentralization that adopt a political economy approach. By a political economy approach, I mean a systematic attempt to think about the behavior of government – whether at the national or local level – taking into account institutions and processes, such as elections and legislatures, which determine the choice of fiscal policies in practice. This is in contrast to the "standard" or traditional approach to the study of fiscal decentralization, which builds on the pioneering work of Oates (1972) and has been since developed by a number of authors.[1] This approach treats each level of government as a benevolent social planner, maximizing the welfare (for example, sum of utilities) of the residents of its jurisdiction.

What is the distinctive contribution of the political economy approach? In discussion of the costs and benefits of decentralization, it is usually argued that the costs of decentralization are due to various kinds of coordination failure: specifically, the failure to internalize tax and expenditure externalities of various kinds, or to exploit economies of scale (Oates, 1999). The political economy approach has little to say about these coordination failures that is distinctive from the standard approach.

There is less of a consensus on the benefits of decentralization, but generally, the idea is that it is beneficial because it is "closer to the people". There are two ways in which this can manifest itself. First, it is claimed to improve allocative efficiency, in the sense that the goods provided by governments in localities will be better matched to the preferences of the residents of those localities. This is sometimes known as the preference-matching argument. Second, decentralization is argued to increase the accountability of government. This term is used in rather a broad sense, and refers to the extent to which undesirable activities of office-holders, such as taking bribes, favoring of particular interest groups and insufficient innovation and effort, are held in check.[2]

It is the thesis of this chapter that the standard approach has little to say about either preference-matching or accountability, but that a political economy approach can give an account of these two effects that is both rigorous and plausible. So, the distinctive contribution of the political economy approach is that it can rigorously explain two of the key benefits that are widely believed to arise from increased fiscal decentralization, and give more precise predictions about when such benefits might be achieved.

To understand the distinctive contribution of the political economy perspective, consider first a simple version of the "standard" model. Assume two levels of government, central and local, for simplicity. Both types of government are assumed benevolent: that is, they maximize the sum (or average) of utilities of the residents in their jurisdiction. The activity of government is to provide local public goods, which may generate externalities (positive or negative) for other regions.

With decentralization, regional governments fail to internalize these spillovers. On the other hand, with centralization, as the government is benevolent, such spillovers are internalized. So, the standard model easily captures the "coordination failure" cost of decentralization. But, to capture the preference-matching benefit, it is forced to make the ad hoc assumption of policy uniformity: central government is assumed to set a uniform level of local public good provision in all regions. Moreover, as policy-makers are assumed benevolent, the "problem" of non-accountability is not even defined within the standard model.

The newer political economy approach can address both these shortcomings. First, models of legislative decision-making with centralization developed by Lockwood (2002) and Besley and Coate (2003) explain why, even when regional delegates are benevolent in the sense that they represent the interests of the voters in the regions from which they are elected, levels of regional public good provision decided upon by the legislature can be insensitive to regional preferences; in other words, why there is reduced preference-matching with centralization.

Again, models of electoral control developed by Besley and Case (1995), Persson and Tabellini (2000), Besley and Smart (2007) and others study the degree of accountability of elected policy-makers to voters in an environment where (1) policy-makers may not represent the interests of the voters, for example, they may be motivated by rent-seeking, and (2) initially, voters do not know whether the incumbent policy-maker is good or bad, but can make inferences about the incumbent's type from the fiscal policy he or she chooses. In this environment, Persson and Tabellini (2000) and Hindriks and Lockwood (2005) have studied how the degree of electoral control voters have differs between centralization and decentralization. Besley and Case (1995), Bordignon et al. (2004) and Besley and Smart (2007), amongst others, have investigated how tax and yardstick competition between jurisdictions (with decentralization) might improve accountability.

Another dimension of accountability is the extent to which governments are prone to capture by special interest groups. There is also an emerging literature on decentralization and lobbying by special interest groups, for example, Bardhan and Mookherjee (2000), Bennedsen and Feldman (2002), Bordignon et al. (2003), Redoano (2003), Ruta and Brou (2006). This literature explains how capture of government by special interest groups may differ between centralization and decentralization.

Issues of accountability are also central to a very recent literature on partial decentralization. Most of the literature assumes that decentralization is "all or nothing", whereas in reality, there is usually a more complex division of responsibilities between central and subcentral government, with central government often providing funding via general or special purpose transfers, and being responsible for some aspects of service delivery, and subnational government being responsible for others. We call this kind of fiscal arrangement, which is very widespread, partial decentralization. Why do governments only partially decentralize? Ahmad et al. (2005) emphasize a "governance trap"; central governments do not fully decentralize, because they fear that they will in any case be held accountable for the actions of local governments. One or two recent contributions, for example, Bardhan and Mookherjee (2006), Brueckner (2007) and Bordignon and Lockwood (2008), have started to model this formally.

Finally, this chapter also surveys recent work on the political economy of the choice between centralization and decentralization. This is a key part of the political economy perspective: after all, in practice, political institutions determine these choices, as well as the performance of government under a given allocation of fiscal powers.

2 DECENTRALIZATION AND PREFERENCE-MATCHING

The "standard" approach sees the benefit of centralization as internalization of externalities, and the cost of centralization as reduced preference-matching. In this section, we see how the standard approach conceptualizes preference-matching in terms of a uniformity constraint with centralization. This gives rise to Oates's influential decentralization theorem (1972). We then ask how robust this theorem is to the introduction of political economy elements, and we see that political economy arguments allow us to endogenize reduced preference-matching, that is, derive it as an equilibrium outcome.

2.1 A Simple Framework

First, we will set up a simple economic framework, which we will use throughout this chapter. This is a simple version of the "local public goods" model that is widely used in the analysis of fiscal federalism. So far as we can, we will do the analysis without using algebra. Consider a country comprising (for convenience only) of only two regions with equal populations, which we normalize to unity. In each region, government (regional or central) can provide a good that is purely public[3] within the region, but has positive consumption spillovers for other regions. The public good can be produced from a second, private, good, and is financed out of taxes on the private good endowments of households. At the moment, we do not constrain these taxes; they could be different in the different jurisdictions.

Households care about their consumption of the private good, the level of public good provision in their region. Moreover, the level of public good provision in region 1 could affect the well-being of households in region 2, and vice versa. In this case, we say that there are local public good (LPG) externalities. LPG externalities could be positive or negative.

Finally, we make the assumption that the distribution of income does not matter, that is, $1 is always worth the same to all households.[4] While unrealistic, this gives us the considerable simplification that we can analyze efficiency of public good provision without being concerned about the distribution of income. Specifically, under this assumption, any Pareto-efficient allocation of public goods in the economy must maximize the sum of utilities, and is thus unique.

Within this framework, we will consider initially two possible allocations of tax and spending powers:

1. *Fiscal centralization.* A single central government sets both local public good levels and taxes to maximize the sum of utilities across regions subject to the national budget constraint; the total cost of public good provision must be equal to total taxes raised.
2. *Fiscal decentralization.* A local government in $i = 1, 2$ sets the local public good level and tax in its own region to maximize regional utility subject to the regional budget constraint; the cost of public good provision in i must be equal to taxes in i.

2.2 The Decentralization Theorem

As remarked above, in the standard model, the objective of government is to maximize the sum of utilities of residents in its jurisdiction (welfaristic objectives). Then, with fiscal decentralization, in each region the marginal

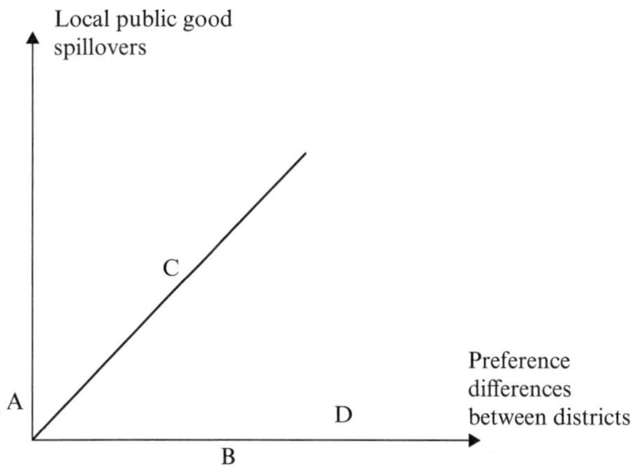

Figure 4.1 Preferences for centralization/decentralization

benefit of the good to that region is equated to the marginal cost of the good, unity. Clearly, regional government i ignores the spillover effect of its public good provision on the other region, and this is a well-known source of inefficiency.[5]

Now consider central government. In this case, without any restrictions on the choice of local public goods, central government will choose the efficient levels, because it internalizes spillover effects. Thus, in order to generate some disadvantage to centralization, the standard approach makes the policy uniformity assumption that public good provision (per capita) must be the same in both regions. Centralization thus has a cost: the level of public good provision cannot now be tailored to each region in the event that the willingness to pay for the public good varies across regions.

Say that one fiscal arrangement is more efficient than the other if it generates a higher sum of utilities.[6] Then, we can state Oates's decentralization theorem. This is in three parts. First, if there are no externalities and regions are identical, it is obvious that centralization and decentralization are equally efficient. Second, if there are no externalities and regions differ in their preferences for local public goods, then decentralization is more efficient than centralization. Third, if there are spillovers and regions are identical, then centralization is more efficient than decentralization.

This result is illustrated in Figure 4.1, where we suppose that both the degree of externality and the difference in the marginal willingness to pay for the public goods can be measured and varied continuously. Then, in region C, where the former is high and the latter is low, centralization is preferred; in region D, where the reverse is true, decentralization is preferred.

Note that the decentralization theorem (DT) rests on the twin pillars of benevolent government and policy uniformity. How good are either of these assumptions, and what happens if they are relaxed?

First, as a positive hypothesis about how government behaves, the hypothesis of benevolent government is clearly wrong. Decisions about taxation and spending are made in legislatures and parliaments, often as a result of commitments made by political parties in election campaigns. So, it is of great interest to know whether the basic insights provided by the DT generalize when some of these more realistic features are allowed for.

As for the policy uniformity assumption, it is clearly incorrect if taken literally, that is, that expenditures on a local public good are the same across districts. For example, in many countries, there is considerable evidence that the level of spending per capita varies across regions in predictable ways. For example, Knight (2004) finds that in the US, funds for projects[7] earmarked in annual House of Representatives and Senate Appropriations Bills are unequally distributed by state, with small states that have higher per capita representation in the Senate and the House have significantly higher per capita expenditure. On the other hand, much central government expenditure is governed by formulae of various kinds based on a small number of observable variables (for example, equalization grants); these grants are typically not sensitive to detailed information about local preferences for public goods, and so on.

We now discuss some recent contributions that replace the unrealistic assumption of benevolent government with more realistic decision-making via voting. It helps to proceed in steps, by first considering the case where policy uniformity is assumed. We then move on to the case where both assumptions are relaxed.

2.3 Political Economy with Policy Uniformity

Two of the most important processes by which public decisions are made are by voting and by the lobbying of interest groups. Does the DT still hold if decisions are made in this way, continuing to assume policy uniformity? This issue is analyzed in Lockwood (2008). He first considers the case where decisions are made by majority voting. It is relatively easy to do this when policy uniformity is assumed, as each district is choosing a single dimension of policy (a level of public good provision) and thus there are no problems with voting cycles.

His main finding is that the DT fails in both "directions". That is, examples can be found where (1) decentralization welfare-dominates centralization even with externalities and identical preferences across regions, and (2) centralization welfare-dominates decentralization with no externalities and different preferences across regions. This can be illustrated using Figure 4.1: even at a point like A on the vertical axis, decentralization may be preferred, and even at a point like B on the horizontal axis, centralization may be preferred.

The intuition is that these are second-best results. Both fiscal regimes have one source of inefficiency, and at the same time, majority voting has a well-known inefficiency, that it does not measure intensity of preference. This inefficiency can interact with the inefficiencies in the two fiscal regimes in such a way as to overturn the DT. For example, it is easy to construct examples where the median voter has a higher preference for the public good than the average voter. This tendency towards over-provision offsets the under-provision with decentralization arising from failure to internalize positive externalities, and can make decentralization superior, even with externalities and identical preferences. It is somewhat more difficult – but possible – to construct examples where majority voting magnifies the heterogeneity across regions, thus leading to levels of public good provision under decentralization that are too heterogeneous. Then, uniform provision under centralization can dominate, even with no externalities and different preferences across regions.

Lockwood (2008) shows, however, that all the problems only occur when preferences within regions are asymmetric, that is, where the households with the median and average willingness to pay for the public good are different. With symmetric preferences, the DT continues to hold, as stated above. Lockwood (2008) also investigates what happens when a benevolent policy-maker is lobbied by a special interest group (a group of households with a specific preference for the public good). Again, he finds that the DT fails in both "directions".

2.4 Political Economy with Policy Differentiation

Lockwood (2002) and Besley and Coate (2003) compare centralization and decentralization, while relaxing both assumptions of the DT. Specifically, they both suppose that policy is determined via bargaining in a legislature with district representatives. That is, the representative from any district i has the preferences of a "representative" household from that district. If there are preference differences within a district, an important issue is how the district representative is chosen; that is the focus of Besley and Coate.

For the moment, we abstract from that complication, and concentrate on the case studied by Lockwood (2002). A simplified example, which makes all the main points, is the following. There are three regions, and in each region, a "project", for example, road, library, police station, and so on can be funded or not. The costs and benefits of each project vary across districts. In districts 1 and 2, the project benefit is 1, and the costs are ¾, whereas in district 3, the cost is 2½, and the benefit is 3. The costs are shared via uniform taxation that is, each district pays ⅓ of the total cost of all projects.

For the moment, suppose that there are no externalities. So, with decentralization, each region gets the full net benefit from its project, which is positive in each case, and all three projects are funded. Moreover, this is also the efficient outcome.

What happens with centralization? We simplify by considering the so-called "one-shot" model of legislative bargaining, which works as follows.[8] With probability ⅓, each of the three district representatives is recognized as "proposer". The proposer can make a proposal about which projects should be funded. This proposal then goes to a vote. If a majority, that is, two or more delegates, vote for it, it is implemented; otherwise, the status quo proposal is implemented, which we take to be no projects.

It is fairly easy to figure out what happens in this case. Every legislator would like his project funded, but he cannot vote it through on his own; he needs the support of another district, which can only be bought by offering that district its own project. But which other vote should the proposer "buy"? If 1 proposes projects in his own district and district 2, the total tax cost of the "package" to either district is ⅓ times ¾ + ¾, which is ½, certainly less than the benefit of 1. But if 1 proposes projects in his own district and district 3, the total tax cost of the "package" to either district is ⅓ times ¾ + 2½, which is 13/12, which exceeds the benefit for district 1.

This has two implications. First, when 1 is proposer, he will buy 2's vote and vice versa. Second, 3 cannot buy the votes of either 1 or 2 to get his own project funded, and so cannot do better than stick at the status quo. So, the outcome is that with probability ⅔, a "minimum winning coalition" of districts 1 and 2 form and get their projects funded, and with probability ⅓, no projects are funded. This is clearly inefficient.

This inefficiency arises for two reasons. First, the "minimum winning coalition" underestimates the true cost of projects; due to national cost-sharing, districts outside the coalition also pay. Second, "minimum winning coalition" may underestimate the true benefit of a project; specifically, they ignore the benefits to districts outside the minimum winning coalition.

These two inefficiencies also imply that the DT does not hold generally. To see this, modify the above example so that project 3 has a small external benefit ε for districts 1 and 2. Then, for $\varepsilon < 1/12$, it is easy to see that the equilibrium just described is unchanged; a "package" including a project for 3 could never be preferred to the status quo by districts 1 or 2. For $1/12 \leq \varepsilon < 7/12$, a "package" including a project for 3 is preferred to the status quo by districts 1 and 2, but is nevertheless worse than a "package" of projects just for regions 1 and 2. So, the outcome is the same as before except that when delegate 3 is recognized, he proposes a package consisting of his project plus one other, which is voted through.

In either case, the outcome is inefficient, while the outcome with decentralization remains efficient, even though externalities are strictly positive. So, the DT does not hold. However, in this environment, it does hold in the other direction, that is, if there are no externalities, the outcome under decentralization is efficient, whereas centralization may not be efficient.

2.5 Endogenously Reduced Preference-matching

Finally, note that this approach generates endogenously, in equilibrium, a reduced level of preference-matching with centralization. Specifically, funding decisions in the legislature are driven by cost-minimization, and are relatively insensitive to the benefits of projects. In equilibrium, the two least-cost projects are funded, not the project with highest net benefit, which happens to be project 3. This bias towards cost-minimization is ultimately generated by two exogenous – and realistic – forces; the sharing of costs via national taxation, and the use of majority voting as a decision rule.

So far, the analysis has assumed that all households within a region are the same. Besley and Coate (2003) argue that in a version of the legislative model, if there is heterogeneity within regions, strategic choice of delegates by voters can cause centralization to be inefficient.[9] Specifically, as Besley and Coate show, if region *i* chooses a delegate to the legislature who places a high value on the local public good, this delegate will be more "aggressive" in the legislature in demanding a higher level of that good. This works to the benefit of citizens of *i* because part of the cost is borne by the other region. But, of course, if both regions delegate to "aggressive" delegates, this will be self-defeating: the end result is that both public goods will be higher than their efficient levels. This can be thought of as a second form of endogenous reduced "preference-matching" with centralization.

3 DECENTRALIZATION AND POLITICAL ACCOUNTABILITY

As remarked in the introduction, although the argument that decentralization "improves" accountability is frequently made, the concept of "accountability" is difficult to pin down precisely. In order to focus the discussion, we will focus on two possible aspects of accountability. The first aspect is the degree to which (de)centralization allows voters electoral control over government officials. This is an issue when there is an agency problem between officials and voters, that is, when officials have private incentives to act against the wishes of voters, for example, take bribes, and so on.

A large literature in economics takes the view that such agency problems are important, especially where media scrutiny and the rule of law are weak. As emphasized by Besley and Smart (2007), there are two aspects of electoral control. First, elections allow voters to de-select bad incumbents (selection effects). Second, the selection effect provides an incentive for incumbents to improve their behavior in order to increase the probability of re-election (incentive or discipline effects). A key question, therefore, is what effect (de)centralization will have on these two accountability mechanisms.

The second aspect of accountability is the degree to which institutions allow special interest groups to distort government decision-making by lobbying. Concern about "capture" by local elites with decentralization goes back a long way. For example, in the *Federalist Papers* (1787–88), Madison said:

> The smaller the society, the fewer probably will be the distinct parties and interests composing it: . . . the more easily will they concert and execute their plans of oppression. Extend the sphere and you take in a greater variety of parties and interests: you make it less probable that a majority of the whole will have a common motive to invade the right of other citizens.

Another key question, therefore, is whether this "elite capture" problem really is more severe with decentralization.

3.1 Decentralization and Electoral Control

We begin by surveying recent work that looks at the first aspect of accountability, control over elected officials. This work adopts the following common framework, which really just extends the basic framework described above. There are a number of districts $i = 1,\ldots n$, each with a local public good. The economy evolves over two periods. With decentralization, the order of events in any region i is as follows. In period 1, an incumbent policy-maker is in power, and chooses fiscal policy (the tax and the local public good), taking public good supply in regions as given. At the end of period 1, there is then an election: all citizens in i can vote for the policy-maker or a challenger. In period 2, the winner then again chooses fiscal policy. With centralization, everything is the same, except that there is (1) only one incumbent policy-maker, who chooses fiscal policy in all regions, and (2) a national election with only one challenger.

This model has three additional key features. First, both the incumbent and challenger can be "good" or "bad" from the point of view of the citizens[10]. Specifically, it is usually assumed that the incumbent's and challenger's types (good or bad) are random draws, so that each is good with some fixed probability. A good type, following Oates (1972), maximizes voter welfare.[11] A bad type maximizes rent, that is, the excess of tax revenue over expenditure on public goods.

Second, citizens are initially uniformed about the type of both incumbent and challenger, whereas (usually) the incumbent and challenger know their own type. The result of this information asymmetry is that the bad type may either imitate the good type in order to be re-elected (a pooling equilibrium), or act in his or her short-run best interests, thus revealing his or her type, and losing the election (a separating equilibrium). The more pooling there is, the weaker is the selection mechanism of electoral control, but the stronger is the discipline mechanism.

Third, unlike the classical "local public good" model of fiscal federalism, there are no LPG spillovers, or difference in preferences for the public goods between regions. This allows a clean focus on electoral control issues. A number of papers use this framework. They can be classified according to the assumptions that they make about voter information.

3.2 Full Voter Information: Yardstick Competition

Suppose that voters are well-informed, that is, can observe fiscal policy in other regions, and that the costs of producing public goods across the different regions are positively correlated. Then, the key difference between centralization and decentralization is that, with the latter, yardstick competition between fiscal jurisdictions occurs. The basic idea is that voters can compare fiscal policy set in neighboring districts to the policy set by their own incumbent policy-maker, to make inferences about whether their own policy-maker is "good" or "bad". Formal theoretical models of yardstick competition have been developed by Besley and Case (1995), Bordignon et al. (2004) and Besley and Smart (2007); these are variants of the electoral control model outlined above.

To understand the basic mechanism, assume further for convenience only that there are only two districts, that the costs of local public goods in the two districts can only be high or low, and finally that these costs are perfectly positively correlated. By definition, good politicians set high (low) taxes only if the cost of the public good is high (low). Second, suppose that bad politicians pool when the cost of the public good is low.[12] That is, they imitate the good incumbent by setting the tax that would be set by the good incumbent if the cost were high, and pocket the difference between tax revenue and the cost of public good provision.

Then if a voter observes his politician setting a high tax, but his neighboring politician setting a low tax, then he will reason as follows: "The neighboring politician is certainly good, with a low cost. So, because of perfect correlation, it is certain that the cost in my region is also low. A high tax plus a low cost implies that my own politician is bad; so my own politician is definitely bad. So, I will vote him out of office". A similar argument applies in the more general case where costs are sufficiently highly correlated. So, with strongly correlated costs, a bad incumbent knows that he will be voted out of office when he sets a high tax and his neighbor sets a low tax.

So, from a theoretical point of view, yardstick competition has the following effects on electoral control. First, it discourages pooling on the part of bad incumbents, because pooling via setting a high tax when the cost is low, rather than separating, may now result in being fired by the voters anyway. So, the alternative strategy of setting a very high tax and providing no public good (full rent-diversion) in the first period, and then being fired by the voters, now becomes more attractive. In the first period, this is, of course, worse for voters, but in the second period, it is better, because the bad incumbent is now replaced by a new incumbent of average quality. In the terminology of Besley and Smart (2007), yardstick competition has a negative effect on (first-period) discipline, but a positive effect on selection. As voters value both discipline and selection, the overall effect of yardstick competition on voter welfare is ambiguous.

How does this relate to the choice between fiscal regimes? Recall that unlike the classical "local public good" model of fiscal federalism, there are no LPG spillovers, or difference in preferences for the public goods between regions. So, the only effect of fiscal decentralization is that yardstick competition is introduced. Thus, decentralization can have ambiguous effects on welfare, but for different reasons than in Oates's (1972) classic analysis.

One attractive feature of the yardstick competition model is that it can be empirically tested. The key prediction is that the probability that the incumbent is voted out of office depends not only negatively on his own tax, but also (positively) on the taxes in "neighboring" jurisdictions. So, the most straightforward test of the model is to estimate a popularity equation, relating some measure of incumbent popularity in district i at election date t, π_{it} (whether defeated or not, vote share and so on) to the incumbent's tax rate, and those of the "neighbors". Specifically, the popularity equation is:

$$\pi_{it} = \alpha + \beta\tau_{it} + \gamma\tau_{-it} + \text{controls} + \text{error}$$

where τ_{it} is the tax rate in jurisdiction i at time t, and τ_{-it} is a weighted average of taxes in neighboring jurisdictions at time t. The theory predicts $\beta < 0$, $\gamma > 0$, with $\gamma > 0$ being the distinctive prediction of yardstick competition. In empirical work, the taxes studied are taxes with "high visibility" to voters such as income taxes (Besley and Case, 1995) or local property taxes (Revelli, 2002). Also, "neighbors" are usually assumed to be geographical neighbors. Both these studies find that $\gamma > 0$, that is, evidence of yardstick competition.

3.3 Limited Voter Information: Selective Rent-diversion

The assumption that voters are well-informed, that is, can observe fiscal policy in other regions, is necessary for the yardstick competition mechanism to operate. Surprisingly, there is very little empirical evidence as to whether voters really have this information. But, what evidence there is suggests that they do not. For example, Teske et al. (1993) surveyed households in Suffolk County, New York, which contained 71 school districts. Only 21 percent of all respondents were well-informed[13] about the tax and expenditure of their own school district relative to others in the county.

What is the effect of decentralization in the electoral control model when voters are not well-informed, and so the yardstick competition mechanism does not work? This question has recently been addressed[14] by Hindriks and Lockwood (2005). Here, it is more convenient to think of what the effect of centralization might be.

The key effect is that a national incumbent is less accountable than a local one, in the sense that he only has to satisfy a majority of districts in order to be re-elected.[15] Specifically, as voters do not observe fiscal policy outside their own jurisdiction, then with centralization, if the incumbent wishes to win the election and stay in office, he can do so by a strategy of selective rent-diversion; only imitating the good incumbent in a "minimum winning coalition" of $m = (n + 1)/2$ regions, and can take unconstrained rent in the other regions.[16]

Thus, as shown by Hindriks and Lockwood (2005), centralization has two effects on voters. First, other things being equal, if the incumbent diverts rent selectively, this makes voters worse off; with probability $1 - (m/n)$, any region will be outside the minimum winning coalition and thus suffer maximum rent-diversion. But, things are not equal, because the lower cost of pooling under centralization causes the incumbent to pool more often, increasing the probability of fiscal restraint. So we have the subtle effect that centralization raises the probability of fiscal restraint but limits the extent of this fiscal restraint to a bare majority of regions. Voters may prefer this if they value discipline over selection.[17]

3.4 Decentralization and Lobbying

As already mentioned above, there is a belief, going back to the US *Federalist Papers* in the 18th century, that local government is more susceptible to "capture" by powerful special interest groups. Capture by special interest groups can be measured in three ways: by the degree to which policy is distorted away from the benchmark in the absence of the special interest group; by contributions paid by the special interest group, at least part of which is usually viewed as a deadweight loss; and finally, if interest group formation is endogenous, by the number of groups that form. Recently, there have been a number of theoretical studies investigating these ideas, for example, Bennedsen and Feldman (2002), Bardhan and Mookherjee (2000, 2006), Bordignon et al. (2003), Redoano (2003), Ruta and Brou (2006). They can be classified by the sophistication and realism by which they model the lobbying process.

Bordignon et al. (2003), Redoano (2003) and Ruta and Brou (2006) suppose that special interest groups can just make direct payments to a policy-maker to buy the "vote" of that policy-maker.[18] Indeed, in Bordignon et al. (2003), and Ruta and Brou (2006) voting over policy is not explicitly analyzed. When choosing policy, the policy-maker maximizes a weighted sum of his own payoff – social welfare in his jurisdiction – and that of the special interest group. Overall, conditions can be found under which policy distortions and contributions are larger with decentralization, confirming Madison's hypothesis, but these are rather model-specific.

These papers, however, suffer from a basic limitation. First, in mature democracies, buying the votes of legislators is usually explicitly illegal, and is in fact very rare. As stressed by Grossman and Helpman (2001), the main activities of special interest groups are (1) money donations to election campaign funds, which are legal and (2) "informational lobbying", that is, provision of relevant information to legislators. Two important papers capture these dimensions of lobbying.

Bardhan and Mookherjee (2000) suppose that in each political jurisdiction, one special interest group lobbies two political parties, by making campaign contributions. Some voters vote rationally, and some randomly ("noise" voters). Campaign contributions are valuable because they influence noise voters. They identify several effects of decentralization. One of these clearly confirms Madison's hypothesis, that of regional favorites. Assume that party A is the strong favorite in region 1 and party B is the strong favorite in region 2. Then, at the national level, the special interest group does not have a strong incentive to lobby either party, as both are equally likely to win the election. But with decentralization, the special interest group has a strong incentive to lobby the party that it knows is very likely to win.

Bennedsen and Feldman (2002) focus on informational lobbying of members of a legislature. The economic environment is similar to the legislative bargaining set-up of Lockwood (2002) and Besley and Coate (2003), before, except that there is uncertainty on the part of individual legislators about benefits from the public goods in each region. Special interest groups can provide information to the policy-maker about these benefits at some cost. With decentralization,[19] there is a single policy-maker and the model set up so special interest groups provide no information in equilibrium.

But with centralization, the decision about public good provision is made in a legislature composed of regional delegates, as in Lockwood (2002) and Besley and Coate (2003). In this case, information provided by the special interest group can influence the formation of the minimum winning coalition in the legislature and thus the choice of aggregate public good supply. Specifically, the special interest group reveals which regions have a high benefit of the public good. These regions will form a "minimum winning coalition" in the legislature and choose a relatively high level of public good provision for themselves. Thus, by revealing information, the special interest group can increase aggregate public good supply (which it likes, by assumption). The special interest group trades off this benefit against the cost of getting the information, and will engage in informational lobbying under a wide range of conditions.

4 PARTIAL DECENTRALIZATION

We noted above that most of the literature on fiscal decentralization assumes that decentralization is "all or nothing", whereas in reality, there is usually a more complex division of responsibilities between central and subcentral government, with central government often providing funding via general or special purpose transfers, and being responsible for some aspects of service delivery, and subnational government being responsible for others. For example, in Mexico, central government designs the secondary school curriculum, supplies textbooks and finances much of secondary school education via special purpose grants, while provincial governments build and maintain schools, and hire teachers. Following Devarajan et al. (Chapter 5, this volume) we call this kind of fiscal arrangement, which is very widespread, partial decentralization. This can be contrasted with full decentralization, as studied above, where local governments have full autonomy over both service provision and taxes.

The question then arises as to whether the "standard theory" of fiscal federalism, based on the ingredients of inter-district externalities and policy uniformity, can explain why we observe partial decentralization so widely. The explanation offered by the standard theory is that effective taxes at the subnational level are often not available, so it is economically efficient to have taxes raised by central government; at the same time, it is efficient to have services provided by local government, to improve preference-matching. However, some recent political economy models can provide a richer story about why some forms of partial decentralization can dominate full centralization and decentralization.

One perspective on partial decentralization is provided by Bardhan and Mookherjee (2006). They study the provision of a public good under three different regimes, full centralization, full decentralization and partial decentralization. The last is defined as a situation where local government has full autonomy over the allocation of the public service, but is restricted to financing the (variable) costs of the service via user fees.[20] The basic inefficiency with full centralization is that central government does not observe local demand and cost conditions, and thus turns over provision of the service to national and local bureaucrats. Each type of bureaucrat cannot perfectly price-discriminate, due to limited information, and thus services are underprovided, especially to the poor.

The basic inefficiency under centralization is that large users of the service lobby local government, that is, a form of "elite capture". With tax finance, that is, full decentralization, service provision is inefficiently biased towards large users, with the poor (small users) being more heavily taxed and thus subsidizing the large users. But, this inefficient cross-subsidization will be eliminated by restricting local government to user fees, as the latter are voluntary. So, partial decentralization is always more efficient than either other fiscal regime.

More recently, Brueckner (2007) considers a model where partial decentralization (centralized taxation, but with local governments setting local public good levels) can also dominate full (de)centralization. This occurs under the rather specific circumstances where local governments are "partial Leviathans", that is, each maximizes the weighted sum of welfare and spending on public goods, but central government is benevolent. The fully centralized outcome is inefficient because of policy uniformity, and the fully decentralized outcome is inefficient because of over-taxation and over-spending. Partial decentralization can be an optimal compromise.

However, neither of these papers really captures what Ahmad et al. (2005), based on their practical experience with the World Bank, identify as the "governance trap". This is that citizens hold higher-level governments responsible for service quality – or lack of it. Knowing this, upper-level governments do not decentralize whole budgets and service responsibilities, only bits and pieces. So, citizens continue to hold national governments, not local governments responsible when things go wrong. A formal analysis of the "governance trap" requires an explicit agency model of the relationship between national government, local government and citizens. Bordignon and Lockwood (2008) make a start in this direction.

5 POLITICAL ECONOMY AND THE CAUSES OF DECENTRALIZATION

We now turn to the second question raised in the introduction: how – if at all – does the political process by which decisions are made determine the degree of fiscal decentralization? Broadly speaking, there are two ways in which a (re-)allocation of fiscal powers between center and regions can be made: by voting in the national legislature, and by referendum. Both methods are used in practice. An important example is the European Union, where ratification of treaties – which often lead to centralization of powers at the EU level – can be done in any member country by either a national referendum or a vote in the legislature. For example, in the UK, the Maastricht Treaty was ratified by a vote in Parliament, but in Denmark and France, it was ratified via referendum.

An additional important issue is that whether a vote in legislature or a referendum is used, the use of either procedure is often quite different in federal and unitary states. In federal states, the allocation of powers is usually specified in the Constitution and may require a constitutional amendment.[21] Constitutional amendments are used routinely in Switzerland, and less frequently in the US, Canada and Australia, to reallocate tax and spending powers (Wheare, 1963). In all major federal states, rules for constitutional amendment require that at least a majority of regions must approve the amendment, either by vote in the regional legislature, or by referendum.[22]

5.1 Unitary Versus Federal States

Cremer and Palfrey (1996) and Lockwood (2004) compare the choice between decentralization and centralization via unitary and federal referenda. A unitary referendum on two alternatives is a one-stage vote by all the citizens in the nation. A federal referendum on two alternatives is a two-stage vote where first, all the citizens in a region vote to determine the preference of the region, and then the regions vote to determine national preference. These capture in a stylized way the differences between procedures in federal and unitary states.

In Cremer and Palfrey's model, the cost of centralization is that the policy variable must be set at the same level in all regions (Oates's policy uniformity): the benefit is that "extreme" policies are less likely.[23] They obtain a remarkable result: as the number of (equal-sized) regions become large, whenever the national referendum selects centralization, the federal referendum also selects centralization (but not necessarily vice versa), so federal referenda unambiguously lead to more centralization. They call this result the principle of aggregation.

Lockwood (2004) addresses the same question in a model of discrete regional public goods, much closer to the legislative model described above. There are no spillovers, so the benefit of centralization is in economies of scale. Policy uniformity is not assumed. The outcome with centralization is modeled in a legislative bargaining framework. Finally, unlike Cremer and Palfrey (1996), the model avoids imposing strong assumptions on the distribution of preferences for projects within regions and between regions. The finding is that Cremer and Palfrey's result is confirmed when distribution of median project benefits across regions is single-peaked. But, when this condition does not hold, or when there is a small number of districts, the result could go the other way.

5.2 Voting in the Legislature Versus Referendum

This is a case that is of particular interest in the context of the European Union, where as already remarked, ratification of EU treaties can be done via referendum or vote in the legislature. Redoano and Scharf (2004) were the first to study this choice. The main insight from their model is that (relative to a referendum), the delegation of the choice of centralization to the legislature can effectively act as a precommitment device by a pro-centralization region to induce the delegate from an anti-centralization jurisdiction to agree to centralization. So, centralization is more likely under representative democracy.

Lorz and Willman (2005) build on Redoano and Scharf. There, the focus is on which (of a continuum) of public goods should be provided centrally. Regions do not differ in preferences for the public goods, but legislators can make side-payments when bargaining over which goods to decentralize. So, voters strategically delegate to legislators who have a relatively low willingness to pay for the public good in order to win higher side-payments. This leads to too few goods (relative to the efficient benchmark) being provided centrally. As a referendum over which public goods to decentralize leads to the efficient outcome, voting in the legislature (representative democracy) leads to less centralization than a referendum. So, while these papers yield interesting insights, there is no robust empirical prediction.

5.3 Empirical Evidence

There are now a number of empirical studies on the determinants of decentralization, for example, Oates (1972), Panizza (1999), Arzaghi and Henderson (2005), Strumpf and Oberholzer-Gee (2002), and Stegarescu (2005), but with the exception of the last study, these studies focus on the economic determinants of decentralization. In cross-country studies, the main factors found to be positively associated with decentralization are: population size, land area, income per capita and ethnolinguistic fractionalization.

Stegarescu (2005) is the first attempt to test for the role of political institutions as determinants of decentralization. He runs regressions for a group of 23 OECD countries where the control variables include not only the usual economic ones but also looks at political institutions.

His first political variable is a measure of federalism. Specifically, in the sample (OECD countries), all federal countries, and some unitary countries (for example, Italy, Netherlands), have regional representation in the upper house of Parliament, that is, a fixed seat allocation, where representatives may be chosen by direct election in the region, or by the regional Parliament. Stegarescu constructs an index of subnational representation based on these features.

His second political variable is a measure of direct democracy. Many OECD countries use referenda or citizen's initiatives at the national level as part of the process of choice either for constitutional amendments, or for ordinary legislation. The importance of these instruments depends (1) on how widely they can be applied; (2) how easy it is to initiate them (for example, number of signatures required to trigger a citizen's initiative) and (2) whether the outcome of the referendum or initiative is binding or not on the legislature. Stegarescu constructs an index of direct democracy based on these features.

His third variable is Persson and Tabellini's (2000) well-known classification of countries as either parliamentary or presidential. His findings are as follows. First, presidential countries are significantly more decentralized on both the tax and expenditure side than are parliamentary countries. This is a very robust result: interestingly, there is as yet no theoretical explanation for this. Second, countries with a higher degree of subnational representation in the second chamber are significantly more decentralized on both the tax and expenditure side. Third, the degree of direct democracy has no effect; this is perhaps consistent with the theoretical literature, where no very robust results emerge.

6 CONCLUSIONS

This paper has surveyed some recent contributions to the study of fiscal decentralization from a political economy viewpoint. The unifying theme of the survey is that the standard approach, based on the idea of benevolent governments and policy uniformity, cannot give a rigorous account of the preference-matching and accountability benefits of decentralization, but the political economy approach can do this. It can also give insights into the empirically important fiscal arrangement of partial decentralization, and can explain why several types of political institution, along with economic determinants, affects the choice of decentralization.

NOTES

1. The policy uniformity assumption is widely used in papers on many topics in fiscal federalism, including: work by Alesina and Spolare (1997) on the size of nations, Bolton and Roland (1997) on the effects of threat of secession, Alesina et al. (2001) on endogenous international unions. While these papers do not assume a benevolent social planner, they use the policy uniformity assumption as an easy way of generating some cost of fiscal centralization.
2. This argument goes back to Buchanan and Brennan's "Leviathan" hypothesis, in which they "envision a monolithic government that systematically seeks to exploit its citizenry through the maximization of tax revenues that it extracts from the economy" (Oates, 1985). They argue that decentralization checks the ambition of a Leviathan government.
3. This is the conventional assumption, but the results below go through if the good is a congestible public good, or even private.
4. Technically, we are assuming quasi-linearity, that is, the utility of any household is linear in private consumption.
5. An objection sometimes made to this argument is that the two regional governments can bargain with each other to improve on the non-cooperative outcome. So, to be non-trivial, the standard approach must assume that Coasian bargaining between regions to internalize externalities is impossible or prohibitively costly. This seems plausible in many cases, for example, sulfur dioxide pollution crossing state boundaries in the US.
6. Given our special assumptions on preferences, it is well-known that the more efficient fiscal arrangement can make everybody better off, given a suitable redistribution of income.
7. These projects correspond very closely to the theoretical concept of a local public good, as they are items such as public buildings, transportation projects, and so on.
8. Lockwood (2002) considered a more complex bargaining procedure, which allowed for amendments by all representatives to the original proposal, with the amended proposal being finally voted on against the status quo.
9. Although strategic delegation through elections is a well-understood effect (Persson

and Tabellini, 1992), it seems to have been so far mainly studied in the context of tax competition.

10. Other political agency models allow politicians to vary in competence in producing the public good (Rogoff, 1990; Persson and Tabellini, 2000).
11. For simplicity, all voters are assumed alike.
12. In this model, it can easily be shown that the bad incumbent never pools when the cost of the public good is high, as pooling only delays the taking of rent by one period.
13. "Well-informed" is defined as correctly identifying whether their school district tax, and expenditure, was above average, below average or about average for the whole county.
14. The paper, Gonzales et al. (2006) extends this analysis to an environment where politicians differ in competence, not benevolence.
15. This basic point about weaker accountability was made by Seabright (1996), in a model of pure moral hazard, where incumbents are all "bad" and choose only the level of effort (or rent-diversion). In that environment, elections only have incentive effects.
16. Of course, ultimately, the reason why selective rent-diversion is possible only with centralization in our model is that public goods are regional, so expenditure can be targeted at specific groups within the electorate only with centralization. But, all we require for our qualitative results to go through is that targeting should be easier with centralization: as long as regional goods are not purely public at the national level, this will be the case.
17. With less than perfect spatial cost correlation, an additional effect comes into play, that is, that the statistical distribution of costs the incumbent will face changes with the size of the relevant jurisdiction (either the region or the nation). This cost distribution effect implies that the selection effect can be stronger under centralization. This changes the conditions under which voters prefer centralization.
18. In this category, one could also add Bardhan and Mookherjee (2006). This paper however, has a different focus, and is discussed in the section on partial decentralization.
19. Bennedsen and Feldman (2002) did not explicitly consider centralized and decentralized fiscal regimes in their paper. However, following both Lockwood (2002) and Besley and Coate (2003), it is very natural to take the case of the single policy-maker as decentralization, and that of the legislature as centralization.
20. Bardhan and Mookherjee do not characterize this case as "partial decentralization", but it clearly can be classified as such. See also Bardhan (Chapter 3, this volume).
21. However, the degree to which reallocation of powers leads to constitutional amendment varies considerably across federal countries. In the US, there has only been one constitutional amendment for this purpose (in 1913, to allow a federal income tax), whereas in Switzerland there have been a large number of amendments over the last 100 years, enhancing the tax powers of central government (Wheare, 1963, Chapter 6).
22. For example, in the US, any amendment to the Constitution must be approved by at least three-quarters of all state legislatures. Constitutional amendments in Australia and Switzerland require majority approval of the population as a whole, and also majorities in all the regions, that is, unanimity among the regions (Wheare, 1963). Moreover, in some federal states, a "double hurdle" must be cleared for a constitutional amendment: for example, amendments in Australia and Switzerland require majority approval of the population as a whole, and also majorities in all the regions.
23. They assume that voters are incompletely informed about the preferences of other voters, both in their regions and in other regions. It turns out in this set-up that the benefit of centralization is policy moderation. That is, when the number of regions becomes large, the subjective probability for any particular voter that the policy variable will, in voting equilibrium, take on an extreme value (that is, far from that voter's most preferred value) is lower with centralization.

REFERENCES

Ahmad, J., S. Devarajan, S. Khemani and S. Shah (2005), "Decentralization and Service Delivery", The World Bank, Policy Research Working Paper Series No. 3603.

Alesina, Alberto, Ignazio Angeloni and Federico Etro (2001), "The Political Economy of International Unions", Cambridge, MA: Harvard Institute of Economic Research Working Papers, No. 1939.

Alesina, A. and E. Spolare (1997), "On the Number and Size of Nations", *Quarterly Journal of Economics*, **112** (4), 1027–56.

Arzaghi, M. and V. Henderson (2005) "Why Countries are Fiscally Decentralizing", *Journal of Public Economics*, **89** (7), 1157–89.

Bardhan, P. and D. Mookherjee (2000), "Capture and Governance at Local and National Levels", *American Economic Review*, **90** (2), 135–9.

Bardhan, P. and D. Mookherjee (2006), "Decentralisation and Accountability in Infrastructure Delivery in Developing Countries", *Economic Journal*, **116** (508), 101–27.

Bennedsen, M, and S.E. Feldman (2002), "Lobbying Legislatures", *Journal of Political Economy*, 2002, **110** (4), 919–46.

Besley, T. and A. Case (1995), "Incumbent Behavior: Vote-seeking, Tax-setting, and Yardstick Competition", *American Economic Review*, **85** (1), 25–45.

Besley, T. and S. Coate (2003), "Centralized Versus Decentralized Provision of Local Public Goods: A Political Economy Approach", *Journal of Public Economics*, **87** (12), 2611–37.

Besley, T. and M. Smart (2007), "Fiscal Restraints and Voter Welfare", *Journal of Public Economics*, **91** (3–4), 755–73.

Bolton, P. and G. Roland (1997), "The Break-up of Nations: A Political Economy Analysis", *Quarterly Journal of Economics*, **112** (4), 1057–90.

Bordignon, Massimo and Ben Lockwood (2008), "Vertical Imbalances and Electoral Accountability: Who Do the Voters Blame?", Unpublished paper.

Bordignon, Massimo, Floriana Cerniglia and Federico Revelli (2004), "Yardstick Competition in Intergovernmental Relationships: Theory and Empirical Predictions", *Economics Letters*, **83** (2004), 325–33.

Bordignon, Massimo, Luca Colombo and Umberto Galmarini (2003), "Fiscal Federalism and Endogenous Lobbies' Formation", CESifo Working Paper No. 1017.

Brueckner, J.K. (2007) "Partial Fiscal Decentralization", CESifo Working Paper No. 2137.

Cremer, J. and T. Palfrey (1996), "In or Out? Centralization by Majority Vote", *European Economic Review*, **40** (1), 43–60.

Gonzalez, P., J.J.G. Hindriks, B. Lockwood and N. Portiero (2006), "Political Budget Cycles and Fiscal Decentralization", CEPR Discussion Paper No. 5646.

Grossman, G.M. and E. Helpman (2001), *Special Interest Politics*, Cambridge, MA: MIT Press.

Hindriks, J. and B. Lockwood (2005), "Centralization and Political Accountability", CEPR Discussion Paper No. 5125.

Knight, B. (2004), "Legislative Representation, Bargaining Power, and the Distribution of Federal Funds: Evidence from the US Senate", NBER Working Paper Series No. 1038.

Lockwood, B. (2002), "Distributive Politics and the Costs of Centralization", *Review of Economic Studies*, **69** (2), 313–37.
Lockwood, B. (2004), "Decentralization via Federal and Unitary Referenda", *Journal of Public Economic Theory*, **6** (1), 79–108.
Lockwood, B. (2008), "Voting, Lobbying, and the Decentralization Theorem", *Economics and Politics*, **20** (3), 416–31.
Lorz, O. and G. Willman (2005), "On the Endogenous Allocation of Decision Powers in Federal Structures", *Journal of Urban Economics*, **57** (2005), 242–57.
Oates, W. (1972), *Fiscal Federalism*, New York: Harcourt-Brace.
Oates, W. (1985), "Searching for Leviathan: An Empirical Study", *American Economic Review*, **75** (4), 748–57.
Oates, W. (1999), "An Essay on Fiscal Federalism", *Journal of Economic Literature*, **37** (3), 1120–49.
Panizza, U. (1999), "On the Determinants of Fiscal Centralization: Theory and Evidence", *Journal of Public Economics*, **74** (1), 97–140.
Persson, T. and G. Tabellini (1992), "The Politics of 1992: Fiscal Policy and European Integration", *Review of Economic Studies*, **59** (4), 689–701.
Persson, T. and G. Tabellini (2000), *Political Economics: Explaining Economic Policy*, Cambridge, MA: MIT Press.
Redoano, M. (2003), "Does Centralization Affect the Number and Size of Lobbies?", Warwick Economic Research Paper No. 674.
Redoano, M. and K. Scharf (2004), "The Political Economy of Policy Centralization: Direct vs. Representative Democracy", *Journal of Public Economics*, **88** (3–4), 799–817.
Revelli, F. (2002), "Local Taxes, National Politics, and Spatial Interactions in English District Election Results", *European Journal of Political Economy* **18** (2), 281–99.
Rogoff, K. (1990), "Equilibrium Political Budget Cycles", *American Economic Review*, **80**, 21–36.
Ruta, M. and D. Brou (2006), "Special Interests and the Gains from Political Integration", *Economics and Politics*, **18** (2), 191–218.
Seabright, S. (1996), "Accountability and Decentralization in Government: An Incomplete Contracts Model", *European Economic Review*, **40** (1), 61–91.
Stegarescu, D. (2005), "Costs, Preferences, and Institutions: An Empirical Analysis of the Determinants of Government Decentralization", Working Paper No. 05-39, Centre for European Economic Research.
Strumpf, K.S and F. Oberholzer-Gee (2002), "Endogenous Policy Decentralization: Testing the Central Tenet of Economic Federalism", *Journal of Political Economy*, **110** (1), 1–36.
Teske, P., M. Schneider, M. Mintrom and S. Best (1993), "Establishing the Microfoundations of a Macro Theory: Information, Movers, and the Competitive Local Market for Public Goods", *The American Political Science Review*, **87** (3), 702–13.
Wheare, K.C. (1963), *Federal Government*, Oxford: Oxford University Press.

5. The politics of partial decentralization*

Shantayanan Devarajan, Stuti Khemani and Shekhar Shah

1 INTRODUCTION

Despite its promise of achieving a better match between local preferences and public goods, decentralization—be it fiscal, administrative or political—has achieved decidedly mixed results. The reasons for this mixed outcome are many, but fall into two categories. One category assigns blame to the design of the decentralization. For instance, some governments decentralize only one or two of the trio of "funds, functions and functionaries". In Pakistan, responsibility for education was transferred to the districts but teachers remained employees of the provincial government (World Bank, 2004b). Within one of the trio (say functions), there are often mismatches. In South Africa, expenditure responsibility for health, education and social security has been devolved to provincial governments without the corresponding revenue responsibility (Ahmad et al., 2006). In Brazil, it was the reverse—devolved revenue responsibility without expenditure authority. The second category of reasons for the mixed results has to do with the fact that, even with appropriate design, decentralization in practice has turned up a host of problems. The two most commonly identified ones are (1) that sub-national governments do not receive the funds they are due in order to discharge their responsibilities (World Bank, 2004a) and (2) sub-national governments often lack the capacity to manage their newly given financial responsibilities (some local governments in Ethiopia lacked enough numerate and literate people to manage their finances).

In this chapter, we show that the problems with decentralization in practice stem from a somewhat under-emphasized aspect of the design, namely that attempts at decentralization have not led to citizens being able to hold local governments accountable for budgetary allocations and their outcomes. We define such a situation as partial decentralization. Unless local governments have the discretion to choose among competing uses subject to a budget constraint, and citizens know this and have a way of evaluating whether the government's decision was a good one, the decentralization will only be partial. For instance, when one sector such as education is decentralized, the local government is not responsible for allocating resources between education and other sectors. Even when the central government gives untied grants to local governments for, say, current expenditures, but continues to have central-government-led schemes for capital expenditures, the decentralization is partial since local governments are not accountable for the allocation between capital and current expenditures.

When decentralization is partial, citizens continue to place their expectations of service delivery at the door of national governments. They are more likely to punish national politicians at the polls for inadequacies of service delivery rather than local politicians. This in turn weakens incentives of local governments to allocate budgetary resources optimally across competing public needs. Instead, local incentives are likely geared towards serving narrow interest groups or extracting rents, with poor-quality public services being blamed upon insufficient transfers from higher tiers of government.

Knowing that decentralization is only partial, higher-tier governments have incentives to (1), deliberately withhold resources from local governments, or (2), transfer them under stringent conditions, or (3), transfer them selectively to those local politicians from whom they gain political advantage. Finally, local governments lack the capacity to manage finances because they have no incentive to develop this capacity—since no one is holding them accountable for results.

What we have then is a governance trap. Because local governments are not held accountable by citizens, national governments restrict local discretion to choose among competing allocations, subject to a budget constraint, which in turn continues to hobble local accountability because citizens cannot attribute performance in local resource allocation to their locally elected governments. The existence of this trap has implications for reform and its sequencing. For example, it may not be helpful to recommend that higher-level governments increase their allocations to sub-national governments if there is no change in the accountability of local governments for allocating their budgets. Conversely, it is equally unhelpful to recommend keeping certain essential functions, such as health and education, at the central government level because lower-level governments "lack capacity". They will never build that capacity unless they are held accountable by their citizens for budgetary allocation and management. Finally, it is unlikely that decentralizing individual sectors, such as education, will improve results because it does not strengthen the accountability of local governments for allocating budgets across sectors. Instead, reform programs would benefit from increasing the range of budgetary items for which local governments can be held accountable; and improving the information that citizens have about these budgetary allocations and their outcomes.

In the second section of the chapter, we outline the analytical framework behind these arguments about partial decentralization. We show how lack of accountability of local governments for budgetary allocations leads to inferior outcomes, even if there is adequate resources from the higher-level governments. We also show why partial decentralization creates incentives for higher-level governments to withhold transfers. In the third and fourth sections, we derive the implications of this framework for service delivery and reform, respectively. Section 5 concludes.

2 THE ACCOUNTABILITY FRAMEWORK FOR ANALYZING PARTIAL DECENTRALIZATION

The implications of partial decentralization explored in this chapter emerge from the thinking about service delivery and work done for (and engendered by) the 2004 World Development Report (WDR), *Making Services Work for Poor People* (World Bank, 2004c). The 2004 WDR presents an analytical framework for understanding the relationships of accountability between key actors in the service delivery chain. The essential message of the WDR is: successful services for poor people emerge from institutional relationships in which the actors in service delivery are accountable to each other. When one or more of these relationships are weak, services fail.

Relationships of accountability have five features: delegation, finance, performance, information and enforceability (Figure 5.1). These features are useful to analyze simple transactions such as buying a kilo of rice or running a municipal democracy. Asking for the rice is delegation, paying for it is finance and selling it is performance, eating the rice generates information and enforceability comes from the buyer either going back to the same seller for more rice or getting it from another seller. Similarly, citizens choose an executive to manage their municipality (delegation), they pay taxes that lead to budget decisions (finance), the executive in coordination with others that report to him or her performs services, these services are assessed by citizens based on their experience and information, and they ultimately act to control the executive politically or legally (enforceability).

Weakness in any aspect of accountability can cause failure. But it is

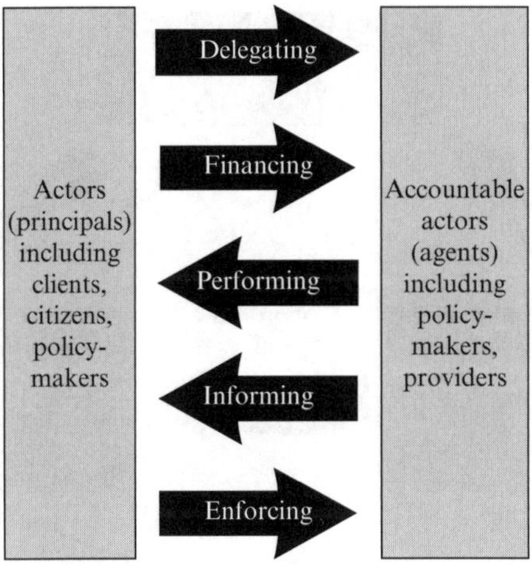

Source: World Bank (2004c).

Figure 5.1 The five facets of accountability

not possible to strengthen one aspect of accountability in isolation; for example, enforceability cannot usually be enhanced without information. If service providers don't receive clear delegation in ways that precisely define and measure desired objectives, increasing enforceability is unfair and ineffective. If they don't receive adequate resources, holding them accountable for performance is also unfair and ineffective. Second, putting finance as the first step in creating accountability stresses that simply caring about an outcome controlled by another does not create accountability. To be a stakeholder, you need to put up a stake.

Unbundling accountability in this way leads to unbundling the service delivery chain into three sets of actors: citizens or clients, policymakers (which includes politicians), and providers (Figure 5.2). Citizens exercise voice over politicians, usually through the political system. Policymakers have compacts with organizational providers, which then manage frontline providers. Clients exercise client power through transactions with frontline providers, including monitoring them. When markets alone are involved and all decisions rest directly with citizens who can enforce them through competition, we have a short route of accountability—citizens holding providers directly accountable. But where the state and the public sector are involved, voice and compacts make up the main control mechanism available to the citizen or client in a long route of accountability. Weaknesses in either the short or the long route of accountability can cause service failures.

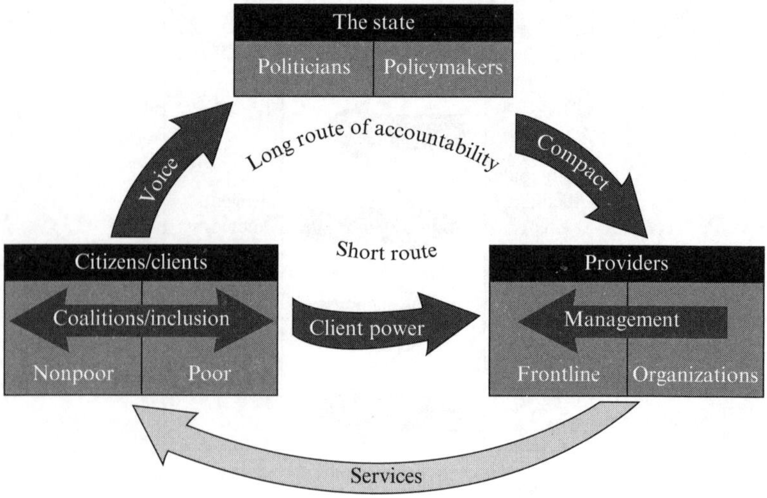

Source: World Bank (2004c).

Figure 5.2 Key relationships of power: the long and the short routes of accountability

Set against this framework of accountability, decentralization introduces an additional actor, sub-national or local government, and at least two new relationships of accountability—between national and sub-national governments, and between citizens and sub-national governments (Figure 5.3). There are, of course, different types of decentralization. Administrative deconcentration affects primarily the compact relationship between central policymakers and their local frontline providers and may have little influence on local voice. At the other end, fiscal devolution implies the handing over of greater resources and power to allocate these resources across different uses to local politicians, and therefore greater scope for strengthening local voice, their compact with local providers and local client power.

In the traditional literature on fiscal federalism, reflecting the ideal situation, mostly relating to the United States, the intergovernmental fiscal system works well with hard budget constraints in place, capacity at different levels of government is not an issue, information and systems to monitor public bureaucracies are in place and lower tiers of government also collect taxes and spend discretionary funds on service delivery.[1] In these situations, local political accountability is strong because citizens associate performance with the spending decisions made, implemented and monitored by their local governments. Under these conditions, the

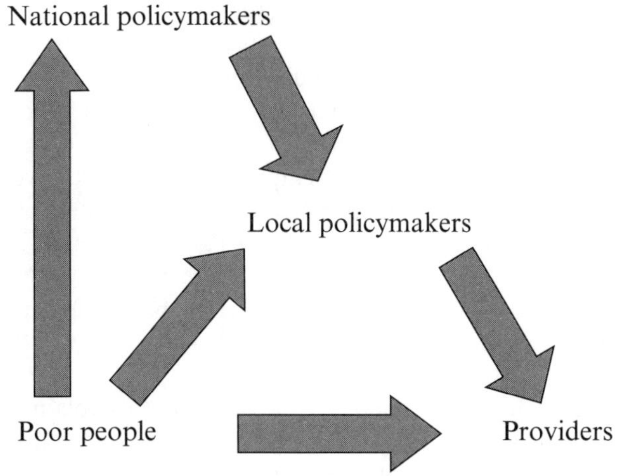

Source: Ahmad et al. (2006, p. 244).

Figure 5.3 Decentralization process

accountability of national and local policymakers to citizens is strong. Citizens look to their local leaders for the quality of their schooling or the cost-effectiveness of garbage disposal, not to their national leaders.

We define as partial decentralization the situation when local governments are not held accountable for a complete set of budgetary allocations and their outcomes. This usually comes about because national governments have not given the local government discretion over all aspects of the budget. For instance, local governments may have discretion over current spending, while capital spending is still the responsibility of the national government. Alternatively, only some sectors such as education have been decentralized. In terms of Figure 5.3, partial decentralization means that the accountability between citizens and local policymakers ("local voice") is weak. But when decentralization is partial, citizens continue to look to their national governments for service delivery. They are more likely to vote in or vote out national political representatives than their immediate local political leaders.

Because local leaders have little discretion, it is hard to pin blame or give credit for performance. Local voice and client power is weak in this setting, precisely the things that are supposed to deliver the fruits of decentralization. Instead, partial decentralization sets up perverse, self-reinforcing incentives for both local and national politicians. Local politicians blame poor services on inappropriate design and insufficient funding from national governments, and their incentives then are to capture the political process for patronage and clientelism. In short, the politics of partial decentralization leads to governance traps when it weakens both the short and the long route of accountability, and often does so in self-reinforcing ways. This is likely to happen irrespective of what is motivating partial decentralization—whether a concern for lack of capacity at lower tiers of government or an attempt by higher-level governments to hang on to political or financial power.

3 FAILURES IN SERVICE DELIVERY UNDER PARTIAL DECENTRALIZATION

The analytical framework laid out above helps to explain why, under partial decentralization, local politics is more likely to be dominated by "clientelist" provision of private benefits to a few citizens, at the expense of broad public services simultaneously benefiting many. We argue that citizens are more likely to mobilize themselves into narrow interest groups and demand benefits targeted to "group" identity, rather than broad collective action for general public goods. Knowing this, higher-tier politicians and bureaucrats, who continue to be held responsible by voters for broad public goods, are likely to restrict local discretion in resource allocation, and provide specific purpose transfers with detailed prescriptions on implementation. This compromises one of the more fundamental benefits expected from decentralization—the tailoring of public services to local priorities.

What should/can citizens expect of local governments under partial decentralization? What criteria should they employ when evaluating their performance, and deciding whether or not to re-elect them? How would citizens organize field candidates for elections to local political office? If local governments have little discretionary authority to make allocations across competing needs, and are not responsible for resultant trade-offs in decision-making, then citizens have incentives to evaluate them largely on the basis of the quantum of public spending they bring. In other words, when local governments do not have ownership over outcomes, or an effective budget constraint, and largely function to distribute benefits from separate pots of funds transferred from above, then citizens have incentives to mobilize themselves to extract private benefits from these funds. Groups could organize at local levels to field their candidates in exchange for targeted benefits or a share in rents from office.

This hypothesis of clientelist local politics, through organization of citizens in narrow interest groups, is at least as tenable theoretically as the alternate arguments that underpin most donor strategies to provide greater resources to local governments (or community-based groups), that citizens will somehow organize in the broader public interest when resources are available with locally elected authorities than with the line ministries of central governments. What we argue here is that faith in the benefits of greater decentralization of public resources is particularly likely to be misplaced when locally elected authorities are merely distributing "goodies" financed from transfers from higher tiers of government that actually control all decision-making authority over revenue-raising and service delivery policy. Expectations for broad public goods continue to be from higher tiers of government as it continues to own the policy space pertinent for such goods.[2]

Analysis of perverse political incentives at local levels has focused overwhelmingly on the risk of "capture" of public resources by local elites for their own benefit, systematically excluding poor and disadvantaged people (Baland and Platteau, 1999; Bardhan and Mookherjee, 2000). An alternate hypothesis we are positing here is that even if "capture" is not salient, and poor and disadvantaged groups are politically mobilized, their incentives, when decentralization is partial, are to demand short-term private benefits from local governments in place of broader public goods. Indeed, in reviewing received evidence on political participation in developing countries, and contributing new evidence from the state of West Bengal in India, Bardhan et al. (2007) conclude that there is little evidence of political marginalization or political exclusion of weaker socioeconomic groups. That is, even if social and economic exclusions persist, under universal suffrage and competitive electoral conditions it would appear that the socially marginal cannot be prevented from becoming politically active.[3]

The existence of historical institutions of social inequality in India makes it a setting from which much evidence has been garnered on relative "capture" by local governments. We review this evidence below to argue that it is equally consistent with political mobilization of disadvantaged groups to demand private goods targeted to members of their "group", at the expense of broad public goods from which all group members would benefit.

Besley et al. (2004) focus on analyzing distribution of access to poverty alleviation schemes, a BPL (Below Poverty Line) card, by village governments (*Panchayats*) in India. They find that legally identified disadvantaged groups, households belonging to the scheduled castes and tribes (SC/STs), are more likely to receive a BPL card and/or targeted home improvement schemes (toilets, drinking water, electricity, repairs) when the elected position of head of the village government, the *Gram Pradhan*, is reserved for members of SC/ST groups.

They also find that a second institutional feature of decentralization in India—the requirement of village-wide meetings, the *Gram Sabhas*, to deliberate upon allocations of public funds reaching local governments—enables targeting of public benefits to disadvantaged groups. Specifically, they find that if a village is the kind of village that holds a *Gram Sabha*, then disadvantaged households are more likely to participate in it than are advantaged households, and they are simultaneously more likely to receive BPL cards.

It is important to note that the impact of political reservations and *Gram Sabhas* is *additional* to overall targeting of BPL cards to disadvantaged households. That is, in general, in all villages a household that is SC/ST, or landless, or poor along other measurable dimensions, is more likely to receive a BPL card than upper caste or richer households, and they are even more likely to be thus targeted when a village has political reservations and holds *Gram Sabhas*.

Besley et al. (2004) interpret this as evidence of appropriate targeting of disadvantaged groups when political decentralization is accompanied by institutional mechanism (political reservations, *Gram Sabhas*) to combat entrenched inequalities. However, from a general political perspective, what these results tell us is that SC/ST *Pradhans* behave no differently than the received evidence for other politicians—they try to target benefits to members of their group, and for all we know they could be targeting these benefits to "elites" within their group rather than to the most needy. Furthermore, we don't know if they could have done better things for larger numbers of SC/STs by generally improving *public* infrastructure in their hamlets (as opposed to privately targeted housing improvement schemes), or in the schools their children attend.

From the perspective adopted in this chapter, we might interpret the body of work produced by Besley et al. on *Panchayats* in India as consistent with the following idea—that *Panchayats* are viewed by citizens primarily as agents from which "private" benefits can be extracted—a BPL card, a job in a public works scheme, a home-improvement scheme—with little or no attention to the role they can play in managing local "public" goods for the benefit of larger groups of citizens. This would not be an irrational position to take for a citizen because India has all the characteristics of partial decentralization. *Panchayats* typically do not have access to regular and significant funds, and are not assigned independent responsibility for local public goods. Indeed, Chhibber et al. (2004) surveyed voters in India and asked which tier of government they held responsible for the public goods they cared most about—medical facilities, drinking water, roads, education. The state governments were indicated as the most responsible agent by the majority of respondents.

Bardhan et al. (2007) contribute recent evidence from the state of West

Bengal in India that voters cite short-term private benefits received from their local governments as most important for their voting decision and support of incumbents, as opposed to longer-term policy initiatives taken by incumbents to promote general public goods.

Foster and Rosenzweig (2001) also provide evidence consistent with Bardhan et al.'s argument that voters place greater emphasis in local elections in India on short-term gains from public spending. They focus on three categories of public goods, which together account for 73 percent of the activities of village governments in their sample in India—roads, irrigation and schools. They find that villages with democratically elected governments are more likely to provide more of all three public goods, but the largest effect is for irrigation, as calculated at the sample average, which is the service most likely to benefit the rural elite. However, in villages with a very high proportion of landless (much above the sample average) public investment shifts from irrigation to road construction (rather than education, which is unaffected by the proportion of landless), which suggests that capture by elites can be ameliorated when the numerical strength of the poor increases, but in a manner that might not be the most efficient for extending benefits to the poor. Roads built by village governments primarily benefit the poor, but largely by raising their (short-term) wages, as local road construction and improvement initiatives in India serve as employment programs for the landless poor. Education, which one expects to have the most profound effect on poverty over the medium and long term, seems least affected by decentralization.

New evidence from India specifically on decentralization of education services further illustrates this point. A central plank of public policy for improving primary education services in India is the participation of Village Education Committees (VECs), which were created in the 1990s, consisting of the head of the elected village government, parents and public school teachers. In a survey of 280 villages in India's most populous and educationally challenged state, Uttar Pradesh, in March 2005, at least ten years after the formal creation of this agency, Banerjee et al. (2006) find that parents do not know that a VEC exists, sometimes even when they are supposed to be members of it; VEC members are unaware of even key roles they are empowered to play in education services; public participation in improving education is negligible, and correspondingly, people's ranking of education on a list of village priorities is low. Large numbers of children in the villages have not acquired basic competency in reading, writing and arithmetic. Yet, parents, teachers and VEC members seem not to be fully aware of the scale of the problem, and seem not to have given much thought to the role of public agencies in improving outcomes.

That is, school failures coexist with public apathy to improving it through public action.

Between September and December 2005, an Indian NGO, Pratham, intervened in 190 of the 280 villages surveyed with different types of information and advocacy campaigns that communicated to village citizens the status of learning among their children, and the potential role that VECs and local governments could play in improving learning. The basic format of the interventions was to organize a village meeting on education, with the attendance of the head of the local village government and the head teacher of the village public school, the key members of the VEC, from whom the village community is urged to ask and receive basic information about local agencies in primary education. The issue raised most frequently in the village meetings, and about which people were most animated, was a government scholarship program intended to provide cash assistance to students from SC/ST groups. SC/ST parents complained that they were not getting these scholarships, whilst teachers complained that parents inappropriately enroll under-age children, who can't and don't attend school, just to lay claim to the scholarships. The second issue that attracted attention was a new government midday meal program. Actual learning levels attracted the least attention, and the facilitators had a difficult time steering the conversation away from scholarships and school meals to the broader issue of learning.

The average attendance in these meetings consisted of about 108 villagers, which seems a large gathering, with village total population (all ages) ranging from 500 to 5000 (Banerjee et al., 2008). These meetings were followed up with small group meetings with VEC members who were provided with pamphlets about their roles and responsibilities in education service delivery. The hypothesis behind these interventions was that once key community members were informed about local agency, they would participate more actively through it to improve services, and citizens at large would thence become informed and aware of it.

Follow-up surveys were undertaken in the same 280 villages in March 2006, three to six months after the information campaigns were implemented, and the most surprising fact emerging is that the campaigns did not lead to any substantial improvement in citizens' lack of knowledge of VECs. Less than 10 percent of citizens are aware of the VECs both before and after the interventions. We also find no effect on public school performance. This contrasts with a dramatic increase in private efforts to improve learning of lagging children in response to information provided—local youth volunteered to hold additional classes outside school, parents of illiterate children in particular chose to participate in these classes, and consequently the children made great strides towards literacy.

However, we don't even have anecdotal evidence that these local volunteers were assisted in their efforts by local government structures—neither the *Pradhan*, nor the village public school teacher, nor any member of the VEC. Indeed, according to anecdotes provided by Pratham's facilitators in the field, the public school teacher and the *Pradhan* in some villages felt threatened by the volunteer activities and attention drawn to learning failures in public schools.

Varshney (2005) provides another argument for why disadvantaged groups in particular would focus largely on the *identity* of candidates competing in local elections rather than their performance in delivering services such as education, health and infrastructure. In environments of poor law and order, historically entrenched social inequalities can lead to harassment of "unempowered" households at the hands of local police and law enforcement authorities that typically come from the dominant social groups. In this context, local elections, especially with political reservations, come as a specific opportunity for the unempowered groups to elect "one of their own" to public office, as an insurance against being victimized by the dominant elites. The proximity argument in favor of decentralization, that local elected representatives are "closer" to citizens, is precisely what makes such identity issues particularly important in local elections. When decentralization is partial, that is, when local governments have limited powers to improve local public services, it becomes all the more compelling for citizens from disadvantaged groups to focus instead on the identity of local politicians.

Some evidence in favor of this identity-based argument can be found in research on incentives of individual politicians to exert effort on public service delivery to their constituencies. Keefer and Khemani (2007) examine a unique public spending program in India—the Member of Parliament Local Area Development Scheme—which entitles every member of the national Parliament, elected from single-member constituencies, to substantial resources to spend on local public infrastructure in their districts. Spending these entitlements, however, requires considerable effort on the part of politicians as they have to work with local bureaucracies to get the projects implemented. Keefer and Khemani find that entrenched incumbents from districts that are reserved for SC/STs, that is, SC/ST politicians who have been elected for consecutive terms, spend 14 percentage points *less* of their entitlement than other politicians. In short, dominant incumbents from reserved districts are not dominant because they exert great effort in providing public infrastructure to their constituencies. Their dominance likely comes from other kinds of identity-based services.

Other examples of how partial decentralization creates perverse incentives for service delivery come from Kenya and Nigeria. Kremer et al. (2002) examine Kenya's mix of centralized and decentralized control over different aspects of education and argue that the system creates incentives for misallocation of public resources. At independence Kenya adopted an education finance system in which local communities were responsible for raising the resources to build schools, while the central government assigned teachers to schools and paid their salaries once the schools were built. Local communities had to provide non-teacher inputs such as textbooks and chalk, which they typically did by levying school fees. Local communities had strong incentives to build new schools, because once they had built one, the central government provided the teachers, which absorbed more than 90 percent of the present discounted cost of operating the school. Thus, many small schools, with small classes, were built close together. In the districts studied in the paper, the median distance between primary schools was 1.5 km, and Kenya's average pupil–teacher ratio was 28 in 1998, which is much lower than the average of 43 for Sub-Saharan Africa in 2000. The system led to excessive spending on teachers relative to non-teacher inputs. For example, a Ministry of Education survey showed that, on average, 17 primary school pupils in Kenya shared one textbook. Kremer et al. (2002) show that substantial service delivery gains could be achieved if resources were reallocated more efficiently.

Under partial decentralization, citizens are likely uninformed about what local governments are responsible for, what resources they have and how they perform their functions. Khemani (2006) presents evidence from Nigeria on the non-payment of salaries of health workers by local governments under the guise of fiscal powerlessness. Nigeria experienced a similar problem of non-payment of salaries of teachers in primary schools in the 1990s, when primary education was decentralized to local governments. Following nationwide agitations by teacher unions, a policy of deducting primary school teacher salaries from federal transfers to local governments was adopted (termed "deductions at source"), with the salaries being directly passed on to the teachers. This "solution" of essentially converting a portion of an untied federal transfer into a specific purpose grant for teacher salaries, although successful in ensuring that teachers get paid, had the unintended effect of undermining overall accountability of local governments. Local governments claim that deductions at source in essence lead to "zero allocations", thereby preventing them from carrying out any of their responsibilities for service delivery. Such uncertainty about resources actually available to local governments facilitates local evasion of responsibility—what local governments do receive as transfers is therefore sometimes treated as the personal fief of local politicians (World Bank, 2002).

In several countries, from Argentina to China, one of the most important responsibilities being decentralized to locally elected governments is beneficiary selection for poverty alleviation schemes funded by higher tiers of governments (Jalan and Ravallion, 1999; Galasso and Ravallion, 2000). Such decentralization has invariably been viewed in the literature as good policy design, in the face of solid evidence of informational advantages of local governments in appropriately identifying the poor or those that have faced particularly negative economic shocks (Alderman, 2002). However, this well-specified role of local governments, to the exclusion of proper specification of their role in general service delivery, might further strengthen clientelist impulses at local levels.

4 IMPLICATIONS FOR REFORM

Many of the reforms being pursued by donors in support of decentralization consist of providing greater revenues or transfers, and building capacity of local governments through training in technical issues such as public financial management. Our arguments suggest that these reforms on their own are unlikely to be successful. If decentralization is partial, greater funds devolved to local governments are more likely to go towards clientelist transfers rather than improvement of public goods. Capacity building can be a complete waste when local politicians have no incentives to develop technocratic skills for better service delivery. Even clarifying expenditure assignments, which is often part and parcel of donor-driven decentralization reforms, might have perverse effects of exacerbating the "partiality" of decentralization if the assignments circumscribe the role of local governments and reduce their discretionary authority in allocating across competing needs.

Our analysis suggests that these favored reform packages might have a greater chance of success if accompanied by a serious information or advocacy component that addresses the root cause of the problem with partial decentralization—low citizen expectations from local governments for broad public goods. The role of information and advocacy in changing political participation of citizens is increasingly being explored in policy experiments around the world, and often specifically in the context of improving local government.

One of the earliest examples from the developing world comes from Brazil. Tendler (1997) describes how the politics of patronage or "clientelism" in municipal governments in the state of Ceara in Brazil was tackled head on through massive information campaigns by a state government that took office in 1987. The state government flooded radio airwaves with messages about how infant and child mortality could be drastically reduced through particular programs of municipal governments, thus bringing political pressure to bear upon the mayors to actually deliver basic health services. The state also created a new class of public health workers through a publicized recruitment effort that conveyed information to communities about the valuable role the workers could play in improving public health through communitywide effort. In only a few years, coverage of measles and polio vaccination in Ceara tripled to 90 percent of the child population, and infant deaths fell from 102 to 65 per 1000 births. The campaigns' success has been attributed to bringing a remarkable turnaround in the politics of the state—from "clientelist" and patronage-based to service-oriented (ibid.).

More recently, Brazil has been the source of another innovative experiment in reducing local political rent-seeking by generating and providing credible information to citizens. In May 2003 the national government of Brazil launched an anti-corruption program based on the random auditing of municipal government expenditures by an independent public agency, and then publicly releasing audit findings on the internet and to media sources.[4] New evidence from more than 600 municipalities covered by the audit suggests that the disclosure of information significantly and substantially reduced the re-election rates of mayors who were found to be corrupt (Ferraz and Finan, 2006). Furthermore, this impact was significantly more pronounced in municipalities with greater access to radio stations.

Similar evidence is provided by Reinikka and Svensson (2005) from a newspaper campaign launched by the Ministry of Education in Uganda to publicize school grants that district authorities are supposed to provide. The Ministry pursued this campaign in response to new evidence that the grants did not in fact reach the schools as intended. Reinikka and Svensson provide evidence consistent with such information disclosure disciplining district authorities and forcing them to release the previously withheld funds: after the newspaper campaign had been launched, schools located closer to newspaper outlets received a larger share of their allocation.

Jenkins and Goetz (1999) and Goetz and Jenkins (2001) describe recent anti-corruption drives organized in India by NGOs, consisting of public audits of particular spending programs of local governments. These NGOs organize large public hearings, or *Jan Sunwais*, in the local language, to inform citizens about resources that were allocated to local officials and how they were spent, thereby exposing local corruption. The impact of these efforts is difficult to discern. Although anecdotal evidence suggests that they had enormous local impact around the hearings that were held, the hearings themselves are rather special events, spearheaded by a group of altruistic, charismatic and visible ex-civil servants with long-term commitment to grass-roots mobilization. The hearings are also limited in focus, providing information about individual public expenditure items, such as a particular road or water body.

These efforts have played a role in getting governments to legislate citizens' "right to information", where information refers to material held by public authorities in any form, including reports, documents, memos, records, opinions, advice, and so on (Goetz and Jenkins, 2001). Such legislation might facilitate greater reductions in corruption than have been documented with the mere existence of a free and independent press (Brunetti and Weder, 2003; Adsera et al., 2003), by allowing media greater access to government documents.

Some contrasting evidence on the role of information in improving local accountability comes from Indonesia. Olken (2005) evaluates a randomized experiment of different mechanisms to combat local corruption, including both grass-roots information dissemination among beneficiaries and announcement of audits from higher-tier government authorities, but without large-scale disclosure of audit results. He is therefore able to contrast the impact of information among local citizens with a more "top-down" institutional mechanism of combating corruption. He finds that audits-from-above were more effective in reducing corruption.

In reviewing the literature on information campaigns and the role of mass media in influencing public policy, Khemani (2007) argues that there are significant gaps in knowledge and experience in this area, and that much work remains to be done in exploring "information" as a tool to strengthen political accountability for development. She argues that local information campaigns whose immediate objective is to generate local participation (as in Banerjee et al., 2008 described earlier) cannot have sustainable or large-scale impact on public services unless they change incentives of politicians who have ultimate authority over the management of public employees and public budgets.

Extending or adapting the arguments made in Khemani (2007), we argue that decentralization reforms might indeed provide the opportunity to change political incentives, through information campaigns about the outcomes of public policies that are the responsibility of the lowest jurisdiction of government. If information on development outcomes that public policies are designed to address are made available in a credible manner to citizens on a regular basis, so they can compare performance in one local jurisdiction compared with another, and monitor improvements (or lack thereof) over time within a jurisdiction, it can potentially lead to voter coordination in evaluating local governments on this basis, and thereby promote yardstick competition between them to improve development performance.

Would such information indeed be retained by citizens and cause them to change their political behavior, emphasizing performance in broad service delivery when making their voting decision? This is a quite open question, but we argue that it is worth addressing rigorously. Systematically experimenting with information and advocacy campaigns as part of donor-driven or supported decentralization reforms would be valuable. If they work, they would assist poor countries in escaping from the governance trap. Theory and evidence suggests that information and advocacy are not a panacea and cannot be expected to achieve success if generally implemented. Specific design elements are critical and must be based on a rigorous understanding of local political economy if such campaigns are to be successful in changing citizen expectations and strengthening accountability of locally elected governments.

5 CONCLUDING THOUGHTS: WHY IS DECENTRALIZATION PARTIAL IN DEVELOPING COUNTRIES?

Almost every paper dealing with decentralization in developing countries begins by citing Tiebout (1956). After paying homage to the originality and power of those early ideas by that brilliant economist, many go on to acknowledge that its application to developing countries is limited because populations are less mobile, and less eager to move across jurisdictions (or accept "outsiders") in search of the "right" public goods. Few acknowledge another factor in the limited applicability of a Tiebout-style theoretical framework to understanding decentralization in the developing world—that long-standing central and/or provincial politicians are consciously deciding to delegate power and finances away from themselves, creating jurisdictions where none existed.

These central/provincial governments have some choice in determining the level of the lowest jurisdiction (based on considerations of capacity, natural tax bases, ethnic composition), expenditure and tax assignments, sharing of national/provincial revenues. What we find most commonly, especially in countries of Africa and South Asia, is a choice of decentralization instruments that results in the creation of very local village-level governments as the lowest tier, with low capacity, limited access to own tax bases, and no ownership over a defined policy space. That is, politicians choose decentralization to be partial. As a result, local agents largely perform functions at the behest of the center/province. When decentralization is thus determined by politicians, we have argued in this chapter that it reduces local government incentives to pursue "publicness" of spending and policies, and results in the provision of narrowly targeted or "club" goods. Donor-driven decentralization in the face of apathy of country governments, or worse still, in the face of widespread opposition by country political elites, can similarly lead to partial decentralization and clientelism, when greater resources are provided to local jurisdictions to distribute among communities, without proper specification of local policy space and budget constraints.

The motivations of national political elites for decentralization appear to be varied. Shah and Thompson (2004) have argued that in Eastern Europe and the former Soviet Union, decentralization was part of the region's political and economic liberalization; in Latin America, it was to reinforce the transition to democracy; in South Africa, Sri Lanka and Indonesia, it was a response to ethnic or regional conflict and in Chile, Uganda and Côte d'Ivoire, it was to improve the delivery of basic services. When national or provincial political elites have incentives to pursue more complete decentralization is a critical question for future research. Only when politicians' hands are forced by citizen pressure—greater demand for improved services—are things likely to be different. Both the institutions of decentralization will be then more complete (greater provision of resources and responsibilities) and citizens will have greater expectations from local governments. A striking feature of the experiments in Brazil discussed above is the critical role of national or large state governments in launching the information campaigns to change expectations of citizens from their local governments. Changing political incentives at higher levels of government can therefore contribute to more effective and successful decentralization.

NOTES

* An earlier version of this paper was presented at the seminar on "Effectiveness of Decentralized Strategies and Outcomes", Moncalieri, 3–4 September 2007.

1. See Bardhan (2002).
2. If a country's politics is particularly clientelist, citizens might not have any expectations of public goods from any tier of government. All we are arguing here is that under partial decentralization, citizens have relatively (and perhaps weakly) greater incentives to demand broader public goods from higher tiers of government than from local governments.
3. The only groups with low participation identified by Bardhan et al. (2007) are immigrants, women and those with low education, not low-caste groups or low-income/wealth groups.
4. This program is called Programa de Fiscalização a partir de Sorteios Públicos, details of which is available from the following website: www.presidencia.gov.br/cgu, accessed 22 March 2009.

REFERENCES

Adsera, A., C. Boix and M. Payne (2003), "Are You Being Served? Political Accountability and the Quality of Government", *Journal of Law, Economics and Organization*, **19** (2), 445–90.

Ahmad, Junaid, Shantayanan Devarajan, Stuti Khemani and Shekhar Shah (2006), "Decentralization and Service Delivery?", in Ehtisham Ahmad and Giorgio Brosio (eds), *Handbook of Fiscal Federalism*, Cheltenham, UK and Northampton, MA, USA: Edward Elgar, pp. 240–68.

Alderman, Harold (2002), "Do Local Officials Know Something We Don't? Decentralization of Targeted Transfers in Albania", *Journal of Public Economics*, **83**, 375–404.

Baland, Jean Marie and Jean-Philippe Platteau (1999), "The Ambiguous Impact of Inequality on Local Resource Management", *World Development*, **27** (5), 773–88

Banerjee, A., R. Banerji, E. Duflo, R. Glennerster and S. Khemani (2006), "Can Information Campaigns Spark Local Participation and Improve Outcomes?", Policy Research Working Paper No. 3967, Washington, DC: Development Research Group, The World Bank.

Banerjee, A., R. Banerji, E. Duflo, R. Glennerster and S. Khemani (2008), "Pitfalls of Participatory Programs: Evidence from a Randomized Evaluation in Education in India", Policy Research Working Paper No. 4584, Washington, DC: Development Research Group, The World Bank.

Bardhan, Pranab (2002), "Decentralization of Governance and Development", *Journal of Economic Perspectives*, **16** (4), 185–205.

Bardhan, Pranab and Dilip Mookherjee (2000), "Capture and Governance at Local and National Levels", *American Economic Review*, **90** (2), 135–39.

Bardhan, P., S. Mitra, D. Mookherjee and A. Sarkar (2007), "Local Democracy in Rural West Bengal: Political Participation and Targeting of Public Services", Working Paper, UC-Berkeley, Department of Economics.

Besley, Timothy, Rohini Pande, Lupin Rahman and Vijayendra Rao (2004), "The Politics of Public Good Provision: Evidence from Indian Local Governments", *Journal of the European Economic Association*, **2** (2–3), 412–26.

Brunetti, A. and B. Weder (2003), "A Free Press is Bad News for Corruption", *Journal of Public Economics*, **87** (7–8), 1801–24.

Chhibber, P., S. Shastri and R. Sisson (2004), "Federal Arrangements and the Provision of Public Goods in India", *Asian Survey*, **XLIV** (3), 339–52.

Ferraz, C. and F. Finan (2008), "Exposing Corrupt Politicians: The Effect of Brazil's Publicly Released Audits on Electoral Outcomes", *Quarterly Journal of Economics*, **123** (2), 703–45.

Foster, A. and M. Rosenzweig (2001), "Democratization, Decentralization, and the Distribution of Local Public Goods in a Poor Rural Economy", Working Paper, Brown University, http://adfdell.pstc.brown.edu/papers/democ.pdf, accessed 22 March 2009.

Galasso, E. and M. Ravallion (2000), "Distributional Outcomes of a Decentralized Welfare Program", Working Paper No. 2316, Washington, DC: World Bank.

Goetz, Anne Marie and Rob Jenkins (2001), "Hybrid Forms of Accountability: Citizen Engagement in Institutions of Public Sector Oversight in India", *Public Management Review*, **3** (3), 363–84.

Jalan, Jyotsna and Martin Ravallion (1999), "Income Gains to the Poor from Workfare: Estimates for Argentina's Trabajar Program", Working Paper No. 2149, Washington, DC: World Bank.

Jenkins, R. and A.M. Goetz (1999), "Accounts and Accountability: Theoretical Implications of the Right-to-information Movement in India", *Third World Quarterly*, **20** (3), 603–22.

Keefer, P. and S. Khemani (2007), "Why Do Some Legislators Pass On 'Pork'?" mimeo, Development Research Group, The World Bank.

Khemani, S. (2006), "Local government Accountability for Health Service Delivery in Nigeria", *Journal of African Economics*, **15** (2), 285–312.

Khemani, S. (2007), "Can Information Campaigns Overcome Political Obstacles to Serving the Poor?", in S. Devarajan and I. Widlund (eds), *The Politics of Service Delivery in Democracies*, Sweden: Ministry of Foreign Affairs.

Kremer, Michael, Sylvie Moulin and Robert Namunyu (2002), "Unbalanced Decentralization", Mimeo, Cambridge, MA: Harvard University.

Olken, B. (2005), "Monitoring Corruption: Evidence from a Field Experiment in Indonesia", NBER Working Paper No. 11753, Cambridge, MA: National Bureau of Economic Research.

Reinikka, Ritva and Jakob Svensson (2005), "Fighting Corruption to Improve Schooling: Evidence from a Newspaper Campaign in Uganda", *Journal of the European Economic Association*, **3** (2–3), 259–67.

Shah, A. and T. Thompson (2004), "Implementing Decentralized Local Governance: A Treacherous Road with Potholes, Detours, and Road Closures", Policy Research Working Paper No. 3353, World Bank.

Tendler, Judith (1997), *Good Government in the Tropics*, Baltimore: Johns Hopkins University Press.

Tiebout, C.M. (1956), "A Pure Theory of Local Expenditures", *Journal of Political Economy*, **65** (5), 416–24.

Varshney, Ashutosh (2005), "Democracy and Poverty", in Deepa Narayan (ed.), *Measuring Empowerment*, Washington, DC: The World Bank.

World Bank (2002), *State and Local Governance in Nigeria*, Sector Report No. 24477, Washington, DC: World Bank.

World Bank (2004a), *Fiscal Decentralization to Rural Governments in India*, Report No. 26554-IN, Washington, DC: World Bank.

World Bank (2004b), *Devolution in Pakistan: An Assessment and Recommendations for Action*, http://go.worldbank.org/DQ5P6ADC50, accessed 21 March 2009.

World Bank (2004c), *Making Services Work for Poor People*, Washington, DC: World Bank.

PART II

What do we know?

6. What do we know? Evidence on decentralization and local service provision

Ehtisham Ahmad and Giorgio Brosio

1 INTRODUCTION

What do we know about the results of decentralized service delivery? Verifying outcomes and results of decentralized policies is a very challenging exercise, given the large number of stakeholders involved. It is understandable that bilateral aid agencies and donors that have recommended decentralization have also stressed the importance of verifying outcomes of decentralized public policies. However, this is quite difficult to achieve in practice, especially in the developing country context. Only the more advanced OECD countries have moved effectively in this direction on a standardized basis, using the tools of performance budgeting (for example, the UK—whereas France is the latest to do so). An approximation may be attempted to evaluate outcomes in the absence of a performance budgeting framework, but this requires the definition of a proper methodology that is common among jurisdictions and levels of government, and using information that may not be readily available. Consequently, the emerging empirical literature on the outcomes of decentralization is heavily focused on OECD countries, and particularly on the efficiency considerations of service delivery (see Ahmad, Brosio and Tanzi, 2008).

Efficiency in decentralized provision is a focal concern for economists and it should be also for citizens, but it is not always the main goal of decentralization. There are distinctive themes concerning decentralized service delivery in different parts of the world. In the developing world, the issue of poverty reduction at the local level has been at the forefront of the policy debate. In Africa, the re-emergence of democratic governance has paralleled poverty reduction as an overarching goal of decentralization. In Europe, both Western and Eastern, decentralization and federalization have been sought to accommodate regional demands for autonomy based on ethnic, or cultural differences. This is the case in Belgium, Spain and some of the countries born out of the break-up of Yugoslavia. In these cases citizens may be ready to trade lesser efficiency with government closer to home.

In countries, such as Peru, decentralization is seen as a mechanism to share political power and prevent a resurgence of centralization (Ahmad and García-Escribano, 2007)—whereas in Pakistan the decentralization efforts by a military government was seen as a mechanism to bypass established political parties (Devarajan et al., Chapter 5, this volume). In Bolivia, decentralization was initiated partly to redress the economic discrimination suffered by the indigenous population, but is sought now by the richest regions to protect the resources coming from the exploitation of natural resources.

From the stylized facts and the recent literature, including some papers included in this volume, we highlight some of the critical elements that are needed to properly assess the outcomes of decentralization with a focus also on distributional issues and poverty reduction. The chapter is organized around three sections. Section 2 tackles definitional issues and presents the various points of view from which the outcomes of decentralization might be analyzed. Section 3 presents stylized trends in decentralization around the world. Section 4 provides a review of the empirical literature. Section 5 concludes.

2 GENERAL CONSIDERATIONS AND DEFINITIONAL ISSUES

Decentralization is understood, in general, as a process through which the role and functions of the subnational governments are expanded. This expansion can take place through three main different processes—these are not necessarily in actual or suggested order of sequence.

The first process is that of political decentralization. In countries with democratic institutions at all levels, political decentralization means devolution of political authority or of electoral capacities to subnational actors. Typical examples are the popular election of governors and mayors (previously appointed by local councils or by central authorities), constitutional reforms that reinforce the political autonomy of subnational governments and electoral reforms designed to augment political competition at the local levels.

The second process relates to fiscal decentralization. This involves a transfer of expenditure responsibilities to lower-level local governments, financed by a combination of own and other sources of revenues, including transfers. Unless complete functions are devolved, the decentralization process may remain incomplete. Also, the manner in which responsibilities are assigned, for example, by unfunded mandates, or earmarked or tied transfers, may reduce the "effective autonomy" of the local governments. Similarly, without own-source revenue at the margin, the local governments may lack incentives for proper "accountability", as they might be able to leverage the federal government or pass on the consequences of their actions to other jurisdictions (see Ahmad and Brosio, 2006 and Ambrosiano and Bordignon, 2006). Further, with access to borrowed resources, and in the absence of credible hard budget constraints, there is a substantial risk that the costs of subnational operations may be transferred to other jurisdictions, particularly at higher levels. Even in developed countries, there are significant risks to subnational operations as the current crisis in credit markets has recently illustrated for developed countries.

The third process relates to regulatory decentralization. This does not imply an appreciable transfer of financial resources or assignments, although its impact may be considerable for citizens (for example, regulation of car emissions). Pure regulatory decentralization is much less frequent than fiscal decentralization. In fact, there has been a substantial centralization of regulations, particularly in the field of environmental policies, health and even financial policies.

Both fiscal and regulatory decentralization imply transfer of some decision-making power over the use of public (fiscal) or private (regulatory) resources from the central to the subnational governments. Recognition that shifting of decision-making power is the essence of decentralization is crucial to the identification and the use of proper indicators of fiscal decentralization. For example, a simple reassignment of health expenditure from the central to regional budgets does not imply per se an increase in the degree of decentralization if it is not accompanied by the transfer of some decision-making power relating to this decentralized expenditure.

If the reassignment is financed by tied transfers, regional budgets would show a higher amount of expenditure, but since regions have to follow centrally set instructions for the use of these resources, no effective decentralization takes place (regions act simply as hierarchical subordinated agents of the central government).[1] Conversely, there can be real decentralization even if the share of regional expenditure or revenues is not changed, but if more decision-making power is devolved to regions concerning the existing resources. This poses a difficulty for empirical work—since the extent to which a spending assignment can be treated as a local responsibility depends on the financing arrangements, in particular whether tied transfers are involved.

Outcomes can be examined within single countries, where local jurisdictions have different degrees of autonomy (asymmetry). Or, if standardized information were available (even the IMF's GFS (Government Finance Statistics) data are not complete in this regard) it might be possible to observe different countries with different degrees of decentralization. Proper analysis requires adequate data on outcomes, efficiency and distributional outcomes. Evaluation of the outcomes of devolution would require assessments over a sufficiently long time frame, given the lags in adjusting policies and assignments.

Another relevant obstacle to the proper assessment of the outcomes of decentralization is that concurrent reforms are often involved. In many cases, decentralization requires changes of policy at higher levels of government that accompany and facilitate the process. A typical example is the reform of the civil service, or of public financial management systems. In these cases it becomes difficult to ascribe success or failure to the lower level of government that implements the reform. Education in Ethiopia provides an extremely relevant example of this difficulty. Progress in school enrollment was substantial after decentralization, and was achieved by using three distinct instruments: construction of schools, use of local languages and adaptation of school calendar to seasonality of crops. The construction of schools lowers barriers to entry by reducing the distance that children have to travel, in addition to providing the necessary expansion in capacity. In Ethiopia, construction of school premises is a typical local task, requiring use of resources and effort at the local level. The use of local languages and the school calendar lower barriers to entry, especially for poor people, and are reputed to have been quite successful in Ethiopia. They are mainly regulatory and have been initiated by the federal government, with some adaptation to local circumstances by subnational governments. Without the two regulatory measures the impact of school construction would have been much reduced.

3 SOME STYLIZED TRENDS IN DECENTRALIZATION OF SERVICE DELIVERY

As mentioned above, most countries have experimented with variants of decentralization reforms in the last three decades, addressing different motivations. A few have embarked in ambitious decentralization processes requiring constitutional revisions. The most notable cases have been the federalization of Belgium and of Ethiopia, the regionalization of Spain, Italy, France and the United Kingdom. The post-Apartheid constitution of South Africa presents an interesting case of a quasi-federal system. The decentralization processes in natural resource-rich countries, including Indonesia, Nigeria and more recently in Sudan and Iraq, are clearly driven by considerations to keep the country together. Noticeable decentralization reforms have also been introduced in almost all Latin American countries. Sub-Saharan Africa presents a wide array of decentralization processes, some instigated by donors, whereas others were political economy solutions to perceived problems of nationhood or governance. In addition to above-mentioned cases of Ethiopia and South Africa, extensive decentralization reforms have been introduced in Uganda and Nigeria.

3.1 European Trends

Increasing efficiency is a motivation of the decentralization in France, and partly in Italy. In Italy, the economic divide between rich and poor regions led to a demand for autonomy from the former. A larger subnational tax autonomy had led to a demand for larger redistributive transfers by the poor regions and to an expansion of public spending. The increased tax burden is resented by the voters of the rich regions. In France, decentralization reforms were started in 1982 (with a Socialist president) with the devolution of functions and the creation, in 1984, of the decentralized public service (Fonction Publique Térritoriale). The powers of the prefects vis-à-vis subnational governments have shifted from control to support. Since 1986 regional councilors are popularly elected. Following the 2001 budget reforms that led to the introduction of performance budgeting, the 2003 constitutional reform (sponsored by a center/right government) aims at increasing the role of subnational governments by introducing the subsidiarity principle, involving both policy and fiscal autonomy (Documentation Française, 2007).

Decentralization has also taken place in all new Eastern EU member countries. Poland, Slovakia and the Czech Republic have introduced a regional level of government, in addition to the initial focus on improved local governments—largely to benefit from the availability of EU structural funds that are made available to intermediate levels of government. In the Balkans, Croatia and Macedonia have also moved expenditure functions down to their subnational governments.

A few countries including Denmark and Norway also recentralized their system of territorial government. Higher education has been recentralized and the most important responsibility of the counties, management of hospitals, has been transferred to newly created regions. Denmark follows a typical Scandinavian trend in health care, where hospitals have been transferred to new and single-function regional entities, while the role of municipalities in primary care has been strengthened (Rico and Léon, 2005). Table 6.1 presents information on decentralization trends.

The motivation to decentralize, or centralize, often reflects complex and not always transparent political debates. In most cases, decentralization is

Table 6.1 Main traits of intergovernmental relations in selected countries

Countries	Share of Subnational Spending in General Government Spending 1985	Share of Subnational Spending in General Government Spending 2001	Main Traits of Intergovernmental Relations	Recent Reforms
Australia		49.9	Federal system	VAT administration by center on behalf of the states
Austria	28.4	28.5	Federal but highly federally regulated system	The Constitutional Convention recently fostered debate on constitutional reform of intergovernmental relations
Belgium	31.8	34.0	Federalization based on linguistic divides	Transformed from unitary to federal state
Bolivia		34.5	Three-layered unitary system	Powers of municipalities have been considerably increased Provinces are presently asking for substantial but asymmetrical powers Creation of autonomous local governments for indigenous people
Brazil		44.5*	Federal system based on three layers of government	National coordination of sales taxes is an urgent priority
Canada	54.5	56.5	Federal system	Asymmetries (Quebec)
China		70.0	Highly decentralized system, amounting to a de facto federation	Recentralization of taxing power
Colombia			Three-layered unitary system	Extensive devolution of resources to provinces
Denmark	53.7	57.8	Unitary system with strong municipal government	Recentralization of higher education and health since 2006

Table 6.1 (continued)

Countries	Share of Subnational Spending in General Government Spending 1985	Share of Subnational Spending in General Government Spending 2001	Main Traits of Intergovern-mental Relations	Recent Reforms
France	16.1	18.6	Regional system	Regulatory, fiscal and political decentralization
Germany	37.6	36.1	Federal system with extended concurrent responsibilities	Reduced intensity of equalization transfers after completion of re-unification
Italy	25.6	29.7		Fiscal, regulatory and political decentralization
Mexico		23.1**	Federal system with high political and low fiscal decentralization	Fiscal and regulatory decentralization since late 1980s, with devolution to states of basic education (1992) and health care (1996)
Poland		33.3 ***	Unitary	Political and fiscal decentralization with emphasis on the local level
South Africa		49.1	The post-Apartheid constitution introduced a quasi-federal system	Devolution of extensive responsibilities for education and health to provinces
Spain	25.0	32.2	Regional, quasi-federal system	Completed transition toward an almost federal system
Switzerland		67.4	Federal system	Equalization transfers from federation to cantons
United Kingdom	22.2	25.9	Regional	Introduction of regional government in Scotland and Wales

Note: * 1998 ** 2000 ***2005.

Sources: Quantitative information derives from OECD (2002), World Bank (2004) and from papers quoted in the text.

a multi-step, long duration process, carried out by different political coalitions, and impacts different layers of government differently. Italy provides an example. Decentralization since 1993 has successively involved: (1) the devolution of taxing powers to municipalities and regional governments: (2) the popular election of mayors and of provincial and regional governors; (3) the devolution of important expenditure responsibilities and legislative functions to regional governments and (4) the elimination of many central government controls on subnational units. These reforms—some of which are constitutional—have been implemented by both center/left and center/right coalitions and have reflected pressures applied by regionally based political movements. There are still very few analyses of the impact of decentralization in Italy on effective service delivery. However, given the complexity of the process, it would be almost impossible to ascribe the results to any one of these specific policy changes.

Spain has almost completed a transition to a quasi-federal system, driven by the goal of accommodating the demand for autonomy coming from the rich, linguistic regional minorities. The process was set in motion by the 1978 Constitution that granted a high level of autonomy to the historical nationalities of Navarra, the Basque County and Catalonia, while recognizing the right of the other regions to attain a similar level of self-government (Agranoff and Gallarin, 1997; Garcia-Milà and McGuire, 2002; Moreno, 2002). Spanish decentralization has been typically asymmetric, thus providing an excellent ground for empirical analyses of the impact of decentralization.

Similarly, federalization in Belgium and regionalization in the UK derive from historical/linguistic/cultural divides. In the Eastern European countries, decentralization has been sponsored by the EU and by international organizations, replicating the pattern observed in many developing countries, where the consolidation of democracy, efficiency reasons and expectation of better governance dominate. The EU, however, does not sponsor a particular model of decentralized governance, although the European Charter of Local Self-government prescribes strict guidelines in favor of subnational autonomy for signatory countries.

Demands for more power and autonomy from local elected officials and bureaucrats are important. All OECD countries have longstanding traditions of decentralized government and thus strong constituencies in favor of decentralization.

3.2 Developing Countries: Indonesia

The path towards decentralization has been more hesitant in Asian countries, with the notable exception of Indonesia since 2000. Indonesia had achieved some success with "deconcentrated" service delivery under the Suharto years (Shah, 1999), and the decentralized model reflects the reaction to the centralized power, and has focused more on a more equitable appropriate "sharing of natural resources". Indonesia has a three-tiered system of territorial government, and the decentralization in the post-Suharto period was focused on the third tier of government, namely districts and municipalities, in order to preserve the unitary structure of the constitution. The sequencing of the devolution of spending responsibilities was governed by practical considerations as well as political economy (with both the Habibi and Wahid administrations relying on the support of regional interests). The success with poverty reduction is more mixed—despite the recent growth, the total number of people in poverty remains stubbornly high (fluctuating between 35 million and the current level of 37 million); the unemployment rate in 2007 was the same as in 2002; and inequality appears to have increased significantly since 2003. Adequate safety nets are needed for the urban poor and landless populations. However, these are not easy to define in Indonesia.

Although the Indonesian government has taken steps to strengthen governance institutions at the central level, including a new budget classification and accounting system, as well as the treasury single account. These are not used by lower-level governments and it is difficult to order standardized and timely information for more effective macroeconomic management. It is also important for the central government to be aware in a timely manner about the quality of the subnational spending in key areas such as education, health and infrastructure. Given the weaknesses in reporting and monitoring of subnational operation, the central government has reintroduced centralized cash transfers to compensate the poor for the recent steep adjustments in the level of food and fuel prices in May 2008.

3.3 China

China presents an interesting case of a unitary country and a single party system, but where provinces enjoyed considerable de facto autonomy (Ahmad et al., 2002; Yagi, 2004). This was further consolidated in the post-1978 economic reforms, and local governments enjoyed increasing autonomy in terms of expenditure and growth-promoting policies (Qian and Weingast, 1997). While the initial informality in intergovernmental relations was an element in "market preserving reforms", declining central revenues and a fuzzy legal framework posed a threat to macroeconomic stability and future growth prospects. As a reaction, the central government moved to centralize its revenue-raising powers and in 1994 established a central tax administration to manage central and shared taxes (traditionally managed by the provinces) with a view to more effective macroeconomic management, and also to reduce the growing disparities among provinces (Ahmad et al., 2002). Given the restructuring of the system of state-owned enterprises, the central government is now moving to clarify spending responsibilities across levels of government and to hold lower levels accountable for their own effectively devolved functions—together with a strengthening of monitoring and evaluation capabilities of the central government, and a standardization of budget classification and treasury single accounts at all levels of government—so that there is better comparative information on who spends what and at what time.

3.4 Indian Sub-continent

The countries in the Indian sub-continent share common institutions and organizational structures that reflected the British colonial past. The Government of India Act (1935) provided autonomy to states/provinces, with the creation of separate and concurrent lists of functions (Singh, 2003). Most of these structures carried over to independent India and Pakistan, which both became federal countries, where individual states/provinces retained a unitary structure. In India, the push towards further responsibilities to responsible local government came in the 1990s, with the *Panchayati Raj*[2] changes to the institutional structure.

A similar push towards local governments in Pakistan by the military government at the end of the 1990s became discredited as it was also seen as a move to bypass the political process and the main parties that were organized at the provincial level (see also Bardhan; and Devarajan et al., Chapters 3 and 5 this volume). Unclear spending responsibilities, together with an absence of own-source revenues continue to hamstring the decentralization process—that is, brought into severe re-evaluation by the failure to improve service delivery in the sensitive tribal regions that also happen to be among the poorest in the country.

3.5 Latin America

A common motivation for the decentralization process in Latin American countries is the reaction to decades of military rule in many of the countries. In other cases, the decentralization is based on the central government's desire to share with other levels the increasing political costs of governance of complex systems. This motivation applies especially to Bolivia (at least, until recent events that signal increasing resistance of the richest regions to the sharing of resources with the poorest ones) and Colombia.

In Mexico, the decentralization process was also seen as a reaction to seven decades of virtual single party "centralized" rule. While the political power of the state governors has grown, on the fiscal side, there is a lack of clarity on spending functions, the states lack effective revenue tools and the transfer system is opaque. The most effective poverty reduction program happens to be central, the "Progresa/Opportunidades" (see Ahmad, Gonzales et al., 2008 and Ahmad, Chapter 12, this volume).

The centralization of revenues, together with overlapping spending responsibilities and extensive earmarking of transfers extend far beyond the federal countries, such as Mexico, to virtually all the unitary countries in Latin America, from Bolivia (one of the earliest countries to decentralize) to Colombia and Peru. In most cases, there are very weak governance institutions with non-standard classifications and accounting frameworks, absence of treasury single accounts and weak reporting. Brazil is an exception—while it also has overlapping responsibilities, it has the most advanced focus on own-source revenues, treasury single accounts and standardized reporting mechanisms. It also has had some success in decentralized service delivery and poverty reduction programs.

3.6 Decentralization and Governance in Sub-Saharan Africa

Sub-Saharan Africa presents the most challenging context for decentralization. The concerned countries are extremely poor and with limited traditions of democratic governance. Huge ethnic, cultural and religious cleavages characterize most of them, originating a demand for strong autonomy and increasing the difficulties of the task of keeping the countries together.

3.6.1 Institutional arrangements and sequencing of decentralization

The institutional/legal framework of a country determines the starting point for assessing the scope for decentralization. A distinction needs to be made between federal countries, such as Nigeria and Ethiopia (or South Africa, which is a quasi-federal country), and unitary states (for example, Mozambique, Niger, Senegal). In addition, there are some three-tier/regional systems (for example, Mali and Uganda).

The emphasis on regional or subnational governance in some cases has been driven by the dictates of a political compromise to solve festering conflicts, as in the DR Congo. In such cases, the emphasis is more on "co-opting regional or ethnic factions" with promises of sharing of natural resources and wealth, with relatively little focus on effectiveness of service delivery.

In the federal context, the subnational assignments and responsibilities are typically divided between regions (states or provinces) and local governments, and may be clearly specified in the constitution or higher-level laws (see, for example, Constitution of South Africa, Act 108, 1996, schedule 5 for exclusive responsibilities, and schedule 4 for concurrent responsibilities between the center and the provinces). It is interesting to note that education and health care are concurrent responsibilities between the center and the provinces in South Africa—these are not municipal responsibilities, as in many other African countries. Nigerian attempts to assign primary education to local governments were constrained by capacity limitations and the absence of clear own-source revenues and governance difficulties (more on this below).

3.6.2 Clarifying assignments

Overlapping responsibilities are the norm in most African states, with a gradual transfer of functions and responsibilities—such as in Uganda. This has led to contradictions between mandates (universal access to free primary education) and the financing available, when the center does not fully control the numbers of persons employed, and the subnational governments do not face a hard budget constraint (Levy and Kpundeh, 2004).

Assigning full responsibility has been attempted in federal countries, such as Nigeria and Ethiopia, for example, for primary education assigned to the lowest tier of government (see Table 6A.1 in the Appendix at the end of the chapter). However, capacity constraints, together with the absence of own-source revenues and other weaknesses in the design of intergovernmental fiscal relations, have resulted in an effective reinstatement of overlapping responsibilities.

In the Nigerian case, after the implementation of the new constitution, several local governments played their main political card—not paying the health workers or teachers (Khemani, 2006). This forced the center to pay these wages through the conversion of municipal transfers into "earmarked grants" for wages. But this again faced the intractable issue of implementation of centrally determined policies at the local level with incomplete or weak information, including on the number of teachers. The "middle-tier" states have been co-opted to assist with the determination of the rolls and ensuring the transfers actually reach the relevant teachers or health workers, involving a return to overlapping responsibilities. The Ethiopian experience, with effective sequencing of decentralization/deconcentration and strong leadership, has been more successful, but the federal government has effectively maintained a firm grip over all levels of governments.

The Kenyan constitution, still under discussion, attempts a clearer delineation of responsibilities for education and health care, making a distinction, for example, between primary and secondary education, assigned to districts, and tertiary education assigned to the center. However, on other crucial issues, such as the role of local governments, the constitutional text is silent.

In South Africa, the critical functions of education or health care were not devolved to local governments, but to the provinces—given the substantial externalities associated with these functions, and the possibility of "game-play" that has become apparent in cases such as Nigeria (and in several Latin American countries). These issues become clearer with the evaluation of public service delivery outcomes in several African countries—where the requisite information is available.

3.6.3 Governance and monitoring

A coherent framework for consistent decision-making across all levels of government would be desirable. However, standard public financial management principles are weak in the African context, as noted in the World Bank-IMF HIPC (Heavily Indebted Poor Countries) tracking exercise and are even weaker at the subnational level in these African countries.

Attempts to involve the local communities to assist with monitoring the use of special purpose transfers and donor funds, as in Uganda, have had some success. However, these do not per se overcome the weaknesses of the design of the intergovernmental fiscal system, and the absences of effective incentives, together with the generation of information and application of sanctions needed for good governance.

Monitoring by citizens at the local level is a positive factor, but has to be based on solid public financial management systems and processes, and is not a substitute for these foundations. Attempts to bypass standardized reporting requirements through the use of contracts and local monitoring are subject to all the uncertainties associated with a weak base line, audit institutions, and limited information or sanctions. This may result in some patchy successes, but cannot be a basis for rapid decentralization. Given significantly enhanced capabilities in certain regions in most countries, such as in capitals and major urban centers, there may be a case for more rapid devolution of responsibilities in these regions—leading to asymmetric solutions.

Several donors and international agencies have emphasized the importance of performance outcomes, especially for subnational public service delivery, in order to achieve more effective poverty reduction. Consequently, several countries are being encouraged to move towards performance budgeting. Desirable as this may be, a shift to performance budgeting, without adequate preparation of the public financial management system, risks a loss of control and information and could paradoxically generate greater corruption and rent-seeking. Again, careful preparation and sequencing is essential.

4 EXPECTED OUTCOMES OF DECENTRALIZATION: A SURVEY OF THE LITERATURE

In this section, we examine some cross-country and single country studies. A number of papers discuss decentralization outcomes in individual countries,[3] others provide international comparisons. The cross-country studies are generally constrained by limited availability of comparable data to using a reduced-form relationship between decentralization and efficiency.[4] Assessments for single countries can, potentially, overcome the control variables issue and provide firmer results. Many studies use data from different sources—mainly budgets, administrative sources and increasingly, household survey data.

The empirical literature on decentralization and efficiency can be arranged in four distinct groups. The first group of studies link decentralization with production efficiency (Table 6.2), and forms the largest group. The OECD evidence is summarized in Ahmad, Brosio and Tanzi (2008).

A second group of a few papers relates decentralization to convergence of service delivery levels (Table 6.2). According to the theory, decentralization should decrease convergence, when heterogeneity of preferences and disparities of economic conditions prevail. However, it does not imply that centralized provision ensures uniformity of levels. For example, in Italy, major differences are commonly observed among regions at different levels of development in the actual levels of centrally provided services, such as tax administration, education, health or the postal service. This may reflect neglect by national politicians, slack and bureaucratic capture in deconcentrated agencies. It is expected that decentralization could bring convergence, particularly if accompanied by introduction of uniform standards and effective transfers.

A third group of papers refers to preference matching and decentralization (Table 6.3). This is an important consideration, the more so when cultural/ethnic motivations are important in the impetus for decentralization. However, there are relatively few papers addressing this issue, and most consider it jointly with growth issues.

Fourth, a large number of papers examine decentralization and growth (Table 6.3). It is hard to argue that overall economic growth could depend on decentralization. However, one of the crucial goals pursued by local politicians is the promotion of growth in their areas, and this may have an impact on overall growth. The origins of the literature linking decentralization to growth can be traced out to Oates (1993), who argued that the gains from decentralization should also apply to a dynamic framework of economic growth. This is because centrally determined policies do not adequately consider local conditions in the provision of public goods and services, such as those regarding infrastructure and education. It is argued that economic growth might be more rapid with decentralization if more resources go to public investment; health and education policies are better targeted to growth, and in sum this produces more growth. In other words, local preferences are growth-oriented. A simpler approach focuses mostly on productive efficiency. The main hypothesis is that if decentralization promotes more efficient use of resources, it should also result in higher rates of growth for the whole economy.

There are also a number of arguments against a positive link between decentralization and growth. For example, decentralization could work against growth if it discourages big investment projects with growth-conducive spillovers across regions. It may discourage the production of genuine public goods. Moreover, political objectives may emphasize equity and not growth—elected politicians want results within their terms in office.

4.1 Production Efficiency

Barankay and Lockwood (2006) (Table 6.2) examine the relationship between educational outcomes and decentralization in Switzerland. They show: (1) that it is possible to overcome most problems associated with information constraints and, (2) that decentralization does in fact contribute to improved outcomes. In Switzerland responsibility for education has always been cantonal, although the federal government equalizes across cantons. Cantons can devolve some of expenditure responsibilities to their local governments and they effectively do so. It is thus possible to observe different degrees of decentralization in education between cantons.

Educational outcomes are measured in the study by the share of the 19-year-old population that passes the final exams (*La Maturité*) to enter university.[5] The index of decentralization is measured by share of education expenditure by the local governments in each canton over the sum of local and cantonal expenditure for education. In other words, the index shows the degree of education expenditure within each canton:

$$D_{ct} = \frac{LE_{ct}}{LE_{ct} + CE_{ct}};$$

where D_{ct} is the index of canton c in year t, LE_{ct} is the sum of education expenditure in all counties of canton c in year t and CE_{ct} is education expenditure at the cantonal level in year t.

The use of a purely fiscal variable, such as the expenditure share, entails the risk that it does not adequately represent the degree of effective autonomy of local government. To solve the problem, Barankay and Lockwood examine cantonal regulations in four crucial areas for education: (1) appointing teachers; (2) determining the pay level of teachers; (3) granting teachers' incentives and (4) organizing the structure of school. Apparently, decentralization of expenditure is closely associated with higher local decision-making power, especially for teachers' incentive pay. Local government expenditure for education is mainly for teachers' salaries. Thus, when the number of teachers or the pay levels increase, the degree of decentralization also varies within cantons. Second, variation in expenditures for teachers' salaries is induced by changes in the size of the student population. If it increases, local government has to provide more teachers, since cantons impose minimum class sizes. Also, changes in student numbers induce changes in the indicator of decentralization. Variations in outcomes can thus be meaningfully associated with changes in decentralization if the number of students does not impact on outcomes.

Finally, Barankay and Lockwood regress for 20 years (1982–2002) the *La Maturité* results on their chosen index of decentralization after adding a number of variables that control use of inputs and canton and year fixed effects. Results show that educational attainment is positively and significantly related to the degree of decentralization. The absolute impact of the latter is also substantial.

According to the estimate, if the decentralization index increases by ten percentage points, the share of students obtaining the *La Maturité* increases by 3.5 percent. Thus, cantons seem to play an important role in ensuring effective outcomes. It should be noted, however, that the system of transfers in Switzerland has been reformed (since this chapter was written) as the authorities felt that the previous system, in which transfers are linked to variables under the control of cantons, provided an incentive to increase costs—generating macroeconomic inefficiencies.

A similar analysis is conducted by Salinas Peña (2007) (Table 6.2) on Spanish schools. Spain provides, through its asymmetric regionalization, unique opportunity for checking the outcomes of decentralization. The central government has retained the responsibility for defining the structure and setting national guidelines and standards for education policies, leaving other competences to the regions. Salinas Peña uses as an indicator of outcomes the share of students who complete post/secondary education (*Bachillerato*) to those enrolled in the last year of compulsory education,

Table 6.2 Selected papers on production efficiency and convergence

Author(s)	Countries of Reference	Period of Reference	Dependent Variable	Decentralization Index	Main Results
Ahlin and Mörk (2007)	Sweden	1989–2000	Convergence in per student spending and teacher–pupil ratio	Regulatory variables	Little evidence on convergence
Balaguer-Coll et al. (2006)	Spain (1315 municipalities)	1995–2000	Output of local services	Range of responsibilities (regulatory and fiscal)	Decentralization increases efficiency
Barankay and Lockwood (2006)	Switzerland (26 cantons)	1982–2000	Education attainment	Fiscal and regulatory: local on cantonal expenditure controlled for regulatory powers	Decentralization increases efficiency
Cantarero Prieto and Pascual Sanchez (2006)	15 EU member countries	1993–2003	Infant mortality ratio and life expectancy at national level	Fiscal decentralization: local on total expenditure	Decentralization improves outcomes
Crivelli et al. (2007)	Switzerland (26 cantons)	1996–2001	Expenditure and input measures for health	No specific decentralization index	Huge disparities associated with decentralization and federalism
Jakubowski and Topińska (2006)	Poland: local governments	1999–2003	Various variables referring to education	Fiscal regulatory decentralization	Mixed results
Jimenez and Smith (2005)	Canada (ten provinces)	1979–1995	Infant mortality rate	Fiscal decentralization	Decentralization reduces infant mortality
Montero-Granados and de Dios Jiménez (2007)	Spain (17 Autonomous Communities)	1980–2001	Life expectancy at birth and infant mortality	Regulatory (before and after devolution of responsibilities)	No clear convergence: regions with low levels improve,

Table 6.2 (continued)

Author(s)	Countries of Reference	Period of Reference	Dependent Variable	Decentral-ization Index	Main Results
					but greater dispersion of outcomes emerges
Robalino et al. (2001)	High-income countries Spain	1970–95	Infant mortality ratio	Fiscal decentral-ization: subnational on total national expenditure	Positive impact declining with increases of GDP
Salinas Peña (2007)	Spain (50 provinces)	1980–2003	Survival rate: proportion of students in last course of compulsory education who access non-compulsory education	Regulatory (before and after devolution of responsibilities)	Decentral-ization is associated with positive outcomes

Source: Ahmad, Brosio and Tanzi (2008).

assuming that a good level of education quality will induce students to stay at school. Typical variables explaining educational outcomes, such as family income, or the size of classes, are used for control purposes, while a few dummies are used to distinguish between regions that acceded to education responsibilities in different years. The fiscal discipline of regions is controlled via the introduction of the surplus/deficit in the regional budget. Different specifications of the chosen model are tested. The results show some problems referring to the control variables, most of which do not show the expected sign. Decentralization is positively and significantly correlated with the survival rate in two out of three specifications. However, earlier decentralized regions are at the same time those with a higher per capita income. As income is also a determinant of the survival rate, the link of the latter with decentralization may be blurred. The dependent variable is also correlated positively with fiscal discipline, supporting a basic tenet of decentralization theory that maintains that the benefits of decentralization are also dependent on the quality of decentralization.

Jimenez and Smith (2005) (Table 6.2) try to trace the impact of decentralization on health care outcomes proxied by infant mortality, with reference to Canada during 1975–95. This shows higher variation among Canadian provinces than life expectancy. First, the authors attempt to check the production efficiency of decentralization with a single-step model, where infant mortality is regressed on a decentralization index and a number of control variables. Second, they proceed to estimate a two-step model. In the first step, provincial expenditure for health is regressed on the index of decentralization and on a number of control variables, such as transfers from the central government, private sector expenditure, birth rates and the like. In the second step, the authors proceed again to check the impact of decentralization on infant mortality by substituting actual provincial expenditure for education with an estimated one. The purpose of the two-step exercise is to control the impact of decentralization on preference matching and then to proceed to control the efficiency effect.

The results show a negative and significant relationship between infant mortality and the decentralization. More specifically, reduction of mortality is closely dependent on provincial expenditure on health: roughly a 1 percent increase in provincial expenditure on health stimulated a 3.8 percent reduction in infant mortality.

Unfortunately, the reliability of the results is reduced by the indicator of decentralization used, which is based on the provincial share of total health care in that province.[6] By not controlling for the effective subnational decision-making power, the index shows mostly the propensity to spend for health by a provincial government and its municipal governments. Moreover, as federal expenditure in each province is not a substitute for subnational expenditure, its relative size is not an indicator of degree of decentralization of expenditure.[7]

Balaguer-Coll et al. (2006) (Table 6.2) examine a sample of Spanish municipalities during 1995 and 2000. They attempt to estimate the impact of decentralization on typical municipal services, that is, those that constitute the backbone of any decentralized system. The study tries to evaluate the gains in production efficiency brought by decentralization by using a non-parametric (FDH [free disposal hull]) estimate of the efficiency frontier. The study links inputs used—more specifically municipal expenditure—to a number of indicators of municipal output, such as the waste collected and surface of public parks, and then select the most efficient units. The authors distinguish between (small) municipalities with fewer responsibilities and medium and large municipalities with extended responsibilities. After controlling for the operation of scale economies, municipalities with wider responsibilities should be ahead in the decentralization process. The results show that average efficiency is higher for large and medium-sized municipalities and that the differences tend to grow larger over time (a proxy for increased decentralization).

Robalino et al. (2001) (Table 6.2) provide one of the few cross-country studies for industrial economies. In their empirical model they regress infant mortality on the ratio of expenditure managed by local governments relative to that managed by the central government. They also introduce a few control variables, which refer to institutional capacity, such as political and civil rights, and corruption. These variables allow the authors to control the quality of political institutions. But without reference to the actual use of inputs one cannot perform a thorough assessment of production efficiency (with the partial exemption of GDP). The sample of low- and high-income countries is not specified. The results show that outcomes are positively correlated with decentralization. They also show that the marginal effects of decentralization diminish as GDP increases. This, if validated with other empirical evidence, would be an interesting result. It would mean that when countries grow, their institutional capacity increases and thus the advantages of decentralization are likely to vanish, since the presumed differences between central and local management of public affairs disappear.

Cantarero Prieto and Pascual Sanchez (2006) (Table 6.2) provide a similar analysis for 15 EU countries. However, their results—positive association between outcomes in health and decentralization—are weakened by, among other factors, their use of nationwide indicators. There is now an increasing use of household surveys for the assessment of the access of poor and disadvantaged individuals and on the personal characteristics of users. When combined with fiscal and administrative data, household surveys can potentially allow for an examination of both efficiency and equity.

Jakubowski and Topińska (2006, and Chapter 9, this volume) (Table 6.2) use this methodology to evaluate the results of decentralization in education and health care in Poland. Their paper in this volume is an illustration of methods that could be used to evaluate the effects of decentralization—and also emphasizes the combination of fiscal and household information that is needed to carry out a proper evaluation. It provides for a before, during and after comparison, and illustrates the complex inter-relationships that arise. The authors show that decentralization in Poland has not been up to the expectations in terms of cost-effectiveness and has brought about a reduction in service delivery in the rural areas. This applies particularly to kindergartens.

All the studies are valuable since they move the debate to practical policy questions, rather than purely political considerations that represent a black versus white perspective on decentralization.

4.2 Convergence of Service Provision Across Areas

There is a small but increasing number of studies analyzing convergence across areas of levels of service provision. Empirical observation seems to confirm the theory—for example, for health care in Switzerland. Switzerland is one of the most decentralized countries of the world. With respect to health care, the role of the federal government is limited to funding of health care to poor people (federal expenditure is 20 percent of total national health care) and to the definition of basic packages of health insurance (Crivelli et al., 2007) (Table 6.2). Provision of health care shows huge disparities between cantons, whether measured in terms of expenditure, use of inputs, or outcomes, such as differences in mortality rates amenable to absence of timely and effective care (ibid.).

One of the arguments used against decentralization is that it will increase disparities in levels of service delivery, if decentralization is not accompanied by the imposition of strict national standards on service levels and if substantial equalization grants are not provided.

Montero-Granados and Juan de Dios Jiménez (2007) (Table 6.2) do not provide an analytical framework, but test the convergence hypothesis with reference to the Spanish regions in the health sector. Health care is provided by a National Health System funded (with the exception of Navarre and the Basque Country) by general taxation and small user co-payments. Standards are determined by the central government, while regional authorities are responsible for planning, organization and management of health care, and are provided with a centrally determined block-grant allocated according to an unadjusted capitation formula. The authors use two measures of convergence derived from the literature on growth. They are the sigma (s) and the beta (b) convergence. The first measure is based on changes of standard deviation over time. When variation declines, there is more homogeneity of outcomes, or of behaviors. According to the second measure, convergence increases when laggard regions improve quicker than more advanced.

Outcomes of health care include life expectancy at birth and infant mortality, while decentralization is measured by access by regions to health responsibilities. The authors also use a host of variables, other than decentralization, that are expected to impact on outcomes. The results show convergence taking place at the extremes. That is, less developed regions improve faster than more advanced regions, while in the middle, there is a big increase in variation. These results are open to interpretation. One could say decentralization fills the most optimistic expectations, as the difference between the rich and the poor regions are leveled and at the same time individual (middle) regions adjust to their preferences. One can also argue that the results confirm the expectations that there is little to expect in terms of homogeneity from decentralization.

Ahlin and Mörk (2007) (Table 6.2) analyze the impact on convergence due to different stages in decentralization in the Swedish education sector. Sweden took three major steps to decentralize its education system. In 1991 formal responsibility for compulsory, upper secondary and adult education was moved to the local government level. Teachers were transferred to municipalities, but salaries were still determined centrally, as well as curricula and national evaluations. Distinct specific grants for education, such as for books and school premises were unified into a single specific grant. In 1993, all sector-specific grants—such as those for education, health and social protection—were unified into a single block-grant, giving municipalities the freedom, for example, to move resources from education to social protection (or vice versa). In 1996, teachers' wages-setting was moved to municipalities and a new block-grant system was introduced, based on revenue and cost equalization. Note that since 1992, the central government introduced public funding for independent schools, thus inserting more competition between public and private education. Convergence is analyzed with reference to two typical input indicators: per pupil spending and teacher–pupil ratio. The paper shows that no appreciable change has taken place in the pattern of per pupil spending, while variation in teacher–pupil ratio has decreased over time. The authors explain the surprising result (challenging traditional theory) in terms of the strategic interactions between local politicians—local choices are constrained by neighboring municipalities' choices. However, they do not control for the varying equalizing impact of different systems of grants. Subsequent regression analysis shows that with decentralization, higher reliance on own-source of revenues had an impact on per pupil expenditure, but this effect may have been neutralized by the equalization grants. Thus, the power given to local governments by decentralization of responsibilities may have been offset by the ability of the central government to influence local choices through the allocation of grants.

4.3 Preference Matching

The empirical literature exclusively devoted to preference matching is still relatively small. In fact, most studies link preference matching with growth, as illustrated below.

A well-structured and accurate analysis is provided by Strumpf and Oberholzer-Gee (2002) with reference to regulation of the liquor sales in the US states between 1934 and 1970. In 1933 the Prohibition Act was repealed and the states were made responsible for liquor control. States then had the choice between centralized/statewide regulation, or devolution of regulation to their local governments (counties, municipalities and towns). Initially, seven states prohibited sale of package liquor, while among non-prohibitionist states 20, and later 34, devolved regulation to their local communities where the issue was decided in local elections.

Strumpf and Oberholzer-Gee construct, and test with regression analysis, a model predicting that decentralization of regulation would be observed in states with huge heterogeneity of preferences on liquor sales, while centralization should prevail with less extreme disparities. The test is conducted in two sequential stages. The first stage refers to (3100) counties where the tastes of the decisive voters are estimated using variables that according to the literature should influence the taste for liquor, such as religious affiliation and socioeconomic variables. Tastes will predict the policy—wet or dry—adopted by the community. The second stage refers to states and is based on regression of decentralization of policy with two measures of within-state taste heterogeneity. The results show that the states with more heterogeneous preferences have been more prone to decentralize.

Arze del Granado et al. (2005) (Table 6.2) provide specific empirical testing of preference matching, also with reference to developing countries. More precisely, the paper analyzes the impact of fiscal decentralization on the provision of publicly provided private goods, such as health and education. The analysis is based on 45 developed and developing countries between 1973 and 2000. The dependent variables are the share of local health and education expenditure on total local expenditure, while the independent variable is the share of local total general government expenditure.

The results show that decentralization brings about an increase of the share of these two categories of expenditure, but the generality of the findings may be questioned. Since there is no evidence—but only a general presumption—in the paper that more expenditure for health and education means effectively better adaptation to local preferences in every country, more spending for these two sectors could simply derive from the fact that these are the sectors where decentralization has taken place.

There are also a few studies of preference matching referring specifically to developing countries. Faguet (2004) and Faguet and Sanchez (2006) (Table 6.3) analyze Bolivia and Colombia. These countries have undergone a far-reaching decentralization process. While Bolivia has relied mostly on strengthening of municipalities, Colombia's decentralization was initially based on strengthening municipalities and has relied subsequently on the regional governments (departments). Bolivia also initiated elections of departmental governors, but the process has run into difficulties over the sharing of natural revenues. In both countries, subnational revenue has substantially been increased through the increased sharing of national tax collections—much of this was earmarked to investments in education and health.

Both studies assess, first, how decentralization affects the composition of local expenditure by sector in line with citizens' preferences, and second, how decentralized spending improves the outcomes of education, although from a partial point of view, namely enrollments. The studies exert a considerable effort in singling out local preferences for expenditure. They argue that, with decentralization, investment priorities shift from typical services such as water, sewerage and roads to education and health. This shift is assumed to be more in line with people's preferences. There is, however, no demonstration of this. In both countries decentralization brought about an increase in school enrollment, as would have been expected considering the increased amount of investment. There is, however, no precise checking of the correspondence between increased expenditure and increased enrollments. In other words, the studies do not provide conclusive evidence about gains in production efficiency reached through decentralization per se.

Inchauste (Chapter 7, this volume) (Table 6.3) uses both fiscal and household survey data to check whether resources channeled to municipalities have been distributed as intended under the enhanced HIPC initiative, and whether there is any evidence of absorptive capacity constraints, particularly by poor municipalities. The paper also investigates whether the resources that actually have been spent have had any impact on short-term social indicators, such as illiteracy rate, rate of unattended respiratory diseases, and home access to electricity and water. Results again do not provide convincing evidence of efficient working of local governments. For example, municipalities, particularly the poorer ones, show substantial problems in transforming increased revenue in effective spending. For education, for example, increases in education transfers do not significantly affect the share of children not attending school. When looking at infrastructure indicators, there is still no significant effect of changes in spending or transfers on the share of homes with access to water and electricity services. More in general, there is no evidence of a clear improvement of conditions in the poorest municipalities, or for the poorest segments of the population.

Solé-Ollé and Esteller-Moré (2005) (Table 6.3) analyze the impact of decentralization on the pattern of investment in roads and education premises during 1977–98 in Spain. The paper is well constructed, although it is not *strictly* a test of preference matching, but rather an efficiency test of spending decisions. The main focus of the analysis is, in fact, testing

Table 6.3 Decentralization: preference matching and growth—summary of selected papers

Author(s)	Countries of Reference	Period of Reference	Fiscal Variables of Reference	Growth Variables of Reference	Decen-tralization Index	Main Results
Akai and Sakata (2005)	US counties	1993–2000		GDP growth rate	Fiscal with emphasis on tax autonomy	Growth is positively related to tax autonomy and specifically to non-bailouts
Arze del Granado et al. (2005)	45 countries Developed and developing countries	1973–2000	Ratio of education and health expen-ditures to total public expen-ditures		Fiscal decentral-ization	Likely increase of expenditure for health and education
Ebel and Yilmaz (2002)	19 OECD countries	1997–99	Public sector's expen-diture share of GDP	GDP growth rate		
Faguet (2004)	Bolivia Sample of munici-palities	1991–96	Investment for education; water and sanitation; watershed manage-ment		Fiscal decentral-ization	Increased spending in poorer areas
Faguet and Sanchez (2006)	Bolivia and Colombia Samples of munici-palities	Mid-1990s early 2000.	Investment in education		Fiscal decentral-ization	Increased spending for education and expanded enrollments
Inchauste (2009) (and Chapter 7 this volume)	Bolivia Munici-palities	2001–2005	Education and public works		No specific index	Provision of additional funds does not bring substantial results
Solé-Ollé and Esteller-Moré	Spain	1977–98 (44 provinces)	Investment: roads and education		Fiscal and regulatory decentral-ization	Better adaptation of investment to local needs

Table 6.3 (continued)

Author(s)	Countries of Reference	Period of Reference	Fiscal Variables of Reference	Growth Variables of Reference	Decen-tralization Index	Main Results
Strumpf and Oberholzer-Gee (2002)	US states	1934–1970	Devolution of regulatory powers to local governments			More devolution in states with heterogeneous preferences
Thiessen (2000)	26 mainly developed countries	1975–95	Annual growth rate of real gross fixed capital formation (as indicator of physical investment)	Growth rate of per capita GDP Total factor productivity growth	Fiscal decentral-ization	Growth initially increases but then declines with decentral-ization
Thiessen (2003)	14 and 21 high-income OECD countries	1973–98	Average annual investment share in GDP	Log difference GDP per working-age person Average annual total factor productivity growth	Fiscal decentral-ization	Growth initially increases but then declines with decentral-ization

if after decentralization investment decisions have been more closely targeted to effective needs, such as, more road construction in congested areas and more school construction in areas with higher student population growth and if investment activities have become more cost-conscious. The results show that with decentralization the regional allocation of investment in these two sectors has become better adapted to local conditions and needs, thus showing a higher level of efficiency than under the previous centralized regime.

4.4 Decentralization and Growth

Although there is a large empirical literature on the link between decentralization and growth, the consensus appears to be that any relationship is relatively weak. A good survey of its main results has already been provided by Breuss and Eller (2004, see, for example, p. 11).

The empirical literature refers to samples of countries, as in Thiessen

(2000 and 2003) (Table 6.3), Ebel and Yilmaz (2002) (Table 6.3) and to distinct countries, such as in the papers by Behnisch et al. (2003) on Germany and by Feld (2004) on Switzerland. The empirical findings are mixed. Negative findings are more frequent for European countries and with a longer-term perspective.

We limit our consideration to the studies of Thiessen (2000 and 2003), which are mostly devoted to OECD countries. The relationship between decentralization and growth is represented by a bell-shaped curve, meaning that when countries move from low to medium levels of decentralization, growth accelerates, but higher decentralization will reduce growth. Part of this explanation derives from the positive impact on capital formation deriving from decentralization. However, the key variables used—average rate of growth from 1973 to 1998 and average indexes of fiscal decentralization—raise a few doubts on the results even after other variables that affect growth are controlled for. Take the case of Italy. Most decentralization reforms were introduced in the 1990s, but growth declined in that period, while lower decentralization and higher growth characterize the previous years. Ireland has the highest rate of growth, but has always been a highly centralized country. Norway has promoted some recentralization, but its high rate of growth is due to oil. Japan is close to Ireland in the sense that no change towards decentralization is observable. However, economic growth had declined in the second half of the period.

4.4.1 Convergence/divergence in regional rates of growth

When countries decentralize, less developed regions fear losing in terms of growth because of lesser support from the central government. This looks prima facie reasonable, although increasing divergence may be associated with the peculiarities of the decentralization process. Akai and Sakata (2005) (Table 6.3) provide good analytical and empirical analysis for the US. They distinguish between two different concepts/impacts of decentralization. The first refers to decentralization of resources. The presumable impact of decentralization is to increase disparities among regions. Here the impact of decentralization will arise mostly through the expenditure multiplier. The second concept refers to decentralization as a commitment device. Decentralization occurs when subnational governments rely on their own sources of revenue with a hard budget constraint. In this case, regional efficiency in spending and self-reliance will be increased, with likely positive effects on growth. Akai and Sakata test their model with reference to an unspecified number of US counties during 1993–2000. They also use a number of appropriate control variables in order to take into account many of the factors that impact on growth. Their results show that decentralization, as a commitment device, has a significant impact on the reduction of regional disparities in growth. The results by Akai and Sakata are confirmed by Rodriguez-Pose and Bwire (2003) with a detailed analysis of a group of five OECD countries (Germany, Italy, Mexico, Spain and the US) plus India.

The exploration of a link between purely regulatory decentralization and growth is also an important one. When subnational, particularly regional, governments are empowered with growth-related responsibilities, there are clearly new potentialities to foster growth, but regional growth-inducing policies can be construed at the expense of other regions. There are also concerns—for example in Italy—about excessive regional regulation in growth-related sectors, such as the environment, health and labor. These issues have been initially explored by Weingast (1995), who maintains that a federal system is market-preserving if it has three characteristics: (1) subnational governments have primary regulatory responsibility over the economy; (2) a common market is ensured, preventing the lower governments from using their regulatory authority to erect trade barriers against the goods and services from other political units and (3) the lower governments face a hard budget constraint, that is, they have neither the ability to print money nor access to unlimited credit. Jin et al. (2005) and Cao et al. (1997) make extensive empirical analysis of market-preserving federalism theory with reference to China. Unfortunately, similar studies for other, and specifically OECD countries, are still missing. Again this may have been the case during the early years of the economic reforms, but increasing inequalities and other potential constraints are likely to have changed the composition of the "growth engine" in recent years.

5 CONCLUSIONS

Confronted with the often-asserted benefits of decentralization for enhanced service delivery, efficiency and preference matching the evidence is not quite conclusive. Despite the number of available empirical studies, general conclusions are still tentative because of the context-specific nature of decentralization processes and of their outcomes. Of course, it is possible to draw firmer conclusions when, as in the case of Spain, there are quite a large number of studies. The studies for Spain show a convergence of positive, although cautious, conclusions, especially concerning preference matching. Also for Switzerland, some positive results emerge, particularly regarding allocative efficiency. In general, the evidence referring to industrialized countries is more positive than that for developing countries, where decentralization has additional goals to meet and where institutions are generally weaker than those in mature economies.

There is also not enough specific evidence to conclude whether ethnically or culturally driven processes of decentralization produce better or worse results than those driven only by efficiency considerations. Surely, the cases of Spain and Switzerland show that cultural and linguistic divides do not necessarily have a negative impact. But the quality of institutions is a critical precondition for the successes seen in Spain and Switzerland.

In theoretical terms, the claims that decentralization enhances service delivery have to be reconciled with the recognition of the joint nature of the spending and revenue constraints. Also, lower levels of administration are neither likely to have adequate own-source revenues for effective hard budget constraints, nor the governance, budgeting and reporting infrastructure to make decentralization effective.

There is relatively poor evidence to characterize effective links between decentralization and growth. Claims of improvements in developing countries may be due to the general development process and growth, perhaps improved central decision-making with local implementation, while linkages with decentralization are tenuous.

Convergence of levels of service delivery does not seem to be a prevailing pattern, but this should be an expected outcome of decentralization, which rewards capacity and availability of resources. Clearly, the poor jurisdictions should also benefit from the growing exposure to efficiency that derives from increased autonomy. There is, however, still little evidence to prove this.

NOTES

1. Of course, this assumes that there is full information on subnational operations, without which tied transfers could degenerate into spending others' moneys without adequate supervision.
2. Decentralized form of government where each village is responsible for its own affairs.
3. There are several papers on Spain. Spain provides excellent opportunities for testing theories about the impact of decentralization. First, Spain has experienced an important process of fiscal decentralization since the re-establishment of democracy and the Constitution of 1978. Second, the timing of decentralization has not been equal for all Autonomous Communities (ACs). Some ACs have assumed devolved responsibilities earlier than others, thus allowing researchers to examine the impact of decentralization with reference to two distinct samples: one with decentralized and the other with still centralized responsibilities.
4. The dependent variable is usually a comparable but simple indicator of policy outcomes, while decentralization is represented by fiscal indicators based mostly on the relative shares of central and subnational governments in total national public expenditure and/or revenue.
5. Some problems have to be noted with regard to the use of this measure of outcome.

Upper secondary education is mostly a responsibility of cantons while local governments are fully responsible for primary education. Their expenditure and policies are thus impacting minimally on *La Maturité*. To partially account for this fact Barankay and Lockwood refer results at *La Maturité* to the degree of decentralization in the years where the concerned students were enrolled in primary schools, but clearly the main impact on *La Maturité* derives from years spent in secondary education. Finally, there is no federal intervention in exams that could ensure uniformity of criteria.

6. The indicator is represented by the formula that follows:

$$D_{pt} = \frac{MEH_{pt} + PEH_{pt} + SSF_{pt}}{MEH_{pt} + PEH_{pt} + SSF_{pt} + FEH_{pt}}$$

where MEH_{pt} is health expenditure by all municipalities in year t; PEH_{pt} is provincial expenditure for health in the same year, SSF_{pt} security funds provincial expenditure and FEH_{pt} is the federal government expenditure in the same province in the same year t.

7. Consider a numerical example: in province A subnational expenditure for health is 80 and federal 20. In province B the same numbers are 10 and 90. The indicator will have a value of 0.8 in A and of 1.0 in B. It means simply that subnational governments in province A spend more on health than the corresponding governments in province B. This could be compensated by lower expenditure for education, but is not referred per se to any difference in decentralization. On the other hand federal expenditure is for native Canadians, military personnel, inmates of federal penitentiaries and the Royal Mounted Police, which has no relationship with decentralization.

REFERENCES

Agranoff, Robert and Juan Antonio Gallarin (1997), "Toward Federal Democracy in Spain. An Examination of Intergovernmental Relations", *Publius, The Journal of Federalism*, **27** (4), 1–3.

Ahlin, Asa and Eva Mörk (2007), "Effects of decentralization on school resources: Sweden 1989-2002", Working Paper No. 2007:9, Uppsala: Dept of Economics, Uppsala University.

Ahmad, Ehtisham and Giorgio Brosio (2006), *Handbook of Fiscal Federalism*, Cheltenham, UK and Northampton, MA, USA, Edward Elgar.

Ahmad, Ehtisham and Mercedes García-Escribano (2007), "Fiscal Decentralization and Public Sub-national Financial Management in Peru", *IMF Working Paper*.

Ahmad, Ehtisham, Giorgio Brosio and Vito Tanzi (2008), "Local Service Provision in Selected OECD Countries: Do Decentralized Operations Work Better?" in G. Ingram and Y.H. Hong (eds.), *Fiscal Decentralization and Land Policies*, Cambridge, MA: Lincoln Institute of Land Policy.

Ahmad, Ehtisham, Li Keping and Thomas Richardson (2002), "Recentralization in China?", in E. Ahmad and V. Tanzi (eds), *Managing Fiscal Decentralization*, London: Routledge.

Ahmad, Ehtisham, José Antonio González Anaya, Giorgio Brosio, Mercedes García-Escribano, Ben Lockwood and Ernesto Revilla (2008), "Why Focus on Spending Needs Factors? The Political Economy of Fiscal Transfer Reforms in Mexico", IMF Working Paper No. 07/252.

Akai, Nobuo and Masayo Sakata (2005), "Fiscal Decentralization, Commitment and Regional Inequality: Evidence from State-level Cross-sectional Data for the United States", Working Paper Cirje F Series, No. CIRJE-F-315, Tokyo: Faculty of Economics, University of Tokyo.

Ambrosiano, Flavia and Massimo Bordignon (2006), "Normative Versus Positive Theories of Revenue Assignments in Federations", in Ahmad and Brosio, *Handbook of Fiscal Federalism*, Cheltenham, UK and Northampton, MA, USA.

Arze del Granado, Javier, Jorge Martinez Vasquez and Robert McNab (2005), "Fiscal Decentralization and the Functional Composition of Public Expenditure", Atlanta: Andrew Young School of Policy Studies, Georgia State University, Working Paper No. 05-01.

Balaguer-Coll, Teresa, Diego Prior and Emili Tortosa-Ausina (2006), "Decentralization and Efficiency in Spanish Local Government", Castellò de la Plana: Department of Economics, University Jaume I, Working Paper No. 206-02.

Barankay, Iwan and Ben Lockwood (2006), "Decentralization and the Productive Efficiency of Government: Evidence from Swiss Cantons", *Journal of Public Economics*, **91** (5–6) 1197–1218.

Behnisch, Alexej, Thiess Buttner and Dan Stegarescu (2003), "Public Sector Centralization and Productivity Growth: Reviewing the German Experience", ZEW Discussion Paper No. 02-03.

Breuss, Fritz and Mark Eller (2004), "Fiscal decentralization and Economic Growth. Is there really a link?", *Journal for Institutional Comparisons*, **2** (1), 3–21.

Cantarero Prieto, David and Marta Pascual Sanchez (2006), "Decentralization and Health Care Outcomes: An Empirical Analysis Within the European Union", Santander: University of Cantabria Working Paper.

Cao,Yuanzheng, Yingyi Qian and Barry Weingast (1997), "From Federalism, Chinese Style to Privatization, Chinese Style", mimeo.

Crivelli, Luca, Massimo Filippini and Ilaria Mosca (2007), "Federalism and Regional Health Care Expenditures: An Empirical Analysis for the Swiss Cantons", Lugano: Università della Svizzera Italiana, MECOO, Quaderno No. 04-07.

Documentation Française (La) (2007), *La Réforme de la Decentralisation: La Révision Constitutionnelle*, http://www.la documentationfrancaise.fr/dossiers/reforme-decentralisation/revision-constitutionnelle.shtml, accessed 22 March 2009.

Ebel, Robert and Serdar Yilmaz, (2002), "On the Measurement and Impact of Fiscal Decentralization", Policy Research Working Paper No. 2809, The World Bank.

Faguet, Jean-Paul (2004), "Does Decentralization Increase Government Responsiveness to Local Needs?", *Journal of Public Economics*, **88** (3–4), 667–93.

Faguet, Jean-Paul and Fabio Sanchez (2006), "Decentralization's Effect on Educational Outcomes in Bolivia and Colombia", Discussion Paper No. 47, Suntory and Toyota International Centres for Economics and Related Disciplines, London School of Economics and Political Science.

Feld, Lars, Gebhardt Kirchgässner and Christoph Schaltegger (2004), "Fiscal Federalism and Economic Performance: Evidence from Swiss Cantons", mimeo.

Garcia-Milà, Teresa and Therese J. McGuire (2002), "Fiscal Decentralization in Spain: Asymmetric Transition to Democracy", mimeo.

Inchauste, Gabriela (2009), "Decentralization in Bolivia: Has it made a Difference?", this volume, Chapter 7.
Jakubowski, Maciej and Irena Topińska (2006), "Impact of Decentralization on Public Service Delivery and Equity. Education and Health Sectors in Poland, 1998–2003", mimeo.
Jimenez, Dolores and Peter Smith (2005), "Decentralisation of Health Care and its Impact on Health Outcomes", Discussion Papers in Economics No. 2005/10, York: University of York.
Jin, Hehur, Yingyi Qian and Barry R. Weingast (2005), "Regional Decentralization and Fiscal Incentives: Federalism, Chinese Style", *Journal of Public Economics*, **89** (9–10), 1719–42.
Jin, Jing and Heng-fu Zou (2002), "How Does Fiscal Decentralization Affect Aggregate, National, and Subnational Government Size?", *Journal of Urban Economics*, **52** (2), 270–93.
Khemani, Stuti (2006), "Local Government Accountability for Health Service Delivery in Nigeria", *Journal of African Economies*, **15** (2), 285–312.
Levy, Brian and Sahr Kpundeh (2004), "Building State Capacity in Africa: New Approaches, Emerging Lessons", Washington, DC: World Bank.
Montero-Granados, Roberto and José Martin Juan de Dios Jiménez (2007), "Decentralisation and Convergence in Health Among the Provinces of Spain (1980–2001)", *Social Science and Medicine*, **64**, 1253–64.
Moreno, Luis (2002), "Decentralization in Spain, Regional Studies", **36** (4), 300–408.
OECD (2002), *Fiscal Decentralization in EU Applicant States and Selected EU Member States*, Centre for Tax Policy and Administration.
Oates, Wallace (1993), "Fiscal Decentralization and Economic Development", *National Tax Journal,* **46** (2), 237–43.
Qian, Yingy and Barry Weingast (1997), "Federalism as a Commitment to Preserving Market Incentives", *Journal of Economic Perspectives*, **1** (1), 83–92.
Rico, Ana and Sandra Léon (2005), "Health Care Devolution in Europe. Trends and Prospects", Working Paper No. 2005-1, Oslo: Health Care Organization.
Robalino, David, Oscar Picazo and Albertus Voetberg (2001), *Does Fiscal Decentralization Improve Health Outcomes? Evidence from a Cross-country Analysis*, World Bank Country Economic Department Series No. 2565, The World Bank.
Rodriguez-Pose, Andrés and Adala Bwire (2003), "The Economic (In)Efficiency of Devolution", London: Department of Geography and Environment, LSE.
Salinas Peña, Paula (2007), "Evaluation of the effects of decentralization on educational outcomes in Spain", *XIV Encuentro de Economía Pública*, Santander: Universidad de Santander.
Shah, Anwar (1999), "Indonesia and Pakistan: Fiscal Decentralization—an Elusive Goal?" in R. Bird and F. Vaillancourt (eds), *Fiscal Decentralization in Developing Countries*, Cambridge: Cambridge University Press, Chapter 4.
Singh, Nirvikar (2003), *Some Economic Consequences of India's Institutions of Governance: Conceptual Framework*, Santa Cruz: Department of Economics, University of Santa Cruz.
Solé-Ollé, Alberto and Alejandro Esteller-Moré (2005), "Decentralization Provision of Public Inputs, Government Responsiveness to Local Needs, and Regional Growth. Evidence from Spain", Working Paper, Barcelona: Institut d'Economia de Barcelona.

Strumpf, Koleman and Felix Oberholzer-Gee (2002), "Endogeneous Policy Decentralization: Testing the Central Tenet of Economic Federalism", *Journal of Political Economy*, **110** (1), 1–36.
Thiessen, Ulrich (2000), "Fiscal federalism in Western European and Selected Other Countries: Centralization or Decentralization? What is Better for Economic Growth?", Berlin: Deutsches Institut für Wirtschanftsforschung (DIW), Discussion Paper No. 224.
Thiessen, Ulrich (2003), "Fiscal Decentralization and Economic Growth in High-income OECD Countries", Fiscal Studies, **24** (3), 237–74.
Weingast, Barry (1995), "The Economic Role of Political Institutions: Market Preserving Federalism and Economic Development", *Journal of Law, Economics and Organization*, **11** (1), 1–31.
World Bank (2004), *Decentralization & Sub-national Regional Economics Thematic Group. Measuring Fiscal Decentralization*, data note.
Yagi, Kinnosuke (2004), "Decentralization in Japan", Keio University Policy and Governance Working Paper Series No. 30.

APPENDIX

Table 6A.1 Expenditure assignments in African countries

Countries	Level of Government	Policy Responsibilities	Functional Responsibilities Education	Functional Responsibilities Health
Ethiopia	Central	Typical functions of federal states	Framework legislation Financing	Framework legislation Financing
	State/ Regional	Regulation of education, health, roads and financing of local government	Regulation, financing and monitoring	Regulation, financing and monitoring
	Local	Education, health, roads, growth promotion and basic urban services (when transition is completed)	Hiring of teachers Administration O&M Infrastructure	Hiring of medical personnel Administration O&M Infrastructure
Uganda	Central	Typical of decentralized systems	Policy Financing (including wages)	Policy Financing (including wages)
	Regional (districts)	Education, health, roads and basic urban services	Hiring of teachers Administration O&M Infrastructure	Hiring of medical personnel Administration O&M Infrastructure
	Local (counties, parishes, villages)	Mostly urban services	Administration O&M Infrastructure	Administration O&M Infrastructure
Rwanda	Central	Most	All	All
	Local	Basic urban services and some economic services (water, agriculture) Devolution of education & health is planned		

Table 6A.1 (continued)

Countries	Level of Government	Policy Responsibilities	Functional Responsibilities Education	Functional Responsibilities Health
Nigeria	Central	Typical functions of federal states	Policy, financing of teachers	Policy, financing of health care
	State/ regional	Concurrent legislative powers with the federal government in education, health, public works	Hiring of teachers Administration O&M	Hiring of medical personnel Administration O&M
	Local	Typical urban infrastructure and services	Some maintenance Responsibility for primary education	Some maintenance Responsibility for basic health care
Ghana	Central	Typical functions of unitary states	Policy, financing, teachers	Policy, financing, medical personnel
	Provincial	Feeder roads, abattoirs	Building and O&M primary, middle and secondary schools	Public health and public hygiene
	Local	Typical urban services		
Tanzania	Central	Typical functions of unitary states	Financing and tight control through standards on inputs and outputs	Financing and tight control through standards on inputs and outputs
	Local	Primary education, health services, water supply, local roads and agricultural extension	Most functions, very tightly controlled	Most functions, but…as for education
Senegal	Central	Most functions	Most	Most
	Local	Typical urban services	Building and O&M for primary education	Building and O&M for health centers

Table 6A.1 (continued)

Countries	Level of Government	Policy Responsibilities	Functional Responsibilities Education	Functional Responsibilities Health
DR Congo	Central	Typical functions of federal states	Policy, financing and teachers	Policy financing and medical personnel
	Regional	Education, health, social protection, sports, culture, roads	Building and O&M, supply of material	Building and O&M, medical supplies and equipment
	Local	Typical local services		Local clinics
South Africa	Central	Typical functions of federal states		
	Regional	Concurrent legislative powers with the federal government concerning roads and transport, economic affairs, social services, health and education, public works	Recruitment of teachers, administration O&M Investment, supply of equipment	Recruitment of doctors, administration, O&M Investment, supply of medical equipment
	Local	Provision of urban infrastructure and basic services, such as water, sanitation, transport and roads	None for localities, but possibly some role for local communities and families	None for localities, but possibly some role for local communities and families

Note: O & M = operations and maintenance.

7. Decentralization in Bolivia: has it made a difference?

Gabriela Inchauste*

1 INTRODUCTION

Decentralization has been promoted as an instrument for improving service delivery in the sectors that are crucial for poverty alleviation, and Bolivia has been quoted as one of the main examples in support of the proposition (Faguet, 2004). A main argument for this is that local authorities are better able to understand and address local needs. With this in mind, the international community has given a boost to the decentralization process around the world by transferring savings obtained from recent debt relief initiatives directly to local governments in poor countries, and Bolivia again was one of the first cases to benefit from this support. However, recent experience across developing countries has often found that lack of local capacity, misalignment of responsibilities and lack of accountability have implied that the hopes raised by the decentralization paradigm have fallen short of its promises.[1] This chapter reviews the detailed data to present a fresh perspective on what has actually happened in Bolivia.

Bolivia was one of the first countries to participate and receive debt relief under both the original Heavily Indebted Poor Countries (HIPC) and the enhanced-HIPC initiatives, and more recently under the Multilateral Debt Relief Initiative (MDRI). The HIPC initiative was designed to reduce to sustainable levels the debt burden of highly indebted poor countries. Participating countries received substantial debt relief in exchange for continued efforts in macroeconomic stabilization, structural reforms and poverty reduction. The enhanced-HIPC initiative, in particular, put a greater focus in directing the *savings* from the debt relief towards pro-poor programs. The more recent MDRI went further by providing full debt relief so as to free up additional resources to help these countries reach the Millennium Development Goals (MDGs).[2] This most recent debt relief initiative has helped reduce Bolivia's total public debt from about 70 percent of GDP in 2005 to about 35 percent of GDP in 2007.

The debt relief initiative in Bolivia, as in other countries, was also ambitious as it was linked to the ongoing devolution of responsibilities to local governments. In particular, resources saved from the enhanced-HIPC initiative were delivered directly to local governments and were earmarked toward poverty-reducing spending. More recently, revenue sharing between different levels of government has become the focus of much of the political debate surrounding the creation of a new constitution, which at its core must address the revenue and expenditures assignments across levels of government. The debate has become crucial in light of large resources that have started to flow from the hydrocarbons sector, both in the form of royalties, as well as oil excise taxes.

This chapter aims to analyze the social impact of transfers and spending by local governments in the Bolivian context, with particular focus on the impact of transfers to local governments from the savings that were generated by the HIPC initiative. To answer this question, the chapter first checks whether resources channeled to municipalities have been distributed as intended under the enhanced-HIPC initiative, and whether there is any evidence of absorptive capacity constraints, particularly by poor municipalities. Then the chapter investigates whether the resources that actually have been spent have had any impact on short-term social indicators. For this purpose I construct a panel of municipalities by combining short-term social indicators from various rounds of household survey data with detailed municipal transfer and spending data. Finally, the chapter asks whether the resources that have been spent were well targeted.

Although local government resources from debt relief have fallen recently, they have now been replaced by resources from the hydrocarbons sector. With this in mind, the chapter aims to examine the impact of the relatively large resource flows made available through debt relief and to point to areas for improvement. The results suggest that the social impact has been minimal between 2001–05. Although there is some evidence that poorer municipalities had capacity constraints, the bulk of the evidence points to the misalignment of revenue and expenditure responsibilities between the central and local governments as the main reason for the lack of progress.

2 THE DECENTRALIZATION PROCESS

The decentralization process started in the late 1980s with an overarching goal of deepening the democratic structures after decades of dictatorship and neglect of Bolivia's poorest regions. An initial stage included the introduction of municipal elections and the development of a legal framework for fiscal decentralization in the mid-1990s. A fundamental change was the introduction of a revenue-sharing agreement, which provided municipalities with a direct transfer of 20 percent of national revenues. The distribution of these "coparticipation" transfers is based solely on municipal population. This broke with past tradition where regional capitals received the vast majority of transfers from the center.[3] In addition, municipalities were given the ability to apply local taxes, mainly on property.

The decentralization system, while providing poorer local governments with greater resources, still suffers from significant vertical imbalances and only partially addressed the horizontal inequalities. Before the reform initiated in 1994–95, only the large regional capitals received almost all devolved revenues, while after 1995 poorer/smaller municipalities saw their revenues increase substantially, as much as 300 percent in some cases. More recently, the 2005 Hydrocarbons Law significantly increased the amount of revenues shared with subnational governments, without a corresponding transfer of expenditure responsibilities. Royalties from hydrocarbons are allocated according to where they are produced, exacerbating existing horizontal imbalances (Simone, 2006). As shown in Table 7.1, local governments remain highly dependent on transfers from the center, with own-revenues representing less than 40 percent of local expenditures. Coparticipation transfers continue to be based on municipalities' population size, with no effective mechanism to address income inequalities and revenue capacity between municipalities. In terms of expenditure responsibilities, the Law of Popular Participation (1994) requires that a large share of the coparticipation transfers be allocated for public investment—with a broad definition of capital expenditures. In 1996, the share for capital expenditure was reduced from 90 to 85 percent, however over time additional earmarking was established from the coparticipation funds, mostly benefiting the health and education sectors.

The status of regional governments (*prefecturas*) was not as well defined under the original framework. While *prefecturas* also received new spending and revenue responsibilities (a share of revenues from natural resources and excise taxes), they were largely under central government control—governors were appointed by the president—with some input from local governments. However, this changed at end-2005, when governors were elected by popular vote. Following the 2005 Hydrocarbons Law, these regional governments have benefited from both the direct tax on hydrocarbons and an increased share in royalties. Beginning in mid-2006, and again in 2008 there were referendums on regional autonomy, which overwhelmingly won support, especially in the rich eastern states. By 2008, the hydrocarbons resources that had been going to the states

Table 7.1 Bolivia: fiscal accounts (in percent of GDP)

	Average 1990–94	Average 1995–2000	2001	2002	2003	2004 preliminary	2005 preliminary
Central government							
Revenues and grants	19.2	21.7	21.8	20.9	20.8	22.6	26.6
Of which grants	1.7	1.5	1.8	2.0	2.5	2.3	2.0
Expenditures	22.4	24.4	29.0	30.0	29.1	28.8	30.9
Overall balance	−3.1	−2.7	−7.3	−9.0	−8.3	−6.3	−4.3
Prefecturas – Corporaciones							
Revenues and grants	2.2	2.2	3.6	2.5	2.5	2.9	4.8
Of which transfers from central government	1.1	0.9	2.0	1.2	1.0	1.0	2.3
Expenditures	2.6	2.4	3.7	2.6	2.2	2.4	3.4
Overall balance	−0.4	−0.1	−0.1	−0.1	0.2	0.5	1.4
Municipalities							
Revenues and grants	1.7	3.9	4.4	5.7	5.3	5.7	5.8
Of which transfers from central government	1.3	2.4	2.7	4.0	3.3	3.7	3.8
Expenditures	1.7	4.2	4.3	5.3	5.1	5.5	5.0
Overall balance	0.0	−0.2	0.1	0.5	0.2	0.2	0.8
Memorandum:							
Own-revenues as share of spending for municipalities	25.6	36.8	40.8	33.7	37.7	36.6	40.0
Nominal GDP (millions of bolivianos)			53790.0	56682.0	61904.0	69626.0	76154.0

Source: Bolivian Ministry of Finance, Unidad de Programación Fiscal, "Dossier Estadistico, 1990–2005".

began to be used at the central government level, in support of transfers to the elderly. The resulting controversy over the distribution of resources intensified, resulting in a referendum on the mandate of the president as well as those of the state governors in August 2008. The results show a country largely divided, and have exacerbated regional tensions. The distribution of resources derived from the wealthy hydrocarbons sector remains the most contentious points underlying the drafting of a new constitution, and the stability of the nation as a whole.

3 THE HIPC INITIATIVE AND DISTRIBUTION OF RESOURCES

An important aim of enhanced-HIPC initiative was to reduce poverty and improve social indicators by freeing up funds and channeling these through local governments. In effect, the enhanced-HIPC initiative led to a new push in the decentralization process, as more funds were directed to municipalities starting in 2001. Under the 2000 National Dialogue Law, all savings from the enhanced-HIPC initiative were redirected to municipalities and distributed based on poverty indicators. These resources represented a windfall for many of the poorest municipalities. The equity criterion introduced with HIPC was meant to compensate for the bias caused by the per capita distribution of resources in effect since 1994.

In this context, it was agreed that HIPC resources would be distributed directly to municipalities based on poverty levels. In particular, the formula stated that 70 percent of HIPC resources would be allocated based on a recalculated population, which gives greater weight to poorer municipalities as described in equation (7.1) below:

$$RPop = A^*(-1) + B^*(0) + C^*(1) + D^*(2) + E^*(3) \qquad (7.1)$$

RPop is the municipal recalculated population, *A* is the number of inhabitants in the municipality with satisfied basic needs; *B* is the number of inhabitants in the municipality who are at the poverty threshold; *C* is the number of inhabitants in the municipality who are moderately poor, *D* is the number of inhabitants in the municipality who are indigent poor; and *E* is the number of inhabitants in the municipality who are marginally poor.[4] Municipalities receive funds based on their share of the total national recalculated population. The remaining 30 percent of funds are distributed equally among the nine departments. Within each department, this 30 percent of resources is then distributed to municipalities again based on equation (7.1).

HIPC resources are first allocated to the Solidarity Fund for School Education and Public Health and the National Solidarity Fund (SUMI). Then the remaining resources are distributed to municipalities using equation (7.1) with the requirement that municipalities use the resources as follows: 20 percent for investment in education, 10 percent for investment in public health services and the remaining 70 percent to socially productive investment infrastructure. Since public expenditure management systems are weak, the funds are transferred directly to three distinct commercial bank accounts for each municipality, one for each of the intended purposes as a sole way of tracking expenditures.

4 TRANSFERS AND ACTUAL SPENDING IN MUNICIPALITIES

4.1 How Large Have Flows to Local Governments Been? The Aggregate Perspective

The aggregate fiscal position in Bolivia has improved sharply over the last few years, reflecting growth in the hydrocarbons sector. At the same time, Bolivia's public debt has declined due to the debt relief under the MDRI (IMF, 2007). The non-financial public sector shifted from a deficit of about 9 percent of GDP in 2002 to a surplus of about 4.5 percent of GDP in 2006, on account of higher hydrocarbons-based and other revenues as well as containment of expenditure growth (Table 7.2).

In this context, total transfers to municipalities grew from 2.3 percent of GDP in 2000 to 3.1 percent of GDP in 2002 on account of HIPC transfers, which amounted to 1 percent of GDP by 2002 (Table 7.3). HIPC transfers have since steadily declined to 0.3 percent of GDP in 2006, overtaken by transfers from the center flowing from the hydrocarbons sector. HIPC resources transferred to the health, education and infrastructure sectors are in line with the law described above. There was a dramatic increase in actual total municipal spending beginning in 2003, as many municipalities were unable to immediately spend the large increase in transfers that began in 2002. Total spending from HIPC peaked at 0.8 percent of GDP in 2003, mostly on infrastructure spending. Total spending by municipalities has declined somewhat in 2006, but there could be important increases in the near future given the additional transfers that have started to flow from hydrocarbons royalties.

One of the conditions imposed by the international community prior to delivering debt relief was that HIPC resources should be additional to existing budgeted amounts for poverty-related expenditures. Table 7.3 shows that between 2000 and 2001, spending on health, education and infrastructure indeed increased in line with HIPC resources. The share of HIPC spending relative to total spending grew substantially in 2002, with HIPC spending on education accounting for over 21 percent of total spending in education by 2003 (Table 7.4). HIPC spending on infrastructure made up over 20 percent of total capital spending in 2003, a dramatic rise from the 3 percent share that it had in 2001. The recent decline in available HIPC resources partly explains the decline in overall spending on health, education, and infrastructure at the municipal level, which fell from about 5 percent of GDP in 2004–05 to about 4 percent in 2006.

Table 7.2 Bolivia: operations of the combined public sector (in percent of GDP)

	2002	2003	2004	2005	Preliminary 2006	Projected 2007
Total revenue and grants	24.5	24.1	26.8	31.3	35.2	32.3
Current revenue	22.2	21.2	24.3	29.1	33.3	30.7
General government	21.6	21.1	23.9	28.7	31.7	25.1
Tax revenue[a,b]	17.8	17.8	20.6	25.4	28.5	22.3
Of which excise taxes of fuel	2.3	1.7	1.6	2.5	2.2	2.1
Other	13.2	13.2	15.6	16.4	16.6	16.5
Non-tax revenue	3.8	3.4	3.3	3.2	3.2	2.9
Grants	–	2.9	2.5	3.5	1.9	1.6
Public enterprise operating balance	0.1	−0.1	0.1	0.1	0.8	4.6
Of which royalties and IDH[c] to general government	0	0	0	0	0	5.7
Central bank operating balance	0.5	0.2	0.3	0.3	0.7	0.9
Total expenditure	33.3	32	32.3	33.6	30.6	31.3
Current expenditure	24.9	23.9	23.2	23.4	20.1	19.9
Wages and salaries[d]	9.3	9.4	9.0	8.7	8.1	9.0
Goods and services	2.9	2.6	2.0	2.0	1.8	2.1
Interest	2.6	2.8	2.9	3.0	2.6	2.4
Transfers (excludes pensions)	1.7	1.5	1.9	2.3	1.6	1.7
Pensions	4.5	4.4	4.3	4.1	3.7	3.5
Other	3.8	3.2	3.1	3.3	2.4	1.2
Capital expenditure	8.4	8.1	9.1	10.2	10.5	11.4
Overall balance	−8.8	−7.9	−5.5	−2.3	4.6	1.0
Financing	8.8	7.9	5.5	2.3	−4.6	−1.0
External	6.0	5.3	3.9	2.3	0.4	1.8
Domestic	2.8	2.6	1.6	0.0	−5.0	−2.8
Memorandum item:						
Hydrocarbons-related revenues		2.8	3.4	6.6	11.1	11.2
Royalties and IDH		2.8	3.4	6.6	9.7	9.3
YPFB[e] participation		0	0	0	1.4	1.9
Non-hydrocarbons balance	−11.1	−10.7	−8.9	−8.9	−6.5	−4.5

Notes:

a. Since May 2007 royalties and IDH are no longer included in the definition of tax revenue of the general government as these funds are now collected and transferred by YPFB.

b. In 2007 tax revenues include only the IDH and royalties that were paid directly by the oil companies to the general government preceding the takeover of this responsibility by YPFB in May 2007.

c. Direct Tax on Hydrocarbons—Impuesto Diracto alos Hidrocarburos.

Table 7.2 (continued)

d. In 2007 the spending on universities initially included in other spending was reclassified. More importantly, the wage bill now includes 1056 million bolivianos of salaries of university personnel while other minor amounts were included in goods and services.
e. State-owned hydrocarbons company.

Sources: Bolivian authorities; IMF (2007).

Table 7.3 Bolivia: municipal transfers and spending, 2000–06 (in percent of GDP)

	2000	2001	2002	2003	2004	2005	2006
Total transfers	2.3	2.5	3.1	2.7	3.0	2.9	4.4
Total coparticipation transfers	2.3	2.1	2.1	2.1	2.4	2.4	2.6
Coparticipation transfers	2.1	1.9	2.0	1.9	2.2	2.2	2.3
SUMI	0.1	0.1	0.1	0.2	0.2	0.2	0.3
Bank commission	0.0	0.0	0.0	0.0	0.0	0.0	0.0
Total HIPC transfers	–	0.4	1.0	0.6	0.6	0.4	0.3
HIPC transfers for health	–	0.0	0.1	0.1	0.1	0.0	0.0
HIPC transfers for education	–	0.1	0.2	0.1	0.1	0.1	0.1
HIPC transfers for infrastructure	–	0.3	0.7	0.4	0.4	0.3	0.2
HIPC bank commissions	–	0.0	0.0	0.0	0.0	0.0	0.0
Direct taxes on hydrocarbons							1.5
Direct taxes							0.9
Compensation							0.6
Bank commission							0.0
Total spending[a]	3.8	4.5	4.4	4.8	5.2	4.8	4.0
Health	0.3	0.3	0.3	0.5	0.6	0.6	0.4
Education	0.5	0.6	0.8	0.8	0.7	0.7	0.5
Capital spending	2.2	2.8	2.8	2.7	2.9	2.7	2.0
Total spending from HIPC[b]	–	0.1	0.7	0.8	0.6	0.4	–
Health spending from HIPC	–	0.0	0.0	0.1	0.1	0.0	–
Education spending from HIPC	–	0.0	0.1	0.2	0.1	0.1	–
Infrastructure spending from HIPC	–	0.1	0.5	0.6	0.4	0.3	–

Sources: Ministry of Finance. See http://vmpc.hacienda.gov.bo/coparticipation.asp. a. Excludes all financing outflows, including amortization payments. b. Ministerio de Hacienda, "Dossier Estadistico", various issues. Accessed 22 March 2009.

Table 7.4 Bolivia: HIPC spending as a share of total, 2001–05 (in percent)

	2001	2002	2003	2004	2005
Total HIPC as share of total spending	2.4	16.8	16.6	10.7	8.4
HIPC health as a share of total health spending	3.1	16.3	12.5	8.6	6.8
HIPC education as a share of total education spending	3.4	19.7	21.1	17.2	12.5
HIPC infrastructure as a share of total capital spending	2.9	19.2	20.9	13.0	12.2

Sources: Bolivian Ministry of Finance. See http://vmpc.hacienda.gov.bo/coparticipation.asp. Accessed 22 March 2009.

4.2 How Much Has Actually Been Spent? A Disaggregated View

One could argue that one reason for the lack of progress in obtaining improved social outcomes is that the resources that have been transferred have not been utilized due to absorptive capacity constraints or other bottlenecks. At the municipal level, the evidence suggests that after initial bottlenecks in 2001 and 2002, utilization of HIPC resources have increased substantially. Table 7.5 compares HIPC transfers to actual spending from these HIPC resources for all municipalities. Utilization of HIPC resources dramatically improved over time, with average utilization rates increasing from 27 percent of HIPC transfers in 2001, to 134 percent in 2003, remaining at around 95 percent in 2004 and 2005. Infrastructure and education are the areas where there seems to be highest absorptive capacity, although by 2003 municipalities were able to absorb more than 100 percent of health transfers for that year.[5]

Between 2003 and 2005, on average, municipalities have managed to spend in excess of 90 percent of transferred resources. The table also shows that the share of HIPC resources in total transfers increased dramatically in the first years of the program, making up 33 percent of total transfers in 2002. However, these transfers have quickly declined in their importance relative to other sources of financing, making up only 15 percent of total transfers in 2005 and only 7.5 percent of total transfers by 2006.

One way to check whether poorer municipalities have greater capacity constraints is a simple correlation between the share of the poor and the utilization of HIPC resources. This correlation is negative for all years for which poverty data is available, –0.04 in 2001, –0.12 in 2002, and –0.06 in 2005, indicating that poorer municipalities were more likely to

Table 7.5 Bolivia: utilization of HIPC resources

	2001		2002		2003		2004		2005	
	Number of Municipa-lities	Average (in percent)	Number of Municipa-lities	Average (in percent)	Number of Municipa-lities	Average (in percent)	Number of Municipa-lities	Average (in percent)	Number of Municipa-lities	Average (in percent)
Health spending as a share of HIPC transfers for health	308	18.7	299	43.0	314	106.2	314	94.8	327	81.8
Education spending as a share of HIPC transfers for education	311	24.0	307	66.9	314	141.2	314	108.9	327	96.8
Infrastructure spending as a share of HIPC transfers for infrastructure	310	28.9	313	71.6	314	138.5	314	94.8	327	98.2
Total HIPC spending as a share of total HIPC transfers	311	26.5	313	66.7	314	133.7	314	96.3	327	94.6
Share of HIPC in total transfers	314	16.7	314	33.0	314	21.5	314	19.3	327	14.7

Source: Author's estimates based on data from the Bolivian Ministry of Finance.

underutilize HIPC resources transferred to them. This could point to greater capacity constraints in the poorest municipalities. However, one would get a similar result even if all municipalities had the same capacity constraints, because the formula over-assigns resources to poorer municipalities. Either way, the fact is that poorer municipalities seem to have had greater trouble in utilizing the resources transferred to them. One could argue that with additional time and training perhaps these funds will have greater impacts on social outcomes.

To assess the relative size of HIPC transfers and spending, Table 7.6 presents the average municipal spending and transfers on health, education and infrastructure as the share of total municipal spending and transfers. In line with the distribution formula discussed above, the largest share of all transfers is for infrastructure, peaking at 65 percent of average municipal spending in 2002. In contrast, the relative importance of spending on health doubled between 2001 and 2005 to about 10.5 percent of total municipal spending. The share of education spending increased from 12 percent in 2000 to 16.5 percent in 2002 and has slightly fallen to about 13.5 percent of municipal spending in 2005. Therefore, in the three areas that were singled out as critical for poverty reduction, one can argue that there have been substantial increases in municipal spending. Note that actual spending is higher than transfers, pointing to the fact that municipalities have their own resources, and have also incurred large debts over the past few years (particularly some of the largest municipalities).

5 THE IMPACT OF DECENTRALIZATION AND HIPC ON SOCIAL OUTCOMES

5.1 Are Observed Transfers Influenced by Poverty Levels?

So far, it is clear that there have been important increases in spending in the areas designated as important by the Bolivian Poverty Reduction Strategy Paper (PRSP). The next question is whether the distribution of HIPC resources actually followed the ideal of giving poorer municipalities a higher share of HIPC transfers. Figure 7.1 illustrates the correlation between poverty levels and HIPC transfers at the departmental level. Unfortunately, the correlation is relatively low. One of the main reasons for this result is the design of the transfer system in the National Dialogue Law. As described earlier, part of the HIPC transfers (30 percent) are distributed equally among departments, independently of their population or poverty levels. This has meant that the least populated regions were the beneficiaries, particularly the smaller ones, for example, Pando

Table 7.6 Bolivia: HIPC transfers and spending

	2000		2001		2002		2003		2004		2005		2006	
	No. of Munic.	Municipal Average	No. of Munic.	Municipal Average	No. of Munic.	Municipal Average	No. of Munic.	Municipal Average	No. of Munic.	Municipal Average	No. of Munic.	Municipal Average	No. of Munic.	Municipal Average
	(percent of municipal total spending)													
Total spending	314	100.0	314	100.0	314	100.0	314	100.0	327	100.0	327	100.0	–	–
Total health spending	314	7.3	314	5.4	314	6.3	314	10.4	327	12.1	327	10.6	–	–
Total education spending	314	11.9	314	12.6	314	16.7	314	16.3	327	14.0	327	13.6	–	–
Total Capital spending	314	58.3	314	63.0	314	65.0	314	56.8	327	56.1	327	49.3	–	–
Total HIPC spending	–	–	311	2.4	313	16.9	314	17.3	314	11.2	327	8.4	–	–
HIPC health spending	–	–	308	0.2	299	1.1	314	1.4	314	1.1	327	0.7	–	–
HIPC education spending	–	–	311	0.4	307	3.4	314	3.6	314	2.5	327	1.7	–	–
HIPC infrastructure spending	–	–	310	1.8	313	12.6	314	12.4	314	7.6	327	6.0	–	–

						(percent of municipal total transfers)								
Total HIPC transfers	–	–	314	16.7	314	33.0	314	21.5	314	19.3	327	14.7	327	11.5
Health transfers	–	–	314	1.7	314	3.3	314	2.1	314	1.9	327	1.4	327	1.1
Education transfers	–	–	314	3.3	314	6.5	314	4.2	314	3.8	327	2.9	327	2.3
Infrastructure transfers	–	–	314	11.6	314	22.9	314	14.8	314	13.3	327	10.1	327	8.0
Total coparticipation transfers	314	100.0	314	83.3	314	67.0	314	78.5	314	80.7	327	85.3	327	88.5
						(percent of GDP)								
National totals														
Total municipal transfers		2.3		2.5		3.1		2.7		3.0		2.9		4.4
Total municipal spending		4.2		4.5		4.1		4.7		5.2		4.7		

Source: Author's estimates based on data from the Bolivian Ministry of Finance and INE (Bolivian National Statistics Institute).

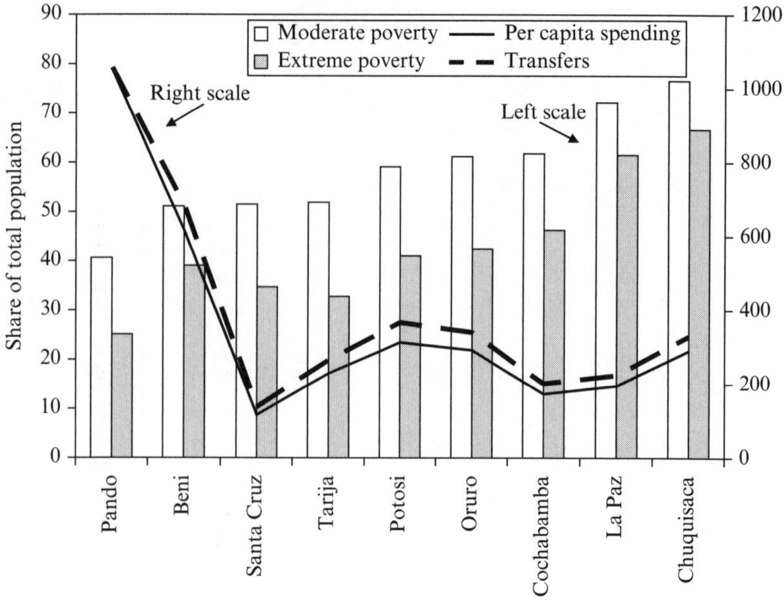

Note: Total per capita HIPC spending from August 2001–September 2006. Population rates from 2001 census.

Source: Ministry of Finance, Unidad de Programación Fiscal (UPF)

Figure 7.1 Bolivia: poverty and municipal spending from HIPC resources

and Beni, in detriment of larger and poorer regions. Two extreme cases are Potosi and Pando. Potosi benefited the least by the pro-poor transfer design, as it has the highest levels of poverty, based on 2001 census, but receives less transfers per capita than most departments, including Tarija—one of the richest. Pando, on the other hand, has been the largest beneficiary, receiving four times more than the poorest regions in per capita terms, largely due to its small population size—less than 1 percent of total population.

The lack of strong links between poverty levels and HIPC transfers is further substantiated with more comprehensive econometric analysis over the years. Table 7.7 shows simple regressions of total transfers to municipalities for 2000–05, controlling for population, a department dummy and the number of poor. Total population in each municipality is positive and significant, and accounts for most of the variation in total transfers to municipalities. The coefficient on the number of poor people, on the other hand, is insignificant beginning in 2002, including for regressions focusing

Table 7.7 Bolivia: transfers to municipalities, population, and poverty[a]

	2000	2001			2002			2005		
	Log of Total Transfers	Log of Total Transfers	Log of HIPC Transfers	Log of Tax Transfers	Log of Total Transfers	Log of HIPC Transfers	Log of Tax Transfers	Log of Total Transfers	Log of HIPC Transfers	Log of Tax Transfers
Log of municipal population	0.931	0.901	0.748	0.933	0.917	0.761	0.988	0.954	0.730	0.996
	(0.019)***	(0.018)***	(0.025)***	(0.018)***	(0.012)***	(0.032)***	(0.004)***	(0.010)***	(0.033)***	(0.008)***
Log of poor population in municipality	0.044	0.033	0.054	0.025	0.016	0.049	−0.001	−0.001	0.013	−0.007
	(0.022)**	(0.017)**	(0.024)**	(0.017)	(0.013)	(0.033)	(0.004)	(0.014)	(0.043)	(0.011)
Regional dummies[b]										
Chuquisaca	−0.126	−0.203	−0.318	−0.168	−0.138	−0.198	−0.087	−0.133	−0.196	−0.109
	(0.066)*	(0.051)***	(0.071)***	(0.051)***	(0.037)***	(0.097)**	(0.013)***	(0.036)***	(0.114)*	(0.028)***
La Paz	−0.199	−0.228	−0.324	−0.200	−0.164	−0.360	−0.056	−0.123	−0.333	−0.075
	(0.068)***	(0.055)***	(0.077)***	(0.055)***	(0.038)***	(0.101)**	(0.013)***	(0.038)***	(0.120)***	(0.030)**
Cochabamba	−0.053	−0.056	−0.066	−0.060	0.065	0.045	0.049	−0.024	−0.084	−0.020
	(0.074)	(0.064)	(0.088)	(0.063)	(0.045)	(0.199)	(0.015)***	(0.040)	(0.128)	(0.032)
Oruro	0.090	0.062	−0.021	0.085	0.085	0.065	0.105	0.018	0.011	0.027
	(0.070)	(0.060)	(0.083)	(0.059)	(0.041)**	(0.108)	(0.014)***	(0.039)	(0.124)	(0.030)
Potosi	−0.074	−0.028	0.063	−0.057	0.063	0.062	0.027	−0.152	−0.129	−0.172
	(0.087)	(0.077)	(0.106)	(0.076)	(0.053)	(0.141)	(0.018)	(0.046)***	(0.145)	(0.036)***
Tarija	−0.120	−0.236	−0.455	−0.180	−0.202	−0.469	−0.044	−0.183	−0.592	−0.096
	(0.068)*	(0.055)***	(0.076)***	(0.054)***	(0.039)***	(0.102)***	(0.013)***	(0.037)***	(0.118)***	(0.029)***

Table 7.7 *Bolivia: transfers to municipalities, population, and poverty*[a]

	2000	2001			2002			2005		
	Log of Total Transfers	Log of Total Transfers	Log of HIPC Transfers	Log of Tax Transfers	Log of Total Transfers	Log of HIPC Transfers	Log of Tax Transfers	Log of Total Transfers	Log of HIPC Transfers	Log of Tax Transfers
Beni	−0.127	−0.166	−0.091	−0.186	0.004	−0.002	0.016	0.085	0.105	0.089
	(0.079)	(0.068)**	(0.095)	(0.068)***	(0.047)	(0.124)	(0.016)	(0.044)*	(0.140)	(0.034)**
Pando	−0.190	0.151	0.690	−0.227	0.601	0.902	−0.014	0.343	0.757	0.004
	(0.104)*	(0.089)*	(0.123)***	(0.088)**	(0.059)***	(0.154)***	(0.020)	(0.052)***	(0.166)***	(0.041)
Constant	4.773	5.308	5.219	4.772	5.448	5.996	4.252	5.111	5.712	4.476
	(0.161)***	(0.149)***	(0.207)***	(0.148)***	(0.097)***	(0.256)***	(0.033)***	(0.090)***	(0.286)***	(0.070)***
Observations	155	211	211	211	213	213	213	153	153	153
R-squared	0.97	0.96	0.89	0.96	0.98	0.85	1.00	0.99	0.84	0.99

Notes:
a. Standard errors in parenthesis. * significant at 10%; ** significant at 5%; *** significant at 1%. Transfers have been deflated by regional GDP deflators.
b. Municipalities in Santa Cruz are excluded.

Source: Ministry of Finance and INE.

on HIPC transfers alone. This provides some evidence that transfers are not a function of poverty levels in practice, despite the intentions laid out in the PRSP. Moreover, the regressions show that some departments, including notably Pando, Beni and Oruro, have seen an increase in transfers relative to Santa Cruz (the richest department), even when controlling for population and the number of poor. Chuquisaca and La Paz, on the other hand, have seen a decline in transfers, despite the fact that they are also those with the highest level of poverty.

6 THE IMPACT OF HIPC TRANSFERS AND SPENDING ON SOCIAL OUTCOMES

The previous section highlights the remaining horizontal inequalities across municipalities. Despite these imbalances, municipalities have seen substantial increases in transfers. An important question is whether social outcomes have improved due to these transfers. To analyze this question, the 1999–2005 household income and expenditure surveys are used to compute average social outcomes by municipality. Given the long lags associated with improvements in social indicators, I concentrate on short-term indicators that could be expected to change relatively quickly. These could be seen as intermediate indicators, rather than final objectives. Averages of these social indicators for municipalities over time are presented in Table 7.8.

These indicators are then combined with time-series data on fiscal transfers and spending by municipality. The end result is a panel data set with around 300 municipalities over the 1999–2005 period containing average social indicators and fiscal transfers and spending information. Unfortunately, annual household surveys are available only for 1999–2002, and 2005. The analysis is therefore split into two parts, beginning with the following random effects regressions models for 1999–2002:

$$\Delta Social\,Indicator_{it} = \alpha + \beta\Delta Transfers_{i,t-1} + \delta\Delta X_{it} + \varepsilon_{it} \quad (7.2)$$

$$\Delta Social\,Indicator_{it} = \alpha + \beta\Delta Spending_{i,t-1} + \delta\Delta X_{it} + \varepsilon_{it} \quad (7.3)$$

where t refers to time, i is an index for municipalities and transfers and spending are deflated by regional deflators. Lagged changes in the log of transfers and spending are included, since it is reasonable to expect that there is a lag between transfers and spending of resources and an actual improvement in the intermediate social target. Finally, changes in a set of control variables, ΔX, which have been shown to be important

Table 7.8 Average municipal social indicators, 1999–2005

	1999	2000	2001	2002	2005
Population characteristics					
Share of income poor	0.72	0.75	0.70	0.72	0.69
Share of indigent population by income		0.49	0.50	0.51	0.50
Share of indigenous/native population	0.45	0.51	0.42	0.53	0.50
Education					
Share of illiterate population	0.18	0.17	0.18	0.11	0.14
Share of school-age children not enrolled in school	0.14	0.14	0.13	0.13	0.08
Share of school-age children not attending school	0.39	0.26	0.56	0.39	0.35
Infrastructure					
Share of households with access to public sewers	0.17	0.21	0.19	0.04	0.23
Share of households with access to phone service	0.09	0.08	0.08	0.08	0.24
Share of households with access to electricity	0.48	0.51	0.48	0.48	0.53
Health					
Share of children vaccinated for polio	0.88	0.89	0.71	0.72	–
Share of children vaccinated for DPT	0.64	0.68	0.59	0.57	–
Share of attended births	0.56	0.56	0.52	0.59	–
Share of hospital births	0.53	0.53	0.49	0.55	–
Share of unattended diarrhea	0.08	–	0.09	0.08	–
Share of unattended respiratory illnesses	0.09	–	0.07	0.09	–
Share of unattended illnesses	0.13	0.23	0.24	0.22	–
Number of municipalities	121	155	211	214	155

Source: Own calculations based on INE: Encuesta de Mejoramiento de Condiciones de Vida (1999, 2000, 2001, 2002) and Encuesta de Hogares (2005).

determinants of poverty for the Bolivian context are included. In particular, the average municipal family size, the share of indigenous people and average municipal illiteracy are controlled for, all of which are correlated with higher poverty rates in Bolivia.[6,7]

The results for 1999–2002 are reported in Table 7.9. First, with respect to the control variables, an increase in average municipal education and a reduction in illiteracy leads to improvements in social indicators, although these effects are not always significant. Changes in family size and in the share of indigenous people are insignificant.

With respect to the results of changes in municipal transfers and spending, the results are mixed, with many instances where spending and transfers have insignificant effects on indicators. Given funds are fungible, separate regressions were run using total transfers, total spending, as well as transfers and spending on health, education and infrastructure for each social indicator.

For health indicators, increases in total spending in the previous period, and in health spending in particular, reduce the share of unattended illnesses. Increased total spending is associated with significantly fewer cases of unattended respiratory disease. However, in regressions not reported here, there is no significant effect of spending on the municipal share of children under age three who were vaccinated for DPT or polio.

For education indicators, increases in education transfers in the previous period are associated with a decline in the share of children not attending school. However, there is no significant effect when looking at the change in education spending. When looking at infrastructure indicators, there is no significant effect of changes in spending or transfers on the share of homes with access to phone service or electricity.

Since there were no household surveys in 2003–04, regressions were slightly modified for 2005 as follows:

$$\Delta \mathit{Social\,Indicator}_{i,2002-2005} = \alpha + \beta\Delta \mathit{Transfers}_{i,2002-2005} + \delta\Delta X_{i,2002-2005} + \varepsilon_{it} \tag{7.4}$$

$$\Delta \mathit{Social\,Indicator}_{i,2002-2005} = \alpha + \beta\Delta \mathit{Spending}_{i,2002-2005} + \delta\Delta X_{i,2002-2005} + \varepsilon_{it} \tag{7.5}$$

The change in social indicators is now defined as the difference between 2002 and 2005 and is modeled as a function of the changes in spending between 2002 and 2005, and the change in the set of control variables, discussed above. Unfortunately, the 2005 survey dropped the section on health, so the results reported in Table 7.10 focus on education and infrastructure indicators. The results run contrary to expectations. In particular, for education, increases in education transfers actually seem to have increased the share of unenrolled children, while they did not significantly

Table 7.9 Bolivia: municipal changes in indicators: 2000, 2001, 2002

	Change in Share of Unattended Illness		Change in Share of Unattended Cases of Respiratory Diseases		Change in Share of Children Not Attending School		Change in Share of Unenrolled Children		Change in Share of Homes with Access to Electricity		
Change in average municipal family size	−0.031 [0.014]**	−0.028 [0.013]**	0.034 [0.013]***	0.033 [0.013]**	0.032 [0.021]	0.03 [0.024]	0.007 [0.006]	0.012 [0.007]*	0.014 [0.014]	0.019 [0.015]	0.019 [0.015]
Change in share of indigenous people	0.000 [0.000]	0.000 [0.000]	0.000 [0.000]*	0.000 [0.000]	−0.001 [0.000]**	−0.001 [0.000]	−0.001 [0.000]	0.000 [0.000]	0.000 [0.000]	0.000 [0.000]	0.000 [0.000]
Change in average municipal education	−0.027 [0.013]**	−0.028 [0.012]**	0.011 [0.012]	0.006 [0.012]	0.01 [0.019]	0.015 [0.022]	−0.011 [0.006]*	−0.02 [0.007]***	0.102 [0.013]***	0.108 [0.014]***	0.108 [0.013]***
Change in average municipal illiteracy	0.369 [0.193]*	0.428 [0.191]**	−0.027 [0.176]	−0.129 [0.178]	0.275 [0.306]	0.502 [0.338]	0.403 [0.096]***	0.356 [0.102]***	−0.285 [0.199]	−0.256 [0.203]	−0.250 [0.202]
Change in total transfers (t–1)											
Change in education transfers (t–1)					−0.021 [0.004]***		0.003 [0.001]**				
Change in infrastructure transfers (t–1)									0.000 [0.002]		
Change in total spending (t–1)	−0.021 [0.010]**		−0.034 [0.009]***							0.015 [0.011]	

Change in health spending (t–1)		−0.021 [0.007]***		−0.011 [0.007]							
Change in education spending (t–1)						0.022 [0.014]		0.000 [0.004]			
Change in infrastructure spending (t–1)										0.012 [0.010]	
Constant	0.016 [0.014]	0.021 [0.014]	−0.002 [0.015]	0.002 [0.014]	0.127 [0.028]***	0.012 [0.025]	−0.005 [0.009]	0.009 [0.008]	−0.023 [0.018]	−0.015 [0.016]	−0.016 [0.016]
Observations	308	303	281	279	387	297	387	297	388	320	320
Number of municipalities	157	154	150	148	193	158	193	158	194	163	164
R-squared – overall	0.12	0.12	0.07	0.05	0.11	0.03	0.15	0.2	0.33	0.35	0.35
R-squared – within	0.13	0.13	0.13	0.07	0.13	0.03	0.14	0.2	0.33	0.35	0.35
R-squared – between	0.15	0.16	0.07	0.06	0.09	0.01	0.18	0.2	0.33	0.34	0.33

Notes: Standard errors in brackets.
* significant at 10%; ** significant at 5%; *** significant at 1%.

Source: Own calculations based on Ministry of Finance and INE: Encuesta de Mejoramiento de Condiciones de Vida (1999, 2000, 2001, 2002).

Table 7.10 Bolivia: municipal changes in indicators: 2002, 2005

	Change in Share of Children Not Attending School		Change in Share of Unenrolled Children		Change in Share of Homes with Access to Electricity		
Change in average municipal family size	0.039 [0.025]	0.045 [0.025]*	−0.006 [0.008]	−0.009 [0.009]	0.026 [0.016]	0.023 [0.016]	0.023 [0.016]
Change in share of indigenous people	0.000 [0.001]	0.000 [0.001]	0.000 [0.000]	0.000 [0.000]	−0.001 [0.000]***	−0.001 [0.000]***	−0.001 [0.000]***
Change in average municipal education	0.031 [0.022]	0.028 [0.022]	−0.021 [0.007]***	−0.026 [0.008]***	0.098 [0.014]***	0.101 [0.014]***	0.099 [0.014]***
Change in average municipal illiteracy	0.779 [0.381]**	0.792 [0.342]**	0.052 [0.128]	−0.149 [0.119]	−0.159 [0.242]	0.021 [0.219]	0.004 [0.221]
Change in total transfers (t–1)							
Change in education transfers	−0.007 [0.034]		0.040 [0.011]***				
Change in infrastructure transfers					−0.043 [0.020]**		
Change in total spending (t–1)						−0.01 [0.011]	
Change in education spending (t–1)		−0.013 [0.014]		−0.001 [0.005]			
Change in capital spending							−0.014 [0.009]

Constant	−0.089	−0.087	−0.029	−0.025	0.038	0.039	0.041
	[0.026]***	[0.028]***	[0.009]***	[0.010]**	[0.017]**	[0.018]**	[0.017]**
Number of municipalities	183	180	183	180	181	180	181
R-squared overall	0.02	0.03	0.08	0.04	0.28	0.29	0.28
R-squared within	0.04	0.05	0.07	0.03	0.34	0.31	0.32
R-squared between	0.01	0.01	0.09	0.06	0.2	0.25	0.23

Notes: Standard errors in brackets.
* significant at 10%; ** significant at 5%; *** significant at 1%.

Source: Own calculations based on Ministry of Finance and INE: Encuesta de Mejoramiento de Condiciones de Vida (2002) and Encuesta de Hogares (2005).

affect the share of children not attending school. Similarly, an increase in infrastructure transfers reduces the share of homes with access to electricity, while there is no significant effect of changes in spending or transfers on the share of homes with access to phone service.

In summary, the results show no strong evidence that increases in spending by municipalities between 2000 and 2005 have had a measurable impact on short-term social indicators. Even when considering infrastructure, where the bulk of resources have been spent, there is no strong evidence that access to public infrastructure in the form of access to electricity, phone service or public sewers has significantly improved. In fact, the 2005 data suggest that there has actually been a decline in access.

7 ALLOCATIVE EFFICIENCY: HOW ARE RESOURCES ACTUALLY SPENT?

An important explanation for the lack of improvement in social indicators despite the increases in transfers is that total spending by all levels of government is poorly targeted. As detailed below, there is evidence that all existing resources are not allocated efficiently. First, at the local level, there may be a lack of sound projects and program evaluations, or simply poor program implementation. Second, spending is inefficiently used due to poorly defined revenue and expenditure responsibilities between different levels of government. Although changes to revenue-sharing agreements increased resources given to departments, there was no corresponding increase in their expenditure responsibilities (Simone, 2006). For example, as detailed below, in the health and education sectors, the central government continues to control the bulk of spending because it is responsible for wages and salaries. This is partly due to the strong health and education sector unions who have opposed any attempt to decentralize wage-setting negotiations. This sharing of expenditure responsibilities has implications for the allocative efficiency of resources and ultimately for the quality of service delivery and the potential for poverty reduction.

7.1 The Aggregate Perspective

From an aggregate point of view, total pro-poor spending in Bolivia increased from about 11 percent of GDP in 2000 to 13 percent of GDP in 2002. It then declined slightly, but has recently rebounded up to over 13 percent of GDP in 2006 thanks to the increase in revenue from the hydrocarbons sector. The largest shares of pro-poor spending have taken place

Table 7.11 Bolivia: pro-poor spending (in percent of GDP)

	2000	2001	2002	2003	2004	2005 Prel.	2006 Prel.
Current spending	6.0	6.7	7.2	7.1	7.4	7.4	6.9
Health (excluding veterans)	2.4	2.6	2.6	2.7	2.8	3.0	2.7
o/w health wages	1.1	1.2	1.4	1.4	1.4	–	–
Veterans	0.4	0.4	0.4	0.4	0.3	–	–
Education (excludes universities)	3.6	4.1	4.6	4.4	4.5	4.2	4.0
o/w education wages	3.0	3.2	3.6	3.9	3.8	–	–
Other social spending	0.0	0.0	0.0	0.1	0.1	0.1	0.1
Capital spending	4.8	5.3	5.7	4.7	4.6	5.1	6.4
Health	0.7	0.6	0.7	0.5	0.6	0.5	0.6
Education	1.0	1.4	1.5	1.1	0.8	0.9	1.2
Basic sanitation	1.1	0.9	0.6	0.5	0.8	0.9	0.6
Urban development	0.6	0.8	0.8	0.7	0.7	0.8	1.9
Rural development	1.3	1.7	2.1	1.8	1.6	2.0	2.0
o/w rural roads	0.5	0.7	0.8	0.8	0.7	0.7	0.8
Total pro-poor spending	10.8	12.1	12.9	11.9	12.0	12.4	13.3
o/w Municipal spending	0.6	0.7	1.2	1.4	1.5	1.3	1.9
Current spending	0.3	0.3	0.3	0.4	0.5	0.4	0.3
Capital spending	0.3	0.4	1.0	1.0	1.0	0.8	1.6
HIPC resources	0.0	0.1	0.7	0.8	0.6	–	–
Own resources	0.3	0.3	0.3	0.3	0.5	–	–
Total pro-poor spending excluding wages	6.7	7.6	7.9	6.6	6.8	–	–
GDP (millions of bolivianos)	51 928	53 790	56 682	61 904	69 626	76 154	89 428

Source: Ministry of Finance: Unidad de Programación Fiscal.

in education and in capital projects. A growing share of total pro-poor spending has taken place at the municipal level, increasing from about 6 percent of total pro-poor spending in 2000 to about 15 percent in 2006 (Table 7.11).

Education is the largest sector of public spending in Bolivia. Pro-poor spending on education increased from about 4.5 percent of GDP in 2000 to over 6 percent of GDP in 2002 but declined to 5.2 percent of GDP by 2006. The expansion in 2002 was due to increases both in the number of teachers, and their average wage, as teacher salaries account for 80 to 90 percent of total education expenditures.[8] Average salaries in the education sector have grown by about 5 percent a year between 1998 and 2002, while inflation grew on average at 3 percent during the same period. Moreover, employment in the education sector increased from 50 to 53 percent of total Bolivian public employment between 1998 and 2002. This increase in employment has been accompanied by steady student–teacher ratios, implying that there has been a large increase in the number of teachers. In terms of resource distribution across education sectors, pre-primary and primary education received between 55 and 60 percent of the education budget in 2002. Tertiary education received around 30 percent of the annual education budget (one of the highest levels in Latin America), the bulk of which goes to supply free university education, mostly for the non-poor.[9] Secondary education, on the other hand, receives the smallest share, only about 12 percent of the education budget, which is well below the average in Latin America (30.5 percent) and even Sub-Saharan Africa (28 percent).

Similarly, pro-poor public health expenditures amounted to around 3.5 percent of GDP in 2006. According to the 2002 World Bank Public Expenditure Review, the central government controlled around 80 percent of public health expenditures, mostly for wages and salaries, while municipalities managed 18 percent and are responsible for variable costs of the public health insurance, while the remaining 2 percent is managed by the Social Investment Fund and other public entities. Significant steps were taken in 2002 in the context of the enhanced HIPC initiative to increase the provision of doctors and nurses. As a result, there was a 37 percent increase in the number of doctors and 8 percent increase in the number of professional nurses. This led to a ratio of 23 doctors per 100, 000 population, twice the number recommended for the delivery of a package of core clinical and public health interventions. In contrast, spending on inputs and drugs remains low, limiting the effectiveness of health services, particularly with regard to vaccines. Moreover, there are substantial imbalances in the allocations of professionals, with half employed at the tertiary care level, and a high concentration of professionals in urban areas while rural facilities are staffed by low-skilled auxiliary nurses.

8 DISTRIBUTION OF HEALTH AND EDUCATION RESOURCES TO MUNICIPALITIES[10]

The misalignment of responsibilities between the central, regional and local governments plays an important role in explaining why resources from debt relief have not led to improvements in social outcomes. Although the central government continues to be responsible for payment of wages and salaries of education and health sector employees, it has weak control of staff. This is because salaries are mostly determined at the local level, on the basis of workload assigned to teachers and health workers by local committees, where departments, municipalities, and popular participation bodies are represented. The problem is that the municipalities and departments are not particularly keen about certifying the hours worked, as they have little incentive to do so.

Construction of school and health premises and their maintenance, on the other hand, is a municipal responsibility. Decisions are made on the basis of needs, on the availability of finance and on the constraints on the use of resources imposed from above. New construction generates new requests for personnel to run the premises and to provide services, but separation of responsibilities leads to frequent discrepancies between building and staffing of new premises. As a result, there is evidence that in some municipalities, the availability of HIPC resources has led to the construction of new schools that are ultimately not staffed and therefore not used due to lack of financing from the center for wages.

Table 7.12 describes how total municipal resources are spent by both economic and functional classification. Although there are important problems with the functional classification of data in Bolivia, if we are to take the data available, it is clear that the biggest areas of municipal spending are housing and community services, economic affairs and education. More importantly, note that the relative shares have changed over time, with education and health gaining ground over the last few years. From the point of view of an economic classification, the most important thing to notice is that the bulk of municipal spending is on capital projects. This is true for all functional categories of spending, including health and education.

9 SUMMARY AND CONCLUSION

The decentralization system introduced in the mid-1990s suffers from significant vertical imbalances and only partially addresses the horizontal inequalities. Coparticipation transfers, and more recently hydrocarbons

Table 7.12 Bolivia: functional and economic classification of municipal spending (in percent of GDP)

	1997	1998	1999	2000	2001	2002	2003	2004	2005	2006
Total spending[a]	4.6	4.4	4.9	3.8	4.5	4.4	4.8	5.2	4.8	4.0
Current	1.8	1.7	1.8	1.6	1.7	1.6	2.1	2.3	2.1	2.0
of which: wages	0.9	0.9	0.8	0.8	0.8	0.8	0.8	0.8	0.7	0.7
Capital	2.9	2.6	3.1	2.2	2.8	2.8	2.7	2.9	2.7	2.0
General public services	1.2	1.1	0.7	0.7	0.8	0.8	0.8	0.7	0.8	0.6
Current	0.9	0.9	0.7	0.7	0.8	0.8	0.8	0.7	0.7	0.6
of which: wages	0.5	0.5	0.4	0.4	0.4	0.5	0.5	0.4	0.4	0.4
Capital	0.3	0.2	0.0	0.0	0.0	0.0	0.0	0.0	0.0	0.0
Defense	0.0	0.0	0.0	0.0	0.0	0.0	0.0	0.0	0.0	0.0
Public order and security	0.0	0.0	0.0	0.0	0.0	0.0	0.0	0.0	0.0	0.0
Economic affairs	0.9	0.9	1.1	0.9	1.0	1.0	1.0	1.2	1.1	0.8
Current	0.1	0.1	0.1	0.1	0.1	0.1	0.1	0.1	0.1	0.1
Capital	0.9	0.8	1.1	0.8	1.0	0.9	0.9	1.0	0.9	0.7
Environmental protection	0.3	0.3	0.3	0.2	0.3	0.3	0.4	0.3	0.3	0.3
Current	0.0	0.0	0.0	0.0	0.0	0.0	0.1	0.1	0.0	0.0
Capital	0.3	0.2	0.3	0.2	0.3	0.3	0.2	0.2	0.2	0.3
Housing and community services	1.0	1.1	1.5	0.8	1.1	0.9	1.0	1.1	1.0	0.9
Current	0.5	0.5	0.7	0.4	0.5	0.3	0.5	0.5	0.5	0.5
of which: wages	0.2	0.2	0.3	0.2	0.2	0.1	0.2	0.2	0.2	0.2
Capital	0.6	0.6	0.8	0.4	0.7	0.6	0.5	0.5	0.5	0.4
Health	0.2	0.2	0.3	0.3	0.3	0.3	0.5	0.6	0.6	0.4
Current	0.1	0.1	0.1	0.1	0.1	0.1	0.2	0.3	0.3	0.3
of which: wages	0.0	0.0	0.0	0.0	0.0	0.0	0.0	0.0	0.0	0.0
Capital	0.1	0.1	0.1	0.1	0.2	0.2	0.3	0.3	0.3	0.1
Culture and sports	0.3	0.2	0.3	0.2	0.3	0.3	0.3	0.4	0.3	0.3
Current	0.1	0.1	0.1	0.1	0.1	0.1	0.1	0.2	0.1	0.1
Capital	0.2	0.2	0.2	0.2	0.2	0.2	0.2	0.2	0.2	0.2
Education	0.5	0.4	0.6	0.5	0.6	0.8	0.8	0.7	0.7	0.5
Current	0.0	0.0	0.1	0.1	0.1	0.2	0.2	0.3	0.2	0.2
of which: wages	0.0	0.0	0.0	0.0	0.0	0.0	0.0	0.0	0.0	0.0
Capital	0.5	0.4	0.5	0.4	0.5	0.6	0.6	0.5	0.4	0.3
Social protection	0.1	0.1	0.1	0.1	0.1	0.1	0.1	0.1	0.1	0.1

Note:

a. Excludes financing, including amortization payments and is presented only for consistency with total outflows of municipalities.

Source: Bolivian Ministry of Finance. ViceMinisterio de Presupuesto y Contaduria; http://vmpc.hacienda.gov.bo/coparticipacion.asp, accessed 16 June 2009.

revenues, are based on municipalities' population size, with no effective mechanism to address income inequalities and differences in revenue capacity between municipalities. The equity criterion introduced with HIPC was meant to compensate for the bias caused by the per capita distribution of resources in effect since 1994. The evidence presented in this chapter shows that this objective has not been achieved. HIPC transfers are not correlated with poverty levels in practice, despite the intentions specified in the PRSP. Indeed, transfers to the least populated department, Pando, have increased, while transfers to La Paz and Chuquisaca, which are among the poorest departments, have declined even when controlling for population and the number of poor.

Beyond the equity criterion that the HIPC was aimed at addressing, an important question is whether the transfers that reached municipalities and the associated spending has led to measurable impact on short-term social indicators. The analysis presented here uses a panel of municipalities that combines average municipal social indicators extracted from multiple rounds of household surveys with time-series data on fiscal transfers and spending by municipality. The results show no strong evidence that increases in spending by municipalities have had a measurable impact on short-term social indicators. Even when considering infrastructure, the area where the bulk of resources have been spent, there is no strong evidence that access to infrastructure has significantly improved.

One possible explanation for this failure is that there may be absorptive capacity constraints at the municipal level. An important point to note is that resources are fungible, and despite the efforts at earmarking and then tracking HIPC spending, there is no one-to-one additionality of HIPC spending on total spending in the priority areas. The evidence presented here shows that after initial bottlenecks in 2001 and 2002, municipalities started to absorb all or most of what was transferred. Although there is some evidence that the poorest municipalities still face absorptive capacity constraints, on average, municipalities have managed to spend in excess of 90 percent of resources transferred to them between 2003 and 2005. The magnitude of the funds spent would suggest that these should have been large enough to make a difference.

The most compelling explanation for the lack of improvement in social indicators is that total spending by all levels of government has been poorly targeted. Inefficiencies in government spending could be explained by poor management and/or execution at local levels and a lack of sound decision-making based on project evaluations. In addition, expenditure inefficiencies are at least partly due to misaligned responsibilities between central and local governments. Unless these issues are addressed, particularly in the areas that have a direct impact on poverty alleviation, it is hard to imagine that new resources flowing from the hydrocarbons sector will have a better impact on improving social services and ultimately reducing poverty.

NOTES

* I am grateful for useful comments on earlier versions of this paper from Alejandro Simone, Enrica Detragiache, Luis Tejerina and participants at an IMF Institute seminar. Radu Paun provided valuable research assistance. All remaining errors are my own.

1. For a recent review of the issues, see Ahmad and Brosio (2006).
2. See www.imf.org/external/np/exr/facts/hipc.htm for more details on the HIPC initiative and http://www.imf.org/external/np/exr/facts/mdri.htm for more details on the MDRI, accessed 22 March 2009.
3. See Faguet (2004).
4. Bolivian Poverty Reduction Strategy Paper, March 2001, pp. 142–3, available at: http://www.imf.org/external/np/prsp/2001/bol/01/033101.pdf, accessed 22 March 2009.
5. In 2003, municipalities were able to run down the build up of transfers in bank accounts. As a result, bank commissions on transfers slightly declined.
6. Previous versions of these regressions included initial poverty levels, but were dropped as they were insignificant.
7. Note that when household data is disaggregated at the municipal level, the calculated social indicators will be noisier, thus potentially generating larger errors in the estimated coefficients than what is assumed by standard theory.
8. See the 2002 World Bank *Public Expenditure Review*.
9. For example, the top two quintiles of the income distribution receive 80 percent of public expenditure on universities, while the poorest two quintiles receive only 5.5 percent of this spending. Primary and secondary education, on the other hand, benefits the poor, as 47 and 32 percent of this spending, respectively, benefits the two poorest quintiles.
10. See Simone (2006).

REFERENCES

Ahmad, Ehtisham and Giorgio Brosio (2006), *Handbook of Fiscal Federalism*, Cheltenham, UK and Northampton, MA, USA: Edward Elgar.

Bolivian Ministry of Finance, Unidad de Programación Fiscal, "Dossier Estadistico 1990–2005", available at: http://www.upf.gob.bo/M2400dos.htm, accessed 22 March 2009.

Bolivian Ministry of Finance, Unidad de Programación Fiscal (UPF), Comportamiento de los Recursos HIPC II (Behavior of HIPC II resources), Boletín Informativo, September, 2006, No. 6, available at: http://www.upf.gob.bo/M2400hipcsep06.htm, accessed 22 March 2009.

Bolivian Poverty Reduction Strategy Paper, March 2001, pp. 142–3, available at: http://www.imf.org/external/np/prsp/2001/bol/01/033101.pdf, accessed 22 March 2009.

Faguet, Jean-Paul (2004), "Does Decentralization Increase Government Responsiveness to Local Needs? Evidence from Bolivia", *Journal of Public Economics*, **88** (4), 867–93.

International Monetary Fund (IMF) (2007), "Bolivia: 2007 Article IV Consultation – Staff Report", available at: http://www.imf.org/external/pubs/cat/longres.cfm?sk=21209.0, accessed 22 March 2009.

Simone, Alejandro (2006), "Fiscal Decentralization" in *Bolivia – Selected Issues*, International Monetary Fund, 30 June.

World Bank (2002), *Bolivia – Public Expenditure Review*, Washington, DC: The World Bank.

8. Uganda: managing more effective decentralization

Ehtisham Ahmad, Giorgio Brosio and Maria Gonzalez*

1 INTRODUCTION

The complex interplay between political economy and fiscal decentralization is clearly seen in the case of Uganda, which has engaged in an ambitious decentralization reform over the last 15 years. Partly designed as an element of the political agreement following the civil war, the process quickly became enmeshed with the country's overarching poverty-reduction strategy, and as a mechanism to improve service delivery, as advocated by bilateral and some multilateral donors.

The program devolved responsibility for a large number of key public services to the local level, including primary education and health services, and with only few exceptions—such as security and defense. In 1994, as the major legislative initiatives were being formulated and expenditure functions delegated, the central government employees working in the local governments officially became local employees, and hence accountable to them. Subsequently, the size of the central government was reassessed in light of the shift of many functions from the center to the local authorities. While the staff were transferred from central to local control, the center retained important financing controls, as well as an ability to determine and require spending at the local level, resulting in unfunded mandates, as discussed further below.

However, the devolution of functions was not paralleled by improved revenue generation capacity, nor by the ability to make significant resource allocation decisions at the local level. It is in this light that available assessments of service delivery in key social sectors have brought, at best, mixed results to the promises of the decentralization process. Indeed, the tension between central financing and administrative controls, and the devolution of local responsibility for spending is at the core of the divergent forces that have prevented the full realization of the decentralization process.

The assessment in this chapter suggests that Uganda has implemented decentralization only partially. While quickly devolving spending, the process was complicated by a subsequent centralization of revenues. Moreover, many of the new mandates were accompanied with a rigid system of conditional grants, possibly to mitigate the risks from low capacity and weak public financial management, and to ensure the appropriate tracking of pro-poor spending. Many of these conditions represented requirements from the donor community that has financed more than half of Uganda's spending over the last ten years. As a result, the model built in a rigid structure of vertical accountability links, but undermined the generation of local autonomy in decision-making, and the system of horizontal accountability links that are at the root of strengthened performance by policymakers in decentralized frameworks.

The chapter is organized as follows. Section 2 presents a brief historical overview of the decentralization process in Uganda. Section 3 analyzes the design and sequencing of the decentralization framework, and reviews the experience with public financial management. Section 4 looks closely into sectoral outcomes, with the support of data from household surveys. Section 5 concludes.

2 UGANDA'S DECENTRALIZATION PROCESS: THE INSTITUTIONS

2.1 Historical Overview: The Sequencing of the Decentralization Process

Uganda's initial experimentation with decentralization was associated with the colonial government, and did not survive independence from Great Britain. During the British rule, elected local officials[1] were tolerated by the colonial administration as a measure to contain pressures for a full independence. At independence in 1962, Uganda had a system of local governments responsible for significant expenditure functions, although effective administrative control was exercised by the center through the district commissioners. This effectively deconcentrated system was, however, dismantled shortly after independence, and replaced by a centralized administration. The subnational governments played only minor implementation roles, as the central government reacted to colonial structures and also sought to contain the unsettled political environment until the mid-1980s (Steffensen et al., 2004).

The end of the civil war in 1986 reopened the door to decentralization. The new government of the National Resistance Movement (NRM) quickly adopted decentralization through a radical reform—to facilitate the reconciliation of political ambitions for all previously warring factions, and to become a cornerstone of a new governance model. Thus, as early as 1987, the government introduced political decentralization by establishing "Resistance Councils" at all subnational government levels, with the objective of increasing local participation in the decision-making processes and strengthening democracy. The program was formalized in 1993 through the issuance of the Local Government Statute, enshrined in the 1995 Constitution, and later in the Local Government Act of 1997.

The number of the local governments increased rapidly with decentralization, largely obeying political considerations, and as a tool to achieve national consensus among different groups. Thus, the need to satisfy regional and tribal demands for political power led the central government to permit a proliferation in the number of districts—originally, the highest subnational government tier.[2] By 2005, the government also reached agreement with regional and tribal leaders to establish regions—a new intermediate tier of local authority comprised of interested districts, de facto representing tribal kingdoms.[3]

The need to effectively ensure service delivery contributed to the strong and continuous expansion of Uganda's local governments. This expansion took root as the government focused its economic program, supported by donors, more intently on poverty reduction in the second half of the 1990s. With the country's grass-roots-based Poverty Eradication Action Plan (PEAP) launched in 1997, Uganda scaled up significantly the resources allocated to delivering pro-poor spending, in particular those identified and tracked under the Poverty Action Fund (PAF), which received strong financial backing and attention from the international donor community. The local governments were, in fact, assigned the responsibility to execute a growing share of expenditures tracked under the PAF—a share that reached 60–70 percent in the early 2000s. Partly to support related service delivery, the number of local civil servants expanded—and the expansion was particularly pronounced in the case of the teachers hired to serve the Universal Primary Education Program (UPE), a frontline in the national program for poverty reduction (see Figure 8.1). The central government was thus confronted with a huge increase in the teachers' wage bill over which it had little control. This put great pressure on the government to manage its macroeconomic constraints. In effect, the UPE effectively imposed unfunded mandates on the local governments, as the additional resources transferred were not commensurate with the mandate.

At the same time, an upward drift in the central government staff outside the ministerial civil service was not contained. Off-ministerial staff includes special independent commissions, secondary and tertiary schools, police, prisons and central government staff delegated to districts (Langseth, 1995; Golola, 2001 and Kjaer, 2004).

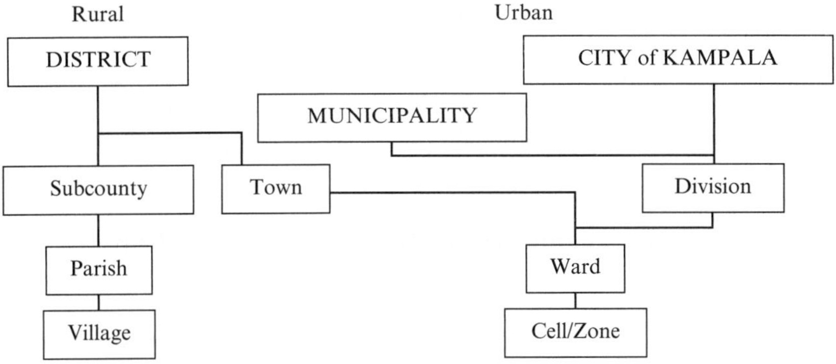

Source: World Bank (2004), *The Republic of Uganda Country Integrated Fiduciary Assessment (CIFA)*, Vol. V.

Figure 8.1 Uganda: government tiers

Throughout the decentralization process, the strategy for local capacity building had a "learning-by-doing" orientation, which lagged behind the devolution of government responsibilities. Wide divergences in capacities across different local authorities quickly presented challenges to service delivery—with the poorest districts facing significant constraints to adequately execute and report spending, in spite of the technical assistance provided by the center and international donors. There are also widespread reports of rent-seeking behavior at the subnational level, compounded by the information and public financial management difficulties at several levels of government. Problems aside, however, many local authorities also made attempts to improve service delivery once they gained autonomy. For example, some studies suggest that the ability to make employment decisions based on block resources assigned directly to districts led a number of them to retrench workers, reorganize their administrative structures and try to recruit better-qualified staff. These reorganizations were based on improvements in the methods of service provision—including by allowing outsourcing to the private sector (Brixiova, 1998).

The design of Uganda's decentralization program has been subject to reassessments, and continues to be refined over time. A first decade of experience allowed the authorities to identify a host of outstanding problems, ranging from capacity weaknesses to institutional design issues that have undermined performance in service delivery—including factors such as intergovernmental resource allocation and flexibility, design and capacity weaknesses in public financial management and policy coordination. To address some of these problems, the government developed the Fiscal

Decentralization Strategy (FDS)—containing a sequenced strategy to improve the grant allocation formulae across districts, and enhance and simplify expenditure management and reporting by the local authorities. The FDS was formally adopted in June 2002, and launched through a number of sequenced pilot phases for its implementation—these are still ongoing.

2.2 Does Uganda's Institutional Design Promote Accountability?

2.2.1 Legislation and administrative structure

Uganda's decentralization scheme is supported by a legal framework under the 1997 Local Government Act, which was drafted to provide a clear description of the key responsibilities to be undertaken by the different tiers of local authorities in the country. In addition, the 1998 Local Government Financial and Accounting Regulations (LGFAR) cover a framework for development planning, budgeting, revenue collection, expenditure management, accounting and audit. The authorities revised the LGFAR in 2005 in line with the 2003 Public Finance and Accountability Act (setting out nationwide provisions on public financial management), and other modernization initiatives, including the FDS itself.

The institutional design of Uganda's decentralization framework is intricate. There are five basic tiers of local governments in Uganda (Figure. 8.1), linked through complex political and administrative arrangements.[4] The highest basic tier is comprised of districts and the city of Kampala. Urban areas are divided into municipalities and towns; both Kampala City and the municipalities are split into divisions, and subsequently, wards and zones. In the rural areas, the districts are split into subcounties, and subsequently into parishes and villages. Most executive decisions are taken at the districts and municipalities; the lower-level authorities are considered to be the subcounties, towns and divisions, while parishes and wards are regarded as administrative units supporting their upper structures (World Bank, 2003a and 2003b). Crucially, there is no formal subordination or hierarchical control across the different local government layers.

The executive bodies at different tiers are designed to be highly representative, but are vulnerable to local pressures. Districts, municipalities and subcounties are headed by an elected executive (the chairperson) and an elected Local Government Council.[5] The Council is formed by directly elected councilors from specific constituencies. In rural areas, chairpersons and councilors are elected at the district, subcounty and village levels, while in urban areas, they are elected at the city, municipality, town, division and cell levels.[6] Operations are conducted through executive committees elected directly by the chairperson, and endorsed by the Council. The presence of Local Council at lower government tiers is meant to ensure a more direct system of accountability of the local affairs by the voters. In practice, however, especially in small communities, the scheme has often been monopolized by special interest groups (World Bank, 2004).

External local government oversight is cumbersome. There are a large number of institutions with overlapping or unclear mandates for monitoring local authorities, working with little or no coordination among them. At the central government level, the Ministry of Finance, through the Treasury Inspectorate Department is responsible for collecting fiscal data and overseeing specific local government grants. The Ministry of Local Governments is responsible for policy design, and for monitoring the adherence of the local authorities to their laws and regulations. The Auditor General is legally vested to inspect the local authorities' accounts. Auditing, scrutinizing and follow-up of the local accounts and performance also fall under the mandate of the Local Government Public Accounts Committees (LGPACs) and the Parliament's Local Government Accounts Committee (LGAC). The Local Government Finance Commission has an advisory role, responding directly to the President on revenue issues. Finally, there are Resident District Commissioners—appointed by the center, and mainly responsible for security issues, but who effectively reflect strong central control over the local governments, as was the case in colonial times.

2.2.2 Expenditure assignments

Uganda's allocation of sectoral expenditure responsibilities between the central and local authorities is broadly along the lines expected in developing countries. In particular, subnational authorities are charged with delivering basic services that affect their communities directly, to strengthen the link between delivery and accountability. These services are: primary education—as well as some services at the secondary and tertiary schooling levels; primary health care and district hospitals; rural water services; most agricultural extension services and district, feeder and municipal roads. The picture is muddied because of the prevalence of unfunded mandates assigned by the center.

The allocation of expenditure responsibilities between local government tiers is more obscure. Generally, only the upper government tiers (including districts, municipalities, towns and subcounties) execute significant expenditures on their own. The only spending taking place at the level of the parishes and urban wards is the remuneration of the local councils. While each of the subtiers has some responsibilities assigned by legislation, most important responsibilities are allocated to districts and municipalities, which have discretion to delegate some of them to lower government tiers. In this context, some of the largest subcounties and towns have been able to take over some functions, for example, to provide primary education, basic health care and agricultural extension. These arrangements may favor accountability between the towns and subcounties and their constituencies, but only when such responsibilities are known by all and well demarcated. At the same time, the districts and municipalities do not have clear legislative ability to impose a strong vertical oversight mechanism, given the lack of direct and legally binding subordination between the different local government levels.

From a sectoral perspective, the devolution of expenditure responsibilities in Uganda has proceeded fast. The local authorities' share of execution of total government expenditure per sector, excluding the share directly financed by earmarked donor projects, rose from some 30 percent in 1997/98 to about 37 percent by 2004/05—with the subnational governments picking up the responsibility for 75 percent of the resources assigned to education, 62 percent of those assigned to the health sector and about half of the budget for water services (Table 8.1). Crucially, once earmarked donor projects—which have increased significantly in Uganda in recent years—are taken into account, the trend moderates significantly. Clearly, specific conditionality by donors has often required implementation by the central government ministries, rather than the local governments.[7]

Development expenditure devolution took place relatively quickly in Uganda. The country allowed its local authorities to handle a significant share of capital expenditure projects from an early stage. As noted below, much of this devolution was made possible through a detailed conditional grant system, which allowed close supervision by the center of the execution of capital projects, but did not favor the build up of horizontal accountability between the local governments and their constituencies. The effectiveness of the central supervision has been open to question.

2.2.3 Revenue and borrowing arrangements

Perhaps the weakest aspect in Uganda's decentralization arrangements is that pertaining to the revenue framework. By generating a large dependence of the subnational governments on the center, and emphasizing hierarchical monitoring mechanisms on the use of the resources, the institutional structure has taken little advantage of the horizontal incentive potential upon which decentralization is based. As a result, it has, de facto, built a system of "deconcentration" rather than one of decentralization—blurring the information available to the constituencies on the extent to which local authorities are truly responsible for their own performance, thus weakening accountability.

Table 8.1 Total sector expenditure executed by local governments (in billions of Ugandan Shillings)[a]

	Excluding Donor Projects				Including Donor Projects[a]			
	2001/02	2002/03	2003/04	2004/05	2001/02	2002/03	2003/04	2004/05
Agriculture	7	11	15	20	7	15	20	22
Education	330	363	393	432	330	363	393	432
Health	98	104	118	135	98	104	118	135
Water	25	26	27	29	25	26	27	29
Roads and works	23	18	21	22	23	18	21	22
Total local government expenditure	611	669	739	819	611	673	744	820
Agriculture	42	49	46	52	42	115	108	120
Education	456	492	517	567	456	561	587	632
Health	163	190	208	220	163	307	383	366
Water	49	55	53	57	49	90	94	108
Roads and works	157	155	146	155	157	223	261	400
Total expenditure	1742	1928	2079	2215	1742	2555	2879	3151
Local government expenditure as a share of total expenditure								
Agriculture	17.6	22.8	32.6	39.2	17.6	13.0	18.3	18.3
Education	72.5	73.8	75.9	76.1	72.5	64.7	66.9	68.3
Health	59.9	54.8	56.8	61.7	59.9	33.9	30.8	37.0
Water	50.1	46.7	50.6	51.3	50.1	28.5	28.7	27.0
Roads and works	14.6	11.9	14.6	14.4	14.6	8.2	8.2	5.6
Total	35.1	34.7	35.5	37.0	35.1	26.3	25.8	26.0

Note: a. In 2001/02, outturns on expenditure including donor projects were not available.

Source: Ugandan authorities and staff estimates.

In contrast to the rapid devolution of spending, decentralization in Uganda has not been very ambitious with regard to local revenue generation. The share of the revenues mobilized locally relative to total resources available to the subnational governments collapsed over time, from about 80 percent at early stages of the decentralization process to about 20 percent by 2004/05. The share of total domestic revenue to GDP has remained stagnant at around 12 percent. With the share of public expenditure on GDP at around 24 percent of GDP, Uganda has had to rely significantly on foreign aid. Expanding revenues and increasing the effectiveness of public expenditure at all levels of government remains a crucial challenge. In the immediate future, there has to be a substitute for the revenue loss, particularly for the local governments, incurred through the suspension of the graduated income tax that used to be assigned to the lower levels.

At the root of the bleak local revenue collections lies the design of the "own-revenue" raising instruments available to the subnational authorities. These encompass several problems:

- They are very limited—the main local revenue instruments at present are a property tax and a series of market dues. This assignment is broadly in line with best practice, but the number of instruments and revenues collected are very small. Moreover, the local authorities have no ability to modify bases or rates—thus, these taxes do not strictly constitute own-taxes—in the sense needed to generate additional revenues at the margin and to impose hard-budget constraints on the local governments.
- They are suboptimal due to design and/or capacity constraints:
  - First, poor administrative capacity and the lack of proper enforcement have generated dubious assessment practices in the collection of the graduated income tax, rendering it burdensome and widely unpopular.[8]
  - Second, the proliferation of lower levels of government may add to administrative constraints—indirectly increasing the dependency on the center.
  - Third, the base of the property tax has remained unnecessarily narrow, as it is confined by the legislation to urban areas—thus accentuating the fiscal imbalances between wealthy urban local governments and the poorer rural districts.
  - Fourth, the specific market dues constitute a widely varying share of the available product prices, generating distortions that fall more heavily on small traders in poorer administrative jurisdictions (Nsibambi, 1998).
- They are subject to political manipulation—for example, due to its widespread unpopularity, the graduated income tax was picked up as a frontline issue in the local and presidential campaigns of 2004/05. As a result, the tax was "suspended" for a ten-year period – which has deprived the local authorities of their largest yielding revenue source.[9]

The revenue-sharing arrangements within local governments are narrow and administratively complex. Given the low level of local revenue collections, transfers among local governments are not feasible. However, local revenues are redistributed within districts and municipalities, after being collected at the lower local levels. This redistribution takes place through a complex transfer system that requires resources to flow back and forth across tiers.[10] These arrangements, aside from being burdensome, have often generated incentives for under-reporting of revenue collections.

Given their weak revenue collections, Uganda's local governments are highly reliant on central government transfers—in particular, on conditional grants.[11] On average, about 80 percent of the central transfers are conditional—that is, earmarked by the center for the provision of specific services. The remaining 20 percent represent equalization and unconditional grants. In practice, the unconditional transfers are mostly used to cover administrative costs—including councilor wages and allowances—rather than to deliver direct services to the public. Therefore, the allocation decisions of the bulk of the funds accruing to the local governments are widely perceived as being largely predefined by the central government. This, coupled with the fact that transfers available for discretionary use are not allocated to service provision, has weakened the degree of accountability of the local authorities to the beneficiaries of such services, at least in what pertains to decision-making in expenditure allocation.

The monitoring mechanism implied by the conditional grants has been key to facilitating the devolution of expenditure mandates. As national social spending grew, on the basis of the PEAP, the delegation of expenditure responsibilities in priority sectors to local authorities with relatively low capacity increased. Corruption remains endemic. Furthermore, bad practices are widespread, such as request of non-official fees for access to services.

The problems described above called for strengthened oversight by the center. Thus, the central authorities established conditionality on their grants to ensure that their use was properly monitored and accounted for. This tendency has been, perhaps, exacerbated by the need to track poverty-related expenditures appropriately, to provide assurances to the donor community that largely financed them that the resources would be used effectively for priority needs, such as basic education or health care. In the event, districts were required to produce monthly accounts on expenditures undertaken with the resources from conditional grants. Grants under the Poverty Action Fund (PAF), which tracks key poverty-reducing spending, were subject to even more stringent requirements.[12] Thus, the framework sought to offset the falling accountability from the local governments to the citizens in their jurisdictions by imposing stronger vertical accountability links between the center and the local governments. In effect, the decentralization process now depends to an even greater extent on centralized controls, and as stated above, this weakens even further the local preferences and accountability,

Horizontal accountability has also been undermined by other weaknesses in the overall system of grant allocation to the subnational governments. For example, the magnitude and distribution of equalization grants are scheduled to be revised in the context of the FDS, in the light of new available indicators and updated data in different jurisdictions. In addition, the allocation scheme of the conditional grants is also to be modified based on new measurements of uncovered needs across local governments.[13] As the local authorities have been able to claim that the need for revision of the allocation formulas has generated unfunded mandates—and provided insufficient discretionary resources for them to assign to the generation of public goods—the ability of their constituencies to monitor and hold them accountable for their performance, and the effectiveness of the decentralization framework to improve service delivery has waned.

The local government resort to formal debt financing has been very limited. Borrowing by local governments is allowed by law, but it has a stringent cap—of 25 percent of locally generated revenue—and is subject to central government conditions and approval. In this context, formal indebtedness by the local authorities has been contained.[14] While this may have limited moral hazard on the side of the subnational governments, it has also eliminated the subnational authorities' ability to access additional resources to finance investments needed for service delivery based on local needs.

2.3 Capacity Constraints: The Experience with Public Financial Management

The public financial management (PFM) system at different levels in Uganda is coherent, but has suffered from flaws in capacity and institutional design. The system is based on the principle of civil society participation, relying on a scheme in which lower government tiers are expected to seek grass-roots feedback, to define expenditure priorities at the country level. These inform the PEAP—which is periodically revised—as well as the national medium-term framework and budget, prepared annually. This bottomup approach is expected to entrench ownership of the budget in every jurisdiction, and favor accountability for the decisions made by local policymakers. A full scheme of arrangements has been set in place to facilitate budget execution and reporting, as well as ex post auditing, although some of these arrangements can be seen as transitory mechanisms that compensate for more fundamental weaknesses in the PFM system. Poor performance has often been observed at the various stages of the financial management cycle, partly because of faulty arrangements, but also due to the lack of human capital, especially in the most disadvantaged districts and municipalities.

Budgeting and planning have proved challenging to Uganda's local authorities. The weakest element of the local budget cycle has been the effort to link the chosen policies and plans to the budget. Districts are expected to reflect their own development priorities in three-year district development plans that serve as a basis for local budgets, which are later integrated at the national level. However, the quality of the development plans is generally low—even when presenting coherent objectives and strategies, the plans are often not properly costed and are poorly linked with the local budgets (World Bank, 2003b). As a result, the local government input into the final national budget exercise does not effectively reflect local priorities, thus undermining ownership.

Budget implementation by the subnational authorities has suffered from serious problems of under-execution, often driven by capacity constraints. Assessments of the quality of public financial management by the donor community have reported frequent discrepancies between budget ceilings and effective outturns, with the latter being significantly below budget ceilings.[15]

Expenditure controls are very weak, reflecting low capacity and institutional loopholes. Most importantly, the local authorities have constantly experienced very serious difficulties in managing and updating their wage payrolls and pension registries. This has caused large wage arrears, especially for the primary teaching service with the introduction of UPE,[16] as well as a large stock of pension arrears that had to be absorbed by the central government given its size.[17] Further, non-wage arrears are also a problem, since no commitment control system for expenditure is used at the local government level, except under pilot programs, to strengthen public financial management in selected local governments.[18] According to some reports, some subnational authorities hold stocks of arrears of up to 20 percent of their budget expenditures (World Bank, 2004).

Local authorities lack an effective cash planning system. In fact, most subnational governments do not forecast their intra-year disbursements or plan their use—rather, they wait for cash to arrive, and then choose how to spend it. Conditional grants are usually transferred promptly to the appropriate sectoral account, while—as previously noted—unconditional and equalization grants are allocated to pay salaries. Cash received from the local government's own revenue collections is disbursed as soon as it is received, typically in an ad hoc manner (World Bank, 2003b). While most districts hold meetings to discuss spending priorities, the budget rarely serves as a basis for these discussions—possibly as a reflection of the weaknesses observed during budget formulation.[19]

Complicated cash management arrangements are in place to compensate for the lack of effective monitoring mechanisms, posing strains on the local governments with lowest capacity. In particular, conditional grants are disbursed and managed through a large number of separate bank accounts. This facilitates the tracking of their use, by allowing for the reconciliation between the balances in the accounts and the financial reports submitted by the local authorities to the center. Additional bank accounts are used for projects funded by donor sources. These arrangements, while providing assurances on use of funds, have resulted in the creation of 30 or more separate bank accounts in each district—a costly arrangement, particularly when capacity is weak. Under the FDS, the number of accounts is being streamlined to bring the total number of bank accounts to less than ten in each district.

Overall, the severe weaknesses in the PFM systems have hampered service delivery. Moreover, they have also flagged the limited capacity of the local authorities to respond to the strong demands placed by the heavy devolution of spending that has taken place, especially as they have entailed burdensome reporting requirements to satisfy the vertical oversight mechanisms. Perhaps more worrisome, however, are the weaknesses observed when the local governments had greater autonomy—for example, in the cases of payroll management, cash planning or the decision-making process for the allocation of their scarce local revenues. These results suggest, on the one side, that low PFM capacity reduced the effectiveness of the decentralization process. But, perhaps more importantly, they also hint at the presence of institutional design flaws that might prevent an adequate level of performance in service delivery to emerge, even if greater degree of autonomy in decision-making were granted to the local authorities.

3 ACCOUNTABILITY AND GOVERNANCE

3.1 Accountability

Generally, the available tools for holding the local authorities accountable for their performance are as weak as other aspects of the public financial system. The strongest mechanisms in place are vertical. In contrast, the public rarely demands accountability from its local authorities directly, and Local Councils have remained largely passive and ineffective at holding their administrations responsible for their performance. However, recent donor assessments suggest that a few local service commissions have become more active in disciplining staff, especially in cases of misappropriation of resources.

Vertical accountability mechanisms are complex, and narrow in scope and effectiveness—although they are gradually improving. External audit by the executive is performed by the Office of the Auditor General (OAG), which is mandated to audit the accounts of all higher and lower local governments at the end of each financial year. While timely preparation of these reports has improved over time, the OAG has continuously faced severe staff and resource limitations, which have hampered both the coverage and depth of its assessments. The LGPACs are mandated to review internal and external audit reports on local government performance, and make recommendations for follow up. The LGPACs reports are, however, of varying quality and limited in scope, since they focus mostly on non-compliance with the regulatory framework, rather than on correcting the underlying faults of the system. In Parliament, the LGAC is active in reviewing the scrutiny and performance reports prepared by the LGPACs. The LGAC's investigations have resulted in some prosecutions, demotions and recommendations for withdrawal of status of accounting officers. There is some debate, however, as to the relevant authority of the LGAC relative to the LGPACs (World Bank, 2004).

Public Expenditure Tracking Studies (PETSs) have been increasingly used to assess performance in service delivery at the local government level. Since 1999, PETSs have been carried out in the education, health, water and sanitation sectors (World Bank, 2004). PETSs are useful to assess issues of central concern to the local authorities with respect to the achievement of national objectives. However, since they are carried out on a sample basis, they cannot be seen as a mechanism for identifying systematic problems in local governments. In this context, they can only complement the system of monitoring and assessing individual local government performance. Moreover, follow up on the results of the PETSs remains at the discretion of the central government ministry that spearheads them.

3.2 Corruption

Corruption in Uganda is widespread, but modest improvements have been reported for local administrations. In parallel with the implementation of the PEAP, and under pressure from the international donors, the authorities have implemented policies to strengthen governance and curb corruption in the recent years. Data from the surveys on corruption and bad government practices prepared by Uganda's Inspectorate General of

Table 8.2 Incidence of bribery in contacts with public officials, 1998 and 2002

	Percentage of Contacts with Payment of Bribes		Average Bribe (in Ugandan Shillings)	
	1998	2002	1998	2002
Health	28.0	24.5	11 998	12 178
All police	63.0	46.0	50 453	42 211
Local governments	39.0	16.0	15 322	13 948
Judiciary	50.0	29.0	106 542	87 436
Education	n.a.	8.5	n.a.	10 245

Source: Inspectorate of Government, *National Integrity Surveys*, 1998 and 2003.

Government suggest that these efforts have achieved some success (Table 8.2). Corruption in education appears to be less than in other sectors.

4 SPECIFIC OUTCOMES IN SERVICE DELIVERY

There is still limited evidence on preference matching with decentralization. Azfar (2006) presents an analysis of preference matching in Uganda, combining information from household surveys with information from questionnaires submitted to local officials. The results show that there is both a statistically and economically significant variation in demand across districts and that there are also differences across subcounties within districts. However, no evidence is found of correlation between household demands and either public officials' knowledge of these demands or resource allocation decisions at the district level. When repeated at the subcounty level, the exercise shows a tiny evidence of some congruence between household and public official preferences. The paper also conducts an analysis of whether actual resource allocation has been adjusted in response to preferences, with very weak results showing a positive, but insignificant relationship between household demand and subcounty-level resource allocation.

There is mixed evidence on the effectiveness of local service delivery. As noted in the following sections, data analysis from a range of household surveys suggests that the improvements observed in the service provision in three key sectors—education, health and water services—have not been steady or widespread across the country's different jurisdictions. Further, in sectors in which comparisons can be made, it is clear that the quality of public services remains lower than that of private services. More broadly, there is no system in place to allow for comparisons on performance in service delivery across sectors.

The analysis of service delivery outcomes presented here has two main caveats. In particular, while a number of household surveys is available, they have little disaggregation even at the territorial level, limiting the depth of the analysis. Moreover, even in cases in which performance improvements have been registered in the assessed sectors, it is not possible to disentangle whether these were generated by the decentralization process itself, or by the nationwide scaling up of social expenditure in the sectors examined. Thus, the outcomes presented should be used to shed light on key aspects of the decentralization framework that may have triggered them. The analysis also draws attention to factors that might be relevant in making local service delivery more effective in the future.

4.1 The Outcomes: Education, Health and Water Services

4.1.1 Education

Primary education has been a top policy priority in Uganda, and the most important expenditure responsibility assigned to local governments (Jeppson, 2001). The institutional assignment is, however, complicated. As noted earlier, while local governments are formally mandated to provide primary education and some services at the secondary and tertiary education levels, the central government has the entire responsibility for the funding of the sector. Thus, districts have full responsibility for teacher recruitment, but salaries are determined and paid by the center; further, the center provides conditional grants that can be used for other non-wage school needs.[20] Second, districts are permitted to devolve the primary education mandate to lower government tiers at their discretion, which further blurs the assignment of responsibilities. In effect, the central government has little control over the numbers or quality of teachers hired, and the local governments hiring the teachers do not face the financial consequences of their actions.

Performance monitoring in education has evolved gradually. As in the case of other priority sectors, the tracking of education outcomes against nationwide priorities has relied heavily on the national budget for the identification of performance indicators. Some progress has been made in moving away from purely quantitative targets, such as the number of exercise books, to contextual targets, such as the ratio of textbooks to pupils, but even these new targets remain input-oriented. Focused monitoring through PETSs has also become systematic.[21] A widely quoted PETS found that during the first half of the 1990s only some 30 percent of funding for non-wage education spending reached the schools

Table 8.3 Primary school net enrollment, 1995–2004

	1995			2000				2004			2006		
	Total	M	F	Total	M	F	Poverty Incidence	Total	M	F	Total	Male	Female
Central	79	77	80	77	77	78	20	n.a	n.a	n.a	n.a	n.a	n.a
Eastern	68	70	67	87	88	86	28	n.a.	n.a.	n.a	n.a	n.a	n.a
Northern	55	62	44	70	69	70	37	n.a.	n.a.	n.a	n.a	n.a	n.a
Western	64	65	63	78	76	79	65	n.a.	n.a.	n.a	n.a	n.a	n.a
Total	67			79			35	90	93	88	92	94	92

Source: *Education Profile and Education Statistics Abstract* and 1999/2000 *Uganda National Household Survey* (UNHS).

(Ablo et al., 2008; Reinikka, 2001).[22] This share improved sharply, to about 90 percent in 1999/2000, through strengthened transparency and procurement procedures.

Survey data confirms that the heightened attention paid to education in Uganda since the mid-1990s has yielded positive results. The introduction of the UPE program in 1997, aimed at providing free primary education to Ugandan children, generated a boom in primary school enrollment almost immediately. Across the country, the net enrollment ratio climbed from 67 to 79 percent between 1995 and 2000, reaching 92 percent by 2006 (Table 8.3). Moreover, regional data also show a reduction in the disparities in enrollment over time. The poorest regions—identified as those with higher shares of people in the lowest quintile of the income distribution—have increased enrollment faster than other regions, and no gender disparities are apparent.[23]

Secondary school net enrollment remains extremely low, increasing only from 10 percent in 1995 to about 14 percent at the country level in 2000 (Table 8.4). In addition, there are large regional differences—ranging from 5 percent in the northern region—which is the poorest one and plagued by a guerrilla war—to 22 percent in the central region, which has the lowest poverty rate. Moreover, enrollment in secondary schools has not substantially increased in the recent years. Net enrollment rates are expected to rise, however, as the bulk of students attending primary education graduate to secondary school levels, putting additional demands on this service, and stretching available resources further.

School attendance has been undermined by a host of constraints, especially in rural areas. Physical and financing restrictions are the main reasons deterring children's continuous attendance at primary school. Results from the *National Delivery Survey* for 2004, reported in Table 8.5,

Table 8.4 Secondary school net enrollment

	1995			2000			2004		
	Total	Male	Female	Total	Male	Female	Total	Male	Female
Central	16	18	14	22	20	24	n.a	n.a	n.a
Eastern	9	10	8	14	13	15	n.a	n.a	n.a
Northern	5	8	2	5	7	4	n.a	n.a	n.a
Western	9	10	8	10	10	10	n.a	n.a	n.a
Total	10			14			15	16	14

Source: *DHS Education Profile and Education Statistics Abstract 2004.*

Table 8.5 Reasons for not attending school, 2003

Age	Too Young	Long Distance	High Cost	Lack of Interest	Disability	Need to Work	Other	All
6	62.5	40.4	32.4	13.8	19.7	6.3	17.2	47.6
7	19.7	15.2	18.1	25.8	19.8	15.1	28.3	19.8
8	9.8	20.7	17.6	14.7	19.6	18.3	12.7	12.6
9	3.7	4.7	5.2	10.1	7.9	12.9	26.2	5.8
10	2.4	10.1	15.0	17.0	18.6	19.3	4.1	7.1
11	1.2	1.5	3.3	7.1	6.4	5.9	6.3	2.6
12	0.7	7.4	8.4	11.5	7.9	22.2	5.3	4.5
Total	100.0	100.0	100.0	100.0	100.0	100.0	100.0	100.0

Source: *National Service Delivery Survey, 2004.*

suggest that the need to cover long distances between the place of residence and the school is a significant disincentive for attendance, particularly at young ages.[24] High education costs also reduce attendance—while under UPE, public schools are supposed to provide free services, the 2004 survey revealed that two-thirds of the interviewees declared to be paying non-specified fees, including for building development and lunch provision.

Finally, nearly a quarter of the oldest children drop out of school because they need to work—a problem that is likely affecting secondary school enrollment and attendance as well.

The public sector is the main but not the only provider of education in Uganda. In 2004, it owned almost 80 percent of primary schools, but less than 30 percent of secondary schools. Quality of public school is lower than that of private schools, as indicated by the much higher pupil-to-teacher

Table 8.6 Indicators for government and private primary schools, 2003–04

Indicator	Type of School					
	Public		Private		All	
	2002	2004	2002	2004	2002	2004
Pupil-to-teacher ratio	56	53	28	n.a.	52	50
Pupil-to-classroom ratio	94	n.a.	41	n.a.	87	n.a.

Source: Uganda Ministry of Education, *Statistical Abstract 2003–2004.*

and pupil-to-class ratios, although the ratios at public schools are slowly improving (Table 8.6).

The indicators on the quality of public education vary widely across districts. For example, in 2003, the pupil-to-teacher ratio ranged between 39 to 90, suggesting significant stress on the capacity of the available teachers, especially in the rural areas (Table 8.7).[25] Huge disparities were also present with the pupil-to-classroom ratio, which varied from 33 to 187, reflecting the capacity of districts to comply with their responsibility of building and equipping schools. Sizable pupil-per-classroom ratios are a clear indicator of lower quality and constraints on teachers as well as physical infrastructure—the rate of construction of new premises does not follow adequately the rate of growth of pupils. From 2003 to 2006 (the indicators for 2006 are reported in Table 8.8) there does not seem to have been an improvement in the reduction of spatial disparities, as evidenced by the contradictory change in the value of the standard deviation coefficients referring to the two distinct indicators.

4.1.2 Outcomes in health care

Health care has also been a social priority in Uganda. The sector has experienced a growing inflow of resources, in line with the implementation of the PEAP. In this context, local governments were assigned increasing resources to finance service delivery related to primary health care centers and district hospitals and referral hospitals. As in the case of the education sector, these funds were channeled mainly through a number of conditional grants—which also covered the salaries of primary health care workers and other district health workers. However, as noted earlier, the overall resource delivery of the health sector has become more centralized over time, once the earmarked donor resources for specific projects are taken into consideration. As in the case of the education, the dependence on funding and policy

Table 8.7 Uganda: indicators for government primary schools per district, 2003

	District	Pupil–Teacher Ratio (September Payroll)	Pupil–Class-room Ratio		District	Pupil–Teacher Ratio (September Payroll)	Pupil–Class-room Ratio
1	Adjumani	74	59	30	Kyenjojo	61	92
2	Apac	62	119	31	Lira	56	84
3	Arua	63	130	32	Luwero	50	70
4	Bugiri	61	103	33	Masaka	48	82
5	Bundibugyo	54	88	34	Masindi	51	87
6	Bushenyi	56	78	35	Mayuge	57	128
7	Busia	57	89	36	Mbale	55	110
8	Gulu	59	96	37	Mbarara	50	92
9	Hoima	53	71	38	Moroto	45	53
10	Iganga	62	118	39	Moyo	52	64
11	Jinja	58	91	40	Mpigi	66	81
12	Kabale	43	77	41	Mubende	59	100
13	Kabarole	52	97	42	Mukono	46	77
14	Kaberamaido	61	84	43	Nakapiripirit	77	104
15	Kalangala	39	33	44	Nakasongola	38	60
16	Kampala	46	61	45	Nebbi	70	105
17	Kamuli	67	103	46	Ntungamo	56	80
18	Kamwenge	53	93	47	Pader	80	154
19	Kanungu	50	82	48	Pallisa	64	103
20	Kapchorwa	50	95	49	Rakai	41	84
21	Kasese	57	101	50	Rukungiri	43	65
22	Katakwi	56	93	51	Sembabule	55	97
23	Kayunga	68	98	52	Sironko	59	95
24	Kibaale	56	83	53	Soroti	60	98
25	Kiboga	51	80	54	Torero	62	187
26	Kisoro	53	70	55	Wakiso	48	68
27	Kitgum	71	122	56	Yumbe	69	185
28	Kotido	72	115		National total	56	94
29	Kumi	56	90		Standard dev	9.29	27.45

Source: Uganda Ministry of Education, *Statistical Abstract 2003.*

priorities predefined from the center, as well as the recentralization tendencies observed in the overall flow of sectoral resources, have likely reduced the horizontal accountability of the local authorities regarding service delivery.

Detailed information on health care outcomes in Uganda is scant. There

Table 8.8 Uganda: indicators for government primary schools per district, 2006

	District	Pupil–Teacher Ratio (September Payroll)	Pupil–Class-room Ratio		District	Pupil–Teacher Ratio (September Payroll)	Pupil–Class-room Ratio
1	Adjumani	47	55	41	Mubende	52	80
2	Apac	58	98	42	Mukono	46	65
3	Arua	60	119	43	Nakapiripirit	83	78
4	Bugiri	55	82	44	Nakasongola	35	48
5	Bundibugyo	48	74	45	Nebbi	64	95
6	Bushenyi	46	57	46	Ntungamo	48	64
7	Busia	51	75	47	Pader	90	156
8	Gulu	57	83	48	Pallisa	63	92
9	Hoima	48	96	49	Rakai	43	68
10	Iganga	57	94	50	Rukungiri	42	53
11	Jinja	46	72	51	Sembabule	42	78
12	Kabale	37	56	52	Sironko	50	75
13	Kabarole	51	75	53	Soroti	55	78
14	Kaberamaido	57	70	54	Tororo	61	88
15	Kalangala	32	28	55	Wakiso	40	57
16	Kampala	39	55	56	Yumbe	50	96
17	Kamuli	57	96	57	Abim	54	75
18	Kamwenge	50	68	58	Lyantonde	44	72
19	Kanungu	47	63	59	Mityana	42	62
20	Kapchorwa	38	63	60	Nakaseke	55	68
21	Kasese	45	84	61	Amuria	54	80
22	Katakwi	52	76	62	Budaka	61	84
23	Kayunga	52	76	63	Bududa	61	94
24	Kibaale	49	68	64	Bukedea	53	84
25	Kiboga	45	59	65	Butaleja	68	102
26	Kisoro	46	56	66	Manafwa	50	95
27	Kitgum	94	106	67	Namutumba	62	108
28	Kotido	60	75	68	Bukwo	46	74
29	Kumi	53	80	69	Amolator	64	89
30	Kyenjojo	55	76	70	Amuru	70	107
31	Lira	67	88	71	Dokolo	59	88
32	Luwero	54	66	72	Kaabong	88	95
33	Masaka	48	77	73	Koboko	65	149
34	Masindi	51	79	74	Maracha-Terego	61	129
35	Mayuge	61	100	75	Oyam	70	134
36	Mbale	49	86	76	Buliisa	75	100
37	Mbarara	37	56	77	Ibanda	42	72
38	Moroto	51	50	78	Isingiro	42	66
39	Moyo	48	62	79	Kiruhura	40	64
40	Mpigi	54	73	80	National total	52	78
					Standard deviation	11.92	21.61

Source: *Uganda, Ministry of Education and Sports Education Sector Factfile, 2006.*

Table 8.9 Mortality indicators

	1995	2000	2006
Infant mortality (per 1000 live births)	81.3	88.4	75.0
Neonatal mortality (per 1000 live births)	27.0	33.2	29.0
Post neonatal mortality (per 1000 live births)	54.3	55.2	46.0
Maternal mortality (per 100,000 live births)	527.0	505.0	435.0

Source: Uganda Demographic and Health Survey (UDHS), 1995, 2000, 2006.

is little that may allow for territorial disaggregation or intertemporal comparisons, and hence it is difficult to draw definite conclusions about the impact of decentralization in this sector.[26]

There are a couple of detailed studies on the impact of decentralization on health care spending by Akin et al. (2005) and Hutchinson et al. (2006). Both reach the same results; namely, that decentralization has led to an increase of expenditure for curative services at the expense of primary health care. This is questionable, but not necessarily bad, per se. However, the results are not robust. For example, Hutchinson et al. examine changes in local health budgets in two different but very close years, 1995 and 1997, and are not able to control for changes in both fiscal and regulatory decentralization over the period. They recognize that much of the central transfers for health remained earmarked for specific activities, such as salaries, equipment and hospitals, and cannot be reallocated. Donors also attach strings to their funds.

A less detailed but more prolonged view on basic outcomes of health care (see Tables 8.9, 8.10 and 8.11, which are built on results from Household Surveys) shows that, countrywide, mortality indicators have generally deteriorated from 1995 to 2000, but have improved thereafter, to 2006. Information on infant and child mortality by regions shows wide geographical variations, reflecting the structural characteristics of the regions. Most strikingly, while some reduction of mortality in the richest regions is apparent, the impact of the war and other adverse factors seems to have seriously worsened the health outcomes in Northern and Western Uganda, particularly in respect to the child mortality rate.[27]

Data also suggest that the quality of service provision has been weak. According to the *National Service Delivery Survey* (2004), the government is the only provider of health services—but about one-third of sick people did not make use of such services, owing to the "lack of drugs, demand for payment, and the long distance to the facilities". Data also indicate that the illegal charge of fees and other payments appears to have

Table 8.10 Infant mortality by region, 1995–2000

	1995	2000	Incidence of Poverty 2000
Central	77	72	20
Eastern	98	89	28
Northern	99	106	37
Western	75	98	65

Source: UDHS, 1995, 2000.

Table 8.11 Child (under-five) mortality by region, 1995–2000

	1995	2000	2006	Incidence of Poverty 2000
Central	141	135	n.a.	20
Eastern	176	147	n.a.	28
Northern	190	178	n.a.	37
Western	131	176	n.a.	65
National Total	156	158	137	

Source: UDHS, 1995, 2000, 2006.

increased—from about 40 percent of patients, according to the *National Integrity Survey* of 2002, to 50 percent according to the *National Service Delivery Survey* for 2004.

Also according to the available literature, access to health care facilities has not greatly improved after decentralization. For example, Kasirye et al. (2004) examine, using the 2002/03 *Uganda National Household Survey*, the nature and determinants of individuals' decisions to seek care on condition of illness reporting. The major finding is that cost of care is regressive and substantially reduces the health care utilization for any formal provider by the poorer individuals after controlling for other factors.

4.1.3 Access to safe water

Uganda's spending in water services has been relatively modest compared with that in education and health, although spending on water and sanitation is often perceived as a key factor for improving health outcomes—including infant mortality. In Uganda, the share of expenditure in water and sanitation executed directly by the local authorities—particularly, the districts and municipalities—is relatively large, even when the financing of earmarked donor projects is taken into account.

Table 8.12 Access to safe water by income quintile and by region, 1992–2002

Region/Quintile	I	II	III	IV	V
National total					
2002	20.8	22.9	20.6	15.4	20.3
1996	20.5	21.5	21.7	13.6	22.7
1992	16.9	18.7	21.9	13.8	28.8
Central region					
2002	8.7	11.2	21.5	23.3	35.4
1996	6.0	10.6	20.5	20.5	42.4
1992	2.0	9.6	19.0	21.2	48.2
Eastern region					
2002	29.2	29.3	18.0	8.6	15.0
1996	24.9	31.3	20.9	10.0	12.9
1992	22.8	22.6	21.7	12.0	20.9
Northern region					
2002	42.3	26.1	17.7	10.2	3.7
1996	53.5	17.3	16.1	8.8	4.3
1992	52.7	19.4	14.4	7.5	6.0
Western region					
2002	13.4	31.0	24.3	15.3	16.0
1996	13.8	35.0	29.3	8.8	13.0
1992	11.6	33.6	34.3	5.5	14.9

Source: Rudaheranwia et al. (2003). Original sources of data are *National Health Surveys* (in particular that for 2002).

As in the case of education and health, the funds are allocated by the center in the form of a conditional grant to the local authorities. At the same time, the weight of the water sector as a share of total general government spending has been very small—at about 3 percent—suggesting that the sector has not received particularly high attention by the center.

The information on water outcomes is better than that available for the health sector. Variations on the distance of access to safe water are a crucial indicator of the impact of policy, particularly from the point of view of the poor. Distant access uses time and energy and hampers the effort exerted by individuals to overcome their poverty conditions.[28]

The data suggest a significant improvement in water service provision, especially in the poorest jurisdictions. At the national level, the wealthiest quintiles have seen their importance in the share of access to water services reduced, while the poorest quintiles have seen it increase (Table 8.12). This pattern is supported by the regional data—in most regions, accessibility

Table 8.13 Uganda: distance of access to water by communities, 1992–2002

Communities with Access to Safe Water Within a Distance of Less Than 1 km				
	1992	1996	1999	2002
Central urban	20.8	17.1	9.8	13.5
Central rural	22.3	21.5	20.5	20.7
Eastern urban	5.7	4.8	9.9	9.3
Eastern rural	12.5	16.9	16.9	17.3
Northern urban	5.9	5.8	6.2	5.2
Northern rural	12.1	12.6	12.3	11.4
Western urban	7.6	8	12	8.2
Western rural	13.2	13.4	12.5	14.3

Source: Rudaheranwia et al. (2003).

to safe water has increased for the lowest quintile of population, while decreasing for the highest quintile. Access to water for the lowest quintile is quite high in the Northern region, which is poor and ravaged by war, and low in the Central region, which is the richest.

Perhaps surprisingly, the regional variations in service provision are relatively mild. There are no substantial discrepancies in the distance to access to water by communities (Table 8.13), with the exception of the Central region, where the share of communities situated at a distance of less than 1 km from a safe source has decreased slightly.

5 CONCLUSION: POSSIBLE EXPLANATIONS OF THE OUTCOMES

In summary, the survey data shows an improving performance in the education and water sectors, partly opposed to that observed in the health sector, where improvements are more recent. Three main factors appear to be behind this outcome:

- *National relevance.* The education sector has been at the forefront of Uganda's development priorities since early in the 1990s. As a result, it has received significantly more resources and scrutiny than other sectors—by the central and local governments, and by Uganda's development partners. To this extent, the improvements observed are not directly linked to the benefits of decentralization, but rather to the central government's efforts to strengthen basic education services, including through a heavy monitoring system of the local authorities. To a lesser degree, the achievements in the water sector may also be the result from a well-targeted use of resources—albeit at a much smaller scale—as directed by the center.

- *A sectoral structure that favors horizontal accountability.* According to donor assessments, while the involvement of the direct beneficiaries in the management and monitoring of service delivery usually varies across sectors, the education sector appears to have received the most attention. In particular, school management committees have been reported as the most effective units for horizontal accountability—perhaps because the parent–teacher relationship is strong, and the link between parents and their children's education providers tends to be continuous over the medium term, thus allowing for close supervision. Experience shows that maintaining user committees in other sectors has proven harder, likely because the relationship between the service providers and the beneficiaries tends to be more sporadic (World Bank, 2003a and b). Interestingly, the provision of water services also generates a long-term and constant relation between the service provider and the beneficiaries, creating space for the emergence of horizontal accountability.
- *Relatively higher autonomy in decision-making of the local authorities.* Improvements in the water sector are striking, especially because the relatively small amounts allocated to the sector over time do not support viewing the sector as a headline in the central government's priorities. There is, however, a crucial feature in the sector's financing structure that calls for attention: namely, the resources allocated to the local authorities to finance service delivery under the conditional grant were largely non-wage-related. In fact, the share of development expenditures exceeded 95 percent throughout the 1990s. This situation is almost opposite to that observed in the cases of education and health sectors, where recurrent spending—mostly to serve politically sensitive and rigid wages—has consistently neared 70–80 percent. Therefore, the capital-intensiveness of the water sector, as well as its relative unimportance, seems to have brought significant flexibility to the local authorities, allowing them to allocate resources for specific water projects more efficiently and significantly improving delivery, while still meeting the requirements imposed by the central government's conditional grants.[29]

While there was much initial enthusiasm, Uganda's decentralization process became subject to "central directions" taking it more towards deconcentration in certain areas. Indeed, the initial model implemented focused ambitiously on the devolution of significant spending functions to the local authorities. However, the center soon imposed a revenue structure that made the local authorities overly dependent on the center. Also, with the flow of donor funds for priority spending on education and health care, there was greater pressure on the center to ensure that the funds were being effectively spent and tracked. By creating a strong arrangement to ensure vertical accountability to the center and the donor community, the government may have undermined local autonomy, as well as the horizontal accountability links on which decentralization frameworks rely, thus hampering effective service delivery. Capacity constraints and loopholes in the PFM system also contributed to this result.

In this light, Uganda's decentralization reform appears to have fallen short of its promise in key areas of public service delivery. The assessment of service outcomes in key priority sectors—including education, health and water services—tend to provide only mixed results. The close examination of sectoral outcomes appears to support these conclusions. The sector that has performed best—water services—received only a minimal share of the overall government expenditure over the last 15 years, but has structural features that favor the creation of grass-roots monitoring mechanisms and horizontal accountability. In addition, by being largely capital-intensive and domestically financed, it has escaped from the decision-making restrictions faced by other sectors dealing with a largely rigid and politically sensitive wage component.

Clearly, national policies and national problems—the border conflicts and the civil war in the North—have impacted hugely on sectoral performances by putting a strain on human and financial resources. In fact, national data for education and health show improvements of indicators over the recent years (specifically from 2004 to 2006).

Going forward, Uganda has the option of providing greater responsibilities in the key sectors to the local authorities. The process should be adequately sequenced to avoid failures in service delivery, especially in the poorer areas. Strengthening devolution and accountability, together with the ability to reallocate resources in line with local priorities and needs, will create incentives for the effective provision of public services. Preconditions include enhanced information flows, and an improved public expenditure management cycle—including a budget process owned by the local authorities, more careful execution and better and more streamlined reporting. This should satisfy the voters, central governments as well as requirements for quality assurance for Uganda's development partners. The alternative will be an increasingly greater reliance on central mandates and deconcentrated operations. It is evident that political economy concerns will be important in the choices that are eventually taken in Uganda.

NOTES

* We thank Maria Albino-War and Jiri Jonas for useful comments on an earlier draft.
1. An Ordinance introducing democratic local governments was issued in 1949.
2. The total number of districts jumped from 33 in 1980 to 44 in 1997, 56 in 2000 and 78 by 2006.
3. In addition, political discussions have increasingly concentrated on developing a federal government framework, commonly referred to as FEDERO.
4. As noted earlier, since 2005, districts are allowed to group voluntarily to form regions. These regions would be able to establish a regional assembly with elected representatives, and a regional government with ministers appointed by the regional kings, and approved by the regional assemblies. The regional governments would control the policies currently devolved to the districts.
5. At lower government tiers, the administrative role of the chairperson and local government is insignificant, as it involves little use of financial resources.
6. To avoid political influences, councilors are not allowed to campaign on a party basis.
7. For example, total spending in the health sector is increasingly reliant on earmarked funds provided by international donors and administered by the Ministry of Health, such as the Global Fund for AIDS, Tuberculosis and Malaria.
8. In general, wealthier people have usually been able to easily evade payment, while the poorest have been forced to pay the highest rates because the appropriate payment tickets were not available.
9. The graduated tax represented some 60 to 80 percent of local tax collections prior to its suspension. A very accurate account of the reasons behind the practical elimination of the tax is provided by Cammack et al. (2007). The tax was widely unpopular due to the harsh methods (inherited from colonial times) of collection and its regressive character. However, no attempt was made to find a local tax instrument to replace it.
10. According to the Local Government Act, 35 percent of the collections attracted by the villages and parishes (and submitted to the subcounties) must be transferred to the upper-level district. Of the remaining 65 percent, 5 percent stays at the subcounty councils, 5 percent to the parishes and 25 percent to the villages; urban authorities have a different sharing formula.
11. These grants are financed from taxes collected at the national level, and from resources provided by Uganda's international development partners to the country.
12. These include the submission of quarterly work plans and execution reports by the districts, detailing expenditures made and the associated activities undertaken on the basis of agreed work plans prior to each quarterly release of resources. These requirements under the PAF grants have provided assurances to donors, who have channeled a large amount of budget support through this virtual fund. The World Bank provided financial and technical support to the authorities in this area.
13. Some other issues, such as the lack of an allowance for the poorest and remote jurisdictions—particularly, districts—to pay higher wages and incentives to attract qualified staff, and resources to compensate for insecurity in the regions affected by armed conflict are also to be resolved.
14. There are, however, no official figures on aggregate local government borrowing.
15. For example, the World Bank's CIFA (World Bank, 2004) reported that, on the basis of a benchmarked average for districts, aggregate expenditures were at 87 percent of the budget, and total revenues at 91 percent, although local revenue collection was well below budget, averaging just 76 percent of the projected amount (2002/03). On the basis

of a sample, deviations between budgeted and actual amounts were most significant at a departmental level—while most sector departments underspent against budget, the problem was chronic for those departments funded by locally generated revenues.

16. The problem is particularly acute in the case of primary school teachers assigned to rural areas. A particularly strong increase in arrears took place in 1997 with the expansion of the UPE—reports at the time suggested that about 89 000 teachers were working in public schools, while only 74 300 were registered on the payroll. These arrears had to be partly cleared through a World Bank credit. See IMF (1998).
17. The stock amounts to about 17.5 billion Ugandan shillings.
18. Two main pilot programs are in place. The most important is the roll-out of a computerized Integrated Financial Management Information System (IFMIS) both at the central and local-government level, intended to improve cash planning and management, and imposing automatic expenditure control and auditing—a sound initiative that will only be fully in place over the medium term. In this light, technical assistance from the International Monetary Fund has intended to develop a manual Commitment Control System for the use of the local authorities, to serve as a transitory mechanism while the IFMIS is rolled out to all jurisdictions.
19. As an exception, the district of Kabale has developed its own cash management systems. The district has a cash-flow budget that sets out the expected timing of inflows, from different revenue sources and the department expenditure ceilings, over a two-month period. The district also keeps quarterly cash projections and schedules for disbursement of the spending departments.
20. Including several conditional grants covering the primary, secondary and tertiary education levels.
21. The education sector has had at least five PETSs since 1996. Every year, an area of concern identified during the semi-annual sector review is evaluated through PETSs. The last four assessments have covered: (1) two studies on the status of Universal Primary Education system; (2) the Teachers' Recruitment, Deployment and Payroll Management; (3) the Value-for-Money of the School Facilities Grant and (4) the Cost-effectiveness and Efficiency of Education Spending, for which the terms of reference are currently being prepared.
22. The first PETS in the Ugandan education sector, undertaken in 1996, disputed official records, which seemed to understate the increase in primary enrollment during 1991–95, following an increase in funding. Despite the increases in primary enrollment, the study also showed a significant amount of leakage of resources before they reached schools, and serious accountability problems on non-wage education spending (World Bank, 2003b).
23. Unfortunately, no distinction between rural and urban areas is available in regional data.
24. In fact, according to the Ministry of Education survey for the year 2001, distance to school represents for 24 percent of the persons interviewed the main reason for not attending school.
25. The problems with updating the payroll data may either overstate or understate these indicators. On the one hand, there may be teachers providing services not incorporated in the registry; at the same time, the authorities have often recognized the presence of "ghost" teachers on the payroll.
26. The health sector has also had several surveys to track performance in specific areas. Specifically, PETS have been implemented for: (1) funds under the primary health care conditional grant (2001); (2) drugs (2002) and (3) conditional grant for shared services (2003). For example, the study by Anokbongg et al. (2004) uses a mixed method evaluation design, involving both quantitative and qualitative methods and refers to two district hospitals in Northern Uganda. The authors maintain that decentralization policy led to increased utilization of health facilities. The perception was that the policy was good because it empowered the community in terms of creating a sense of responsibility in the stakeholders, and a sense of ownership that facilitated sustainability of public

institutions. However, the policy failed to improve drug shortages, inefficient utilization of resources and low morale among hospital staff.

27. There is widespread public recognition that Uganda has been one of the most successful countries in fighting HIV/AIDS. This fight has been engaged by both the central and the local governments, but there is no information on the specific actions at the subnational level.
28. The water and sanitation sector has also implemented PETSs. In 2002, at the request of the Ministry of Finance, Planning and Economic Development, a technical audit/value-for-money study was initiated for the rural water and sanitation conditional grant. While some questions arose about the methodology and overall quality of both studies, their completion allowed the Ministry to focus its efforts on a deeper analysis of areas of concern.
29. Interestingly, the share of donor-earmarked financed projects in the total development budget for the water sector has also been quite modest, at rates below 10 percent of total spending.

REFERENCES

Ablo, E. and R. Reinikka (1998), "Do Budgets Really Matter? Evidence from Public Spending on Education and Health in Uganda", World Bank Policy Research Working Paper No. 1926, Washington, DC: World Bank.

Akin, John, P. Hutchinson and K. Strumpf (2005), "Decentralization and Government Provision of Public and Private Goods: The Public Health Sector in Uganda", *Journal of Development Studies*, **41** (8), 1417–43.

Anokbonggo W.W., JW. Ogwal-Okeng, C. Obua, O. Aupont and D. Ross-Degnan (2004), "The Impact of Decentralization on Health Services in Uganda: A Look at Facility Utilization, Prescribing and Availability of Essential Drugs", *East African Medical Journal*, **81** (12), S2–S7.

Azfar, O. (2006), "Giving Citizens What They Want: Preference Matching and the Devolution of Public Service Delivery", paper for EGDI Conference in Stockholm, April.

Brixiova, Z. (1998), "Public Service Reform", *Uganda: Selected Issues and Statistical Appendix, IMF Staff Country Report No. 98/61*, Washington, DC: International Monetary Fund.

Cammack, D., F. Goolob-Mutebi, F. Kanyongolo and T. O'Neil (2007), "Neopatrimonial Politics, Decentralization and Local Government: Uganda and Malawi in 2006", Irish Aid, Working Paper No. 2.

Golola, M. (2001), "Decentralization, Local Bureaucracies and Service Delivery in Uganda", WIDER Discussion Paper No. 2001/115, Helsinki: World Institute for Development Economics Research.

Government of Uganda (2004), *Poverty Eradication Action Plan, 2004/05*.

Hutchinson, P., J. Akin and F. Ssengooba (2006), "The Impacts of Decentralization on Health Care Seeking Behaviors in Uganda", *International Journal of Health Planning and Management*, **21** (3), 1–32.

IMF (1998), *Uganda Enhanced Structural Adjustment Facility Policy Framework Paper, 1998/99–2000/01*, Washington, DC: International Monetary Fund.

Jeppson, A. (2001), "Financial Priorities under Decentralization in Uganda", *Health Policy and Planning*, **16** (2), 187–192.

Kasirye, I., S. Ssewanyana, J. Nabyonga and D. Lawson (2004), "Demand for health care services in Uganda: Implications for Poverty Reduction", unpublished MPRA paper, University of Munich.

Kjaer, A.M. (2004), "Old Brooms Can Sweep Too!: An Overview of Rulers and Public Sector Reforms in Uganda, Tanzania, and Kenya", *Journal of Modern African Studies*, **42** (3), 389–413.

Langseth, P. (1995), "Civil Service Reform in Uganda: Lessons Learned", *Public Administration and Development*, **15** (4).

Nsibambi, A. (1998), "Financing Decentralization", in A. Nsibambi (ed.), *Decentralization and Civil Society in Uganda: The Quest for Good Governance*, Kampala: Fountain Publishers.

Reinikka, R. (2001), "Recovery in Service Delivery: Evidence from Schools and Clinics", in R. Reinikka and P. Collier (eds), *Uganda's Recovery: The Role of Forms, Firms, and Government*, Washington, DC: World Bank.

Rudaheranwia N., L. Bategeka and M. Banga (2003), *Beneficiaries of Water Services Delivery in Uganda*, Economic Policy Research Centre, Kampala.

Steffensen, J., P. Tideman, H. Naitore, E. Ssewankamb and E. Mauaipopo (2004), *A Comparative Analysis of Decentralization in Kenya, Tanzania, and Uganda*, Final Synthesis Report, NCG.

World Bank (2003a), *Decentralization Policies and Practices: Case Study Uganda*, Washington, D.C.

World Bank (2003b), *Uganda Public Expenditure Review 2003*, Washington, D.C.

World Bank (2004), *The Republic of Uganda Country Integrated Fiduciary Assessment* (CIFA), Volumes I and V, Report No. 29377-UG.

9. The impact of decentralization on education in Poland

Maciej Jakubowski and Irena Topińska*

1 INTRODUCTION

Poland represents a laboratory for the evaluation of decentralization, and there is evidence regarding changes in accessibility, public and private expenditures and teaching quality after more than 15 years of decentralization. The preschool, primary and lower secondary school levels were decentralized in different years under different frameworks and this is used to compare the effects of various policy approaches. The assessment is based on fiscal and school system data available at the *gmina* (lowest local government) level, as well as on household budget survey data. The latter show how decentralization affects households and individuals. In the case of research on teaching quality, national examination data combined with school system and fiscal data for almost all local governments and students in Poland are explored.

The analysis focuses mainly on comparing the situations in 1998 and 2003. These dates were chosen to assess the impact of reforms in 1999 and 2000, which directly affected primary and lower secondary education and could be interpreted as the real beginning of decentralization. Though preschool education was decentralized in 1991, detailed data are only available for 1995–2006, precluding a comparison of what was before the decentralization. The important point is that decentralization is an ongoing process and one should not expect to observe any effects at the very beginning. Thus, trends observed after several years of decentralization are analyzed and the impact of reforms conducted in 1999/2000 is discussed. Finally, we address the question of whether, after more than ten years of decentralization, the variation in expenditures affects teaching quality. Thus, the focus is on the effectiveness of decentralized expenditures but no comparison is possible with a counterfactual situation where some schools are still run in a centralized manner. Instead, short panel data random effects models are employed to explore variations in expenditures and teaching quality within and between *gminas*.

It should be emphasized that the research concentrates not only on average efficiency effects, but also on distributional issues. The question of the impact of decentralization on disadvantaged households and poorer local governments is addressed. The use of household budget surveys, together with sub-national fiscal data, provides an opportunity to deepen our understanding of how decentralization affects the situation of households.

The chapter is organized as follows: Section 2 describes datasets used in the study; we then provide an overview of the process of decentralization and reform of the education sector in Poland during the transition period; Sections 3, 4 and 5 present research results for preschool education and for school education; the final section summarizes the main findings and gives several policy-relevant conclusions.

2 DATA SOURCES

Four data sources were used: (1) Regional Data Bank (Bank Danych Regionalnych or BDR), (2) Household Budget Surveys (HBSs), (3) examination results from the Central Examination Board (CKE) and (4) Ministry of Finance budgetary data (MoF). The first two datasets are maintained by the Central Statistical Office (Główny Urząd Statystyczny or GUS). However, they are different in nature and cannot be analyzed together in a straightforward way.

Regional Data Bank (BDR) contains a few thousand variables aggregated to the level of sub-national governments (in some cases with the rural/urban split). In this research, data on *gmina* expenditures and revenues (fiscal data), the number of students and schools and the number of children in kindergartens (school system data) have been explored. This is administrative data collected for the Ministry of Education or the Ministry of Finance. BDR data are available for the period 1995–2006, but in some cases fiscal data had to be supplemented with MoF datasets on sub-national budgets. This is particularly true for data on expenditures on kindergartens, which do not go beyond 2000 in BDR, and were completed with MoF data.

Household Budget Surveys (HBSs) have been conducted every year for over two decades. Each year, the HBS sample contains over 30 000 households and 100 000 individuals. Every household is surveyed for one month; therefore, the annual sample consists of 12 monthly sub-samples of fairly equal size (over 2500 households each). The HBS sample is representative of virtually the whole population, excluding those who live with foreigners or outside "standard" households (in dormitories, welfare homes and so on). Data over the period 1998–2003 is comparable, although some methodological changes have been implemented each year.

HBSs provide data on household incomes (by various sources), expenditures (over 200 items), type of residence, housing conditions, durables, land area (if any) and so on. Detailed information is also given for each household member: age, sex, education, relation to the household head, individual source of income. At the household level, various categorizations submitted by GUS are also available. Education expenditures include expenditures on services (from nine in 1998 up to 12 items in 2003) and on goods (for items such as textbooks, copybooks and so on). Services are grouped by education level and type of service (fees for service at school or out of school). Expenditures on books, copybooks and so on cannot be assigned to an educational level. Moreover, HBSs do not include information on expenditures involved with child/student transportation to and from school. It should be pointed out that no information about preschool enrollment is available. Therefore, preschool enrollment or the "use" of kindergarten should be established on the basis of expenditure alone.

The measurement of some important impacts of decentralization – such as the poverty impact for instance – requires the use of combined datasets merging sub-national fiscal data with household surveys. This cannot be directly done in Poland because of confidentiality issues. Therefore, the merging process has been done in the following way.

Given the information available in HBSs, each household may be located according to the following territorial characteristics: (1) *voivodship* (region), (2) area of residence, rural or urban, the latter with the indicator of the urban size according to the number of inhabitants (under 20 000; 20 000–100 000; 100 000–200 000; 200 000–500 000; above 500 000). Since there are 16 *voivodships* in Poland and six types of place of residence are recorded, a maximum of 96 territorial units can be set. In fact, only 73 territorial units (TUs) exist, because in some *voivodships*, cities of a particular size do not exist. HBS and BDR datasets have been merged through these 73 units. BDR fiscal variables (expenditures) expressed as means of sub-national governments for 73 TUs have been added to household records in HBSs. Also, BDR has been supplemented with HBS statistics, that is, means for 73 TUs. Using statistical information on 73 TUs instead of 2500 *gminas* involves a substantial loss of information regarding variation within *gminas*. The same is true in the case of aggregated household data. However, this is the only way to merge HBS and BDR datasets. Further details of the merging process can be found in Jakubowski and Topińska (2007).

Fiscal and school system data were also merged with national examination data to conduct a value-added analysis of teaching quality. In this case, merging was easily done for most of the *gminas* and schools because of the common indicator system. However, the biggest cities like Warsaw or Cracow were differently coded in the BDR and CKE datasets and had to be excluded from the analysis. This is not a real problem, having in mind that for the biggest cities fiscal data are not really helpful because they tell almost nothing about the differences in resources available to schools (in Warsaw there are more than 100 schools and we would have to assign one number to each of these). Nevertheless, for more than 90 percent of students and more than 95 percent of schools, the data were merged successfully.

3 DECENTRALIZATION AND REFORMS OF THE EDUCATION SECTOR IN POLAND

3.1 Main Trends

In Poland, decentralization started in 1991, at the very beginning of transition, and was strongly supported by the newly elected democratic government. It was believed that decentralization would boost the development of civil society and would increase the efficiency of locally provided services. The usual arguments were made that local representatives better understand local conditions and needs, are more able to supervise service provision and can be held accountable by citizens. However, the main motive for decentralization was political, because democratic powers saw decentralization as a way to dismantle the communist state and its local bureaucracy, and as a vehicle for establishing a political base for their new political agencies (see Regulski, 2003).

The law to conduct local government elections was passed quickly as early as in 1990. A few weeks before the election of 1990, the law defining the division of responsibilities between *gminas*, the lowest level of the sub-national government, and the central government authorities was adopted. About 2500 *gminas* were established in 1990. This number has slightly changed during the transition period. In 2006, there were 2478 *gminas*, of which 307 were urban, 1591 rural and 580 mixed (rural/urban). The smallest *gmina* has less than 1500 inhabitants, while the largest has more than 1.5 million (Warsaw). Most *gminas* have between 5000 and 10 000 inhabitants.

In 1999, a major administrative reform introduced a new middle level of government – *powiat* – and scaled down the number of *voivodships* constituting the highest sub-national level of government. In 2005 there were 314 *powiats* and 16 *voivodships*. Most *powiats* have between 80 000 and 100 000 inhabitants and *voivodships* have between 1 and 5 million inhabitants. Additionally, there are 65 city-*powiats*, which are the biggest cities combining the responsibilities of *gmina* and *powiat*. Typically, city-*powiats* are analyzed together with other municipal *gminas*, and we follow this strategy.

The focus of this chapter is on the *gmina*, the lowest level of local government in Poland. *Gminas* differ from other sub-national governments not only in their areas of responsibilities and their role in social services provision but also in the way in which they are financed. Thus, the findings that follow do not necessarily apply to *powiats* and *voivodships*. *Gmina* expenditures are much bigger than expenditures at other levels of sub-national government. In recent years, *gminas* have spent as much as 8 percent of GDP, while *powiats* have spent less than 2 percent and *voivodships* less than 1 percent of GDP. In *gmina* budgets, education is the biggest single category (depending on the year, education accounts for between 35–40 percent of total expenditures and around 50 percent in rural areas). *Gminas* also spend substantial amounts of money on social welfare (10–15 percent). On the other hand, health care accounts for only a small percentage of *gmina* budgets (almost nothing after 1999) and other expenditures are related mainly to infrastructure and administration.

The Local Government Act of 8 March 1990 states that the scope of *gmina* activity extends to all public matters not reserved in legislation for other entities and defines *gminas'* own responsibilities to include spatial order, local infrastructure and public transport, water supply, sewage and waste removal, health care, education, municipal housing, social welfare, culture, public order, fire departments and others. This list of responsibilities is quite general and in some cases without practical significance. At the end of 1990 the Law on *Gmina* Revenue and Subsidization was passed and at the beginning of 1991 the Law on Local Taxes and Fees was passed. *Gminas* were guaranteed independent budgets and revenues from own taxes, shares of income taxes (PIT and CIT), subsidies and grants. Thus, at the very beginning of transition, sub-national governments were established as politically and fiscally autonomous authorities.[1]

In 1991, newly established *gminas* were given the right to collect local taxes and fees. However, these rights were quite limited and have not been significantly extended. Still, local taxes and fees are centrally regulated and more than half of a typical *gmina's* budget comes from the central budget in the form of shares in income taxes (PIT and CIT) and subventions. The shares of PIT and CIT assigned to *gminas* changed during the transition and its relative importance in sub-national budgets has varied. PIT and CIT are central taxes and *gminas* have no right to modify them. *Gminas* can alter the tax base for local taxes or increase local fees but this otherwise limited opportunity is rarely used.

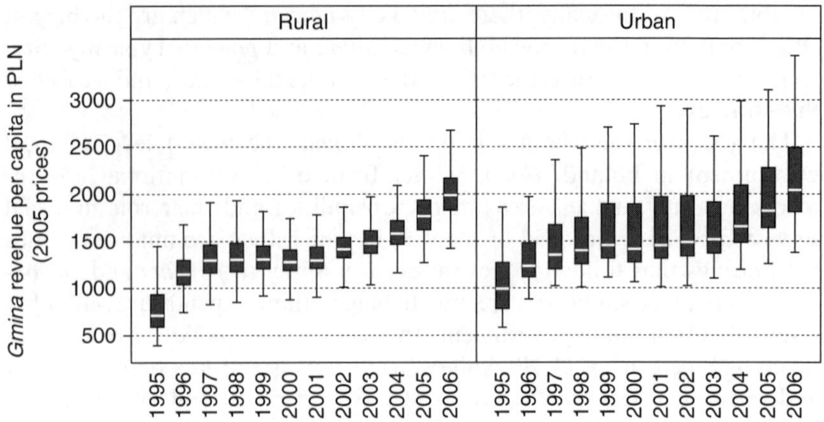

Source: Own calculations based on data from Central Statistical Office (GUS).

Figure 9.1 Rural and urban gmina *revenues per capita in 1995–2006 (in 2005 prices)*

The most important point is that *gminas* have some flexibility in allocating money from their own income, local taxes and fees, shares of PIT and CIT and funds transferred through the general subvention (from which around 90 percent is a so-called "educational subvention"). The autonomy of *gminas* in allocating this money is limited by obligatory payments such as teacher salaries, which are set centrally and which are one of the most important categories in *gmina* budgets. *Gminas* can freely allocate funds from these sources if obligatory payments are fulfilled. These payments importantly limit the potential benefits of decentralization, which could be achieved when local authorities exercise their rights to determine revenues and expenditures trying to satisfy local preferences. In general, Poland is a fairly decentralized country based on a relatively high share of local expenditures and a long list of sub-national responsibilities. But these figures can be misleading. Some very important tasks are still regulated centrally (again the best example is teacher salaries) and most sources of *gmina* revenues are also centrally set, even if they are classified in the budgetary category as "own resources". The essential fact is that such limitations could weaken the expected effects of decentralization.

Nevertheless, the decentralized system has its own dynamic distinct from the centralized one and an important question is whether local revenues and expenditures as well as accessibility and quality of services changed because of decentralized decision-making. The box plot in Figure 9.1 above shows the level and variation of *gmina* total revenue per capita for 1995–2006 (in 2005 fixed prices), separating rural and urban *gminas*.[2] It is easily seen that variation among urban *gminas* is much bigger. Obviously urban *gminas* differ from their rural counterparts in expenditure assignment. However, while the variation of rural *gmina* revenue was roughly equal during these years (with a noticeable change in 1999 and 2000 when some responsibilities were transferred to the newly introduced *powiats*), the variation among urban *gminas* increased significantly. If we expect that revenues affect expenditures and service quality, then these dramatic changes should have visible impact on services provided. One would particularly expect that an increased variation in revenues should increase variation in spending, accessibility and quality of services.

3.2 Reforms of 1999/2000

The Act on Local Government of 1990 stated that preschool and primary education is the responsibility of the *gmina* level of government. Responsibility for non-obligatory preschool education was assigned to the *gminas* to be financed from their revenues as early as 1991. *Gminas* were allowed to set the network of kindergartens in their area and to collect fees from parents. The process of decentralizing primary schools was more gradual. During the period 1991–96, some *gminas* took over responsibility for primary education and some city-*powiats* became responsible for secondary schools. In 1996, ownership rights for almost all public schools were finally transferred to the *gminas*. In 2005, 98 percent of primary school students attended schools run by *gminas* and only 0.2 percent attended schools run by the central government. Private schools also exist, but in 2005 they served less than 2 percent of students (1 percent in schools run by non-profits, 0.3 percent in schools with religious affiliation and 0.5 percent in schools run by other entities, mostly teachers or private business).[3] The gradual process of decentralization and the importance of distinct providers are presented in Figure 9.2.

Thus, it can be said that, by the end of the 1990s, local governments had taken over responsibility for preschool and primary education. However, up to 1999, *gmina*-run schools were still financed on the basis of historical costs and incentives to modify local school systems were limited. The education reform of 1999 (which took effect in the school year 1999/2000) introduced major changes. It modified the organization of the school system and introduced new ideas regarding curriculum, school assessment and teacher development. However, its strongest impact on *gmina* policies was due to the new method of calculating educational subsidies from the central government.

The need for a new method to calculate educational subsidies was

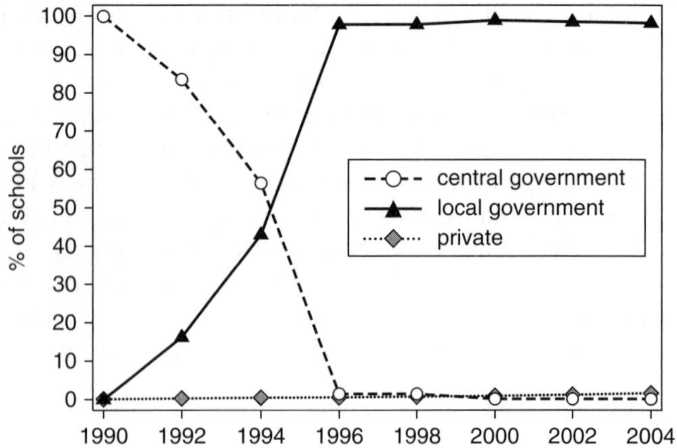

Source: Central Statistical Office (GUS).

Figure 9.2 Primary school structure

reflected in the new Law on *Gmina* Finance, which was passed in 1993 and which made the Ministry of Education responsible for developing a special algorithm (rule) that would allocate subsidies to cover *gmina*-run school operating costs. There were various political and technical difficulties in developing the algorithm.[4] Basically, it was not possible to cover historical costs and at the same time to calculate a subvention that would reflect objective measures of school costs. Thus, before 1999, the algorithm allocated funds to *gminas* according to the number of pupils, teachers and historical costs. Importantly, despite the algorithm, there were "hold harmless" clauses stating that the total subvention for any *gmina* should not be less than 100 percent or more than 110 percent of the previous year's subvention (inflation adjusted). In fact, many *gminas* received subventions based on historical costs. Per student cost differences between jurisdictions remained dramatic and unjustified. Such allocations could not be seen as "just" and at the same time did not guarantee full coverage of teacher wages. The need for some objective criteria in calculating subventions was apparent.

In 2000 a new algorithm was introduced that was truly based on a per-pupil formula. The most important change was that the "hold harmless" clause was changed to mandate that subvention per student (not the total amount of subvention, as before) should be kept within a given range. This made an important difference. Second, more funds were allocated to *powiats* that had limited "own" revenues and were made responsible for upper secondary education. The algorithm, which in a modified version is still in use today, comprises several coefficients (weights) adjusting the final allocated amount. The most important weighting regards students in rural schools, reflecting higher average costs of service provision in rural *gminas*. However, this weight coefficient changes almost every year because of political battles between representatives of urban and rural *gminas*.[5]

Obviously, the development of an algorithm based on measures of objective costs should be supported by legislation defining minimum and maximum class or school sizes, teacher/student ratios, teacher salaries, normative employment and other basic standards of service provision. Only teacher salaries are centrally fixed, but other standards have not been stated until now. This made the whole system problematic, because teacher salaries were not reflected in the algorithm. Thus, the system was seen by many as an unfunded mandate, forcing some *gminas* to cover rising wage costs with limited means of adjustment at hand.

A new financing scheme, fully introduced in 2000, had tremendous impact on many *gminas* because it was no longer based on historical costs. Thus, the year 2000 can be viewed as a major inflection point, during which decentralization was boosted and *gminas* were forced to think about schools in their areas. To make this important point clear, we claim that even though all *gminas* were finally assigned responsibility for schools in 1996, decentralization produced the incentives to manage their property more efficiently only after 2000, when per-pupil funding was introduced. Before that time, most local governments were not incentivized to change anything because the central government fully covered the cost of elementary education. Thus, there was no financial incentive to reorganize local schools.

The process of decentralization of education finance during the whole transition period is shown in Figure 9.3. In 1990, all funds were transferred from the central budget directly to schools, but only a small percentage of total expenditures has been allocated this way recently. Since the late 1990s, about two-thirds of total expenditures were transferred to sub-national budgets through the general subvention and about 30 percent is financed directly from sub-national governments' own revenues. Notice that while in 1996 almost all schools were already assigned to *gminas*, some funds were still transferred without using the subvention. After 1999, almost all funds for public education were transferred to *gminas* through the general subvention (Figure 9.3).

Another important change introduced by the 1999 education reform was the establishment of the "*gimnazjum*", that is, the lower secondary school run by *gminas*. In 1999, the first student cohort went to the first grade of *gimnazjum* instead of the seventh grade of primary school. Since

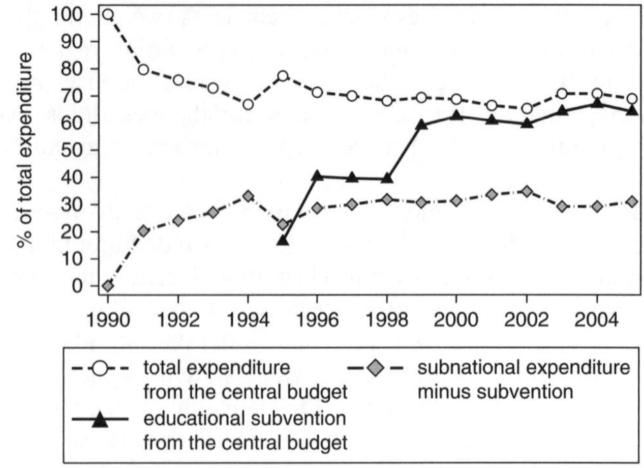

Source: Central Statistical Office (GUS). Subnational governments: 1990–1998 *gminas*; after 1999 *gminas* and *powiats*.

Figure 9.3 Financing of primary education

2001, all students financed by *gminas* were in six-year primary schools or three-year *gimnazjums*, while students financed by *powiats* were in three- or four-year upper secondary schools. The idea was that lower secondary schools would guarantee a better quality of education because *gimnazjums* were less numerous, bigger and better equipped than primary schools. The common belief was that small primary schools in rural areas are of poor quality and that *gimnazjums* create the opportunity to collect students from a wider area to improve efficiency by lowering overall costs and enabling investments to boost the quality of teaching. Importantly, the introduction of *gimnazjums* forced local governments to rethink their education policies because new capital investments and strategic choices were needed.

By the end of the 1990s responsibilities for kindergartens, primary and lower secondary schools had finally been transferred to the *gminas*. The central government, however, still regulated teachers' professional requirements, contracts and salaries, supervised schools, defined curricula and authorized textbooks. Local governments' (also *powiats* in the case of secondary education) own schools, in principle, are responsible for the manner in which educational services are provided. In practice, their rights are importantly limited by law, by decisions of the Ministry of Education, and by the high degree of autonomy afforded to school principals. Local governments have to act according to central rules, which in some specific cases will affect their spending decisions differently from others. However, at the margin *gminas* are responsible for school expenditures and organization.

The most important point, though, is that the level of *gmina* autonomy is different in the case of preschool, primary and lower secondary education. We will use this fact to assess the potential outcomes of decentralization in situations where there is no possibility to observe different "intensities" of decentralization at one level of education. More precisely, in the case of non-obligatory preschool education, *gminas* have the highest degree of autonomy and can even shift a substantial part of costs to households. In the case of primary education, *gminas* are bound not only by the central authorities but also by historical practice, or in other words, path-dependence. In the case of lower secondary education, the relevant rules are similar to those in primary schools, but *gminas* were solely responsible for establishing these schools since 1999/2000. Thus, one could expect that their organization will more visibly reflect local choices than in the case of primary schools. Schooling is also obligatory and *gminas* are not allowed to collect any fees from parents (at least in public institutions, which constitute the overwhelming majority of all schools). This is not the case at the kindergarten level.

To sum up, we have three levels of education at which decentralization plays a different role. Preschool education is the most decentralized, lower secondary education is moderately decentralized and primary education is an example of decentralization heavily limited by centrally set rules and path-dependence. We want to explore this variability in the "intensity" of decentralization to see how it correlates with private and public expenditures, service accessibility and teaching quality.

4 PRESCHOOL EDUCATION: ACCESSIBILITY AND COSTS

4.1 *Gmina* Expenditure on Preschool Education

Data from before 1995 is not available, as already mentioned. At the preschool level, expenditure data for 2004–06 is unreliable because of changes in the nomenclature. Nevertheless, we were able to calculate *gmina* expenditures for the period 1995–2003, which shows trends during the period of educational reform. There are two indicators that could be of interest here. One measures the expenditure per child in preschool institutions, showing differences in the cost of preschool services. This indicator compares the efficiency of service provision between *gminas*. Another indicator

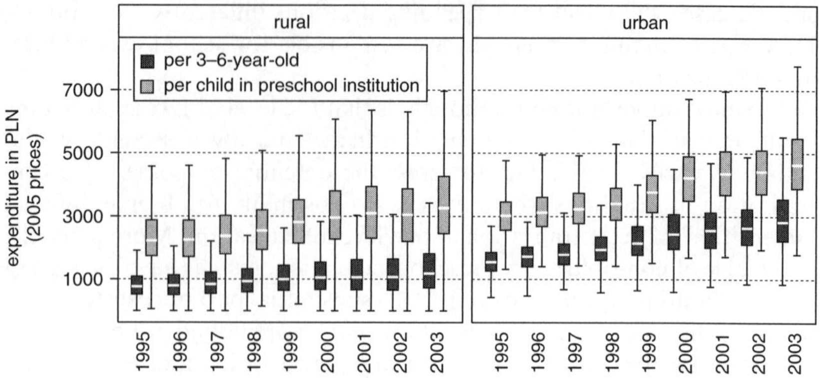

Source: BDR, Central Statistical Office (GUS).

Figure 9.4 Preschool expenditures per child for all three- to six- year-old children, 1995–2003 (2005 prices)

measures expenditures on all children of preschool age (three to six years of age in Poland) for each *gmina*. Thus, it compares the level of subsidy for preschool education between *gminas*. *Gmina*-level distribution of both indicators is pictured in Figure 9.4, separately for rural and urban *gminas*.[6] Preschool expenditures were calculated as the sum of expenditures on kindergartens and preparatory "zero classes" in schools.

From Figure 9.4, it is clear that *gminas* differ in the cost of preschool services as well as in the level of support for preschool education calculated as spending per child of relevant age. Expenditures per capita measured through both indicators steadily increased over the investigated period, but what is more interesting is that variations in these indicators also increased. The coefficient of variation of expenditures for three- to six-year-olds was 0.54 in 1995, compared with 0.59 in 2003.[7] However, variation of expenditures increased only in rural areas, while in urban *gminas* we observed an even greater homogeneity of preschool costs in 2003 than in 1998. These differences are more dramatic when one considers spending on kindergartens and three- to five- year-olds where *gminas* are almost completely free to establish networks of institutions and parental fees. In this case, the coefficient of variation was almost the same in 1995 and 2003 in urban *gminas* but increased from 1.02 to 1.21 in rural areas.

This simple analysis of trends in preschool spending suggests that rural *gminas* exercised their rights given by decentralization to limit their support for preschool services. In this way, decentralization may have increased educational inequalities because these services are needed most

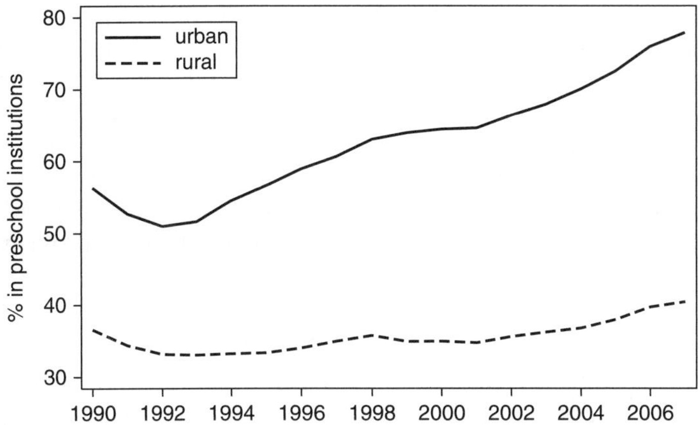

Source: Central Statistical Office (GUS).

Figure 9.5 Participation of three- to six- year-olds in preschool education

in poorer *gminas* that, because of budgetary pressures, frequently decided to close kindergartens (see below) or lower their preschool expenditures.

A simple regression analysis of preschool expenditures shows that these are significantly correlated with *gmina* revenues. This correlation was stronger in 2003 than in 1998 (see Jakubowski and Topińska, 2007, for details). All of this suggests that decentralization has increased inequalities in preschool education, and that the reforms of 1999/2000 indirectly affected the capacity of poorer *gminas* to support kindergartens.[8]

4.2 Overall Trends in Accessibility

We turn to the analysis of aggregate data on the accessibility of preschool facilities during the transition. Using data from the Central Statistical Office (GUS), one can calculate separate indicators for rural and urban areas, which is of importance because these two types differ in many characteristics, mainly in the objective costs of provision of educational services. In Figure 9.5, the participation of three- to six-year-olds is described. We see that at the beginning of transition when preschool education was decentralized, participation rates decreased dramatically. This was the response of local governments that had to deal with an unfunded mandate and had no funds to cover preschool education costs. After a few years, participation rates started to increase in municipal *gminas*. In rural *gminas*, however, they remained low until recent years, despite a population decline.

The observed increase in recent years was due to central government regulation in 2004, which made so-called "zero-classes" obligatory (these are preparatory classes for six-year-olds). Thus, it has nothing to do with local government policies. The participation level among three- to five-year-olds is still dramatically low, and much lower in rural *gminas* than in urban areas (16–18 percent compared with 36–38 percent). Thus, most *gminas* did not seize the opportunity created by population decline to maintain existing networks of preschool facilities and to improve participation levels. The data shows that in many *gminas* the opposite happened. The percentage of *gminas* with kindergartens decreased from 82 percent to 78 percent (73 percent to 66 percent in the case of rural *gminas*). In effect, between-*gmina* variation in preschool accessibility slightly increased, with some dramatic regional differences.[9]

The common view among experts is that preschool education is one of the most effective tools to increase equity in educational systems or, in other words, to enhance educational opportunities for children from disadvantaged or poor families (see Zahorska, 2003, for discussion in the context of Poland). We should emphasize that decentralization had no positive impact in this regard. While the situation is not worsening, the level of participation in preschool education in Poland is one of the lowest among OECD countries (see OECD, 2008, Table C2.1). Increasing the financial burden on *gminas* and making kindergarten expenditures non-obligatory forced many *gminas* to completely withdraw from providing education for three- to six-year-olds. Partial and inadequate central government policies have not improved the situation.[10]

4.3 Household Expenditure on Preschool Education

HBS data allow for the measurement of the cost per one child enrolled in kindergarten using a proxy, since there is no direct information on actual enrollment in the questionnaire. This was done as follows. Households with children at the preschool age of three to six and with positive expenditure on preschool education have been selected. For this subsample, the monthly average per child (age three to six) was computed for 1998–2003. The results are presented in Figures 9.6–9.7 below, separately for rural and urban households, and for households in different equivalent consumption quintiles.

According to the HBS data, a child in kindergarten required about PLN90 per month of private payment in 1998. This amount increased steadily over time, reaching PLN108 in 2003 (in constant prices). Private expenditure always has been much higher in urban than in rural areas.

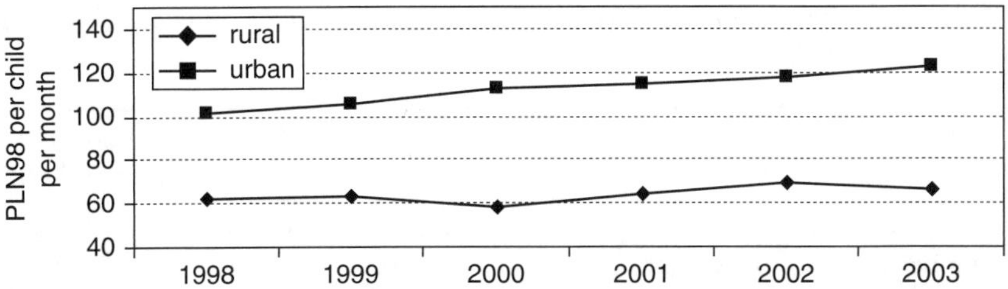

Figure 9.6 *Household expenditure per child at kindergarten, 1988–2003, by place of residence*

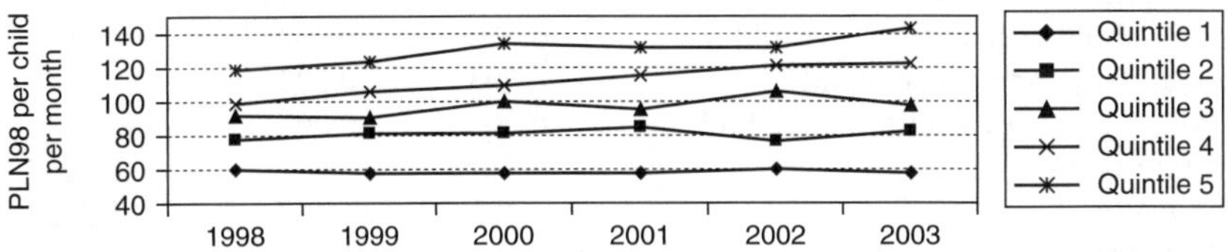

Figure 9.7 *Household expenditure per child at kindergarten, 1988–2003, by hh quintile*

This discrepancy has become more pronounced over time. In 1998, it was equal to PLN40, whereas in 2003 it was close to PLN60 (in constant prices). The most visible finding from the analysis of preschool costs by household quintiles is that the gap between quintiles increased. This is due to an increase in spending by rich households, while spending among the poorest households remained constant. At the same time, there is no visible impact from the 1999/2000 reforms on the household cost of education. Thus, while analysis of the trend for this period reveals an increasing gap in household preschool expenditures, it is not clear whether the peak of decentralization in 1999/2000 had any impact on this.

4.4 *Gmina* Expenditures and Preschool Enrollment: 1998 and 2003 Compared

By using household budget data we were able to study the impact of decentralization on access to education through enrollment indices. HBS, combined with BDR data, enables the application of econometric methods such as probit analysis. Probit functions help establish determinants of the probability of some event. In this research, this analysis has been applied to measuring the impact of *gmina* preschool expenditures on the preschool

Table 9.1 Results of probit regressions for preschool enrollment, 1998 and 2003

Probit (enroll = 1)	1998	2003	Pooled 1998 + 2003
Place of residence: urban	0.210	0.079**	0.390
Number of three- to six- year-old household members	0.210	0.151	0.154
Number of non-working household members	−0.360	−0.209	−0.301
Education: higher	0.304	0.249	0.375
Education: secondary	0.245	0.099**	0.220
Household expenditure per child	0.000	0.000	0.001
Gmina expenditure per child	0.003	0.003	
Poor * *gmina* expenditure per child	−0.003	−0.002	
Dummy for 2003			0.126
Constant	−1.383	−1.507	−1.302
Number of observations	4616	3809	8425
LR chi2(df)	696.22	645.42	1153.8
Pseudo-R^2	0.146	0.156	0.129
Log likelihood	−2036.02	−1752.03	−3891.84

Note: All non-tagged coefficients are significant at less than 1% level. Coefficients marked with ** are not significant at 10% level. Sample restricted to households with children aged three to six years.

Sources: HBS and BDR, own computation.

enrollment rate (more precisely – on the probability of sending a child to kindergarten), both before and after the 1999/2000 decentralization peak. Accordingly, probit functions for preschool enrollment with a special set of regressors were estimated for the years 1998 and 2003 and then for the pooled dataset 1998 and 2003.

We wish to see whether expenditures affect enrollment decisions and if the effect was similar in 1998 and 2003. Additionally, if expenditures affect enrollment, we examine if this is the same for rich and poor households. Probits were run on the HBS sub-sample restricted to households with children at the "preschool age" (age three to six). The dependent variable was equal to 1 for households spending on kindergarten, and equal to 0 for households with zero expenditure.

Given the data available and general knowledge regarding family behavior, the following variables have been chosen as "regular" determinants of the probability of having a child in kindergarten: place of residence (dummy, urban = 1, rural = 0), the number of children aged three to six, the number of adults 18+ who can take care of a child (that is, non-working, except agriculture, and not at regular school), education of the household head (dummies for higher and secondary) and per capita household expenditure indicating the standard of living. *Gmina* expenditure has been measured as average spending on kindergarten per child aged three to six in 73 territorial units (data from BDR). The poverty variable (poor) was given a value of 1 for every household considered to be poor, that is, whenever its equivalent expenditure has been lower than 60 percent of the 1998 median (kept constant in real terms).[11] For the pooled regressions, the year indicator has been set equal to 1 in 2003, 0 in 1998. All expenditure variables have been expressed per month, in constant 1998 prices (CPI deflator has been used) whenever the probit regression was run on a pooled dataset. These were expressed in current prices, and we use household weights provided by GUS. The results are displayed in Table 9.1.[12]

The results are reasonable from both a statistical and a methodological point of view. The estimators of all parameters are significant (with the exception of place of residence and secondary education in 2003) and all carry a proper sign. The only statistical deficiency is the level of pseudo-R^2, indicating that goodness of fit is low. This is not surprising, given the dataset (individual households), the type of function (probit) and the way in which regressors have been introduced (many dummies).

For the purpose of this study, the most important estimation is for the *gmina* expenditure coefficient: for the *gmina* expenditure variable alone as well as combined with poverty indicators. First, notice that this coefficient is positive in both years under investigation for *gmina* expenditure variable but it is negative for this variable combined with the poverty indicator. This implies that the higher the spending of *gminas*, the higher the preschool enrollment rate, or strictly speaking, the higher the probability of sending a child to kindergarten. However, this impact was much weaker or even negligible for poor households (the sum of the coefficient discussed is lower, close to zero).

This finding seems important from the point of view of the effectiveness of local policies in the education sector. The coefficients of *gmina* expenditure are almost identical for the 2003 and 1998 probits. Additional estimation based on the pooled 1998 and 2003 data with interaction terms confirmed through statistical tests that no visible change occurred (these results are available in Jakubowski and Topińska, 2007). However, the dummy for 2003 was positive and significant (the third column in the table) proving the overall increase in probability of enrollment.

5 PRIMARY AND LOWER-SECONDARY EDUCATION

5.1 Trends of *Gmina* Expenditures: Level and Variation

Figure 9.8 describes the change in average expenditure per student and its variation among *gminas* in 1996–2006. This is a period for which *gmina*-level fiscal and school data are available in the Central Statistical Office (GUS) Regional Data Bank. All expenditures were deflated using the HICP Eurostat index with 2005 as a reference year. In Figure 9.8, we show expenditures per primary school student and separately per lower secondary school student. For transitional years 1999 and 2000, expenditures were calculated as the sum of primary and lower secondary school expenditures because it is not possible to separate them due to changes in fiscal nomenclature in the period of lower secondary school establishment.

It is clear from the box plots below that average *gmina* expenditure (in constant prices) was much higher in 2006 than in 1996.[13] Note, however, that as a percentage of GDP, those expenditures were almost the same in 2006 as in 1996. Thus, the increase in costs was in line with the overall development of the Polish economy. What is more interesting is the substantial variation in *gmina* expenditures. It is also worth observing the lower average cost in lower secondary schools. This can be explained in two ways. First, those schools are bigger and could benefit from economies of scale, which are easier to achieve in the case of secondary education. Second, and more importantly, those schools were organized from the beginning

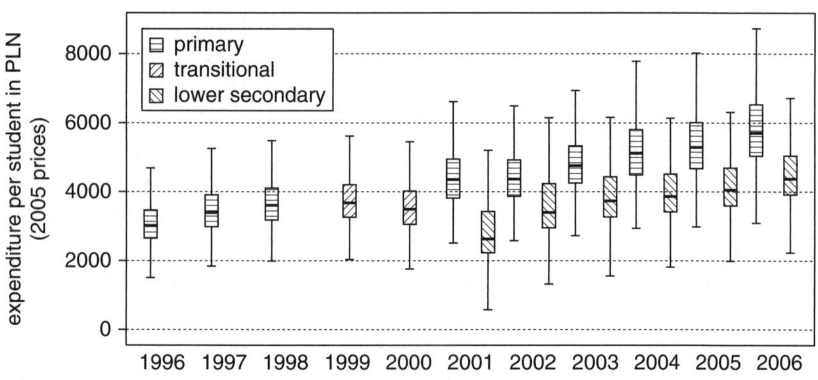

Source: Own calculations based on the Regional Data Bank.

Figure 9.8 Variation of gmina *expenditures on primary and lower secondary schools (expenditures per student in 2005 prices)*

by local governments, which were not bound by historical practice. Thus, expenditures on lower secondary schools depend more heavily on local government choices and therefore are the best source to analyze the impact of decentralized decision-making. Thus, in the next section, we will see whether variation in lower secondary schools affects teaching quality.

Compared with the cost of a child in kindergarten, the private cost of a student at primary or lower secondary school is low. For example, in 1998, households spent on average about PLN6 per month per student enrolled (less than $3). Certainly, this was expected, since in general public education at this level is free. Richer households spend slightly more (up to PLN20 in the biggest cities) but these numbers are still negligible.

In the case of primary education, an important question is whether differences in expenditures are caused by objective factors or just reflect *gmina* preferences. In practice, it is rarely possible to separate these two factors, especially using solely fiscal or school system data. We used regression analysis to show that *gmina* spending per student is affected by class size as well as by *gmina* revenues per capita. Class size depends on objective factors (for example, population density), but depends also on local government decisions (for example, via internal organization of schools or their local network). Nevertheless, it was demonstrated that *gmina* revenues are positively correlated with expenditures. This can be interpreted positively, because one of the goals of decentralization is to utilize local resources, and negatively, because it shows that decentralization increases differences in service quality. However, it is not possible to conclude which factor is more important here (see Jakubowski and Topińska, 2007, for details).

5.2 Distributional Impact of *Gmina* Expenditure – the Household Perspective

A more interesting question is whether the introduction of cost-adjusted per pupil funding in Poland had an equalizing impact on household budgets. We answer this question through an analysis of imputed income.[14] Imputation has been conducted on the basis of HBS and BDR data. For each household, the number of students of a primary school recorded in HBSs was multiplied by the *gmina's* expenditure per student, evaluated as an average for 73 territorial units (BDR). In this way the imputed transfer (or subsidy) was computed for 1998 and 2003. The analysis of quintile distributions as well as concentration coefficients may show what has changed after the implementation of per-pupil funding in 1999/2000.

This has been supplemented by two benchmark simulations of the imputed education subsidy in each year. The first one assumed equal

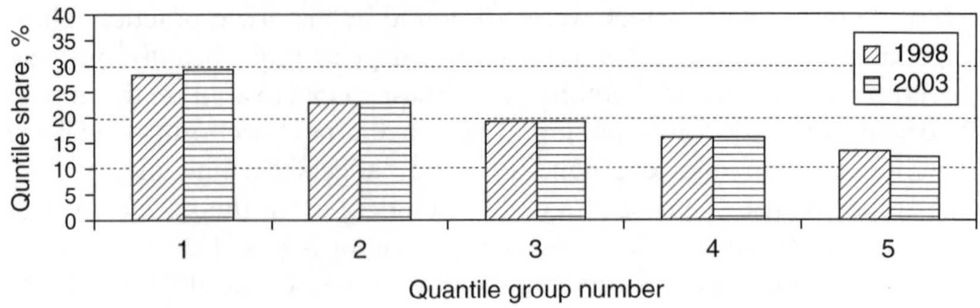

Figure 9.9 Imputed public transfers of TU73 on primary education: quintile shares

spending on primary education throughout the whole country, while the second assumed equal spending between all rural and all urban *gminas*, respectively. The argument for such simulations relies on the assumption that centralization may be associated with more equal distribution of funds in the whole country (although this is not necessarily the case). Therefore, it might be interesting to observe the extent of the actual distribution from such a benchmark. An additional simulation was also run for 2003. This consisted of the 1998 distribution of *gmina* expenditure on primary schools for imputing household income in 2003. This has been done in order to see what would happen if the reform had been postponed and 1998 *gmina* spending had remained unchanged. Selected results are displayed in Figures 9.9, 9.10, 9.11, 9.12 and Table 9.2. Additional results can be found in Jakubowski and Topińska (2007).

As Figure 9.9 shows, the primary education subsidy goes mainly to the poorest households. They receive almost 30 percent of the total transfer, while the richest households receive over 10 percent. This pattern has not changed between 1998 and 2003. In 1998, the poorest 20 percent of the population received 28.3 percent of the transfer while in 2003 this share amounted to 29.5 percent. In the same period, the share of the transfer going to the richest 20 percent decreased from 13.6 percent to 12.1 percent. This slight change is visible through analysis of the quintile shares and may be confirmed with the use of the concentration coefficients, shown in Table 9.2.

All concentration coefficients computed for 1998 and for 2003 have a negative sign indicating that *gmina* subsidy on primary education diminishes inequality among households, both in relative and in absolute terms. However, the coefficients for the two years under investigation are close to each other. This shows that there were no major changes between 1998 and 2003 regarding the impact of public spending on income (or total expenditure) inequality. The concentration coefficient of the imputed

Table 9.2 Concentration coefficient of imputed primary education transfer

Distribution of *Gmina* Expenditure on Primary Education	1998	2003
Actual level of spending (different for TU73)	−0.076	−0.079
Unique level of public spending for the whole country	−0.072	−0.076
Two levels of spending: average for rural and average for urban	−0.078	−0.080
1998 distribution imputed for 2003	–	−0.080
Memo: Gini coefficient for household total expenditure per child	0.335	0.360

Note: Concentration coefficients are computed with respect to the total household expenditure (without education transfer).

Source: HBS + BDR, own computation.

transfer for the actual level of *gmina* spending was equal to −0.076 in 1998 but was somehow higher in absolute terms in 2003, reaching −0.079. This means that a small positive change regarding equity may have occurred.

It is quite possible that this has been the effect of the 1999 reforms. This change, however, was really very small – indicating that the pattern of distribution of primary education subsidy was rather stable.

Comparing these results with the simulated public expenditure distributions selected as benchmarks, one can see that equal spending throughout the whole country (that is, equal for all 73 TUs) would be less favorable for poor households. This may be read from the concentration coefficients, which are lower in absolute terms for the benchmark case.

On the other hand, the two-level distribution of public spending on primary education, higher in rural than in urban areas, would be more favorable to the poor. Such a distribution of funds would equalize household income (total expenditure) more than any other distribution discussed.

The findings presented above should be treated with caution. Concentration coefficients are in fact very similar for all versions of public spending considered. Almost no difference is seen in quintile shares, no matter which version of public spending is analyzed.

One more indicator of the impact of *gmina* expenditure on equity is worth noticing, namely the ratio of imputed subsidy to actual household expenditure. This ratio is displayed in Figures 9.10 to 9.12 below (detailed data are available in Jakubowski and Topińska, 2007). On average, households received as much as 6 percent of their expenditure in the

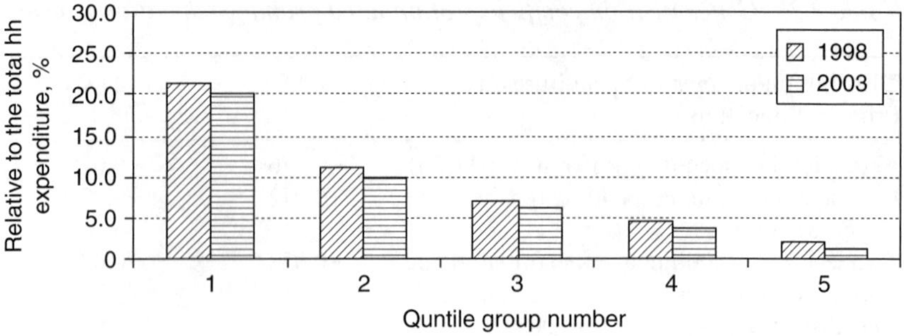

Figure 9.10 *Relative imputed transfer of TU73 on primary education: all households*

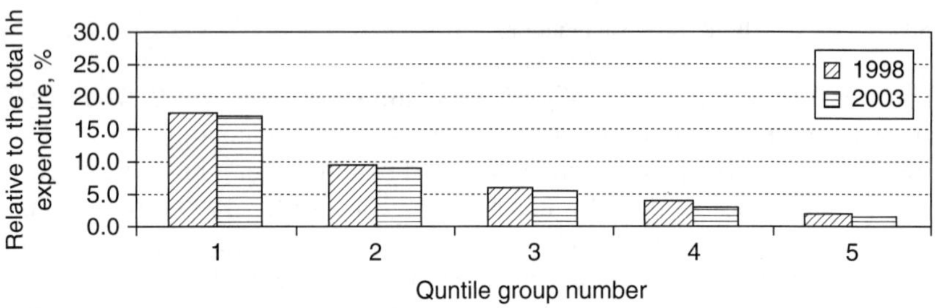

Figure 9.11 *Relative imputed transfer of TU73 on primary education urban households*

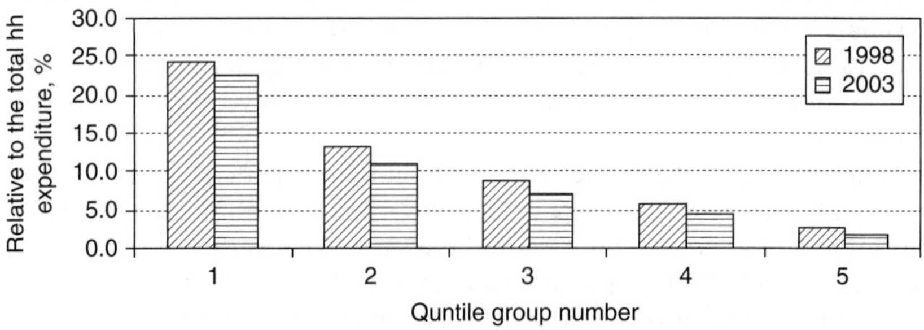

Figure 9.12 *Relative imputed transfer of TU73 on primary education rural households*

form of imputed primary education transfers in 1998. In 2003, this ratio decreased to 5 percent. This decrease affected all quintile groups, in rural and in urban areas. It seems, however, that it was more pronounced in rural areas. On average, *gmina* transfers relative to household expenditure declined from 9.8 percent to 7.9 percent in rural areas and from 4.4 percent to 3.7 percent in urban areas. This may be cautiously interpreted as an effect of the 1999/2000 reform.

In general, the poor benefit more than the rich from the public fund on primary education. This is a result of the demographic composition of households: the share of primary school students is usually higher in poor households. Both in 1998 and in 2003, households of the first quintile group received implicitly more than 20 percent of additional income, while the most affluent households of the fifth quintile received less than 5 percent (see Jakubowski and Topińska, 2007, Annex tables ATEQ2). These coefficients slightly decreased over the period 1998–2003, affecting all groups of the population. Changes were similar in rural and in urban areas. In 1998, the rural poor received 24 percent of their initial expenditure in the form of public transfers. In 2003, this ratio was equal to 23 percent. In urban areas, primary education subsidy was equal to 17.5 percent of household expenditure in the first quintile, and it went down by 0.5 percent.

The main findings of the imputed income analysis may be summarized as follows. *Gmina* expenditure on primary education has a visible equalizing impact on household income (total expenditure). This may be seen through the concentration coefficients, quintile shares of public spending as well as through the ratio of imputed subsidy to actual household expenditure. The reforms of 1999/2000 had a very small effect on household inequality. It seems that this effect has been positive, meaning that the equalizing effect of public spending slightly increased. One of the drivers of this effect is the stable pattern of spending on primary education. The analysis has also shown some methodological deficiencies connected with the (enforced) use of the average *gmina* spending for 73 territorial units. Certainly, there is a need for the use of special surveys in order to study the distributional impact of education expenditure.

5.3 Decentralized Spending and Lower Secondary School Teaching Quality[15]

Decentralization is rarely assessed through empirical research relating to service quality. Problems with quality measurement of public services have made any attempts to assess the effectiveness of public expenditures problematic. In the case of education, the typical research uses data on accessibility, which is the only measure usually available in developing countries, or on student test scores. However, student test scores used as they are in the regression framework could be misleading when one treats them as a measure of teaching quality. Test outcomes depend more on family characteristics than on school or local government efforts. Additionally, if not nationally conducted, such test scores are often unhelpful in an analysis of decentralization. Thus, it is often the case that empirical analyses of decentralization do not consider quality or provide unreliable and biased estimates, because of the hidden correlations between family and local government characteristics and test scores.

This section shows how one can use test scores in a more reliable way, namely, by incorporating value-added models and nationwide examination results. Value-added models explain achievement growth – not achievement level – because they control for student intake scores. They are able to estimate the effects of interest on teaching quality during the period of education at a particular school level. The endogeneity problem is not completely solved this way, because earlier inputs and other hidden characteristics are not fully reflected in intake scores, but without doubt these models offer a much more reliable way to assess policy effects, including the impact of decentralization on teaching quality.[16] Here they were employed to assess the effects of local government educational spending on lower secondary schools teaching quality after several years of decentralization in Poland.

The research explores fiscal and national examination data for the whole population and for a three-year period. This limits the impact of regional or local effects on final results. The main empirical question was whether decentralized educational expenditures affect achievement growth, which is assumed to depend in a systematic way solely on teaching quality.[17] Additionally, we tested whether expenditures affect students similarly despite their intake score level. While these kinds of questions have often been analyzed in the economics of education literature and there is no consensus on the effects of different types of inputs (see Hanushek, 2003 and Krueger, 2003, for opposite views), the focus of this research was not on the general impact of expenditures but on the impact of *decentralized* expenditures on teaching quality. In other words, the research answers the question as to whether decentralized expenditure affects teaching quality if at the margin local governments decide how much to spend on schools each year. If there is no effect then one could claim that fiscal decentralization is not beneficial in this regard.

The value-added model used in the research employs random slopes and random intercepts at the *gmina* level and is given by the equation below:

$$y_{isg} = \pi_0 + \mathbf{X_{isg}\beta_k} + \eta_0 w_g + (\pi_1 + \eta_1 w_g + \varsigma_g)\widetilde{spr}_{isg} + \pi_2 spr^2_{isg} + u_g + \varepsilon_{isg} \quad (9.1)$$

where y_{isg}, is the score of *i*-th student on the exam at the end of primary or lower secondary school *s* in *gmina g*, X_{isg} is a vector of individual, school and *gmina* characteristics, w_g is the expenditure per lower secondary school student in *gmina g*, $\widetilde{spr}_{isg}$ is the intake score of *i*-th student, namely the score obtained at the end of primary school. Therefore, we control for intake scores, which means that the remaining variation in final scores could be attributed to what has happened during the time of lower secondary education. Intake score was centered around the "grand mean" (population mean) or around the 10th percentile of *gmina* intake score distribution. Intake score centering is necessary if one wants to obtain interpretable results. Centering around the average for the whole population, the so-called "grand mean", does not change the model but makes the results directly interpretable: the effects of interest are calculated for the average student in the population. Centering around the group's 10th percentile creates a distinct model that measures the effects for relatively low achieving students in each *gmina* (see Raudenbush and Bryk, 2002; de Leeuw, 2005). A quadratic term of intake scores was added to fit the nonlinear relationship between intake and final scores caused by discrepancies in measurement and score distribution (see Jakubowski, 2006). Individual characteristics included in the model were limited to gender, presence of dyslexia (two dummies for primary and secondary school), and a dummy for students who passed the exam with maximum points without writing it because they succeeded in the national competition in science or language. Inclusion of these variables decreased the unexplained variation but have no impact on the estimates of interest at the *gmina* and school level.

This model allows intake score slopes and intercepts to vary between *gminas*. In equation (9.1) ε_{isg} is the individual error term, u_g is the *gmina* random effect. As usual it is assumed that $\varepsilon_{isg} \sim N(0, \sigma^2_\varepsilon)$ and $u_g \sim N(0, \sigma^2_u)$. To make estimation more feasible, we allowed only *gmina* intercepts to vary and did not seek to estimate school effects. However, we checked that this did not affect final conclusions. The parameter of interest is η_0, which measures the effect of expenditures on student achievement growth in lower secondary education. The positive estimate of this parameter means that higher expenditures positively affect teaching quality. Expenditures per capita were calculated in thousands of polish zloty (comparing mean expenditure of around PLN4000).

Regarding intake score slopes, π_1 is an average slope, ς_g is a random effect allowing slope variation between *gminas*, and η_1 reflects the effect of expenditures on intake score slope. A negative sign for η_1 is expected if the expenditures have an "equalizing" effect on learning outcomes. A positive sign would support the conclusion that the higher the expenditure the steeper the intake scores line, which means that expenditures benefit high achievers more. Note that the equalizing effect could be accompanied by overall higher growth or just the opposite. Thus, we do not make any assumptions about the correlation between intercepts and slopes, but make an attempt to estimate it from the data. Thus, we assumed that $\text{cov}(u_g, \varsigma_g) \neq 0$ and, as usual, that random slopes are normally distributed.

All regressions were estimated using the restricted maximum likelihood, which is a default option in the procedure in the STATA statistical package (see Rabe-Hesketh and Skrondal, 2005). The direct advantage of the random effects model is that standard errors were calculated correctly taking into consideration the clustering of students at the *gmina* and school levels. While a three-year period is too short to run a fixed effects panel data model, the random effects model benefits from the within and between variation to estimate the effect of interest. However, in this case the researcher has to include all important fixed covariates correlated with the variable of interest and an outcome. In our case, we had to control for differences in *gmina* funding and the objective costs of education. We did this by including "type of *gmina*" dummies, which are also included in the educational subvention algorithm. In this way, we almost fully control for systematic discrepancies in the level of central funding. Additionally, we included the number of students in a school or *gmina*, which strongly correlates with objective costs of providing educational services (see Swianiewicz et al., 2005). It should be noted, however, that *gminas* can modify school networks, close schools and define class sizes, although their rights in this regard are limited. The point is that the effect of the number of students should be treated with great caution because it reflects the mixture of *gmina* policy effect, objective costs and pure class size effects, which are also non-negligible (see Jakubowski and Sakowski, 2006). Thus, in our case it serves as an additional control variable rather than exogenous factor directly affecting the learning environment. *Gmina* revenues per citizen were also added to the regression to additionally control for wealth effects.

The results are presented in Table 9.3 Columns (1) and (3) contain two models with intake scores centered around the grand mean. Columns (2) and (4) contain similar models but with intake scores centered around the 10th percentile. For clarity, we omitted from the table several control variables used in estimation, namely, all individual characteristics except intake scores, and several dummies controlling for type of school, area and region (see Jakubowski, 2008, for details). We added school average

Table 9.3 Value-added random slope lower secondary school regression results

Dependent Variable: Total Score from the Lower Secondary School Exam				
	(1)	(2)	(3)	(4)
Intake score	1.254***	1.240***	1.239***	1.213***
Grand mean centered: columns (1) (3)	(0.010)	(0.010)	(0.010)	(0.010)
10th percentile centered: columns (2) (4)				
Intake score * year = 2006	−0.009**	−0.009**	−0.009**	−0.009**
	(0.003)	(0.003)	(0.003)	(0.003)
Intake score * year = 2007	0.050***	0.049***	0.049***	0.047***
	(0.003)	(0.003)	(0.003)	(0.003)
Intake score^2	0.013***	0.013***	0.013***	0.013***
	(0.000)	(0.000)	(0.000)	(0.000)
Lower secondary school expenditure per student	**−0.074***** (0.020)	**−0.055**** (0.024)	**−0.097***** (0.020)	**−0.105***** (0.024)
Expenditures * intake score	**−0.005****	**−0.001**	**−0.004***	**−0.002***
	(0.002)	(0.002)	(0.002)	(0.002)
Natural log of school size			0.279***	0.279***
			(0.022)	(0.022)
Natural log of a number of students in *gmina*			−0.207*** (0.054)	−0.172*** (0.055)
Natural log of *gmina* income per citizen			1.589*** (0.220)	1.648*** (0.221)
IQR of intake scores			−0.128***	−0.128***
			(0.006)	(0.006)
School's average intake score			0.179***	0.180***
			(0.006)	(0.006)
Area type, school type, region and year dummies	Yes	Yes	Yes	Yes
Constant	14.553***	4.372**	−0.201	−0.215
	(0.258)	(1.654)	(1.67)	(1.67)
Random part estimates				
SD of intake score slope (*gmina* level)	0.11	0.10	0.11	0.11
SD of *gmina* intercept	2.38	2.32	2.41	2.36
COV(slope, intercept)	0.31	−0.17	0.30	−0.18
SD of residuals	10.47	10.47	10.46	10.46
Log restricted-likelihood	−4992993	−4993013	−4991941	−4991958
N of students	1324076	1324076	1324076	1324076

Note: Some regressors were not presented in the table (see text for details). ***, **, * stand for significance at the 1%, 5% and 10% level, respectively.

intake scores and the interquartile range (IQR) of intake scores to regressors in columns (3) and (4) to take into account compositional effects (Goldstein et al., 2000).

Observe that the estimated impact of expenditures on random *gmina* intercepts is negative, despite the way intake scores were centered. This means that expenditures negatively affect average students and low achievers. However, these effects are non-distinguishable from zero from a practical point of view. The estimate of around −0.10 means that a change in expenditure by PLN1000 decreases achievement growth by 0.1 exam points. One can compare this with average expenditure of around PLN4000 and standard deviation of *gmina* intercepts around 2.4 points to see that these effects are very small.

We also examine the impact of expenditures on intake score slopes, namely, in the coefficient of interaction term of expenditures and centered intake score. Our estimates of this effect were consistently negative, which means that increasing expenditures lowers the intake score slope. This can be interpreted as an equalizational effect of expenditures, because it suggests that in lower secondary schools on which local governments spend more, low achievers progress more. However, these effects are very weak and from the practical point of view are negligible. This seems to be true despite the intake level of students. The large sample and use of proper statistical methods make these findings precise and robust. Thus, the findings can be summarized as showing no effect of *gmina* expenditure on teaching quality.

6 SUMMARY AND CONCLUSIONS

This chapter provides evidence about the impact of decentralization on the education sector in Poland. The focus was on the *gmina*, the lowest level of local government, which is responsible for preschool, primary and lower secondary education. The progress of decentralization after the beginning of transition in 1990 was discussed using simple statistics. Basic facts about decentralization and educational reforms were presented.

While pre-decentralization data is not available, we analyzed trends in expenditures and accessibility at the *gmina* level over a long period to assess the dynamics of the decentralized system. Furthermore, we used fiscal data to calculate indicators at the *gmina* level and relate these to the situation of households. However, the main problem is that it is not possible to directly merge data on fiscal, school system and household variables because of confidentiality issues. Simply, no indicator of local government exists in household survey datasets available to the public. Thus, the method of merging data at the aggregated level of 73 artificial territorial units was implemented in empirical analyses. Several research examples show how such data could be analyzed, making clear the benefits and boundaries of this approach. Among the benefits, we emphasize the possibility of analyzing decentralization impacts on household situations. The most important drawback, however, is that the analysis of 73 units limits the power of statistical inference. Nevertheless, several policy-relevant conclusions can be made based on the research.

Regarding preschool education, it was found that decentralization decreased accessibility in rural areas. Poorer, mostly rural, local governments decided to close kindergartens and lower their spending while richer, mostly urban, *gminas* were able to increase participation rates during a period of population decline. From the analysis of household budgets, we learnt that financial involvement in the provision of preschool education increased only in the case of urban and richer households. Preschool expenditure for poor and rural households remained at the same level. Thus, in the case of preschool education where local governments are quite independent in deciding about coverage and private/public sharing of costs of provided services, the gap between rich and poor increased significantly. While it is not fully valid to blame decentralization for this, it should be clear that decentralization did not help in this case. Obviously, without additional support during times of fiscal stress, poorer local governments tried to cut their spending. Educational or social services are usually first among those for which local support will be limited.

It is important to emphasize, however, that preschool education is really needed in rural poor *gminas* to enhance educational opportunities for disadvantaged children. Decentralization did not help in this regard. Without clear central government policy and support, one should not expect any positive change here. It does not seem reasonable to expect poorer households to be more conscious of the future returns on early education investment than richer households, especially when preschool fees are responsible for a substantial share of their budgets. Thus, one should expect that decentralization will increase the gap between poor and non-poor in this case, because local government policy in poor areas reflects the attitude of its citizens.

There is a very interesting solution to the problem of low preschool participation in rural Poland. Non-governmental organizations have in recent years established hundreds of kindergartens that benefit from less stringent regulations for non-public institutions. They provide basic preschool services at lower cost in poor and mostly rural areas. The model is often one of cooperation with local governments, which usually allow them to use buildings remaining after public kindergarten closure. Important financial support for these institutions is now offered by the European Structural Funds. However, it has to be assured that the services provided without public regulations are of similar quality and, more importantly, that non-profit involvement is stable enough to replace public institutions.

It is difficult to say whether in the long run similar solutions could be used on a larger scale to increase preschool accessibility. This may be hard to maintain without some involvement of the central government on the financial or regulatory side. Nevertheless, implementing similar solutions could be seen as grass-roots decentralization where services are provided through locally based organizations with the limited involvement of central and local governments, albeit with external financing. However, it is too early to say whether this policy is sustainable and financially viable without support from EU funds. It is hard to imagine that this kind of decentralized policy would be successful without some kind of central government financial support.

In the case of primary and lower secondary education, *gminas* are more limited in their choices but the central government supports them financially by covering two-thirds of current costs. The increase in costs was observed during the investigated period but the reform of school finance in 2000 narrowed the differences in school expenditures among *gminas*. In this case, the introduction of a strict formula based on per-pupil funding has helped to limit inequalities in local government expenditure. Consequently, imputed income analysis shows that primary education expenditure has a visible equalizing impact on household income. Poor households benefit more from the new system because of their demographic composition and higher expenditures in rural areas.

Importantly, lower secondary schools founded in 1999–2001 have lower per student costs, which could be interpreted as a sign of the positive effects of decentralized decision-making, because local governments were solely responsible for establishing them and usually were not bound by historical solutions as in the case of primary schools. However, the scale of this positive effect is not clear, because it is well known that transport costs have also increased and important capital investments were not fully considered. One needs to analyze local government budgets from a wider perspective to fully account for expenditures on newly established institutions.

More importantly, the research conducted for lower secondary schools suggests that this system is not effective, and more precisely, that variation in decentralized expenditures is not correlated with variation in teaching quality. This essential observation could be interpreted in several ways. It could be claimed that the system is overregulated and central government should further decentralize decision-making processes if any beneficial effects of decentralization are to be achieved in this regard. On the other hand, it could be claimed that local governments are not really effective and for some reason they are not able to influence teaching quality via expenditures. It could be that local governments affect teaching quality without spending additional resources, but that cannot be tested using this data.

Nevertheless, it seems that decentralizing expenditures has no effect and that decentralization in education should not concentrate on the financial side. Further research is needed here but it seems clear that the decentralized system in Poland is not able to boost the quality of services to the extent expected at the beginning of transition. There are good arguments to support this view. One is that local governments lack expertise in the area of teaching. Local officials could lower costs and reorganize service provision to better fit citizen needs, but usually they are not experts in education or they are simply teachers from local schools. In the latter case, it is hard to separate teacher group interests from citizen preferences. Locally proposed solutions to enhance learning outcomes usually mix teacher and student interests. Clearly, without additional information about teaching outcomes available to citizens, it is difficult to envision local action substantially increasing teaching quality. Thus, the central government or its agencies should provide citizens with detailed information about teaching outcomes. In fact, such a system was recently developed in Poland. However, it is too early to assess its effects. At this moment it can be said that, without additional information or expertise available to local governments and citizens, decentralization will not increase teaching quality while local governments will spend their money ineffectively.

NOTES

* The chapter draws extensively on two research reports: *The Impact of Decentralization on Public Service Delivery and Equity: Education and Health Sectors in Poland 1998–2003* prepared for UNDP by CASE (Jakubowski and Topińska, 2007) and "Teaching Quality and Decentralization" (Jakubowski, 2008). We would like to thank the participants of seminars in Budapest (October 2006), Moncalieri (September 2007) and Hangzhou (November 2007) for extremely helpful comments. All remaining errors are solely ours.

1. For more about the development of decentralized government in Poland see Regulski (2003). Interesting information and data on fiscal decentralization in Poland can also be found in Levitas (1999). Recent discussions about decentralization in Poland and social policy can be found in Golinowska and Boni (2006).
2. The graph box summarizes revenue per capita distribution by showing the distance between adjacent values (the vertical line segment) and the 25th and 75th percentile (the box). The Horizontal line within the box shows respective median. The longer the vertical line and the box the more spread is the distribution. Notice that "rural/urban" *gminas* have been excluded in order to make the graph clearer. The revenues were deflated using the HICP [Harmonised Index of Consumer Prices] Eurostat index, except that for 1995 HICP is not available and CPI based on older formula was used.
3. GUS (2006).
4. See detailed description of the reform and its political background in Levitas and Herczyński (2002).

5. At the same time, the category of "rural" *gmina* is very heterogeneous. Some rural *gminas* are quite rich (for example, *gminas* where huge mining companies are placed). There is also a large group of rural *gminas* with many farmers and very limited sources of own revenues (farmers do not pay income taxes). Thus, it is claimed that the educational subvention algorithm is not really based on objective categories and this put some *gminas* into financial troubles (see detailed analysis in Swianiewicz et al., 2005; Jakubowski, 2006).
6. For clarity the graph omits rural/urban *gminas*.
7. This is true regarding all indicators of preschool expenditures and even more dramatic differentiation is observed in indicators measuring expenditures in kindergartens (see Jakubowski, Topińska, 2007, for details).
8. To make this point clearer, the school finance reform of 1999/2000 increased the financial burden on local government budgets. Thus, poorer rural *gminas*, which were already spending more than half of their budgets on education, decided to limit their support for kindergartens to cover school costs. This rarely happened in cities where additional sources of revenues were used to cover school costs.
9. In the Opolskie region 51 percent of three- to five- year-olds use kindergartens while in the Podlaskie region this is less than 26 percent.
10. Many view obligatory "zero" (preparatory) classes as inefficient policy that forces all families to send children to school while for many of them this is not really needed. Strictly, in situations of fiscal stress, preschool support should be more concentrated on poor or disadvantaged families. There are several non-profits that recently used European Structural Funds to establish non-public but free kindergartens in rural areas. However, their number is too low to change the situation in a substantial manner and their future is not secured.
11. See Jakubowski and Topińska (2007), for more details on poverty measurement and poverty rates in 1998–2003.
12. Additional results are available in Jakubowski and Topińska (2007).
13. The boxes in Figure 9.8 represent the 25th (lower hinge), median (line in the middle), and the 75 percentile of expenditures per student in a particular year, while lines range from the lowest to the highest adjacent values. Outliers are not presented.
14. Notice that inequality impact of public spending through the imputed income analysis has been already studied in Poland several times. See, for instance, Styczeń and Topińska (1999), Topińska (1991) and World Bank (2003, pp. 97 and 104–5). However, none of these studies used subnational data for the evaluation of the imputed income nor did they cover a longer period of time.
15. This section presents main findings from the research project summarized in Jakubowski (2008). Readers are referred to this paper for methodological details and additional results.
16. See McCaffrey et al. (2005) for detailed discussion of value-added models in education.
17. This is crucial assumption in value-added models. While we can expect that this assumption is often violated there is no point in expecting that other than expenditures factors affect achievement growth. In an important and systematic way. Nevertheless, causal relation could not be estimated this way and it is hard to point possible sources of bias (see McCaffrey et al., 2005; Jakubowski, 2006).

REFERENCES

de Leeuw J. (2005), "Centering in Multilevel Models", in Brian Everitt and David Howell (eds), *Encyclopedia of Statistics in Behavioral Science*, Wiley and Sons.

Goldstein, H., P. Huiqi, T. Rath and N. Hill (2000), *The Use of Value-added Information in Judging School Performance*, Perspectives on Education Policy Series, London: Institute of Education.
Golinowska, S. and M. Boni (2006), "Nowe dylematy polityki społecznej" (New Dilemmas in Social Policy Making), CASE – Center for Social and Economic Research, CASE Report 65/2006.
GUS, (2006), Oświata i wychowanie w roku szkolnym 2005/2006" (Education in the School Year 2005/2006); Warsaw: Central Statistical Office (GUS).
Hanushek, E.A. (2003), "The Failure of Input-based Schooling Policies", *Economic Journal*, **113** (485), 64–98.
Jakubowski, M. (2006), *Developing Value-added Models of School Assessment in Poland*, report for the OECD expert group in the project "Development of Value-added Models in Education Systems".
Jakubowski, M. (2008), "Teaching Quality and Decentralization", working paper, Faculty of Economic Sciences, Warsaw University.
Jakubowski, M. and Sakowski P. (2006), "Quasi-experimental Estimates of Class Size Effect in Primary Schools in Poland", *International Journal of Educational Research*, **45** (3), 202–15.
Jakubowski, M. and I. Topińska (2007), *Impact of Decentralization on Public Service Delivery and Equity. Education and Health Sectors in Poland 1998–2003*, UNDP report, CASE – Center for Social and Economic Research.
Krueger, A. (2003), "Economic Considerations and Class Size", *Economic Journal*, **113** (485), 34–63.
Levitas, T. (1999), *The Political Economy of Fiscal Decentralization and Local Government Finance Reform in Poland 1989–1999*, Washington, DC: USAID.
Levitas, T. and J. Herczyński (2002), "Decentralization, Local Governments and Education Reform in Post Communist Poland", in K. Davey (ed.), *Balancing National and Local Responsibilities. Education Management and Finance in Four Central European Countries*, Budapest: OSI/LGI.
McCaffrey, D., J. Lockwood, M. Koretz and L. Hamilton (2005), *Evaluating Value-added Models for Teacher Accountability*, Santa Monica, CA: Rand Corporation MG-158.
OECD (2008), *Education at a Glance 2008*, Paris: Organisation for Economic Co-operation and Development.
Rabe-Hesketh, S. and Skrondal A. (2005), *Multilevel and Longitudinal Modeling using Stata*, College Station, TX: Stata Press.
Raudenbush, S.W. and A. Bryk (2002), *Hierarchical Linear Models*, 2nd edition, Newbury Park, CA: Sage Publications.
Regulski, J. (2003), *Local Government Reform in Poland: An Insider's Story*, Budapest: OSI/LGI.
Styczeń, M. and I. Topińska (1999), *Padatki I wydatki socjalne jako narzędzia redystrybucji dochodów gospodarstw domowych w Polsce w okresie transformacji* (Redistribution of Household Incomes through Taxes and Social Transfers During the Transformation), Warsaw: Instytut Pracy i Polityki Socjalnej (IpiSS).
Swianiewicz, P., M. Herbst and W. Marchlewski (2005), *Finansowanie i realizowanie zadań oświatowych na obszarach wiejskich* (School Financing and Management in Rural Areas), report for the Union of Rural Local Governments of the Republic of Poland.
Topińska, I. (1991), *The Impact of Social Transfers on Income Distribution: Poland*

1989, Research Report for the World Bank, Research Paper Series no. 2, Washington, DC: World Bank.
World Bank (2003), *Poland: Toward a Fiscal Framework for Growth. A Public Expenditure and Institutional Review*, Report No. 25033-POL, Washington, DC: World Bank.
Zahorska, M. (ed.) (2003), *Opieka przedszkolna w Polsce – szanse i zagrożenia* (The Pre-school Education in Poland), Warszawa: Instytut Spraw Publicznych.

10. Evaluating the effects of decentralization on public service delivery: the Spanish experience

Albert Solé-Ollé*

1 INTRODUCTION

In the last three decades, a substantial number of developed and developing countries have initiated processes of decentralization of responsibilities regarding the provision of public services (Shah and Thompson, 2004). The exact meaning of the word decentralization differs from country to country. In some cases, decentralization means to transfer administrative responsibilities to decentralized agencies, while in many cases it involves the creation of elected lower-tier governments (Shah, 1998). Even in the case of politically autonomous entities, the transfer of responsibilities is often partial (Ahmad et al., 2006), in the sense that the central government retains important regulatory and/or financing powers over service provision,[1] so there is wide variation both in the kind and depth of the decentralization reform. But the motives for decentralization are as varied as its meaning. In many cases, decentralization is a crucial ingredient of a democratization package, as in Latin America or the former communist countries (Jakubowski and Topińska, 2009). In other cases, decentralization is seen as a way to appease secessionist regions and reduce the level of ethnic and regional conflict, as in Indonesia or South Africa (see, for example, Inman and Rubinfeld, 2005). There are also a few cases where the aim was to improve the delivery of public services, and the World Bank and other donors used to emphasize this goal (World Bank, 1999). But, as long as democracy and good governance are a precondition for the improvement of public services (Shah, 2006), even those cases that do not mention efficiency do implicitly pursue this goal.

This has in fact been the case in Spain, where political decentralization must be seen as a result of complex political negotiations that took place in order to set the 1978 Constitution which began the democratic period. The main driver of the creation of the 17 Spanish Autonomous

Communities (ACs) was the need to satisfy the Basque and Catalan demands for self-government, making decentralization of political power a premise of Spanish democracy (Moreno, 1997). However, because the fear that asymmetric federalism would foster instead of appease secessionist movements in these regions, the creators of the Constitution decided to apply the system to all Spanish territory but allow a faster access to the devolved responsibilities to the historic regions. The political will of the Socialist Party at the beginning of the 1980s, and, later, the pressures of non-historic regions – which wished to emulate the historic ones – were the drivers of the effective decentralization of important service responsibilities (for example, health and education) to the whole country (Hanson, 2000). The process was to be completed by 1992 but did not end until 2002.

Many authors qualify the Spanish transition to democracy as a success, and identify decentralization as one of the instruments that helped to reach the initial agreement and to guarantee that it is self-enforcing (see, for example, Weingast, 2004).[2] Moreover, Spain is one of the few countries that have implemented a far-reaching decentralization reform of such large scale systematically and completely, avoiding the transfers of responsibilities to sub-central governments in a haphazard way, as can be observed from other experiences (see for example, Ahmad et al., 2006). The mere fact that such a big decentralization process took place over nearly two decades, with continuous bargaining between central and regional governments and between political parties, should be considered as an indicator of success.

Of course, with expenditure decentralization reaching its end a few years ago, some voices also started to ask about the cost-effectiveness of the reform. Do outcomes in the educational (for example, school drop-out rates) or health (for example, people waiting for interventions) improve after decentralization? Are these services more expensive after decentralization? Do citizens in different parts of the country enjoy a similar standard of service? There is, however, a great scarcity in Spain of both governmental evaluations and academic studies on this topic. This lack of information about the effects of decentralization can be explained by several factors. First, given the long period decentralization took and the magnitude and complexity of the process (we will provide more details on this in the next section) it is quite understandable that nobody really paid attention in Spain to the quality of service delivery. Second, the central ministries have lost most of their traditional responsibilities without developing new tasks that are needed for decentralization to work well, sure as, for example, collecting and standardizing information on service delivery in order to allow yardstick competition to operate (Salmon, 1987).[3] Third, most ACs are reluctant to be evaluated and compared against the others.[4]

This reluctance to be evaluated is in accordance with the general lack of evaluation culture in Spanish budgeting, which has been documented by several authors (see, for example, Zapico, 2002). Fourth, note in any case, that to evaluate a decentralization reform that has lasted many years one would need before-after information on public service outcomes; even if information was available nowadays, it would very difficult to obtain the data for the beginning of the 1980s.

There are a few academic papers that tried to perform partial evaluations of the reform. Most of them, however, focus on equity rather than on efficiency. Several papers have analyzed the effect of decentralization on inter-regional equity for the cases of health care, income support transfers and education. Costa-i-Font et al. (2005) and Costa-i-Font and Rico (2006a) examine the effects of health system decentralization on the emergence of inter-territorial inequalities in health care expenditure and outcomes, concluding that besides significant heterogeneity, once region-specific needs are taken into account, inequalities in inputs and outcomes, although more "visible" with decentralization, do not appear to have increased. In the case of regional income support transfers, Ayala et al. (2001) illustrate the high level of heterogeneity of these programs, ACs with unreasonably high financial resources (Navarra and the Basque Country; see the explanation of the reason in the next section) and some rich urban regions with high concentrations of urban poverty (Madrid and Catalunya) applying both higher standards and spending more money. Moreover, these authors also illustrate, however, that the conclusion reached regarding the effect of decentralization on inter-territorial equity depends very much on accounting or not for purchasing-power differences between regions, which is something that central transfers do not consider in Spain. So, similar to what happened with health care, once one takes into account differences in needs, it is by no means clear that decentralization harms inter-regional equity.

Regarding efficiency, Costa-i-Font et al. (2005) provide evidence supporting the idea that the decentralization of the health system has led to more experimentation in health reforms related to regional diversity. Costa-i-Font and Rico (2006b) document a wide array of cases of horizontal and vertical diffusion of innovation in health care management. Moreover, Costa-i-Font et al. (2005, p. 221) argue that "decentralization of health care has allowed health care reforms to break an arguably monolithic (centrally managed) organization of services by placing financial pressures on politically and fiscally accountable regions", suggesting therefore that the degree of innovation and institutional change has been higher under decentralization than it would have been under the counterfactual of a centralized system. Bonal et al. (2005) also document differences in the strategies different ACs have regarding school management. Many other papers show that decentralized spending does react to local conditions and needs, that is a necessary precondition for decentralization to better match the preferences of residents: Costa-i-Font and Moscone (2008) for health care, Castells and Solé-Ollé (2005) for infrastructure investment and Castells and Solé-Ollé (2001) for a wide array of expenditure categories are examples.

But the only papers that do explicitly evaluate service performance under decentralization versus centralization are those by Salinas and Solé-Ollé (2008) and Esteller-Moré and Solé-Ollé (2009)[5]. The first paper focuses on educational services and examines the effects of decentralization on the survival rate at the age of 16 (that is, the proportion of students enrolled in the last course of compulsory secondary education who access non-compulsory post-secondary education). The second paper examines the effects of decentralization on the degree of government responsiveness to local demands and needs, focusing on the cases of education and roads. Both papers reach the conclusion that decentralization has improved service delivery. In the third section we will provide more details regarding those two papers.

The remainder of the chapter is organized as follows. In the second section we provide a description of decentralization in Spain, providing both a picture of the actual degree of decentralization and a description of the process. The third section describes the two aforementioned papers that are the only examples performing a real before-after evaluation of the decentralization reform. The fourth section concludes with a general assessment of the merits of Spanish decentralization.

2 DEVELOPMENTS IN DECENTRALIZATION IN SPAIN

In this section, we provide an outline of the main traits of the decentralization in Spain, focusing on the distribution of responsibilities among layers of government, the very process of decentralization of spending responsibilities that took place during the 1980s and 1990s and the main traits of revenue assignment and intergovernmental grants.[6] As will be evident through the explanation, until very recently decentralization in Spain meant devolution of spending responsibilities, with little tax autonomy. This trait is important to assess the results regarding the evaluation of decentralization that will be shown in Section 4, since they should be attributed only to the incentives introduced by expenditure decentralization (Brueckner, 2007).

2.1 Distribution of Responsibilities

Strictly speaking, Spain does not qualify as a federal state, as Article 2 of the Spanish Constitution declares the sovereignty and unity of the Spainish state and "recognizes and guarantees the right to self-government of the nationalities and regions of which it is composed". However, Spain can be described as a politically decentralized country with three tiers of government (central, regional and local) in which the distribution of functions and the system of governance are very close to those of a federal state (see, for example, Moreno, 1997). Regional governments (ACs) have their own legislature and executive and, thus, carry state qualities. Moreover, the right of existence of ACs is not merely derived from the Spanish Constitution but is grounded in a basic law for each AC (called "Statute of Autonomy"), which is subordinated to the Constitution but is not an ordinary law.

Spain is comprised of 17 ACs, which were established from 1978 to 1983. Actually, the powers devolved to each one are very similar. This was not the case at the beginning, since the ACs with past history of self-governance received all the responsibilities in the 1980s, while the rest of ACs received the additional responsibilities (basically education and health) at the end of the 1990s. The Spanish Constitution specifies two different sets of responsibilities. On the one hand, Article 148 specifies the responsibilities that may be adopted by the regions. On the other hand, Article 149 specifies the responsibilities that are the exclusive competence of the center. Matters not enumerated include the residual power of the center if the region does not claim the competence in the "Statute of Autonomy". The Constitution also specifies the intensity of responsibility, in a continuum going from full legislative and executive powers, to limited legislative but complete executive powers, to only executive powers.[7]

Table 10.1 presents the different responsibilities attributed to both tiers of government by the Constitution. Note that, apart from these responsibilities, the Constitution (Article 150.2) also envisages the possibility of transfer or delegation of exclusive responsibilities by the center. This possibility requires a qualified majority in the central legislature and has been used to transfer new competences to the ACs (for example, health and education in the 1990s). Although the text says that the center could specify the conditions of the delegation, these new responsibilities are usually attributed to the ACs without any special conditions.

2.2 Decentralization Process

The decentralization process in Spain was very complex and difficult to manage administratively. Note that because the ACs were created from

Table 10.1 Distribution of responsibilities between the state and the ACs

State	ACs
S1. *Exclusive legislative and executive competences:* Immigration and emigration International affairs Defense Justice Commercial, penal, labor, industrial and intellectual property and civil law (except matters regulated by traditional regional law) Foreign trade Monetary system, exchange regime and state treasury and debt Infrastructures of a national scope (that is, inter-regional roads, railroads and water transportation and commercial ports and airports) Sea fishing	AC1 *Exclusive legislative and executive competences:* General organization of self-government Changes in municipal boundaries and creation of supra-municipal bodies Land use planning and housing Infrastructures of a regional scope (that is, intra-regional roads, railroads and water transportation and non-commercial ports and airports) Agriculture, forestry and river fishing Domestic trade and fairs Tourism Culture (that is, museums, libraries, historical heritage, cultural promotion, and so on.) and sports (that is, facilities and promotion) Social services Environmental policy Others listed in the 'Statute of Autonomy' and not included in S1
S2. *Power to set basic legislation*: Banking and insurance activities Health care Social security Education	AC2. *Competences subject to basic state:* "Economic development within the national economic policy framework" Others listed in the "Statute of Autonomy" but included in S2 or S3
S3. *The state also has the power to:* Coordinate and promote scientific and technical research "[Set] the basis for and [coordinate] the general planning of economic activity" "[Guarantee] the equality of all Spaniards in the exercise of their constitutional rights and duties"	AC3. *In addition to this the ACs have:* Any competence delegated by the state

Source: Spanish Constitution of 1978 and own elaboration.

scratch the very process of decentralization demanded the cooperation of both layers of government. The national government and each AC should sit together and bargain on the interpretation of these tasks and the physical and financial means related to them. This bargaining procedure was institutionalized in bilateral cooperation forums (called *Comisiones Mixtas de Valoraciones*). For each specific transfer of responsibilities an agreement (*Acuerdo de Traspaso*) was signed between the state and the AC concerned, specifying the exact nature of the responsibility and the resources transferred. This process must be bilateral because the decentralization process was quite asymmetric, due both to the constitutional asymmetry in the level of competences and to bargaining delays and the difficulty in implementation, which recommended a gradual approach. Although the process was not without problems, it was successful in decentralizing a huge amount of expenditure, personnel and assets in a very short period of time.[8]

Summing up, the Spanish ACs actually have responsibilities in a wide range of policies: health care, education, social services, environment, housing, economic promotion, agriculture, tourism, and so on. They have legislative competences in most of them, but the decisions of their parliaments are subject to the central basic laws. As a result of this decentralization process, the spending power of ACs is also considerable. This government tier, born at the beginning of the 1980s, represented in 2005 42 percent of Spanish public expenditure (spending on pensions aside), a number higher than the 41 percent of the central government (and of the 17 percent of local governments). In addition to this, most of the funds received by the ACs are unconditional, so this spending is relatively unconstrained.

However, decentralization in Spain is not without problems. For example, there is a general feeling by some ACs that sometimes the state's basic laws are too detailed, not providing opportunities to further develop substantial aspects of the policy. Some ACs (especially Catalunya and the Basque Country) consider this as an encroachment by the center over their competences. Moreover, the central government is starting to make use of its responsibility on guaranteeing social rights to pass new laws that impose spending mandates on the ACs (for example, education, elderly care, housing, and so on). The ACs complaints about unfunded mandates have been successful in forcing the center to partially finance the costs imposed by these laws. However, this procedure has also been criticized on the grounds that the center is using its spending power to attach strings to matters that are the exclusive competence of the ACs.

2.3 Financing Arrangements

Spanish ACs are subject to two different financing regimes. On the one hand, there are the 15 ACs of the "common regime", whose services are financed by a mixture of taxes and tax-sharing arrangements and with an unconditional transfer with a strong equalization component. The "common regime" financial system is devised by the center, but there is bargaining in a multilateral forum (Council of Fiscal and Financial Policy). On the other hand, the Basque Country and Navarra belong to the so-called "foral regime". The Constitution recognized a special status to these ACs on the basis of historic rights. Accordingly, both the Basque Country and Navarra collect all the taxes and then pay a quota to finance the services still provided by the center to the citizens of these regions.[9] The quota is bargained bilaterally from time to time and, therefore, these two regions do not participate in the multilateral bargaining process. As a result of this separate procedure these two ACs do not contribute to the equalization fund and end up with a much higher per capita level of resources (Zubiri, 2004; Castells et al., 2005).

The ACs of the "common regime" have the following revenue sources: (1) own taxes are created by law of the AC but are restricted to tax fields not occupied by the center and are, therefore, marginal in quantitative terms. (2) Taxes ceded by the center now have full regional legal and collecting powers (that is, wealth tax, inheritance tax, wealth transmission tax). (3) A 33 percent share of the income tax, where sub-nationals have substantial legal powers on the tax rates and deductions but without collecting responsibilities. (4) A 35 percent share of the VAT and excises, but without any collection responsibilities and with the possibility of a surcharge on gasoline taxes earmarked for health financing. (5) An equalization grant (called *Fondo de Suficiencia*) covers the difference between estimated expenditure needs and resources obtained from items (2) to (4). (6) Some specific transfers are provided for the center's direct initiatives, from agreements between the center and the ACs (*Convenios*), or from regional policy funds, both at the European level (for example, FEDER, Cohesion Fund) and at the national level (for example, the so-called *Fondo de Compensación Interterritorial*). (7) Debt finance is possible, although this has been strongly restricted since 2001 (see, for example, Giorno and Joumard, 2005).

Until the beginning of the 1990s the degree of tax autonomy of common regime ACs was quite low. The share on central taxes started in 1994 with a 15 percent share in the income tax without legal powers, and the last significant increase occurred in 2001. Nowadays, the state is considering further increasing the share in taxes: 50 percent of income tax and VAT

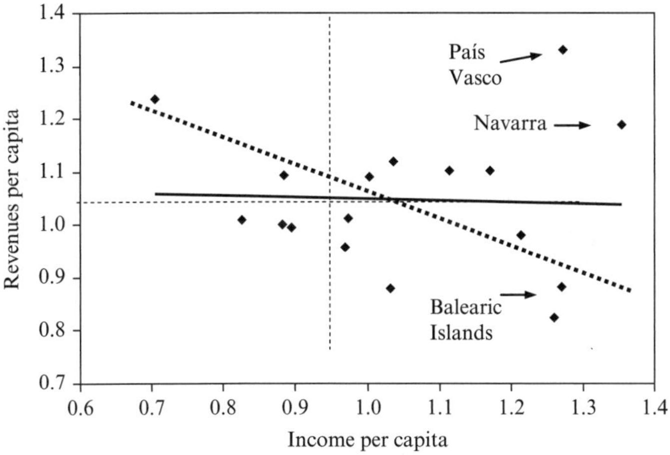

Notes:
1. Revenues per capita = own revenues + tax sharing + general and specific transfers + transfers for health and social services, for the year 2005, expressed with respect to the Spanish unweighted average.
2. Bold regression line includes all the 17 ACs (slope = −0.03 and R^2 = 0.02); dotted regression line excludes País Vasco and Navarra (slope = −0.36 and R^2 = 0.30).

Source: BADESPE, Instituto de Estudios Fiscales, www.ief.es, accessed 1 April 2009.

Figure 10.1 Revenues per capita of the 17 ACs in 2005

and 58 percent of excises. For the moment, the ACs have not used the possibility of modifying the income tax rates, although they have introduced tax credits and deductions. The effect of these changes has been modest on average but can be substantial for some specific types of taxpayers (Esteller-Moré and Durán, 2004). The state is also considering the possibility of giving more tax powers on the excises and on the retail phase of the VAT, although this last option is subject to some problems (Gimeno, 2008), both technical (the retail level is not recognized in Spain) and legal (it may be contrary to EU regulations).

The equalization grant is also being reformed. Although expenditure needs were computed theoretically with objective data, the reality is that political considerations made the formula very redistributive during the 1980s and 1990s. Figure 10.1 plots revenues per capita against income per capita for the 17 ACs for 2005. Revenues include all the different sources except debt – own taxes and user charges, tax-sharing and intergovernmental grants (both conditional and unconditional). This means that the observed relationship refers to the moment where all the equalization mechanisms have been applied.

Once we exclude the two "foral regime" ACs (Navarra and Basque Country, which both have high income and much more fiscal resources) there is a negative relationship between income and the amount of resources an AC has for similar responsibilities (the transfer of health and education was completed in 2005). The slope of the regression is statistically significant. This means that not only between common regime and foral regime ACs, but also inside the 15 ACs' common regime, there are striking differences in per capita resources that are difficult to justify on equity grounds (see Castells et al., 2005, for a discussion). Thus, some ACs with similar income levels end up with very dissimilar levels of resources, and some ACs that are income-rich (above average) end up being revenue-poor (below average) and vice versa. The rich ACs, not belonging to the foral regime (and specially Catalunya), are claiming that this is unfair and pushing for the reform of the system in the direction of a partial equalization system like the German or Canadian ones (Castells, 2001). As we will discuss in the next section, these funding inequities might have profound impacts on the ability to improve service outcomes by means of decentralization.

3 THE EFFECT OF DECENTRALIZATION ON SERVICE DELIVERY IN SPAIN

As we explained at the beginning of the chapter, there are very few papers properly analyzing the effect of decentralization of public service outcomes. In this section we review the evidence provided by Salinas and Solé-Ollé (2008) and Esteller-Moré and Solé-Ollé (2009). Both papers exploit two facts of the Spanish decentralization reform. First, decentralization took place in an asymmetric fashion and over a long period of time (that is, although at the end all the ACs received the same responsibilities, some of them received them early and others late). Second, the year in which an AC received a given responsibility did not depend on factors related to the performance of this service but on broader political considerations (for example, historic ACs received education and health earlier than the other ACs simply because this was mandated in the Constitution and because there were higher demands for self-government).

The first paper evaluates the impact of education decentralization on the survival rate at the age of 16 (which is actually the compulsory schooling age in Spain). The second paper studies whether policy responsiveness improved after decentralization of education and roads, by looking at the

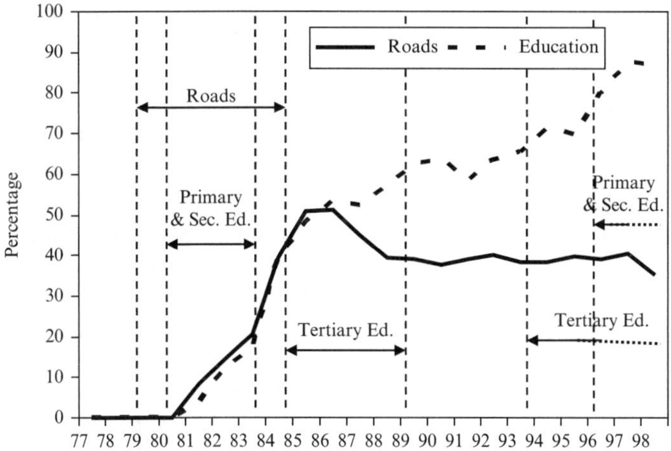

Note: Investment by local governments ("municipalities") not included

Source: Esteller-Moré and Solé-Ollé (2009) with data from Fundación BBVA, *Capital Stocks and Income in Spain* (1964–2000), http://w3.grupobbva.com/TLFBU/tlfbu/esp/areas/econosoc/bbdd/capital.jsp#1, accessed 22 April 2009.

Figure 10.2 Share of regional investment in regional + central investment: investment in roads and education in 1977–98

correlation between investments in these services and demand and need variables. In both cases, the analysis uses data from the decades of 1980 and 1990, thus covering pre- and post-decentralization periods.

Figure 10.2 shows the share of regional investment in regional + central investments in education (all levels) and roads for the period 1979–98. Note that the share of road investment made by the ACs grows during the period 1980–85; that is, until the last of the 17 ACs received road responsibilities regarding intra-regional roads (inter-regional roads are still a responsibility of the central government). In that year, the regional share declined due to the higher effort made by the central government in building inter-regional roads (thanks to the greater share of EU funds retained by this level of government). In the case of education, the share of investment made by the ACs grew steadily throughout the period, as different groups of ACs received the responsibilities. The historic ACs (Catalunya, País Vasco and Galicia) plus some others that decided to join the fast route to decentralization early (Andalucia, Valencia and the Canary Islands) received the responsibilities for primary and secondary education during 1981–85, Navarra received them in 1990, while the remaining ones had to wait until 1997–2000. Most of the ACs in the first group also received responsibilities regarding tertiary education in the 1980s, some received them early in the 1990s and the remaining ones had to wait until the last round of decentralization.

It is important to note what decentralization meant in this context, in order to be able to draw some lessons from these evaluations. In the case of roads, it meant that the ACs received the responsibilities on funding, building and maintaining intra-regional roads. This means that the ACs had full autonomy regarding a sub-set of the road network of the region.

In the case of education, the ACs received the responsibilities on funding and managing the education system. The regulation of the system was shared between the central government and the ACs; the central government was able to fix minimum standards regarding the curriculum, parents rights to education, teachers salaries, and so on (see, for example, Hanson, 2000). However, the autonomy of the ACs both in setting spending priorities and on the design of the system should be qualified as high.

Note also that in no case does decentralization imply a substantial degree of autonomy to raise taxes, since the move to revenue decentralization in Spain did not occur until recently. So, the improvement or not of service delivery should be attributed only to the introduction of spending autonomy. Finally, recall that we are analyzing decentralization to an intermediate level of government, with some very big units (for example, Andalucia, with 8 million people), and not to local communities.

3.1 Production Efficiency in Education

In this section, we provide some evidence that decentralization of education to ACs in Spain had a positive impact on some service outcomes. We begin by discussing the argument we wish to analyze and the empirical evidence that exists for other countries, in order to be able to assess appropriately the insights offered by our analysis.

3.1.1 The argument

Production efficiency means that the same outcomes require fewer inputs, or the same quantity of inputs produces more outcomes. The main reason why decentralization will imply higher production efficiency is improved accountability. Political scientists and economists alike have provided arguments that justify this link. First, as Dahl and Tufte (1973) early pointed out, democracy can work better under decentralization, since regional populations tend to be relatively more homogeneous than the state ones. Small size and low heterogeneity would make it relatively easy to develop public deliberation to identify common interests and the aggregation of citizens' preferences into acceptable collective decisions. Second, decentralization could also foster political participation, since voters have more knowledge about the services provided in close proximity and also have more incentives to participate (Shah, 1998). Third, as Seabright (1996) has pointed out, a majority of local voters can dismiss a politician if dissatisfied with the policy delivered. This is not generally true in the case of centralized provision, since a single jurisdiction has little chance of being able to cause a government reversal.[10] Fourth, if there is mobility of residents and factors, decentralization will put some additional pressure on politicians (Weingast, 1995), forcing them to provide public services in a cost-efficient manner. Fifth, decentralization could foster efficiency by promoting innovation in public service delivery and institutional change (Volden, 2006).

However, it is true that some authors suggest that decentralization also has negative effects on efficiency. First, some authors argue that state capture by interest groups can be higher under decentralization (Prud'homme, 1995; Bardhan and Mookherjee, 2005). However, detailed theoretical work (Bardhan and Mookherjee, 2000) suggests that this is context-specific, depending on the degree of cohesiveness of local versus national interest groups and on the degree of information that voters have regarding local versus national issues. In a recent review, Shah (2006) suggests that interest group capture and corruption can be a real concern precisely in settings where governance institutions are weak and income inequality strong, suggesting that in these cases it is better to foster governance before decentralizing. But, according to this author, once governance reaches a given quality threshold, decentralization will contribute to strengthening accountability (for the reasons above) and thus to reducing corruption and waste in government. Second, of course if there are spillovers in the provision of the service or economies of scale, there could be efficiency losses that outweigh the gains obtained from increased accountability.

3.1.2 Empirical evidence

The evaluation of the effects of decentralization on production efficiency is fraught with many difficulties. First, studies of outcomes have to control for the inputs/resources/expenditure used to produce these outcomes. If these controls are not introduced the results can not be ascribed to the effects of decentralization on efficiency, but to an increase in the amount of resources devoted to the policy that goes in parallel to decentralization. Second, and more generally, the observed results may be attributable to decentralization or to other contemporaneous policies or events. So what is needed for the evaluation of decentralization (as for any other policy) is not only before-after data on the outcomes of the service, but some assurance that the decentralization reform is exogenous.

Although recent, there is a growing literature that provides some evidence on this link. First, some papers using data on a cross-section of countries suggest that decentralization leads to lower levels of perceived corruption (Huther and Shah, 1998 and Fisman and Gatti, 2001), although these results are controversial because there are also some papers that find the opposite (Treisman, 2002). Second, other papers study the effects of decentralization on policy outcomes; for example, the paper by Treisman also finds that decentralized countries also provide health care services and infrastructures less effectively. There are a number of country studies that analyze the impact of decentralization on productive efficiency of educational services (which will be the ones analyzed in this section for Spain). For example, Habibi et al. (2001) report a positive impact of decentralization on educational outcomes in Argentina when using the ratio of students enrolled in secondary school per 1000 primary students as their dependent variable. Galiani and Schargrodsky (2001) and Galiani et al. (2005) likewise describe a positive impact of a decentralizing process in the same country using standardized test scores, but only in provinces that do not report a very large fiscal deficit. Similar results are reported in Barankay and Lockwood (2007) in their analysis of Switzerland, using the percentage of the secondary student population that gets into university.

3.1.3 The Spanish case: education

The work by Salinas and Solé-Ollé (2008) analyzes the effect of decentralization of education on the survival rate at the age of 16, defined as the proportion of students enrolled in the last course of compulsory secondary education (ESO) who move on to (non-compulsory) post-secondary education (either *Bachillerato* or vocational training) in a given year. This educational attainment measure has some advantages. First, it is the only one that can be consistently measured for the whole period, allowing a before-after comparison of the effects of decentralization.

Although it would have been more interesting to use the results obtained in some standardized test, like the university entrance exams (called PAAUU in Spain), or the results obtained from PISA (the OECD program for international student achievement), this has not been possible. On the one hand, the PAAUU data were not available for the full period and geographical level (they use the 50 provinces, not the 17 ACs). On the other hand, the data from PISA and other similar projects are only available for recent years, so that it was not possible to perform a before-after evaluation of the effects of decentralization.

Second, in a country where the enrollment rates in compulsory education are near 100 percent, as in Spain, it is also interesting to use a variable that measures the permanence of students in schools after this period. It is assumed that a good level of educational quality will make students stay at school, instead of going into the labor market, so that we can say that if decentralization implies an increase in the percentage of pupils staying on at school, it is because it has raised the quality of education. Third, the percentage of pupils leaving school at 16 in Spain is quite high in comparative terms (20 percent and lower than the OECD average; Instituto de Evaluación, 2006) and to increase it is actually a real goal of Spanish educational policies. Fourth, this kind of measure has also been used in previous studies such as, for example, Habibi et al. (2001) and Barankay and Lockwood (2007).

The approach used by Salinas and Solé-Ollé (2008) consists of exploiting the availability of information before and after decentralization. First, they use a difference-in-differences estimator, which compares the growth in the outcome variable (survival rate) of the treated provinces (that is, those that belong to an AC that has already received the education responsibilities) with the growth in the outcome of the non-treated ones, being the difference between them in the effect of the treatment (that is, decentralization) on the treated (Blundell and Costa, 2000). Second, they use a random-trend model, which allows them to relax the assumption of common temporal effects by adding a provincial-specific trend. Finally, they use a triple-differences model, by comparing the growth in outcomes of public and private schools after decentralization. Several tests performed by the authors show that the most appropriate model is the random-trend one. On the one hand, it seems pretty clear that specific provincial trends make it unnecessary to include common time effects in the equation. On the other hand, it seems that the private school treatment group it is not appropriate, something that could be due to the fact that in Spain most private schools are also publicly funded (called *Concertadas*) and can thus also be affected by decentralization.

Table 10.2 presents the main results obtained when using the difference-in-differences (first two columns) and random-trend specifications. The equations include variables that aim to control for the level of school inputs (that is, pupil–teacher ratio) and the educational background of pupils (that is, income per capita, unemployment rate, average years of education of the population). Admittedly, some of these variables also control for the factors that push students out of schools and into the labor market (see, for example, Petrongolo and San Segundo, 2002).

For each of the two methods, we show the results controlling or not for the school inputs. As we said above, the preferred estimations include the provincial trends and suggest that decentralization increased the survival

Table 10.2 Effects of education decentralization on the survival rate at age 16. Difference-in-differences estimates. Sample: 50 provinces (NUTS3 regions) during 1980–2003

	(1)	(2)	(3)	(4)
Decentralization dummy	1.070	0.926	2.008	2.119
	(2.960)***	(2.381)**	(30.841)***	(29.010)***
Pupil–teacher ratio	−0.460	–	−0.317	–
	(−7.495)**		(−18.180)***	
Income per capita	−0.430	−0.196	0.417	0.434
	(−4.765)***	(−1.380)	(13.361)***	(16.670)***
Unemployment rate	−0.012	−0.058	0.071	0.065
	(−0.450)	(−1.842)*	(8.712)***	(8.452)***
Average years of education	0.113	0.144	0.008	0.020
	(2.321)**	(2.499)**	(0.700)	(1.860)*
Year fixed effects	YES	YES	NO	NO
Provincial-specific trend	NO	NO	YES	YES

Notes:
1. Dependent variable is the survival rate at age 16 and has been computed as the ratio between students who access post-secondary education (*Bachillerato*) and the students enrolled in the last course of compulsory education (ESO); students who access post-secondary education are calculated as enrolled pupils in the first course of *Bachillerato* less pupils who repeat.
2. Wald tests for the provincial fixed effects and provincial-specific trends have been computed, suggesting these should be added to the equations; the same test suggests that year fixed effects should be included only when there are no provincial-specific trends.
3. Heteroscedasticity, correlation between panels and autocorrelation have been considered in all the estimations.

Source: Salinas and Solé-Ollé (2008); data from either National Institute of Statistics or Ministry of Education and Science (after 1985).

rate by two percentage points. Since the average sample value for the survival rate is 73.5 percent this seems to be a very modest result. Note however, that the within-group standard deviation of this variable is 5.3 percent, meaning that a 2 percent increase due to decentralization indeed seems very high. The between-group standard deviation is around 4.5 percent, meaning that having the education responsibilities or not might have an important effect on the relative educational outcomes of a given AC. In the preferred specification, the impact of the control variables is also the expected one. The outcomes improve with the level of income and education of the population, the more teachers there are per pupil and the higher the level of unemployment (since there are less incentives to go into the labor market).

Another interesting result of the paper by Salinas and Solé-Ollé (2008) is that the effect of decentralization on educational outcomes is mediated by the financial situation of the AC. They re-estimate the model – interacting the decentralization dummy with both per capita revenues and surplus/deficit of each AC – and find that the impact of decentralization is much higher when the AC is rich in resources and has a sound financial situation (that is, a high surplus/low deficit). Simulations performed by these authors for each of the 17 ACs show that the effects of decentralization on the survival rate runs from a 1 percent increase in the case of Madrid or 1.2 percent for the Balearic Islands to 3 percent in the case of Navarra or 2.7 percent for Extremadura. Therefore, decentralization has improved the educational outcomes in all the ACs without exemption, but in an uneven fashion. Part of this effect seems to be related to the unequal distribution of resources made by the financing system of the ACs, as we documented in the second section (recall Figure 10.1). In any case, the differential effect that decentralization of education could have across the country, depending on features related to the amount of resources available, has also been documented by previous studies (see, for example, Galiani and Schargrodsky, 2001 and Galiani et al., 2005, on Argentina).

3.2 Preference Matching in Education and Roads

In this section, we provide some evidence that decentralization of education to ACs in Spain also had a positive impact on the ability or wish of the government to match regional preferences and/or needs. We also begin here by discussing the argument we wish to analyze and the empirical evidence that exists for other countries.

3.2.1 The argument

One of the main arguments in favor of decentralization is that local policies match better to the preferences of the residents than policies by higher levels of government. For example, according to the well-known "decentralization theorem" (Oates, 1972, p. 54):

> in absence of costs-savings from the centralized provision of a good and of inter-jurisdictional externalities, the level of welfare will always be at least as high (and typically higher) if Pareto-efficient levels of consumption are provided in each jurisdiction than if any single uniform level of consumption is maintained across all jurisdictions.

Note however that, for this prescription to hold, it is necessary to assume that the central government is not able to differentiate its provision among regions. Oates (1999) justifies it by means of the supposed better knowledge of state and local governments about the preferences and economic conditions of their constituency, caused perhaps by the difficulty of controlling distant bureaucrats from the center. Without that precise knowledge, and just having an "average" description of the preferences and economic conditions of all the citizens of the federation, the central government may be "forced" to provide a uniform level of public goods across all territories.

Nevertheless, it could be asked why a central layer of government cannot make an effort to achieve the same level of information as sub-central governments? Some authors (Cremer et al., 1996) consider that the process of information acquisition is endogenous, with the incentives of sub-central governments to gather information being greater than those of the center. Even if the information about local circumstances is accurate, central politicians might be less responsive because it is more difficult to create electoral contracts with them. How these incentives work depends on the nature of the political institutions. If local public goods are decided by a central legislature (Lockwood, 2002; Besley and Coate, 2003), the common pool problem caused by centralized finance (Weingast et al., 1981; Knight, 2004) might cause over-provision in some jurisdictions (those that have higher political power) and under-provision in others. Decentralized provision could provide the level of public good demanded by local voters. When the allocation of the local public good across regions is made by a unified central executive, the incentives depend on the nature of the electoral system. Seabright (1996) and Gehlbach (2007) show that, in a variety of electoral systems, the central government has fewer incentives to cater to the demands of a particular region due to the relatively small electoral weight of that region in the federal election process. Thus, the lack of influence on policy decisions taken under centralization not only make it easy for politicians to extract rents (increasing waste and productive inefficiency) but make them less responsive to local demands and needs.

3.2.2 Empirical evidence

There are many problems in trying to assess the preference matching argument. First, one needs to observe changes in the responsiveness of policy to local preferences or circumstances. However, it might be difficult to obtain information on before-after policy or spending patterns and on local preferences. Even if one has this information, changes may tell only part of the story, as better adaptation could derive simply from the massive transfer of resources from central to local levels, or to a change in the criteria used to allocate resources across jurisdictions, that might occur simultaneously with decentralization.

Moreover, when decentralization is partial, in the sense that the center also retains some responsibilities, service delivery could also improve at the central level through a process of bottom-up diffusion (Volden, 2006). Second, the observed effect on policy responsiveness may have nothing to do with better incentives on the part of the regional governments, but may be related to the amount of resources available to regional governments or to the way grant resources are allocated across regions. For example, decentralization may occur in parallel with an increase in the magnitude of funds available for devolved services. In this case, and taking into account that it is difficult to change budget priorities without funding increases, it would be natural to observe an increase in policy responsiveness, because regional governments need additional moneys to increase the relative weight of some programs. Similarly, decentralization may occur at the same time that a more stringent inter-territorial equity criterion is implemented. In this case, more grant money will flow with decentralization to poor regions; if the demand/needs for the service are directly (inversely) related to income we will observe less (more) policy responsiveness.

3.2.3 The Spanish case: roads and education

Esteller-Moré and Solé-Ollé (2009) address the question of whether decentralization of the provision of public infrastructures in Spain improved the matching between funds allocated to different jurisdictions and preferences and/or needs. The approach they use consists of estimating an equation of the determinants of public investment in two main investment categories, roads and education, allowing the response of investment to preferences/needs to differ depending on the layer (central or regional) that bears the responsibility. They observe that coefficients on preferences/needs are higher with decentralization, suggesting a better matching with decentralization.

The extreme but asymmetric decentralization made Spain a good testing ground for this hypothesis. Moreover, Spain also provides a very good database on public investment and capital stock at a regional level, suitable for this exercise. This unique database is provided by Fundación BBVA (2002, "El Stock de capital público en España y su distribución territorial") and provides road and education investment and capital stock series for the period 1965–98. The authors use the democratic period, 1977–98, including years in both regimes (centralization and decentralization), and data at the "*provincia*" level (NUTS3), which is lower than the ACs' jurisdiction (NUTS2) and allows them to analyze investment allocation inside each AC, purging the effect of the overall amount of resources allocated to each AC, which could also have been affected by decentralization.

The authors posit an equation for the per capita capital stock that the government desires for a given jurisdiction:

$$c^*_{st} = \beta_{1s}x_{st-1} + \beta_2 r_{rt} + \beta_3\delta_{st} + \beta_4 z_s$$

where c^*_{st} is the desired per capita capital stock (either in roads or education) in province s, and year t, x_{st-1} are preference or needs variables assumed known with a lag, r_{rt} are resources allocated each year to each AC labeled r (and that has several provinces under its jurisdiction), both in the centralized and decentralized regimes, δ_{st} is a decentralization dummy, z_s are time invariant cost and political variables, $\beta_{1s} = \alpha(1 + \sigma\delta_{st})$ is a coefficient that measures the impact of a preference or needs variable on the desired capital stock and which depends on the decentralization status.

In order to obtain an estimable equation, the authors substitute $\ldots + \beta_2 r_{rt} + \beta_3\delta_{st} + \beta_4 z_s$ for $\ldots + f_{rt} + f_s + \delta_{st} \times f_s$, where f_{rt} are time × sub-central government effects, controlling for overall amount of resources devoted to the jurisdiction of each sub-central government, both in the centralized and decentralized regimes, f_s are regional effects, controlling for omitted variables (for example, politics), and which also interact with the decentralization dummy, $\delta_{st} \times f_s$, controlling for the possible higher impact of decentralization in some places. After assuming an adjustment process for per capita investment, $i_{st} = \kappa(c^*_{st} - c_{st-1})$, the authors obtain the following equation:

$$i_{st} = \gamma_{1s}x_{st-1} + \gamma_{2s}c_{st-1} + f_{rt} + f_s + \delta_{st} \times f_s + \varepsilon_{st}$$

This equation is estimated by GMM (generalized method of moments) after taking first-differences to eliminate both sets of regional effects (f_s and $\delta_{st} \times f_s$) and using several lags in the level of the capital stock as instruments. In the case of roads, the variables included in x_{st-1} are private capital per capita, workers per capita, trucks and vans per capita, distance run by vehicles per year/km of road and cars per capita. In the case of education, these variables are private capital per capita, workers per capita, population between six and 24 years per capita, population older than 65 years per capita, average years of education of the population[11]. Endogeneity of some of these variables is an obvious concern, especially in the case of roads. For example, the better the roads, the more trucks, cars and km run, and there may simply be more economic activity in the region. It is less clear in the case of education, since the age and educational traits of the population can safely be considered as exogenous. The authors argue, however, that this problem is attenuated by two facts. First, they look at the effect of one-period lagged regional traits on changes in the

Table 10.3 Responsiveness of Spanish road investment to regional needs and preferences before and after decentralization. Sample: 50 provinces (NUTS3 regions) during 1977–98

	(1)	(2)	
		Decentralized	Centralized
Private capital per capita	0.134	0.123	0.089
	(3.560)***	(2.553)**	(3.210)**
Workers per capita	0.013	0.011	0.006
	(1.239)	(1.654)	(1.456)
Trucks per capita	0.057	0.115	0.033
	(2.439)**	(4.091)***	(1.573)
Km run per year/km of road	0.017	0.012	0.007
	(2.100)**	(2.273)**	(1.754)*
Cars per capita	0.054	0.088	0.033
	(2.453)**	(2.432)**	(2.091)**
Road capital stock	0.394	0.399	
	(14.676)***	(14.098)***	
R^2-adj.	0.706	0.737	

Notes:
1. Dependent variable is regional + central road investment per capita.
2. Decentralized = dummy equal to 1 if the regional government has received the responsibility for providing intra-regional roads and 0 if not, centralized = 1 – decentralized.
3. The equation has been estimated in first differences by the GMM method and using as instruments lags of the endogenous variable.
4. The equations also include time ×region ("Autonomous Community") effects.

Source: Esteller-Moré and Solé-Ollé (2009). Investment and capital stock data come from Fundación BBVA (2002), capital, workers and population data come from Regional Accounts and Population Statistics, Instituto Nacional de Estadística (INE: www.ine.es), data on trucks, cars and km driven come from the Ministerio de Fomento (www.fomento.es).

infrastructure stock (that is, investment) over time, not a given point in time. Second, they focus on the difference between the coefficient of a given variable in the two regimes (centralized versus decentralized), and there is no motive to think that the possible endogeneity bias of a variable differs from one regime to another. The authors claim, therefore, that even accepting that the size of the coefficient estimated for a variable is not reliable, the comparison between the impact in the two regimes can still be made.

Tables 10.3 and 10.4 present the results for the cases of roads and education, respectively. In each table, the first column shows the results not allowing for different coefficients in each regime, while the second and third columns presents regime-specific estimates. In both cases, roads and

Table 10.4 Responsiveness of Spanish education investment to regional needs and preferences before and after decentralization. Sample: 50 provinces (NUTS3 regions) during 1977–98

	(1)	(2)	
		Decentralized	Centralized
Private capital per capita	0.065	0.079	0.064
	(3.124)***	(2.309)**	(2.310)**
Workers per capita	−0.024	−0.025	−0.020
	(−2.178)**	(−1.761)*	(−1.981)**
Population age 6 to 24 per capita	0.289	0.355	0.234
	(6.845)***	(4.765)***	(5.321)***
Population older than 65 per capita	−0.037	−0.071	−0.029
	(−2.123)**	(−2.081)**	(−1.498)
Average years of education	−0.210	−0.232	−0.160
	(−2.234)**	(−2.344)**	(−2.127)**
Education capital stock	0.365	0.387	
	(9.874)***	(10.184)***	
R^2-adj.	0.511	0.564	

Notes:
1. Dependent variable is regional + central education investment per capita; education included both primary, secondary and tertiary education.
2. Decentralized = dummy equal to 1 if the regional government has received the responsibility for providing primary and secondary education and 0 if not, centralized = 1 – decentralized.
3. See Table 10.2.

Source: Esteller-Moré and Solé-Ollé (2009).

education, the coefficients are higher in the decentralized than in the centralized regime. In the case of roads, the coefficients are nearly twice under decentralization, while in the case of education the decentralization coefficients are more or less 50 percent higher. This suggests that preference matching and policy responsiveness increased as a result of decentralization.[12] The authors then perform a variety of robustness checks in order to assure that these results do not reflect some other event that is contemporaneous with decentralization. They show that the differential impact of the variables with decentralization has not been caused by the EU funding of projects since 1986, since it also occurs in regions that do not receive these funds. This impact is also not due to a democratization trend, since the responsiveness of central government spending to preferences or needs did not increase with time.

4 CONCLUSION

During the 1980s and 1990s Spain experienced one of the most extensive decentralization reforms that can be found both in developed and developing countries. The process was initiated as part of a democratization package and was long and difficult, but ended with 17 ACs enjoying a considerable degree of autonomy in very important public services, such as health and education. In Spain, academics, politicians and lay people consider this process a success, and are generally not able to dissociate it from the success of Spanish democracy and even from the parallel improvement of living conditions. There are, however, practically no evaluations of the direct impact of decentralization of the delivery of public services, aside from those that focus on inter-territorial equity.

In this chapter, we have surveyed the few papers that have attempted to evaluate the efficiency consequences of decentralization. Concretely, we have focused on two papers: one of them evaluating the impact of education decentralization on the survival rate at the age of 16, or percentage of pupils entering post-secondary education (Salinas and Solé-Ollé, 2008), the other analyzing whether preference matching has improved or not as a consequence of the decentralization of both roads and education (Esteller-Moré and Solé-Ollé, 2009). Both papers show that decentralization had positive effects on efficiency. Without decentralization the survival rate would have been on average 2 percent lower, and investment would have been allocated between jurisdictions in a manner less responsive to local needs and demands. Of course, these results are by no means conclusive, and should be taken with caution, given the scarcity of studies and limitations of data and analysis.

These results do not show in any case that the Spanish decentralized system is free from problems. One of the main problems of the Spanish system is the inequity generated by the transfer system and the lack of consensus on the criteria that should guide the distribution of grants. As Salinas and Solé-Ollé (2008) show, differences in resources available to ACs affect educational outcomes. Moreover, the evidence of better matching of decentralized policies to regional preferences or needs has (Esteller-Moré and Solé-Ollé, 2009) been obtained after imposing the constraint that the overall level of resources available to an AC does not change after decentralization. So, this evidence shows that decentralization has the potential for a better matching of regional preferences, but this potential would not be realized in practice if the revenues at the disposal of some ACs are severely constrained.

NOTES

* I acknowledge financial support from SEJ2006-15212 research funding. I am grateful to participants at the Seminar on Effectiveness of Decentralized Strategies and Outcomes (Collegio Carlo Alberto, Moncalieri, 3–4 September 2007), and especially to Giorgio Brosio and Stuti Khemani, for valuable comments.

1. In fact, as has been pointed out by a recent OECD study (Blöchinger, 2008), the observed trend in expenditure decentralization is matched by an analogous one of revenue centralization.
2. This notwithstanding, some authors consider that the system is not fully stabilized, in the sense that the historic regions are not satisfied with a level of responsibilities that is nowadays very similar to that of the other regions. So, cultural heterogeneity in Spain seems to demand some sort of asymmetric federalism, but competition between regions forces convergence in decentralization levels, fostering again the demands from the historic regions.
3. For example, a central agency responsible for collecting information regarding health services (Observatiorio del Sistema Nacional de Salud) was not created by law until 2003. The corresponding agency in the case of education (now called Instituto de Evaluación, http://www.institutodeevaluacion.mec.es, accessed 2 April 2009), was created in 1994 but has remained basically inactive until the beginning of this century, although it is true that it is actually well staffed and has started doing serious work on the topic.
4. For example, only a few ACs actually ask PISA (Program for International Student Assessment of the OECD) to study a specific sample of schools under its jurisdiction (something that costs little) and the central government only pays for a country-representative sample. Unsurprisingly, the few ACs that demand a regionally representative evaluation perform better than the Spanish average.
5. There are also some papers that evaluate the effects of decentralization on growth for the Spanish case, the best example being Carrión-i-Silvestre et al. (2008), which finds a positive but modest effect.
6. We will provide only an overview of the main issues. For an extended analysis of spending decentralization in Spain see, for example, Molero (2001); the main issues regarding revenue assignment and intergovernmental grants can be found in López-Laborda et al. (2006).
7. Some responsibilities are attributed by law to the municipalities. In Spain there are more than 8000 municipalities, most of which are rather small (90 percent of them have less than 5000 inhabitants). The responsibilities of Spanish municipalities are similar to the ones attributed elsewhere to local governments (for example, garbage collection, water supply, street paving and cleaning, parks and recreation, and so on) with the exception of education, which is a regional responsibility in Spain. In addition to municipalities, there is an upper tier of local government called *Diputación Provincial*, with the basic responsibility of giving technical and financial support to municipalities.
8. Note, for example, that just from 1980 to 1993 (before the final round of transfer of responsibilities began) more than 600 000 public servants were transferred from the central to the regional governments. Although public servant unions were sometimes reluctant to decentralize, they did not block the entire process. Moreover, the transfer of personnel implies that the new regional bureaucracies started with a capability level akin to that of the central one (see Hanson, 2000, for a development of this argument in the case of education).
9. See Zubiri (2004) for a more complete description of the foral system.
10. Although this author shows that this is the case in electoral-college systems, recently Gehlbach (2007) has extended the results to majoritarian elections. Note that while in the electoral-college case the central politicians have to please at least 50 percent of the districts, in majoritarian elections they need to please at least 50 percent of the voting

populations. In both cases, the central politician could disregard the demands of a given region without risking losing office.

11. In both cases, a wider set of variables were considered, but those mentioned above are the ones that have some explanatory capacity. Have a look at Esteller-Moré and Solé-Ollé (2009) for more details about the variables and the data sources.
12. The sign of the different variables can be interpreted, although as was mentioned above the size is probably not reliable, due to possible endogeneity problems. For example, road investment increases the more private capital and workers, the more trucks and cars and the more km run by vehicles; and education investment also increases the more private capital (but the less workers) and the more young the population, and decreases the more old the population (priorities are shifted to health and care for the elderly) and the more educated is the population; this last finding is a little bit intriguing, but it might be due to either home inputs being substitutes for the school ones or to the fact that the more educated demand more private education.

REFERENCES

Ahmad, J., S. Devarajan, S. Khemani and S. Shah (2006), "Decentralization and Service Delivery", in E. Ahmad and G. Brosio (eds), *Handbook of Fiscal Federalism*, vol. II, Cheltenham, UK and Northampton, MA, USA: Edward Elgar.

Ayala, L., R. Martínez and J. Ruíz-Huerta (2001), "La descentralización territorial de las prestaciones asistenciales: efectos sobre la igualdad" (The territorial decentralization of income support transfers: effects on equality), Papeles de trabajo del Instituto de Estudios Fiscales. Serie economía, No. 16, pp. 1–39.

Barankay, I. and B. Lockwood (2007), "Decentralization and the Productive Efficiency of Government: Evidence from Swiss Cantons", *Journal of Public Economics*, **91** (5–6), 1197–218.

Bardhan, P. and D. Mookherjee (2000), "Capture and Governance at Local and National Levels", *American Economic Review*, **90** (2), 135–9.

Bardhan, P. and D. Mookherjee (2005), "Decentralization, Corruption and Government Accountability: An Overview", in S. Rose-Ackerman (ed.), *Handbook of Economic Corruption*, Cheltenham, UK and Northampton, MA, USA: Edward Elgar.

Besley, T. and S. Coate (2003), "Centralized Versus Decentralized Provision of Local Public Goods: A Political Economy Approach", *Journal of Public Economics*, **87** (12), 2611–37.

Blöchinger, H. (2008), "Tax Assignment and Tax Autonomy in OECD Countries", in N. Bosch and J.M. Durán (eds), *Fiscal Federalism and Political Decentralization: Lessons from Spain, Germany and Canada*, Cheltenham, UK and Northampton, MA, USA: Edward Elgar.

Blundell, R. and M. Costa (2000), "Evaluation Methods for Non-experimental Data", *Fiscal Studies*, **21** (4), 427–68.

Bonal, X., X. Rambla, E. Calderón and N. Pros (2005), *La descentralización educativa en España. Una mirada comparativa a los sistemas escolares de las Comunidades Autónomas* (The decentralization of education in Spain. A comparitive overview to the schooling systems of the Autonomous Communities), Colecció Estudis 18, Barcelona: Fundació Pi i Sunyer.

Brueckner, J.K. (2007), "Partial Fiscal Decentralization", CESifo Working Paper

No. 2137, University of California at Irvine, http://papers.ssin.com/s013/papers.c£m?obstract-id=1029581, accessed 1 April 2009.
Carrion-i-Silvestre, J.Ll., M. Espasa and T. Mora (2008), "Fiscal Decentralization and Economic Growth in Spain", *Public Finance Review*, **36** (2), 194–218.
Castells, A. (2001), "The Role of Intergovernmental Finance in Achieving Diversity and cohesion: the case of Spain", *Environment and Planning C: Government and Policy*, **19** (2), 189–206.
Castells, A. and A. Solé-Ollé (2001), *Cuantificación de las necesidades de gasto de las Comunidades Autónomas* (Quantification of the expenditure needs of the Autonomous Communities), Madrid: Instituto de Estudios Fiscales.
Castells, A. and A. Solé-Ollé (2005), "The Regional Allocation of Infrastructure Investment: The Role of Equity, Efficiency and Political Factors", *European Economic Review*, **49** (5), 1165–205.
Castells, A., P. Sorribas and M. Vilalta (2005), *Las subvenciones de nivelación en la financiación de las comunidades autónomas: análisis de la situación actual y propuestas de reforma* (Equalization transfers in the financing system of Autonomous Communities: analysis of the current situation of reform proposals), Madrid: Instituto de Estudios Fiscales.
Costa-i-Font, J. and F. Moscone (2008), "The Impact of Decentralization and Inter-territorial Interactions on Spanish Health Expenditure", *Empirical Economics*, **34** (1), 167–84.
Costa-i-Font, J. and Rico, A. (2006a): "Devolution and the Inter-regional Inequalities in Health and Health Care in Spain", *Regional Studies*, **40** (8), 1–13.
Costa-i-Font, J. and A. Rico (2006b), "Vertical Competition in the Spanish National Health System (NHS)", *Public Choice*, **128** (3–4), 477–98.
Costa-i-Font, J., G. Lopez-Casasnovas and I. Planas (2005), "Diversity and Regional Inequalities: Assessing the Outcomes of the Spanish System of Health Care Services", *Health Economics*, **14** (1), S221–S235.
Cremer, J., A. Estache and P. Seabright (1996), "Decentralizing Public Services: What Can We Learn From the Theory of the Firm?", *Revue d'Economie Politique*, **106** (1), 37–60.
Dahl, R.A. and E.R. Tufte (1973), *Size and Democracy*, Palo Alto, CA: Stanford University Press.
Esteller-Moré, A. and J.M. Durán (2004), "El ejercicio de la capacidad normativa de las CCAA en los tributos cedidos: una primera evaluación a través de los tipos impositivos efectivos en el IRPF (The use of the tax powers in ceded taxes by the Autonomous Communities: a first evaluation through the effective personal income tax rates)", *Papeles de Trabajo* No. 20/2004, Madrid: Instituto de Estudios Fiscales.
Esteller-Moré, A. and Solé-Ollé, A. (2009), "Decentralization and Government Responsiveness. Evidence from Spain", Working Papers No. 2009/25, Barcelona: Institut d'Economia de Barcelona (IEB).
Fisman, R. and R. Gatti (2001), "Decentralization and Corruption: Evidence Across Countries", *Journal of Public Economics*, **83** (3), 325–45.
Galiani, S. and E. Schargrodsky (2001), "Evaluating the impact of school decentralization on education quality", *Journal of the Latin American and Caribbean Economic Association*, **2** (2), 275–314.
Galiani, S., O. Gertler and E. Schargrodsky (2005), "School Decentralization:

Helping the Good Get Better, But Leaving the Rest Behind", mimeo, World Bank.

Gehlbach, S. (2007), "Electoral Institutions and the National Provision of Local Public Goods", *Quarterly Journal of Economics*, **2** (1), 5–25.

Gimeno, J.A. (2008), "Tax Assignment and Regional Co-responsibility in Spain" in N. Bosch and J.M. Durán (eds), *Fiscal Federalism and Political Decentralization Lessons from Spain, Germany and Canada*, Cheltenham, UK and Northampton, MA, USA: Edward Elgar.

Giorno, C. and I. Joumard (2005), "Getting the Most Out of Public Sector Decentralization in Spain" OECD Economics Department Working Papers, No. 436.

Habibi, N., C. Huang, D. Miranda, V. Murillo, G. Ranis, M. Sarkar and F. Steward (2001), "Decentralization in Argentina", Yale Economic Growth Center Discussion Paper No. 825.

Hanson, M.E. (2000), "Democratization and Educational Decentralization in Spain. A Twenty Year Struggle For Reform", Country Studies. Educational Reform and Management Publication Series No. 1/3, The World Bank.

Huther, J. and A. Shah (1998), "Applying a Simple Measure of Good Governance to the Debate on Fiscal Decentralization", World Bank Policy Research Working Papers No. 1894.

Inman, R.P. and D.L. Rubinfeld (2005), "Federalism and the Democratic Transition: Lessons from South Africa", *American Economic Review*, **95** (2), 39–43.

Jakubowski, M. and I. Topińska (2009), "Impact of Decentralization on Education in Poland", this volume.

Knight, B. (2004), "Parochial Interests and the Centralized Provision of Local Public Goods: Evidence from Congressional Voting on Transportation Projects", *Journal of Public Economics*, **88** (3–4), 845–66.

Lockwood, B. (2002), "Distributive Politics and the Costs of Centralization", *Review of Economic Studies*, **69** (2), 313–37.

López-Laborda, J., J. Martínez-Vázquez and C. Monasterio (2006), "The Practice of Fiscal Federalism in Spain", ISP Working Paper No. 06-23, Atlanta: Georgia State University.

Molero, J.C. (2001), "Analysis of the Decentralization of Public Spending in Spain", *Public Finance and Management*, **I** (4), 500–56.

Moreno, L. (1997), *La federalización de España: poder político y territorio*, Madrid: Siglo XXI editores.

Oates, W.E. (1972), *Fiscal Federalism*, New York: Harcourt Brace Jovanovich.

Oates, W.E. (1999), "An Essay on Fiscal Federalism", *Journal of Economic Literature*, **37** (3), 1120–49.

Petrongolo, B. and M.J. San Segundo (2002), "Staying-on at School at 16: The Impact of Labor Market Conditions in Spain", *Economics of Education Review*, **21** (4), 353–65.

Prud'homme, R. (1995), "The Dangers of Decentralization", *The World Bank Research Observer*, **10** (2), 201–20.

Salinas, P. and A. Solé-Ollé (2008), "Evaluation of the Effects of Decentralization on Educational Outcomes in Spain" Paper presented at the 64th Congress of the International Institute of Public Finance (IIPF), Maastricht, The Netherlands, 22–25 August 2008.

Salmon, P. (1987), "Decentralisation as an Incentive Scheme", *Oxford Review of Economic Policy*, **3** (2), 24–43.
Seabright, P. (1996), "Accountability and Decentralization in Government: An Incomplete Contracts Model", *European Economic Review*, **40** (1), 61–89.
Shah, A. (1998), "Balance, Accountability, and Responsiveness: Lessons About Decentralization" World Bank Policy Research Working Papers No. 2021.
Shah, A. (2006), "Corruption and Decentralized Public Governance", World Bank Policy Research Working Papers No. 3824.
Shah, A. and T. Thompson (2004), "Implementing Decentralized Local Governance: A Treacherous Road With Potholes, Detours, And Road Closures", Policy Research Working Paper Series No. 3353, The World Bank.
Treisman, D. (2002), "Decentralization and the Quality of Government", mimeo, Department of Political Science, UCLA, http://www.sscnet.ucla.edu/polisci/faculty/treisman/, accessed 1 April 2009.
Volden, C. (2006), "States as Policy Laboratories: Emulating Success in the Children's Health Insurance Program", *American Journal of Political Science*, **50** (2), 294–312.
Weingast, B. (1995), "The Economic Role of Political Institutions: Market Preserving Federalism and Economic Growth", *Journal of Law, Economics and Organization*, **11** (1), 1–31.
Weingast, B. (2004), "Constructing Self-enforcing Democracy in Spain." in J. Oppenheimer. and I. Morris (eds), *From Anarchy to Democracy*, Palo Alto, CA: Stanford University Press.
Weingast, B., K. Shepsle and Ch. Johnsen (1981), "The Political Economy of Benefits and Costs: A Neoclassical Approach to Distributive Politics", *Journal of Political Economy*, **89** (4), 642–64.
World Bank (1999), *World Development Report: Entering the 21th Century*, Oxford: Oxford University Press.
Zapico, E. (2002), "Budget for Results in Spain: Lessons Learned After Two Decades of Reform", OECD, http://www.oecd.org/dataoecd/4/13/2497137.pdf, accessed 1 April 2009.
Zubiri, I. (2004), "La equidad en el sistema actual de financiación de las comunidades autonómas: sistema común versus sistema foral (Equity in the current system of financing of the Autonomous Communities common versus foral system)", Papeles de economía española No. 99, 198–207.

PART III

Selected normative and policy issues

11. Decentralization and public service provision—a framework for pro-poor institutional design

Regina Birner and Joachim von Braun*

1 INTRODUCTION

The effective provision of basic services, such as water and sanitation, health, education and agricultural extension, is a major challenge for development. In many developing countries, the poor—especially the rural poor—receive poor services in terms of access, quantity and quality (World Bank, 2004). Due to a combination of "supply-side" and "demand-side" factors, rural areas—where most of the world's poor still live—are particularly disadvantaged in terms of rural service provision: the unit costs to provide services are relatively higher, especially if population densities are low. Rural areas are less attractive for skilled staff, which leads to human resource constraints in service provision. And the rural poor face higher transaction costs than the urban poor in organizing interest groups to demand better services and hold service providers accountable.

Among the governance reforms that aim at improving public service provision, one type of reform has attracted particular attention in recent decades: decentralization. Some 80 percent of all developing countries have experimented with some form of decentralization in recent decades (Work, 2002). A common argument in favor of decentralization is that it will improve public service provision, and in particular rural service provision, "by bringing government closer to the people".[1] The classical economics literature on decentralization (Oates, 1972)—the "fiscal federalism" literature—has been relatively favorable to decentralization as well. It stressed the role of differential information at different levels of government and identified the advantages of inter-jurisdictional competition and of aligning policy with tax authority.

Yet, the empirical experience with decentralization in developing countries has been rather mixed (Bardhan, 2002). "Bringing government closer to the people" has not universally led to better service provision in rural areas. Partly, this may be due to the fact that decentralization—as a major reform of the structure of the state—needs time to take effect. The literature has focused on a variety of challenges associated with decentralization. Trying to come to grips with the reality of decentralization in developing countries, the current literature places strong emphasis on the question of local political economy. Unlike in the earlier fiscal federalism literature, the state is no longer seen as a maximizer of people's welfare, which is capable and benevolent at all levels. Next to the problems that local governments face in terms of capacity and coordination, local elite capture has been one of the major concerns—a prime reason why the poor may receive even poorer services in a decentralized setting (Bardhan, 2002; Mansuri and Rao, 2004). This problem has been analyzed both from a theoretical perspective, using public choice models (Bardhan and Mookherjee, 2000; Besley and Coate, 2000), and from an empirical perspective, with a strong emphasis on India (Bardhan and Mookherjee, 2006; World Bank, 2006)

In spite of the advances in the theoretical and empirical literature to better account for the reality of decentralization in developing countries, the empirical micro-foundation of such approaches has remained rather incomplete. There are comparatively few studies that take into account that local governments typically consist of *several* tiers, and not much is known about the types of interactions that take place across different tiers of local government. A related complexity—which is not well captured in the current literature on decentralization either—is the fact that even for the same sector, different tasks are assigned to different levels of government. How does this complexity affect the effectiveness of service delivery and the prospects of reaching the poor?

The objective of this chapter is to throw light on this question by developing a conceptual framework that can guide future research and policy design regarding the decentralization of public service provision. Applying a cost-effectiveness approach developed by Williamson (1991) to compare different governance structures, the approach of the chapter is to disaggregate rural service provision in different types of transactions and to identify the factors that influence the appropriate level of government and the appropriate degree of delegation for carrying out the respective transactions. This approach makes it possible to integrate insights from different branches of the economic and the political science literature when assessing the appropriateness of different levels of government for decentralized service provision.

The chapter is structured as follows: Section 2 develops a conceptual framework based on the transaction cost approach sketched above. In

Section 3, the literature relevant to this approach is reviewed. Section 4 discusses the research agenda that follows from this approach, and Section 5 concludes.

2 CONCEPTUAL FRAMEWORK

2.1 Public Services

The framework developed here focuses on basic services that are important for the poor, such as water and sanitation, basic health care, primary education and agricultural extension. As indicated in the introduction, the framework addresses the specific challenges of providing such services in rural areas. The term "public services" is used here, because the framework refers to services that require public sector involvement, either because of market failure, or because there is a societal consensus that access to such services is a right of all citizens, regardless of their income. This chapter does not deal with the question as to which extent state intervention is justified in basic service provision, both for reasons of scope and because this question involves political value judgments and is context-specific.

2.2 A Transaction Costs Perspective on Public Service Provision

The conceptual framework proposed here is based on transaction costs theory, specifically the work on economic transaction costs by Williamson (1981; 1985; 1991; 1999). The chapter applies Williamson's discriminating alignment hypothesis, according to which transactions that differ in their attributes are to be aligned with governance structures that differ in their costs and competence so as to effect an economizing result. Williamson's approach is based on a cost-effectiveness analysis, which aims to identify the governance structures that make it possible to achieve a specified outcome at lowest possible costs. Improving the cost-effectiveness of service provision makes it possible to reach a larger number of citizens with the same level of resources. However, to ensure a focus on poverty in the cost-effectiveness analysis proposed here, it is essential to specify the provision of services to the poor as an element of the outcome to be achieved with the lowest possible costs.

To apply the transaction costs perspective to decentralization, one needs to disentangle service provision into different types of transactions (Ostrom et al., 1993; World Bank, 2007). For the purpose of this framework, five types of activities or transactions are distinguished:

1. *Planning transactions*: decision-making processes regarding the quantity and quality of the service provided and regarding the target groups who should be able to access and use the service.
2. *Production transactions*: activities necessary to construct and maintain the necessary infrastructure and to manage the staff and the daily operations needed for the provision of respective services.[2]
3. *Financing transactions*: activities involved in raising the revenues necessary to provide the service and managing all financial aspects of service provision.
4. *Monitoring and evaluation transactions*: activities related to collecting and analyzing data regarding the quantity and quality of the services provided.
5. *Transactions at the user level*: activities that users need to undertake to access a service, including travel and waiting. The costs of access (and non-access) to the services are part of the total economic costs of the service activities.

In designing governance structures for public service provision, policymakers need to decide which level of government should be responsible for each of these types of transactions. This question is related to other important questions of institutional design: to which extent should different types of transactions be delegated to autonomous public agencies? To which extent should they be outsourced to private service providers, or devolved to local user groups? The framework developed here focuses on identifying the appropriate level of government for public service provision.

Appling Williamson's discriminating alignment hypothesis mentioned above, a more decentralized governance structure x will be considered to be more efficient than a more centralized governance structure y, if the outcome—including the outcome in terms of reaching the poor—of this transaction can be achieved at lower total costs under governance structure x than under governance structure y. The term "governance structure" refers to the institutional set-up used for carrying out the respective transaction, in this case specifically the level of government responsible for the transaction. Figure 11.1 illustrates this approach.

The figure shows hypothetical cost curves for the provision of a service under a more centralized governance structure x and a more decentralized governance structure y. The vertical axis indicates the total costs arising for the provision of the service. We develop a classification of these costs. The total costs include the production costs (PC) that arise from providing this service under governance structure x or y, and the costs of using the respective governance structure (GC). The horizontal axis displays a

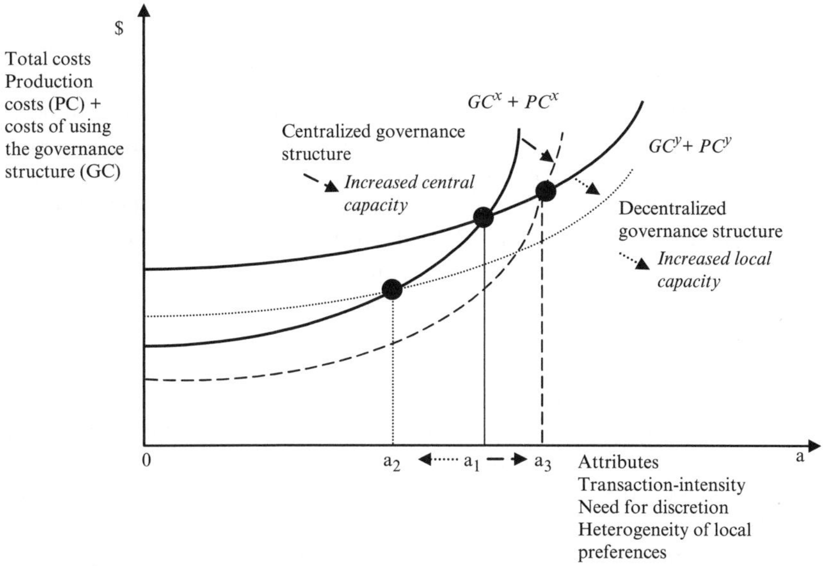

Source: Based on Williamson (1991) and Birner and Wittmer (2004).

Figure 11.1 Comparative cost-effectiveness of different governance structures

combination of attributes, which increase the comparative advantage for decentralized service provision. These attributes will be discussed below in more detail, based on a review of the literature. They include, for example, the heterogeneity of local preferences with regard to the respective service, and the frequency and spatial distribution (transaction-intensity) of the activities that are necessary to provide the service. The more important these attributes are, which is indicated by a move to the right on the horizontal axis, the faster is the increase in the costs for providing the respective service under a centralized governance structure.

In the case of a decentralized service provision (governance structure *y*), these transaction costs increase less rapidly, which is indicated by the reduced slope of the respective cost curve. If these attributes are not relevant (moving to the left-hand side on the horizontal axis), a centralized service provider has a comparative advantage over the decentralized provider, for example, due to the possibility to use economies of scale. From point a_1 onwards (characterizing a certain level of the relevant attributes), a decentralized governance structure has a comparative advantage over a centralized governance structure for performing the respective transaction.

Figure 11.1 also displays the effect of contextual factors. For example, if the capacity of the local government is increased, it will be able to supply the same service at lower costs, indicating a downward shift of the respective cost curve. Accordingly, the point from which a decentralized organization of the respective transaction has a comparative advantage over a centralized one moves from point a_1 to a_2. Likewise, if the capacity of the central administration is increased, this results in a downward shift of the cost curve that indicates central-level provision. Accordingly, the point from which decentralized provision is more efficient moves to point a_3.

This framework makes it possible to derive hypotheses on the appropriate level of governance for different types of transactions, taking the frame conditions into account. It requires the identification of (1) relevant attributes of transactions and (2) contextual factors. The next section will derive attributes and contextual factors from different branches of the decentralization literature. As Williamson (1991; 1999) has pointed out, this framework is not designed to identify "the most efficient" of all possible governance structures. The goal of applying a transaction costs approach is more modest: to compare a limited set of governance structures with regard to the question as to which one is the most cost-effective among those compared, taking the contextual frame conditions into account.[3] While limited, this perspective is highly policy-relevant, because rural services are seldom designed from scratch. In most situations, political decision-makers wish to compare the existing governance structure for providing a public service with a set of alternatives that are considered to be politically feasible.

2.3 Types of Costs to be Considered

Different transactions are associated with different types of costs. Taking the categories of transactions introduced above into account, one can distinguish the following types of costs:

2.3.1 Decision costs

This category can be conceptualized as comprising two types of costs: transaction costs of decision-making and decision-failure costs. The transaction costs of decision-making arising under a governance structure $x(TC_D^x)$ consist of (1) the costs of acquiring the information that is necessary to make appropriate decisions, including information on the preferences of the local population, and (2) the costs of coordinating decision-making if different individuals or groups are involved.

There is obviously a trade-off between the transaction costs incurred for decision-making and the "quality" of the decisions reached. To capture this trade-off, the costs caused by making suboptimal decisions are conceptualized as decision-failure costs. The decision-failure costs arising under governance structure x are denoted as FC_D^x. The sum of the transaction costs of decision-making and the decision-failure costs are subsumed under the term decision costs $(TC_D^x + FC_D^x)$. Note that the category of decision-failure costs is introduced here because a cost-effectiveness framework is applied (Figure 11.1) here. In a cost–benefit framework, one would consider higher benefits due to better decisions instead of the decision-failure costs.

The proposed approach obviously involves the problem of assessing the "quality" of a decision. With regard to operational decisions, for example, on the design of a small-scale reservoir for irrigation, one can conceptualize the decision-failure costs as the damage caused by choosing an inferior design due to a lack of technical expertise. It is more challenging to define the "quality" of allocation decisions, that is, decisions on the amount of a service to be provided, and on the groups of the population who should benefit from it. In this regard, one could define decision-failure costs as the deviation from a social welfare function, but—as shown by Arrow (1950)—there is no procedure that makes it possible to aggregate individual interests to a social welfare function if some basic principles such as the absence of a dictator are met. A classical approach to solve this problem has been developed by Buchanan and Tullock in their *Calculus of Consent* (1962). This approach leads to the development of decision rules that take into account the trade-off between the loss of utility arising for an individual when moving away from unanimity rule and the associated reductions in transaction costs of decision-making.

Next to decision-failure costs that arise because of the challenges of aggregating individual preferences to a social welfare function, decision-failure costs also arise if certain groups can gain an "unfair advantage" in the decision process due to their economic or social position. The negative effects of elite capture are considered as decision-failure costs in this framework. Elite capture problems are a particular constraint for reaching pro-poor results.

2.3.2 Production costs

The production costs PC^x that arise under governance structure x include all costs for the "production" or delivery of a public service that are usually considered in neoclassical economics, such as the costs of material and construction of infrastructure for service facilities, the salary of teachers, and so on. Governance structures affect the production costs. With regard to decentralization, a major consideration is the effect of decentralization on the possibilities of capturing economies of scale so as to reduce the production costs for service provision.

2.3.3 Implementation costs

The production of services is associated with transaction costs. Transaction costs of implementation (TC_I^x) include the costs of supervising, monitoring and evaluating the provision of a rural service. If implementation activities are outsourced to the private sector, the costs arising for organizing the procurement and for the supervision and enforcement of contracts fall under this category of costs, as well. Similar to the case of decision-making, there is obviously a trade-off between the resources spent for monitoring and evaluation, and the quality of service provided. To capture this trade-off, the category of implementation failure costs (FC_I^x) is used here. For example, if corruption in the procurement process for a rural road has the consequence that the maintenance costs are higher than they would have been otherwise, the increased maintenance costs fall under the category implementation failure costs. Ostrom et al. (1993) use the term "strategic costs" to refer to the costs arising in different governance structures due to free-riding, shirking, rent-seeking, corruption and moral hazard. Costs that the service users incur due to implementation failure, such as increased waiting times, bribes or lack of access also need to be subsumed under the implementation failure costs. Costs arising for users due to failed attempts to access a service, for example, because of absenteeism of service staff, also need to be considered in this category. Likewise, this category includes the income lost and damages incurred by service users because of substandard service quality. The sum of the transaction costs of monitoring and evaluation and the implementation failure costs are subsumed under the category of implementation costs ($TC_I^x + FC_I^x$).

2.3.4 Financial management costs

The transaction costs framework can be expanded to take the financing aspects of decentralization into account. The literature on fiscal decentralization has placed strong emphasis on the question of at which level taxes should be raised (Musgrave, 1959). From a transaction costs perspective, one needs to take into account the transaction costs of raising taxes, and the transaction costs of budget management. These two categories may be summarized as transaction costs of financial management (TC_F^x) The transaction costs of financial management include the costs of administering budgets, including the costs of financial transfers, accounting, reporting and auditing. Similar to the case of decision-making, there is a trade-off regarding the amount of resources spent for tax collection and for budget management, and the "quality" of these activities. The tax income forgone due to a lack in the ability to collect the targeted amount of taxes could be labeled financial management failure costs (FC_F^x). The losses arising due to lack of appropriate budget management also fall under this category. The fiscal decentralization literature has paid ample attention to the incentives that different systems of taxation create (Weingast, 2005). Efficiency losses that are caused by misaligned incentives in the tax system can also be considered as a category of costs arising due to financial management failure (FC_F^x).

2.3.5 Access costs

To make appropriate decisions on the institutional design of service delivery, the costs that arise for the users in accessing a particular service (access costs AC) need to be taken into account, as well. These costs include the opportunity costs of time that service users incur to access the service, including the time they spend for getting to the service facility and, if necessary, to wait until the service is provided, and the costs arising from non-access (a forgone value-added). To what extent service users incur opportunity costs of their time is an empirical question, which will be further discussed below. Conceptually, it is important *not* to assume that poor rural households face low or zero opportunity costs of time (Kes and Swaminathan, 2006). To ensure a pro-poor institutional design of public service delivery, these costs need to be taken into account.[4]

2.4 Summing Up: The Costs of Using a Specific Governance Structure

One can consider the sum of the decision costs, the implementation costs, the financial management costs and the access costs as the "costs of using a particular governance structure", or in short "governance costs" (GC):[5]

$$GC^x = (TC_D^x + FC_D^x) + (TC_I^x + FC_I^x) + (TC_F^x + FC_F^x) + AC^x$$

Based on the above considerations, the total costs arising for the provision of a public service (with defined quality, quantity and targeting) under governance structure x are comprised of the sum of the production costs PC^x and the costs GC^x of using governance structure x. As stated above, governance structure y will be considered to be more cost-effective than governance structure x, if the sum of the production costs and the governance costs arising under governance structure y is lower than the sum of these costs arising under governance structure x.

$$PC^y + GC^y < PC^x + GC^x$$

2.5 Distribution of Costs

To ensure a poverty-focus in the design of governance structures for public service provision, it is essential to pay attention to the distribution of the costs involved. In particular, it is important to take into account which share of the costs is incurred by the state, which implies by the tax payers (and, if applicable, by donor agencies), and which share is incurred by the service users. By definition, the access costs (AC^x) are incurred by the users, as discussed above. Service users may also have to cover a share of the costs that fall in other categories. If users participate in decision-making, for example, by serving on user committees, the opportunity costs of their time and other expenses they incur have to be taken into account as share of the transaction costs of decision-making (TC_D^x). If user groups contribute to the management of service facilities, such as drinking water supply, their opportunity cost of time has to be considered as part of the production costs (PC^x) that arise for providing the service. If service users are involved in monitoring and evaluation, they take over a share of the transaction costs of implementation (TC_I^x). As discussed above, service users may also incur a share of the implementation failure costs (FC_I^x), for example, if they have to pay bribes or suffer from substandard quality service provision. They may also share financial management failure costs (FC_F^x), for example, if private tax collectors demand a higher amount than the appropriate tax rate from them.

From a poverty perspective, it is important to identify which share of their income citizens have to spend for the use of basic services, and what differences exist in this regard across different socioeconomic groups. The poor often face particular difficulties in accessing services, because they need to travel longer distances to reach service facilities, and because the transport costs they have to incur constitute a larger share of their income. Current reform approaches have shifted considerable management responsibilities to user groups, especially in rural areas. As argued above, it is important not to assume that the opportunity costs that rural citizens incur for such activities are low or zero. For the poor, the opportunity costs of time are often comparatively high. If they are agricultural laborers, for example, they may lose their daily wage when spending time in village meetings or in organizations created to hold service providers accountable. The poor may also be negatively affected by cost-recovery approaches that shift costs to service users (Bardhan and Mookherjee, 2003). Cross-subsidies for poor households, such as "lifeline" pricing schemes, can help to avoid this problem. Under such schemes, a certain number of essential units of the respective service are provided free (World Bank, 2004).

To capture the gender dimension of service provision, it is important to identify the costs incurred by individual household members for accessing a particular service, rather than looking only at the costs occurring for the households as a whole. Male and female household members may incur different costs of using the same service, for example, if there is gender discrimination in service provision. Moreover, due to the existing gender division of labor, women and girls suffer particular disadvantages from poor access to infrastructure, such as drinking water and sanitation facilities, transport and energy sources. The poorer their access to such infrastructure, the more time they need to spend for fetching water, collecting fuel wood and transporting goods, which limits their possibilities to improve their livelihoods through education, civic participation and income-generating activities (ICRW, 2005; Kes and Swaminathan, 2006).

Measuring the total costs, including the transaction costs, incurred by individuals with different socioeconomic backgrounds in accessing and using a specific service is a promising strategy to capture problems of social exclusion in public service provision. This measure is more objective than reported satisfaction, because this measure avoids the bias that occurs in satisfaction data if the poor have low expectation levels.

From a normative perspective, one needs to acknowledge that it is ultimately a question of distributional justice, which distribution of costs between the state and service users and between different socioeconomic user groups is considered fair, taking into account potential trade-offs between efficiency and equity. To assess the distributional implications of different governance structures, one also needs to assess to what extent the tax system in the country under consideration is equitable. In view of high levels of tax evasion among better-off groups, which is a common phenomenon, inequity can also arise from relying on an inequitable tax system for financing public service provision. The poverty impacts of taxation have, however, received limited attention in the literature, so far (Gemmell and Morrissey, 2005).

3 FACTORS THAT INFLUENCE THE COST-EFFECTIVENESS OF DIFFERENT GOVERNANCE STRUCTURES: INSIGHTS FROM THE LITERATURE

As indicated in Section 2, the transaction costs approach makes it necessary to identify the attributes of the transactions and the contextual conditions that influence the various costs involved in performing the transactions required to provide a public service. This section reviews the literature on decentralization to identify these attributes and contextual factors. The results are summarized in Tables 11.1 and 11.2.

3.1 Fiscal Federalism Literature

As Weingast (2005) points out in his review, the economic classics of federalism revolve around: Hayek's (1939) work on the role of differential information across levels of government; Tiebout's (1956) emphasis on inter-jurisdictional competition and Musgrave's (1959) notions of the assignment of policy and tax authority across jurisdictions. Oates (1972) combined these three ideas, providing a strong normative argument in favor of decentralization. Later studies on the economics of federalism focused on the incentive problems that local governments face due to common-pool situations and opportunities for free-riding. This literature identified externalities and spillover effects, internal trade barriers and soft budget constraints as factors affecting the performance of decentralization (for reviews, see, for example, Bardhan, 2002; Weingast, 2005). Careaga and Weingast (2002) focus on the trade-off faced by local government actors between providing market-enhancing public goods and providing private rents. They show that local governments that raise their own revenue are more likely to focus on market-enhancing public goods, while governments that obtain most of their revenue from the central government are more likely to provide private rents.

This fiscal decentralization literature points to three important attributes of transactions, which influence the appropriate level of decentralization: economies of scale, spillovers and externalities, and the heterogeneity of local preferences. If citizens' preferences with regard to a public service are very heterogeneous, local governments are more likely to incur lower costs of acquiring the information that is necessary to make appropriate decisions on the provision of this service. These information costs are part of the transaction costs of decision-making discussed above. Likewise, local governments are less likely to incur decision-failure costs that may otherwise arise due to lack of information. If economies of scale in providing a rural service are large, a more centralized provision of this service is likely to reduce the production costs of providing the service. A differentiated local government system, which has more than one tier, provides more possibilities to capture differentiated economies of scale in providing rural services. Line agencies often have additional types of service provision areas (for example, areas for which one extension agent is responsible), which leads to even more differentiated possibilities to capture economies of scale. Having more than one tier of government and other types of administrative boundaries also increases the possibilities to adjust the level of service provision to externalities and spillovers that occur at different scales. This is important in natural resource management. Agencies in charge of water resources management, for example, increasingly use river catchments or watershed areas as basic units, even though this may create problems as those typically cut across different administrative areas.

Implicitly, the classical fiscal federalism literature also points to two contextual factors that influence the appropriate level of decentralization (cf. Bardhan, 2002). This literature assumes that the capacities of the national and the local public administration to provide rural services are equal. In the reality of developing countries, this is hardly ever the case. As already highlighted in the introduction, rural areas face particular problems of attracting qualified staff. Another assumption in the fiscal federalism literature, especially in Tiebout's competition model, is the possibility of citizens and business enterprises to move freely between local jurisdictions. In developing countries, this possibility is often restricted, for example, due to social restrictions and the absence of land markets. Farmers constitute a large share of the rural population in developing countries, and their mobility is particularly limited.

A third contextual factor can also be derived from the classical fiscal federalism literature: the ability of local governments to raise tax revenues, which—in this literature—is also assumed to be equal at all levels of governments. As Bardhan (2002) points out, in most developing countries, the more elastic and progressive sources of tax revenue typically lie with the central government. Moreover, local areas may differ considerably in their ability to raise tax revenues due to geographical income disparities, which are often large because of differences in agro-ecological potential and infrastructure development. A study on tax collection in rural Uganda demonstrated a range of problems that local governments may face in tax collection, including serious revenue leakages (tax rendering), negative economic effects caused by distortions of relative prices due to taxation and negative distributional consequences due to a steep regressiveness of local tax systems (Bahiigwa et al., 2004).

With regard to poverty alleviation, the classical fiscal federalism literature draws attention to the fact that decentralization can lead to an under-provision of poverty alleviation programs (Brown and Oates, 1987), an aspect that received rather limited attention in the literature on decentralization in developing countries. The argument made in the classical fiscal federalism literature is quite different from the local elite capture argument. It has two strands. One strand assumes that the non-poor have an interest in assisting the poor. However, when selecting the level of poverty relief in their constituency, they will not take into account the benefits of this support for other non-poor in the nation ("garden-type externality" problem). Hence, even from the sole perspective of the non-poor, decentralization will lead to under-provision of relief programs for the poor. The contextual factor that can be derived from this argument is the variation in poverty across districts. Note that this factor is more relevant for decision-making (standard-setting) rather than implementation. The other strand of the argument focuses on the disincentive effects that arise from the fact that districts with a high level of relief programs may attract poor households to move in. In view of mobility restrictions (see above), this latter strand of the argument appears less relevant for developing countries.

3.2 Public Administration and Institutional Economics Literature

The literature on the institutional dimension of public service provision, which has emerged in administrative sciences and institutional economics, helps to identify further attributes of rural service transactions. Pritchett and Woolcock (2004) emphasize two attributes: they point out that activities that are both inherently "transaction-intensive" and "discretionary" pose particular problems for service provision since it is difficult to codify and control them. The attribute "discretionary" is related to the "specificity" attribute highlighted by Williamson (1985, 1991). It is also related to the care-intensity attribute (Fenoaltea, 1984; Birner and Wittmer, 2004). Discretionary or care-intensive transactions typically require special expertise and diligence. For example, agricultural advisory services that aim at promoting a standardized technology package are less discretionary and care-intensive than those advisory services that aim at promoting farm-specific or community-specific problem-oriented advice. Likewise, teaching becomes more discretionary and care-intensive if the teacher is expected to address the differential learning needs of pupils with different backgrounds. One can hypothesize that reaching the poor is associated with a higher level of care-intensity and discretionary decision-making, because there is a need to overcome problems of social exclusion and address other specific challenges that the poor face.

The attribute transaction-intensity refers to the scale at which specific transactions need to be carried out. It is useful to disaggregate this attribute into two components: (1) frequency and (2) distribution in space. The frequency attribute interacts with other attributes, as highlighted by Williamson (1985): transactions that are subject to monitoring problems (see below) become more challenging if they have to be carried out frequently. Distribution in space is an attribute that is particularly relevant for rural service provision. Primary schools, basic health facilities and wells for drinking water, for example, need to be provided for each cluster of villages throughout the country, which implies a high transaction-intensity in terms of space. The construction of the infrastructure for such facilities is not very frequent. In contrast, the operation of the respective services, such as teaching and health care, is characterized by high transaction-intensity in terms of time. The frequency of such transactions gives scope to the widespread "absenteeism" problem: teachers or health center staff members do not appear regularly to perform their duties (World Bank, 2004).

The New Institutional Economics literature has highlighted another attribute of service transactions: service measurability (Williamson, 1981). This attribute is particularly relevant for monitoring and evaluation transactions. What is important with regard to decentralization is the type of knowledge that is required to observe, or assess, service provision outcomes (World Bank, 2007). Some aspects of service provision are easy to observe by local people, but difficult to observe by a central agency. For example, farmers can easily identify whether an extension agent interacts with them regularly according to their needs, but a central agency has difficulties to collecting this kind of information. Likewise, school children can observe whether the teacher is absent. For some aspects of service provision, however, expert knowledge is required to arrive at an accurate assessment. For example, one needs hydrological expertise to assess whether a reservoir was constructed according to appropriate standards. It is not always apparent, however, which type of knowledge is required. Research from India has shown that the ability of parents to adequately assess the schooling achievements of their children was rather low (Banerjee et al., 2006). The type of knowledge that is required matters not only for monitoring and evaluation transactions, but also for other types of transactions that may be devolved to local governments or to service users. As indicated above, it has been a common reform strategy to pass on management responsibilities to service user groups, such as repairing drinking water facilities. In this case, relevant knowledge can be created through training.

3.3 Literature on Local Political Economy

As indicated in the introduction, a considerable body of literature has emerged in recent years that focuses on the local political economy of public service provision. The debate about elite capture points to an important attribute of service transactions: scope for rent-seeking. Programs that provide private goods, such as housing or agricultural inputs, have a higher scope for rent-seeking than programs that provide local public goods, such as school buildings. Still, in case of the latter, elite capture may still occur, because such infrastructure can be targeted to areas where better-off people reside. The scope for rent-seeking is also high in decision-making about the priorities of service provision, which may take place in village meetings or in local councils. Poor and disadvantaged groups often have other priorities for service provision than better-off households. Likewise, the demand for service may differ between men and women (Chattopadhyay and Duflo, 2004). Elite capture in priority-setting about service provision can increase existing inequality in access to services.

Several authors have highlighted the role of a functioning local democracy as a precondition for avoiding elite capture. Factors highlighted in this literature as determinants of a functioning local democracy include a politically aware citizenry, the absence of high inequality in social status, law and order, the conduct of free and fair elections, effective political competition, reliable information channels for citizens and formal as well as informal oversight mechanisms (Bardhan and Mookherjee, 2006). In terms of the transaction costs framework developed here, the functioning of the local political system, as compared with the political system at higher levels of government, is an important contextual factor, which can shift the cost-curves of decentralized service provision up or down, as explained above (Figure 11.1).

Several countries have implemented affirmative action at the local government level to promote the inclusion of citizens that are subject to ethnic, caste-based and/or gender-based discrimination. India is a prominent example, where seats in local councils are reserved for women and for scheduled castes and tribes. In Pakistan, seats are reserved for women, peasants and laborers. Using the political system to hold service providers accountable has been described as the "long route of accountability" (World Bank, 2004). In contrast, "short routes of accountability" exist if citizens interact directly with service providers, for example, in parent–teacher associations, local health councils or water-user associations.

In both cases, citizens incur a share of the decision costs and the implementation costs of service provision. In terms of the framework developed here, the question is whether these costs are outweighed by an improvement in service outcomes, or—in terms of this framework—by a reduction in the decision failure costs and implementation failure costs. This is an empirical question. A recent study used household and village survey data from South India to study participation in the *Gram Sabha* or village assembly, which is responsible for approving the annual accounts of the village council. This study found that disadvantaged groups were more likely to attend the village meetings, and their attendance improved targeting of resources towards these groups (World Bank, 2006). The same study found that women, however, were underrepresented in these meetings.

3.4 Literature on Corruption

For the framework presented here corruption is defined as an illegal form of taking advantage from public office for private gain, especially through bribery. Rent-seeking, by contrast, often takes place within the legal framework. Scope for corruption is another attribute to be considered in the framework developed here. The scope for corruption differs across transactions. For example, the scope for corruption is high in decision-making and implementation of infrastructure projects, while it is low for agricultural extension as long as extension is not linked with the supply of physical inputs. Some supply-side reforms, such as outsourcing service provision, may create new scope for corruption (bribery by applicants for service contracts). One form of corruption that hurts the poor in particular is the need to pay bribes to receive certain services, such as health services, financial services or land titles. Even if the amounts to be paid are small ("petty corruption"), they can be prohibitive for the poor. Available information on the incidence of corruption in different service areas has increased considerably in recent years. A study by Transparency International India (2005), for example, found that direct experience with bribery varied across service sectors from 9 percent for water supply to 80 percent for police (traffic/crime). The study showed that the sector-specific variation in corruption differed between states, which points to the role of contextual factors.

There is a considerable debate on the question whether corruption is more or less likely to occur if the provision of public services is decentralized (see, for example, Crook and Manor, 1998). On the one hand, it is argued that corruption becomes more visible at the local level, thus creating incentives for people to act against it. Increasing transparency, such as publicly displaying the costs of public infrastructure projects, can help to combat corruption. On the other hand, decentralization may increase the scope for corruption at the local level without creating sufficient incentives for local people to combat it. As a case study in a Sahelian country has shown, poor people may well consider it as legitimate that local leaders appropriate a share of development funds for their personal benefit as a compensation for their efforts to bring such development to their area (Platteau and Gaspart, 2003). Such sociocultural perceptions of legitimacy can be considered as contextual factors in terms of the framework developed here. There is also a debate whether centralized mechanisms of combating corruption, such as auditing by a central office, or local mechanisms, such as community-based or social auditing, are more effective (Olken, 2007).

3.5 Summary: Attributes and Contextual Factors

Table 11.1 summarizes the attributes that have been derived from the literature review in this section.

Three important attributes result from the fiscal decentralization literature: economies of scale, externalities and spillover effects and heterogeneity of local priorities and needs. In the case of these attributes, the implications with regard to decentralization are straightforward. The more the heterogeneity of local needs and priorities matter for the respective transaction, the more appropriate is a decentralized institutional setting, keeping other factors constant. The opposite applies to the attributes, economies of scale, externalities and spillover effects. For two of the attributes derived from the public administration and institutional economics literature, the implications are also straightforward: the more transaction-intensive activities are in terms of space and time, the more appropriate is a decentralized setting, keeping other factors constant. For the knowledge attribute, the direction is equally clear. Decentralized structures gain comparative advantage with increasing relevance of local knowledge. If technical knowledge is relevant, centralized structures are often more appropriate to be able to exploit economies of scale in providing this knowledge.

In case of the specificity attribute (discretion and care intensity), however, the implications with regard to decentralization are less straightforward. This also applies to the two attributes derived from the literature on local political economy and corruption: scope for rent-seeking, and scope for corruption. In these cases, the implications for decentralization depend on contextual factors, which are further discussed below and summarized in Table 11.2. Table 11.1 presents four examples to illustrate the role of these attributes: 1. Small-scale public infrastructure, such as drinking water facilities and school buildings, 2. primary education, 3. agricultural extension and 4. poverty alleviation programs that provide private goods, such as housing and or livestock. For each example, some important types of transactions are listed in the table. Based on the literature reviewed in Section 3, an assessment is made with regard to the role that each attribute plays for the transaction under consideration. The arrows in Table 11.1 indicate whether the respective attribute implies that the transaction should be assigned to a higher (↑) or a lower (↓) level of government. Only attributes that have a high relevance for the respective transaction are considered in this regard.

Table 11.1 shows that in some cases, one can derive rather straightforward implications on whether a transaction should be assigned to a more

Table 11.1 Attributes of transactions involved in rural service provision

Branch of Literature from which Attributes are Derived	Fiscal Federalism Literature			Public Administration and Institutional Economics Literature				Local Political Economy and Corruption Literature	
Types of attributes	Economies of scale	Externalities Spillover	Heterogeneity of local needs/ priorities	Trans-action intensity: spatial dispersion	Transaction intensity: frequency Scope for absenteeism	Type of knowledge required	Specificity Discretion Care-intensity	Scope for corruption	Scope for elite capture
Implication for appropriate level of government, if attribute applies	More centralized	More centralized	More decentralized	More decentral-ized	More decentra-lized	More decentralized for local knowledge	Depending on context	Depending on context	Depending on context
Examples									
(1) Small-scale public infrastructure (wells, village school buildings)									
Planning	Low	Low	Medium	High ↓	Low	Local ↓	Medium	Medium	Medium
Construction	Medium	Low	Low	High ↓	Low	Technical ↑	Low	High	Low
Maintenance	Low	Low	High ↓	High ↓	Medium	Local & tech.	Low	Low	Medium
(2) Primary education									
Curriculum development	High ↑	Low	Low	Low ↑	Low	Technical ↑	High	Low	Low
Teaching	Low	Low	Medium	High ↓	High ↓	Local & tech.	High	Medium	Low

Table 11.1 (continued)

Branch of Literature from which Attributes are Derived	Fiscal Federalism Literature			Public Administration and Institutional Economics Literature				Local Political Economy and Corruption Literature	
Types of attributes	Economies of scale	Externalities Spillover	Heterogeneity of local needs/ priorities	Trans-action intensity: spatial dispersion	Transaction intensity: frequency Scope for absenteeism	Type of knowledge required	Specificity Discretion Care-intensity	Scope for corruption	Scope for elite capture
(3) Agricultural extension									
Location-specific advice	Low	Low	High ↓	High ↓	High ↓	Local & tech.	High	Low	High
Info on new technology	Medium	High ↑	Low	High ↓	Medium	Local & tech.	Med./low	Low	Med./Low
(4) Poverty alleviation program providing private goods (e.g. housing; livestock)									
Planning (identification of beneficiaries)	Low	Low	High ↓	High ↓	Low	Local ↓	Medium	High	High
Construction or delivery	Medium	Low	Medium	High ↓	Low	Local & tech.	Medium	High	Medium

Note: Low, medium and high refer to the relevance of the attribute for the respective transaction; ↓↑ indicates that it has a comparative advantage of assigning the respective transaction to a lower (↓) or higher (↑) level of government, respectively.

Source: Adapted from World Bank (2007, p. 88).

centralized or a more decentralized level. For example, curriculum development is better assigned to a more centralized level, whereas agricultural extension that focuses on location-specific advice is better assigned to a lower level of government. In other cases, however, there are trade-offs. For example, the spillover effects that arise in agricultural extension if general (non-location specific) advice is provided suggests that a more central organization of this type of extension is appropriate. However, the transaction-intensity of extension activities suggests a more decentralized organization. Importantly, trade-offs can also arise if discretion, scope for corruption and/or scope for elite capture have high relevance. In such cases, special attention needs to be paid to the contextual factors. For example, the spatial transaction-intensity of poverty alleviation programs favors a decentralized organization. However, the high scope for corruption and rent-seeking that arises if such programs provide private goods renders the appropriate level of decentralization largely dependent on contextual factors.

Table 11.2 summarizes the contextual factors derived from the literature review above. Examining the assumptions of the fiscal federalism literature leads to the identification of the following contextual factors: differences between the national and the local level regarding administrative capacity and capacity to collect tax revenues, and the ability of citizens and business enterprises to move freely between local jurisdictions. The fiscal federalism literature also implies that a strong variation of poverty levels across districts may lead to the under-provision of poverty relief programs. The literature on local political economy highlights differences between the national and local level regarding the functioning of the democratic system, which is influenced by factors such as the political awareness of the citizenry, and the absence of high inequality in social status, among others (Table 11.2). The literature on corruption draws attention to differences between the national and local level regarding the functioning of anti-corruption mechanisms, such as audit systems. Sociocultural factors, which influence people's incentives to combat corruption, have an influence too, as discussed above.

The contextual factors are not necessarily static. In fact, they can be influenced by policy reforms and public investments. In this regard, it is often a strategic question to identify the level of government at which reforms and capacity strengthening activities should be targeted, taking the political economy of such interventions into account. For example, governments and donor agencies may need to decide whether to concentrate efforts on strengthening national institutions of accountability such as the Auditor General's Office, or invest in community capabilities to perform social audits, or pursue a combination of both.

Table 11.2 Contextual factors

Branch of Literature	Contextual Factors
Fiscal federalism literature	Differences between national and local level regarding capacity of the public administration Differences between national and local level regarding ability to raise tax revenues Ability of citizens and business enterprises to move freely between local jurisdictions Variation in poverty across districts
Local political economy and corruption literature	Differences between national and local level regarding the functioning of the democratic system, which is influenced by: political awareness of the citizenry; absence of high inequality in social status; law and order; conduct of free and fair elections; effective political competition; reliable information channels; formal and informal oversight mechanisms Differences between national and local level regarding the functioning of anti-corruption mechanisms, such as: audit systems (central audit office vs. social auditing) incentives of people to combat corruption (influenced by sociocultural factors)

Source: Authors, based on literature reviewed in the text.

4 A RESEARCH AGENDA FOR THE FUTURE

In Sections 2 and 3, the transaction costs approach has been used to develop a unifying framework to identify the factors that affect the appropriate level of decentralization, based on insights from different branches of the literature on decentralization. The assessments derived from this framework can help policy-makers identify the factors they may wish to consider in decentralizing public service delivery. The World Bank, for example, applies similar considerations when advising policy-makers in India on the question of which role different tiers of local government should play in rural service provision (World Bank, 2007). From a research perspective, the assessments presented in the previous section can be considered as hypotheses. Empirical research will be necessary to test these hypotheses. In those cases where the implications for decentralization are not straightforward, empirical research will be particularly valuable to produce policy-relevant knowledge.

The standard approach in empirical transaction cost economics does not require an empirical measurement of transaction costs (see review by Shelanski and Klein, 1995). The approach is rather to derive hypotheses on the comparative advantage of different governance structures for different situations, depending on attributes and contextual factors. Multinomial logit models or similar statistical techniques are then used to test whether the empirically observed distribution of governance structures corresponds to the hypotheses. This approach is well suited to studying profit-oriented organizations competing in functioning markets, because one can assume that competition will force the enterprises to choose governance structures according to cost-economizing criteria. The transaction costs approach has been used in a similar way to empirically test hypotheses on the decisions of local governments to contract out service delivery (Ferris and Graddy, 1991; Brown and Potoski, 2003). These studies suggest that county governments also have incentives to use cost-economizing criteria when making such decisions.

For the question under consideration here—what is the appropriate level of government for different types of public service transactions—the standard approach of empirical transaction costs economics is less suitable. The empirically observed governance structures for public service provision are the outcome of political decisions rather than a market-driven selection process or decisions of individual managers in the public sector. While efficiency considerations may influence these decisions, political economy factors will be at play, as well, especially since decentralization is a politically contested process. To apply the framework developed in this chapter for the purpose of empirical research, it is, therefore, necessary to empirically measure the transaction costs, together with the production costs, that are incurred both by service providers and service users.

Empirical studies that measure transaction costs directly are still scarce. Yet, the existing literature shows that it is not impossible to measure transaction costs empirically. Those transaction costs that are part of the agency's budget can be derived from available public finance data or collected from the agencies involved. Mann (2007) used such an approach to estimate the transaction costs of administering agricultural investment subsidies. In recent years, survey techniques such as Public Expenditure Tracking Surveys (PETSs), have been developed to account for leakages in public spending (Reinikka and Svensson, 2003). In terms of the framework developed here, such leakages fall in the category of implementation failure costs. The access costs and other categories of transaction costs incurred by the households can be estimated on the basis of household surveys. Mburu and Birner (2002), for example, used a household survey to measure the transaction costs that local people incurred for participating in collaboratively managed wildlife sanctuaries in Kenya. With regard to service provision, survey instruments can be developed that include questions on the time, the transport costs and other expenses that household members incur for accessing and using services. Household surveys are also increasingly used to assess corruption from the perspective of service users (for example, Transparency International India, 2005). To ensure a pro-poor focus in this type of research, it is important to collect data about the socioeconomic status of the households. Moreover, as has been argued above, it is important to collect gender-disaggregated data, as the costs of accessing and using the same service may differ between men and women.

To apply the framework developed here, it is also necessary to collect data on the attributes of transactions, contextual factors, as well as service delivery outcomes. Quantifying attributes of transactions empirically is a challenging task as well. Brown and Potoski (2003) developed a survey instrument for city managers and mayors, who were asked to rate the asset specificity and service measurability of various public services on a scale from 1 to 5. A similar approach could be used to assess other attributes of transactions identified above, such as care-intensity and scope for corruption. For other attributes, such as transaction-intensity, quantitative measures, such as the number of transactions to be performed, can be developed.

The measurement of service delivery outcomes is important for the application of the cost-effectiveness framework developed here. Measurements can rely on research techniques that have been developed for specific services, such as health and education. Even though subjective assessments of service delivery outcomes have become popular with the use of citizen report cards, more objective measures, such as knowledge tests for school children might provide a better basis for applying the framework developed here. To collect data on contextual factors, it will also be useful to rely on the respective literature. For example, in the public administration literature, one can find a range of indicators that can be used to assess administrative capacity at different levels of government, such as staff–client ratios, staff turnover ratios and data from surveys that ask staff members to evaluate their institutional environment (Girishankar, 2001). The political science literature can provide indicators of contextual factors related to the political system, such as voter turnout data, and data from election surveys. There is also an extensive literature that analyzes socioeconomic conditions at the village level, including social hierarchies, which influence the scope for local elite capture.

The design of research projects that apply the framework developed here will also be confronted with the typical econometric challenges found in research on decentralization, especially the endogeneity problem. Hence, research in this field can benefit from the strategies that have been developed in this literature to deal with this challenge, such as studying border areas (World Bank, 2006) and using randomized experimental designs (Banerjee et al., 2006). The framework proposed here can, however, avoid some empirical challenges, because it focuses on the performance of service delivery in terms of quality, quantity and access, not on the ultimate impact of service provision in terms of economic development, which is influenced by a much wider range of factors.

5 CONCLUDING REMARKS

Decentralization and public service provision have been studied for a long time from the perspective of different disciplines, including economics, public administration research and political sciences. As shown in this chapter, a cost-effectiveness approach based on transaction cost theory can provide a framework that makes it possible to integrate insights derived from different branches of this literature. A cost-effectiveness approach can play this integrating role as it can address the diverse types of problems arising due to failure to exploit economies of scale, due to managerial problems within the public administration, or due to problems of political elite capture, all of which ultimately translate into a reduced quantity, quality or targeting of a service that can be provided with a given amount of resources. Therefore, studying the costs, including the transaction costs, at which a service of a defined quality, quantity and pro-poor outcome can be provided, makes it possible to evaluate trade-offs that arise in assigning service transactions to different levels of government.

The chapter emphasizes that, when comparing governance structures in terms of cost-effectiveness, one needs take into account the costs incurred by service providers as well as the costs incurred by service users. Only this perspective makes it possible to ensure pro-poor outcomes and accounting for total costs. The framework supports efforts to improve the cost-effectiveness of public service provision. The more cost-effective a service can be provided to the poor, the easier it is to reach a larger number of the poor with limited public resources. This in fact raises the issue of marginal transactions costs of service provisions, which needs further attention in research. The framework also underlines the need to pay attention to contextual factors, because they influence the appropriate level of government for different service transactions. This focus on contextual factors is supported by the general literature on public sector reforms, which has emphasized the need to move from one-size-fits all or best practice to good-fit approaches (Levy, 2004).

The framework is concerned with a normative analysis of the institutional design of public service provision. It focuses on the appropriate level of government for different service transactions, but the transaction costs economics approach can also be applied to other questions of institutional design, such as contracting out service provision to profit or non-profit organizations (Ferris and Graddy, 1991; Brown and Potoski, 2003).

As shown in Sections 2 and 3, the framework can be used to derive empirically testable hypotheses regarding the cost-effectiveness of assigning service transactions to different levels of government. The empirical challenges of applying this approach are considerable, but the existing literature discussed in this chapter suggests that these challenges can be met. Interdisciplinary collaboration will certainly help to pursue this research agenda. What this framework does not cover is the political economy of decentralization reforms. Reforming public services such as health, education or agricultural extension by decentralizing or re-centralizing service functions to different levels of local government is a political process. This process is often confronted with resistance, both from the bureaucracy and from politicians. Likewise, it is a political process to mobilize service users, especially the rural poor, to effectively use the political space that decentralization can create. Understanding the political economy of decentralization is an important and challenging task, which requires analytical concepts other than transaction costs economics applied here. Hopefully, future research will throw light on both questions: which level of decentralization is appropriate to ensure better public service provision for the poor, and by which political process can necessary reforms be achieved? A better understanding of these questions is needed to benefit the world's poor, including the rural poor, who have suffered far too long from poor service provision.

NOTES

* Paper presented at the seminar on "Effectiveness of Decentralized Strategies and Outcomes" in Moncalieri, 3–4 September 2007. Comments by the participants are gratefully acknowledged. The usual disclaimer applies.

1. In spite of the recent emphasis on decentralization, this is not a new phenomenon. At the end of the colonial period, local governments were seen "as the handmaid of decolonization" (Collins, 2000, p. 4). However, earlier efforts to decentralize mostly focused on administrative decentralization, whereas current trends focus on political decentralization. Political decentralization often precedes fiscal and administrative decentralization (Work, 2002; Ndegwa and Levy, 2004).
2. Ostrom et al. (1993) emphasize the distinction between the "provision" and the "production" of infrastructure. Following their definition, the first, third and fourth sets of transactions refer to the provision of a service, while the second set refers to its production.
3. Identifying "the most efficient" or "optimal" governance structure could be seen as

an extension of the framework proposed here. It would require moving from a cost-effectiveness framework (as in Figure 11.1) to a cost–benefit framework, which compares marginal costs with marginal benefits. Theoretically, such an approach is straightforward, at least if one abstracts from uncertainty and intangible goals in decisions about institutional design. The challenge is the empirical application of such an approach.

4. Due to the cost-effectiveness approach applied here, access costs *AC* refer to the costs that service providers incur if the service is provided at the intended standards regarding quality, quantity and targeting. Additional costs incurred due to substandard service provision are included in the implementation failure costs (FC_I), as discussed above.
5. Transaction costs are often been referred to as the "costs of using the market mechanism". The expression "costs of using a governance structure" is a parallelism, which applies to public sector governance.

REFERENCES

Arrow, K.J. (1950), "A Difficulty in the Concept of Social Welfare", *Journal of Political Economy*, **58** (4), 346.

Bahiigwa, G., F. Ellis, O. Fjeldstad and V. Iversen (2004), *Rural Taxation in Uganda: Implications for Growth, Income Distribution, Local Government Revenue and Poverty Reduction,* Kampala: Final Report, commissioned by DFID Uganda.

Banerjee, A., R. Banerji, E. Duflo, R. Glennerster and S. Khemani (2006), "Can Information Campaigns Spark Local Participation and Improve Outcomes? A Study of Primary Education in Uttar Pradesh, India", Washington, DC: World Bank Policy Research Working Paper No. 3967, World Bank.

Bardhan, P. (2002), "Decentralization of Governance and Development", *Journal of Economic Perspectives*, **16** (4), 185–206.

Bardhan, P. and D.D. Mookherjee (2000), "Relative Capture of Government at Local and National Levels", *American Economic Review*, **90** (2), 135–9.

Bardhan, P. and D. Mookherjee (2003), "Decentralization and Accountability in Infrastructure Delivery in Developing Countries", Boston, Mass: Boston University Economics Department Working Paper.

Bardhan, P. and D. Mookherjee (2006), *Decentralization and Local Governance in Developing Countries – A Comparative Perspective*, Cambridge, MA, London: MIT Press.

Besley, T. and S. Coate (2000), "Centralized versus Decentralized Provision of Local Public Goods: A Political Economy Analysis", NBER Working Paper No. 7084: Cambridge, MA.

Birner, R. and H. Wittmer (2004), "On the Efficient Boundaries of the State – The Contribution of Transaction Costs Economics to the Analysis of Decentralization and Devolution in Natural Resource Management", *Environment and Planning C: Government and Policy*, **22** (5), 667–85.

Brown, C.C. and W.E. Oates (1987), "Assistance to the Poor in a Federal System", *Journal of Public Economics*, **32** (3), 307.

Brown, T.L. and M. Potoski (2003), "Transaction Costs and Institutional Explanations for Government Service Production Decisions", *Journal of Public Administration Research and Theory*, **13** (3), 441–68.

Buchanan, J.M. and G. Tullock (1962), *The Calculus of Consent: Logical Foundations of Constitutional Democracy*, Ann Arbor: University Of Michigan Press.

Careaga, M. and B.R. Weingast (2002), "Fiscal Federalism, Good Governance and Economic Growth in Mexico", in D. Rodrik (ed.), *In Search of Prosperity. Analytical Narratives on Economic Growth*, Princeton: Princeton University Press, pp. 399–435.

Chattopadhyay, R. and E. Duflo (2004), "Women as Policy Makers – Evidence from a Randomized Policy Experiment in India", *Econometrica*, **72** (5), 1409–43.

Collins, P. (2000), "The Last Fifty Years and the Next Fifty Years: A Century of Public Administration and Development", in P.Collins (ed.), *Applying Public Administration In Development – Guideposts To The Future*, Chichester: John Wiley And Sons, pp. 3–14.

Crook, R.C. and J. Manor (1998), *Democracy and Decentralisation in South Asia and West Africa: Participation, Accountability, and Performance*, Cambridge and New York: Cambridge University Press.

Fenoaltea, S. (1984), "Slavery and Supervision in Comparative Perspective – A Model", *Journal of Economic History*, **44** (3), 635–68.

Ferris, J. and E. Graddy (1991) "Production Costs, Transaction Costs and Local Government Contractor Choice", *Economic Inquiry*, **29** (3), 541–54.

Gemmell, N. and O. Morrissey (2005), "Distribution and Poverty Impact of Tax Structure Reform in Developing Countries: How Little We Know", *Development Policy Review*, **23** (2), 131–44.

Girishankar, N. (2001), *Evaluating Public Sector Reform – Guidelines for Assessing Country-Level Impact of Structural Reform and Capacity Building in The Public Sector*, Washington, DC: Operations Evaluation Department, World Bank.

Hayek, F.A. (1939), "The Economic Conditions of Interstate Federalism", *New Commonwealth Quarterly*, **5** (1939), 131–49.

ICRW (2005), *Infrastructure Shortfalls Cost Poor Women Time and Opportunity: Toward Achieving the Third Millennium Development Goal to Promote Gender Equality and Empower Women*, Washington, DC: International Center For Research On Women.

Kes, A. and H. Swaminathan (2006), "Gender and Time Poverty in Sub-Saharan Africa", in M. Blackden and Q. Wodon (eds), *Gender, Time Use and Poverty in Sub-Saharan Africa*, Washington, DC: Working Paper No. 73, World Bank, pp. 13–38.

Levy, B. (2004), "Governance and Economic Development in Africa: Meeting the Challenge of Capacity Building", in B. Levy and S. Kpundeh (eds), *Building State Capacity in Africa*, Washington, DC: World Bank and Oxford University Press, pp. 1–42.

Mann, S. (2007), "Transaktionskosten Landwirtschaftlicher Investitionsförderung – ein Komparativer Ansatz (Transaction Costs of Agricultural Investment Promotion – A Comparative Analysis), *Agrarwirtschaft*, **94** (7), 259–69.

Mansuri, G. and V. Rao (2004), "Community-based and -driven Development: A Critical Review", *The World Bank Research Observer*, **19** (1), 1–39.

Mburu, J. and R. Birner (2002), "Analyzing the Efficiency of Collaborative Wildlife Management: The Case of Two Community Wildlife Sanctuaries in Kenya", *Journal of Organizational Theory and Behaviour*, **5** (3–4), 359–94.

Musgrave, R. (1959), *Public Finance*, New York: McGraw Hill.

Ndegwa, S. and B. Levy (2004), "The Politics of Decentralization in Africa: A Comparative Analysis", in B. Levy and S. Kpundeh (eds), *Building State Capacity in Africa*, Washington, DC: World Bank and Oxford University Press, pp. 283–321.

Oates, W. E. (1972), *Fiscal Federalism*, New York: Harcourt Brace Jovanovich.
Olken, B. (2007), "Monitoring Corruption: Evidence from a Field Experiment in Indonesia", *Journal of Political Economy*, **115** (2), 200–49.
Ostrom, E., L. Schroeder and S. Wynne (1993), *Institutional Incentives and Sustainable Development – Infrastructure Policies in Perspective*, Boulder, CO: Westview Press.
Platteau, J.-P. and F. Gaspart (2003), "The Risk of Resource Misappropriation in Community-driven Development", *World Development*, **31** (10), 1687–703.
Pritchett, L. and M. Woolcock (2004), "Solutions When the Solution is the Problem: Arraying the Disarray in Development", *World Development*, **32** (2), 191–212.
Reinikka, R. and J. Svensson (2003), *Survey Techniques to Measure and Explain Corruption*, Washington, DC: World Bank Policy Research Working Paper No. 3071, World Bank.
Shelanski, H.A. and P.G. Klein (1995), "Empirical Research in Transaction Cost Economics: A Review and Assessment", *Journal of Law, Economics and Organization*, **11** (2), 335–61.
Tiebout, C. (1956), "A Pure Theory of Local Expenditures", *Journal of Political Economy*, **64** (5), 416–24.
Transparency International India (2005), *India Corruption Study 2005*, New Delhi, http://www.transparencyindia.org/publication/IndiaCorruptionStudy 2005inPDF.pdf, accessed 3 April 2009.
Weingast, B.R. (2005), "The Performance and Stability of Federalism: An Institutionalist Perspective", in C.Menard and M.M. Shirley (Eds.), Dordrecht: Springer, pp. 149–72.
Williamson, O.E. (1981), "The Economics of Organization", *American Journal of Sociology*, **87** (3), 548–77.
Williamson, O.E. (1985), *The Economic Institutions of Capitalism – Firms, Markets, Relational Contracting*, New York: The Free Press.
Williamson, O.E. (1991), "Comparative Economic Organization – The Analysis Of Discrete Structural Alternatives", *Administrative Science Quarterly*, **36** (2), 269–96.
Williamson, O.E. (1999), "Public and Private Bureaucracies: A Transaction Cost Economics Perspective", *Journal of Law, Economics and Organization*, **15** (1), 306–41.
Work, R. (2002), "Overview of Decentralization Worldwide: A Stepping Stone to Improved Governance and Human Development", paper presented at the 2nd International Conference on Decentralization Federalism: The Future of Decentralizing States?, Manila, Philippines, 25–27 July 2002.
World Bank (2004), *World Development Report 2004: Making Services Work For Poor People*. Washington, DC: World Bank.
World Bank (2006), *The Political Economy of Gram Panchayats in South India: Results and Policy Conclusions From a Research Project*. Washington, DC: World Bank.
World Bank (2007), *India – Rural Governments and Service Delivery. Volume III: Main Report*, Report No. 38901-IN, Washington, DC: The World Bank.

12. Fiscal policy instruments and the political economy of designing programs to reach the poorest

Ehtisham Ahmad*

1 THE CONTEXT

Reaching the poorest and hungry groups of the population, including those who might be left out of the Millennium Development Goals (MDGs) involves policy-makers at the central and local levels of government. While there has been considerable focus on appropriate targeting mechanisms to reach the poor (see for example, World Bank, 1990; Besley and Kanbur, 1993), attention as to which level of government should be involved, as well as the interactions between levels of government in reaching the poor, is more recent (see Bardhan and Mookherjee, 2000; von Braun and Grote, 2002 and a survey by Birner, 2007).

From the policy perspective, it is important to examine the instruments available at each level of government in order to meet the needs of the poorest. If the responsibility for these groups is seen primarily as that of the central government, then direct federal/central government programs, effectively targeted but building on local information come into focus. If the primary responsibility is local, the policy focus shifts to own-source revenues for financing the expenditures and for greater local accountability, together with a modicum of equalization transfers so that all local governments have similar capacities to provide for the poorest.

Designing central programs to reach the poorest may be difficult without local information. This is because the central government, particularly in large countries such as Mexico and China, lacks the ability to precisely define marginal groups or households that may not benefit from more general growth and prosperity. Yet local officials may not share the objectives of the center—and may prefer to divert central funds to meet objectives that are of higher value to them. This policy dilemma illustrates difficulties with "overlapping" responsibilities between different levels of government and in designing effective special purpose programs, financed by the center and implemented by local governments.

The constraints in designing effective centrally determined special purpose programs in developing countries are legendary. To some extent these are similar to the problems in designing foreign assistance strategies that effectively reach the poorest target groups in the recipient countries—country elites may not share the altruistic objectives of donors. The issue is to design policies that build on local information, yet minimize the incentives at the local level to divert resources from the target groups. Similar issues arise in the context of foreign assistance designed to reach the poorest groups of the population, such as under the Heavily Indebted Poor Countries (HIPC) program.

Local governments with the most limited resources and tax bases may also have the greatest requirements for supporting the poorest groups and individuals. Thus, providing for these groups in the poorer localities may require assistance from the center. However, the center may also have concerns for the poorer groups living in the relatively well-to-do localities. Urban poverty, including in the richer areas, is becoming an increasing problem—in addition to the typical rural poor. Reaching these groups may not be easy, and could generate moral hazard difficulties as local officials may wish to minimize their financing of such activities and shift the burden to the center. A continuation of pockets of extreme poverty in the richer localities tends to reflect divergences of preferences between the center and local officials—local politicians and officials may not be particularly interested in such groups—often the indigent without family support mechanisms that may not have a significant political voice.

Relatively incomplete information is available to the center on the poor and hungry without family support, as well as the budgetary operations at the subnational levels. This generates incentives for subnational governments to divert central funds allocated for the poorest.

This chapter examines the fiscal instruments available to different levels of government and their interactions to enhance the effectiveness of public policies for the poorest and hungry groups. Addressing the leakages associated with central funding and local implementation is based on the design of the programs incorporating competition for resources—both across jurisdictions and over time. This also involves moving budget processes towards greater orientation to results—together with mechanisms for intertemporal feedback in the allocation of resources in the future.

2 SUCCESSFUL PROGRAMS TO REACH THE POOREST: EXAMPLES FROM CHINA AND MEXICO

Depending on the circumstances, either centralized or decentralized approaches may be adopted to address the needs of the poorest. The options are highlighted by the experiences of two large countries—Mexico and China. Mexico has a successful central program to reach the poorest, whereas China has relied on an effective local program. Despite the successes of both programs, there are continuing challenges and difficulties in both cases. There may well be a convergence of solutions in the future—with a more significant role for the center in China, and for state and local governments in Mexico.

Mexico, which is a federal state, has effectively built a safety net on the basis of a central program—the *Progresa/Oportunidades*, a conditional cash transfer program that was created in 1997. The targeting has worked effectively (see Coady and Parker, 2002; Levy and Rodriguez, 2004). However, the *Progresa/Oportunidades* model has been difficult to replicate, even in smaller countries, as administrative overheads are substantive. Also in Mexico, success has been somewhat of a handicap and successive governments have added new objectives and responsibilities that make the program unwieldy and distortive. The question is whether the program with its increased remit can continue to target effectively in Mexico, and be replicated elsewhere in Latin America.

In China, a unitary state, programs such as *wu bao* (see below) were used in the past to provide support for the poorest groups in rural areas. Such programs were predicated on locally generated information and management. With increasing inequality in China since the economic reforms of the 1990s, and dispersion in local government revenues, the issue now is whether local governments have the incentives and resources to continue to effectively provide support to the poorest groups. Each type of program faces challenges and difficulties as described below.

2.1 Centralized Provision

As mentioned, a central government might wish to carry out the social assistance program itself, with or without local identification of recipients. Given the success of *Progresa/Oportunidades*, Mexican administrations have tried to use it as a compensation mechanism for different adjustment policies over time, and the remit and coverage of the program has increased significantly. At end-2005, *Oportunidades* covered 24 million individuals (5 million households)—roughly a quarter of the total population or 70 percent of the rural population (Levy, 2006). In contrast, the Chinese programs were more tightly targeted, with the numbers of people receiving social relief in the early 1990s (including both the *wu bao* and the more extensive poor households support, *pinkun hu*) were around 6 percent of the rural population.

Another federal program in Mexico, the *Seguro Popular*, has also been designed to provide direct support for health care for the uninsured population. It has been criticized on the grounds that it, together with an expanding *Oportunidades* program, encourages an expansion of the informal sector (Levy, 2006) and poses a constraint to the orderly development of formal sector activity. This has a disincentive effect on labor markets and also limits the growth of tax revenues. Thus, these programs may perversely perpetuate the problems that a safety net should solve.

The issue of overlapping responsibilities also creates difficulties in Mexican intergovernmental finances. Whereas the *Oportunidades* program has been effective in meeting its initial objectives, it is seen as encroaching on a typical area of local responsibility. Indeed, given the presence of significant federal earmarked transfers for basic education and health care, states and local governments have begun to treat these areas as effectively the responsibility of the federal government—despite a decade-long effort at decentralization.

It has proved difficult to replicate *Oportunidades* elsewhere in Latin America. Attempts were made, for instance, in the *Red de Solidaridad* in El Salvador, and *Tekoporã* in Paraguay—these are small and homogeneous countries relative to Mexico (see Veras Soares and Britto, 2007). The centrally designed programs in these countries have involved significant administrative costs in establishing eligibility of beneficiaries and effective management. Attempts to involve local governments in the programs have not been particularly successful, as the political benefits are thought to accrue to the "central governments", whereas the political costs are expected to be borne by the localities.

In general, direct provision by the center could be achieved with relatively broad targeting—albeit at a fiscal cost, leakages to the less poor. It may be more efficient to design mechanisms that better utilize the information available to local governments (including at the community level), but with the center equalizing the capacity of the relevant level of governments to undertake the projects. But would the local governments have the appropriate incentives to do so?

2.2 Local Provision

A good example of local identification and provision for the poorest is from rural China. Since the establishment of the People's Republic, a key element in reaching the poorest was the mechanism known as *wu bao*, or five guarantees. It related to a minimum provision of food, health care, shelter and clothing and funeral costs for all citizens—hence the term five guarantees. Its operation is based on local (often village- or community-based) information to identify the poorest groups in society without extended household support, particularly in rural areas where the reach of formal social security instruments is at best limited. As is evident, the *wu bao* families and individuals are often among the poorest (Ahmad and Hussain, 1991). Over time, the term came to denote a special category of persons—those unable to earn a living and lacking relatives for support. These are predominantly the orphans and elderly or disabled, without family support. As is clear, the identification of the vulnerable without family support has to be based on local knowledge. Such individuals also tend not to be associated with elites or interest groups that often have an interest in "capturing" resources accruing to the localities.

The social protection mechanisms in China are undergoing significant change. While the market orientation of the past decade has brought about rapidly rising real incomes, particularly for families able to participate in the labor market, it has generated greater vulnerability for some of the poorest. The social protection system has come under strain as the resources available to lower-level local governments, particularly in the poorer regions, have been subject to greater constraints. On the one hand, there has been a recentralization of the main sources of revenue, and on the other, additional spending responsibilities have accrued to lower levels. Thus, the resources available to provide support or social assistance to the poorest, including the *wu bao*, tend to vary by localities. Moreover, with growing inequalities, "local capture" may begin to be a problem in China, as it is in other parts of the world (see Bardhan and Mookherjee, 2000, 2006).

A more recent intervention, the *Di Bao*, is a largely urban program providing conditional cash transfers to individuals below the poverty line. It started in 1999 and now provides support to around 22 million people, or 6 percent of the urban population (Ravallion, 2007)—or roughly the same magnitude as the rural anti-poverty programs (*wu bao* and *pinkun hu*). Local governments select recipients, and co-financing is available from the center. Central financing varies by province—from zero in the rich coastal regions to 100 percent in Tibet. In principle, the program encompasses two key characteristics: (1) local identification of need, with (2) a degree of equalization in the financing arrangements. Ravallion (2007) however, finds that, despite the central "equalization", the richer localities are able to support higher income levels for program eligibility than poorer ones.

The policy design issues in China are complicated by its multi-tiered administration, in which nested budgeting decisions are made—the center decides how much to allocate to a given province, which then decides on allocations to prefectures, which make transfers to counties and then sequentially down to townships. Allowing the localities to determine eligibility criteria puts the onus on the localities, but at the possible cost of excluding some of the deserving poorest. Tighter central determination of eligibility would move the *Di Bao* closer to the *Oportunidades* model, although still relying on local identification and administration. This could also make the costs to the center open-ended and does not preclude diversion of centrally provided funds.

In the policy options that follow—we examine decision-making in large multi-level countries (reflecting both Mexico and China) based on work by Ahmad, Tandberg and Zhang (2002), and also look at the budgeting model that might be relevant in minimizing leakages (Ahmad and Martinez, 2004).

2.3 The Policy Options

An ideal system of transfers would involve clearly identified criteria provided by the center to local governments to assist them in looking after the poorest (Ravallion, 2007). But, for overall budgetary constraints and efficiency of spending, this requires that local governments disclose information accurately on the extent of need, and also not divert central funds to other uses. It is not clear that they face the incentives to disclose this information—on the contrary, the localities may distort the information in order to maximize transfers from higher levels.

Thus, central governments face a dilemma. Reaching some of the poorest requires local information for effective identification and targeting. This cannot be obtained without the cooperation of local governments. Direct central provision is possible but requires administrative capabilities and resources, and may generate negative effects, such as incentives to remain in the informal sector. Local governments may have the information, but the poorer ones lack the financing to carry out the functions, and in the "game" with the center, may lack incentives to effectively use central transfers.

3 FINANCING INSTRUMENTS FOR SOCIAL PROGRAMS

In this section, we use insights of the new political economy literature on intergovernmental finances (see Lockwood, 2006 for a survey) to examine

Table 12.1 Sources of tax revenues of local governments in selected federal countries, 2001 (percentage of total revenue)

Country	Income Tax and Tax on Profits	Payroll Tax	Property Tax	General Consumption Tax	Taxes on Specific Goods and Services	User Charges	Other Taxes
Australia	0	0	100.0	0	0	0	0
Austria	37.7	19.1	10.0	22.7	3.8	1.7	5.0
Belgium	85.8	0	0	1.4	7.9	4.6	0.3
Canada	0	0	91.6	0.2	0	1.6	6.5
Germany	77.1	0	16.6	5.2	0.5	0.4	0.2
Mexico	0	0.1	88.5	0	1.9	0.9	8.6
Switzerland	83.1	0	16.6	0	0.2	0.1	0
United States	6.2	0	71.5	12.4	5.1	4.8	0

Source: Ambrosanio and Bordignon (2006).

options for improved provision of public services for the poor. This involves the design of taxes at the subnational level, and equally important appropriate transfers. The interaction of instruments matters, as does the budgeting framework, especially the use of contracts together with new multi-year budgeting techniques that focus on the "results or outcomes" of specific programs. These mechanisms build on regional and intertemporal competition, even if there are overlapping responsibilities. Each issue is discussed sequentially below.

3.1 Tax Instruments

A key element in accountable self-governance at the subnational level is access to own-source revenues at the margin, so that a jurisdiction is able to raise additional funds needed for its key local spending. This is also a fundamental precondition for the establishment of hard-budget constraints at the subnational level, without which no-bailout conditions are barely credible (Ambrosiano and Bordignon, 2006). However, whether or not a local jurisdiction has incentives to use its own-tax handles is heavily influenced by transfer design—if a local government could rely on transfers rather than own-source revenues, it probably will, with resulting erosion in accountability. This has been the recent experience in Mexico.

Another drawback with primary reliance on local tax bases is that these tend to vary considerably, especially in large countries (Table 12.1). For instance, in Mexico, the Federal District accounts for roughly half

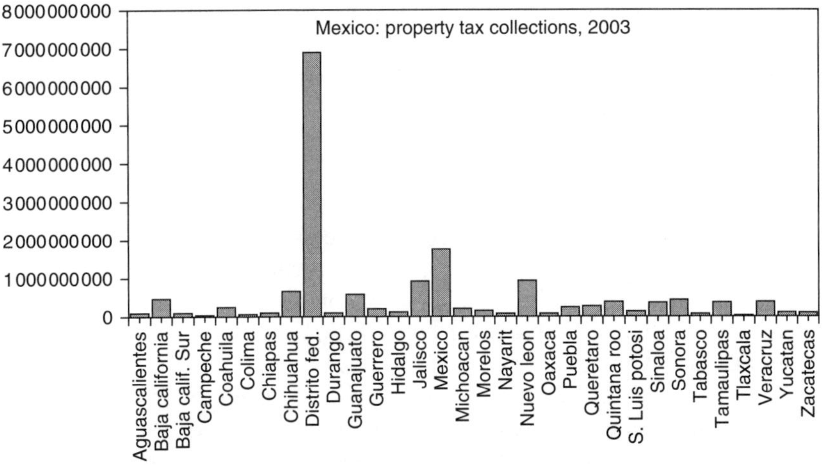

Figure 12.1 Property tax collections in Mexican states (pesos)

of all property tax collections—which are in any case low even by Latin American standards (Figure 12.1). Thus, with considerable local variation in revenue bases, and limited or no control over rate structures, the responsibility for providing a modicum of social services, especially in the poorer regions, generally passes to the higher levels of government.

There is a tendency to administer centrally the broadly based taxes, such as the VAT and the corporate income tax, as in Mexico in the late 1980s, where a number of state-level taxes were abolished on efficiency grounds to make "fiscal space for a centrally administered VAT". The states effectively ceded their tax bases to the center for guaranteed transfers. Also in China in 1994 the establishment of a VAT to be administered by a central State Administration of Taxation was a critical element of the fiscal reforms. More recently, in Australia a range of state taxes was replaced by a VAT, which is administered centrally although all revenues collected are redistributed to the states through the Commonwealth Grants Commission.

In all cases, transfers have been established to compensate for the loss of subnational revenues (particularly state or provincial sales taxes among others) eliminated as a result of the establishment of the VAT. In China, the equalization transfer introduced in 1994 has gradually increased in importance as additional funds have been made available. Mexico had a complex system of untied and earmarked transfers, but did not have an equalization framework. The weak own-source revenues of the lower tiers of government, and limited accountability, together with an opaque and complex transfer design probably explains why a central program in Mexico has been its most successful poverty reduction instrument. Lower levels of government lack the incentives or financing to effectively replicate *Oportunidades* at the subnational level.

3.2 Transfer Design

The central government may try to equalize fiscal capacities, as has been the case in many OECD countries, such that each local government has the capability of providing similar levels of services at similar levels of fiscal effort. This is the basis for equalization transfers in countries like Australia (see Ahmad and Searle, 2006).

The principles of the Australian system—focusing on spending needs and revenue capacities has been adopted in China, and resources available for equalization resources are gradually being increased (Ahmad, Keping and Richardson, 2002). Information flows and the political process are important in ensuring that local officials are held accountable for the use of untied funds. Thus, in less developed countries where information flows are problematic and incomplete, there may not be adequate moral suasion to ensure that the basic services are actually provided at the subnational level with sole reliance on "equalization transfers".

Alternatively, the center may choose to provide such services directly or through special purpose transfers designed to finance local provision of public services, say education or health care. This is the typical case, but it does not guarantee that the poorest will be reached, as the execution is typically by subnational governments. The difficulty is that any earmarked transfer from the center imposes a constraint on the local government. Matching arrangements have been used extensively in some advanced countries, especially the United States, in order to get some "buy-in" from the local governments. However, in developing countries, need is likely to be higher in the poorer localities with weaker sources of own-revenues. Hence, establishing matching criteria might actually exclude some of the poorest localities, and hence deserving recipients.

The linkages between transfer design and accountability as well as incentives to raise own-revenues and manage spending efficiently are complex but very important. Typically, a range of transfers is used for different purposes. If the center also includes "gap-filling" deficit financing among the set of transfers, this could vitiate any of the other "incentives" to ensure accountability of local officials (Ahmad and Searle, 2006).

4 HOW TO MAKE SPECIAL PURPOSE TRANSFERS WORK

Can adequately targeted expenditure programs be designed that are financed by the central government but implemented by the local governments to minimize the incentives of local governments to divert central transfers for their own objectives? This has been a perennial problem in China, for example in ensuring minimum standards in education (for example, number of years of schooling). Can communities determine priorities and monitor implementation? At the one extreme, there is a danger that funds could be diverted, and at the other that unfunded mandates might be created—in both cases it is possible that services would not be provided effectively. Moreover, the priorities may not reflect the interests of the poorest, particularly the most vulnerable members of society without sources of family support—the benefits from the transfers might accrue largely to powerful interest groups or officials.

The central government's (or donor's) problem is to design appropriate targeted or special purpose transfer programs to meet the needs of the poorest but that are executed by recipient agencies (or subnational governments).[1] The objectives of the center and the recipient governments are often likely to be different—the recipients may have less concern with providing for the poorest as the responsibility for these groups may effectively lie with the center. In any case, the recipient local governments receiving funds, in the absence of full information, could use these for other purposes without significant penalty in the traditional single period budgeting framework.

Ahmad, Tandberg and Zhang (2002) model a three-tier hierarchical structure of government that may be relevant for large countries such as Mexico or China: the central government is at the top level of the hierarchy, several provincial (state) governments in the middle layer and a few local or county-level governments within the administrative area of each of the provinces. The interest of leaders of provincial and local governments is to maximize perquisites and their overall budgets.

The central government sets aside a certain amount of financing for specific programs to be carried out by the localities. Ahmad, Tandberg and Zhang (2002) assume that the central government cannot contract directly with the localities, due to high transaction costs or political reasons.

The interaction between the provincial and local governments is nested in the central selection process. Prior to the submission of its bid, the provincial government arranges a bidding process among its localities. Each county within the province offers a bid proposal. The provincial government selects one and formulates the provincial proposal based

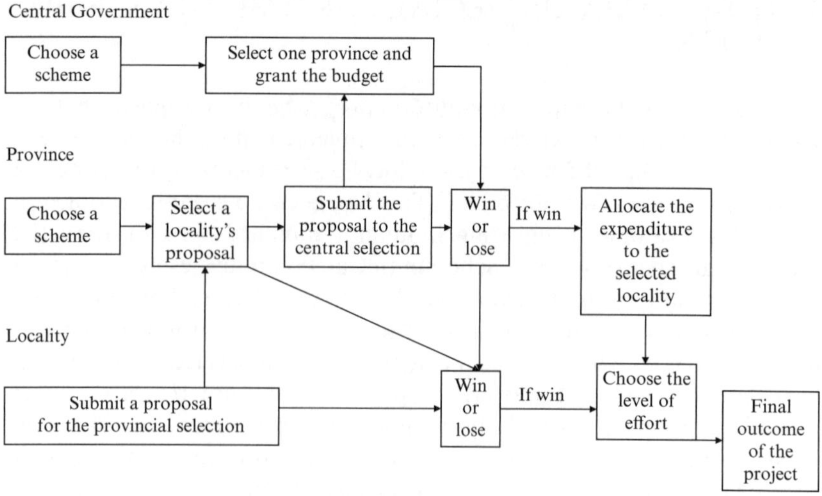

Figure 12.2 Decision diagram for the three tiers of governments

on the selected local proposals. If the province wins the program in the central selection, it will receive the amount equal to its budget bid. Then the provincial government decides the proportion of the budget to be allocated to the locality, to carry out the program. The local government then determines the effort level it will exert to implement the program. This subsumes "local capture" or other diversion of funds, and is not directly observable by the higher levels of government.

Figure 12.2 presents a simplified decision diagram of the three levels of governments. The analysis is similar to the classical "prisoner's dilemma". It is generally not possible to obtain an efficient solution in a one-period game of this type. Unless the game is repeated or constricted in some other way, officials in transfer-receiving jurisdictions will take decisions that are individually rational but which lead to suboptimal solutions and may not meet the objectives of the donor governments. There must be multi-period interactions among the different levels of government. If the game is of only one period, the local governments will bid as low as possible to obtain the transfer; and may not effectively implement the scheme. In a multi-period game, where the governments care for their reputation in the future, it may be possible to identify low-cost agents, and to limit the possibility for a diversion of funds or inefficient implementation.

In order to mitigate problems of asymmetric information, there must be some element of competition between the different governments at the same level. There should be more than one province bidding for the program in the central selection, and more than one locality in the provincial selection. To avoid moral hazard, the transfer scheme must include elements of punishment and rewards from the higher administration to the lower levels of government, based on the evaluation results of the final outcome. This serves as either carrot or stick through its impact on the agents' probability of winning future programs. The scheme also provides a "learning mechanism", where the outcomes in one period have an impact on the central government's assessment of the abilities of lower levels of government to meet their objectives in subsequent periods. Indeed, "reputation" in one set of observable programs might be used as proxy for likely effectiveness in program implementation in general—although there may be more incentive for local governments to implement investment projects rather than provide support to the indigent.

In order to be able to select the program bids through a competitive process, the central government must be able to define the specification of programs very precisely, and to monitor the degree of compliance against these specifications. The objectives of the program should be measurable, standardized across the localities and involve as little subjective judgment as possible. After implementation, it should be possible to evaluate whether objectives are achieved with minimal ambiguity. Unless these conditions are met, agents may be able to influence the central governments' selection of program sites by providing substandard services in areas that are insufficiently defined in the program specifications.

Key elements of the scheme (consistent with what is observed in reality) are that the central government is able to set the policy agenda and also that it is able, in principle, to cut off funds for non-compliance with agreed conditions. However, threats to cut off funds for the poorest groups may not be credible, especially given the overlapping responsibilities found in China or Mexico, but cross-conditionality involving threats to cut off investment funding strongly desired by local officials may be effectively utilized.

The design of policy to provide support to the poorest groups would involve cross-conditionality, where outcomes for provision for the poor could be built into the agreement or contract for investment funds for the localities. Thus, by virtue of setting the agenda, the center can ensure that resources are adequately used for the poorest by threatening to withhold funds for projects or investments that are evidently within the preference function of the localities.

A central result is for future transfers to be made conditional on policy reforms or on past performance. In practice, however, funds distributed by the central government are often independent of the past success of the program—given the typical single-year budgeting framework with little feedback based on outcomes. In many cases, there is an incentive for a donor government to continue to give transfers for the program, not just because of incomplete information, but because funds that are not distributed might lapse. This places the emphasis on clearly identifying "outcomes" of policy actions that could be monitored, and in ensuring that future budgets are linked to the achievement of the outcomes—in a repeated game perspective. In more advanced cases, this has led to the development of "contract federalism" (see Spahn, 2006). The findings of the model echo those from the foreign aid literature. Svensson (1999, 2003) suggests that the donor government's ineffectiveness in providing incentives to improve the performance of targeted expenditure programs may be the consequence of a time-consistency problem.

A policy option is to increase the effectiveness of targeted expenditure programs by introducing competition among local governments in different districts and across time. This formulation echoes the recent developments in the fiscal federalism literature that based efficient outcomes on enhanced competition (Breton, 2002; Ahmad and Martinez, 2004). This allows the central government to distribute all the available transfers and is shown to solve the time-consistency problem described before. The funds that local governments will receive depend implicitly on the central government's confidence in their ability to use these effectively. Therefore, even without explicit contracts, a local government may be induced to consider the central government's interests when deciding on its own actions. This increases the local government's likelihood for receiving more transfers in the future. In a one-period game approximating an annual budget process, recipient governments have incentives to cheat. Horizontal competition helps but is not sufficient to eliminate incentives to cheat.

A combination of both horizontal and intertemporal competition eliminates incentives to divert resources from the objectives of the central government. The competition elements have implications for the information flows and budget models that might be relevant to ensure that funds for programs to reach the poorest are not diverted to other uses.

4.1 Budget Processes and Transparency: Ensuring Accountability

The flow of standardized information is critical in providing a basis for evaluating how monies are used within and across jurisdictions. This involves the establishment of a common structure for the budget classification, for example, based on the IMF's standard for the economic classification: the *Government Financial Statistics Manual 2001* (GFSM 2001) and the UN's classification of the functions of government. These need to be harmonized across all jurisdictions. In addition, most advanced countries use systems of Treasury Single Accounts to manage and track the government's cash. In multi-level countries, it is also critical to set up standards for disclosure and reporting by subnational governments. These requirements are described in Ahmad et al. (2006).

Efforts to establish all of these requirements for information flows are underway in China, but are only beginning in Mexico. In both countries, the immediate issue remains to formulate policies and implementation plans in the context of incomplete information on the use of funds. To some extent, the use of multi-year budgets and competition for the use of funds across local governments and over time should be feasible in the relatively short term, even if the main public financial management reforms are likely to take time to implement fully.

Attempts by central governments to introduce performance budgeting at all levels of government, without adequate systems to track and account for financial flows, are unlikely to be very successful. Indeed, experience has shown that this may even delay the basic information building blocks that are needed in the longer term. Without standardized information that can be used by households to compare performance across jurisdictions, and to use this to discipline local officials, it is not clear that reliance on citizens' action groups and communities to self-police spending will be sufficient to prevent misuse or divergence of funds, except perhaps in egregious cases.

The longer-term goal must remain to establish standards for information flows and reporting that lead to transparency across and within governments. These are critical in achieving accountable operations at all levels of government. However, an immediate measure that can be implemented in most cases is to begin to use feedback mechanisms in the budget process system that take into account the effects and outcomes in meeting the needs of the poor.

5 POLICY IMPLICATIONS

Direct central provision of programs to support the poorest may be feasible in some countries, but may pose significant administrative difficulties in most countries. Local design and implementation use the advantage of local information—but the variance in resource levels across localities in large countries may make it essential for there to be some central transfers for the poorest. The difficulty is that with central earmarked transfers, recipient governments have incentives to divert resources.

The typical one-period budget process encourages inefficient use of central transfers, even if diversion is not intended. The central government would generally like to make transfers conditional on policy reforms or past performance. One of the key policy implications is that a multi-year budget framework, including multi-year appropriations, would greatly facilitate the achievement of central government objectives, since this opens up the possibility of intertemporal competition across lower-level jurisdictions. Within-year and intertemporal competition across lower-level governments is important in mitigating the problems of asymmetric information. This also helps in controlling costs and ensuring efficiency in spending.

Cross-conditionality in the design of transfers is important to address political economy issues. Threatening to withhold funds for the poorest groups of society might not be credible. However, it is feasible to withhold investment funds if the poverty-reduction objectives are not met. This cross-conditionality affects elements that are generally important in the preference functions of local officials and politicians.

The central government must define precisely the specifications of programs and the conditions to be met, and to monitor the degree of compliance against these specifications. While it might take time to establish proper government financial information management systems at all levels of government—this applies to Mexico as well as to China—both outputs and outcomes should be defined carefully to prevent misuse or misallocations of resources.

It would also be helpful to be able to draw up actionable contracts between the center and the local governments. Given that the allocation of inputs is not easily observable, as far as possible the contracts should be able to specify identifiable outputs (even if the outcomes may not be simple to specify or monitor in many developing countries).

In more advanced countries, there may be a possibility of moving towards performance budgeting at all levels of government, although the preconditions for this are quite demanding. But, in the short run, there is considerable promise in clarifying responsibilities, defining outcomes and using targeted transfers within a multi-year budgetary context.

NOTES

* Paper presented at a conference in Beijing in October 2007, on "Reaching the Poorest", organized by the Chinese Leading Group on Poverty Reduction of the State Council and the International Food Policy Research Institute. The views expressed are personal. Helpful discussion with Giorgio Brosio, Mercedes García-Escribano, Stuti Khemani, Jean-Phillipe Platteau, Ugo Panizza and Joachim von Braun are acknowledged.

1. A similar problem exists when an international agency or donor country provides financing for special purposes to be implemented in a recipient country.

REFERENCES

Ahmad, Ehtisham and Athar Hussain (1991), "Social Security in China", in Ehtisham Ahmad, Jean Drèze, John Hills and Amartya Sen (eds), *Social Security in Developing Countries*, Oxford: Clarendon Press.

Ahmad, Ehtisham and Leo Martinez (2004), "On the Design and Effectiveness of Targeted Expenditure Programs", IMF Working Paper, Washington, DC: International Monetary Fund.

Ahmad, Ehtisham and Bob Searle (2006), "On the Implementation of Transfers to Subnational Governments", in Ehtisham Ahmad and Giorgio Brosio (eds), *Handbook of Fiscal Federalism*, Cheltenham, UK and Northampton, MA, USA: Edward Elgar, pp. 381–404.

Ahmad, Ehtisham, Maria Albino-War and Raju Singh (2006), "Subnational Public Financial Management: Institutions and Macroeconomic Considerations," in Ehtisham Ahmad and Giorgio Brosio (eds), *Handbook of Fiscal Federalism*, Cheltenham, UK and Northampton, MA, USA: Edward Elgar.

Ahmad, Ehtisham, Li Keping and Thomas Richardson (2002), "Recentralization in China?", in Ehtisham Ahmad and Vito Tanzi (eds), *Managing Fiscal Decentralization*, New York: Routledge.

Ahmad, Ehtisham, Eivind Tandberg and Ping Zhang (2002), "On National or Supranational Objectives: Improving the Effectiveness of Targeted Expenditure Programs", IMF Working Paper No. 02/209, Washington, DC: International Monetary Fund.

Ambrosiano, Flavia and Massimo Bordignon (2006), "Normative Versus Positive Theories of Revenue Assignments", in Ehtisham Ahmad and Giorgio Brosio (eds), *Handbook of Fiscal Federalism*, Cheltenham, UK and Northampton, MA, USA: Edward Elgar.

Bardhan, Pranab and Dilip Mookherjee (2000), "Relative Capture of Government at Local and National Levels", *American Economic Review*, **90** (2), 135–9.

Bardhan, Pranab and Dilip Mookherjee (eds) (2006), *Decentralization and Local Governance in Developing Countries – A Comparative Perspective*, Cambridge: MIT Press.

Besley, Tim and Ravi Kanbur, (1993), "The Principles of Targeting", in Michael Lipton and Jacques van der Gaag, (eds), *Including the Poor*, Washington DC: The World Bank.

Birner, Regina (2007), "Decentralization and Public Service Provision – How to Meet the Needs of the Poorest?", paper presented at a conference on Effectiveness of Public Service Delivery, Moncalieri, Italy.

Breton, Albert (2002), "An Introduction to Decentralization Failure", in Ehtisham Ahmad and Vito Tanzi (eds), *Managing Fiscal Decentralization*, London and New York: Routledge, pp. 31–45.

Coady, David and S. Parker (2002), "A Cost-effectiveness Analysis of Demand and Supply-Side Education Interventions: The Case of PROGRESA in Mexico", Discussion Paper No. 127, International Food Policy Research Institute.

Levy, Santiago (2006), *Productividad, crecimiento y pobreza en México: Que sigue después de Progresa-Oportunidades?*, Inter-American Development Bank.

Levy, Santiago and Evelyne Rodriguez (2004), *Progresa-Oportunidades*, InterAmerican Development Bank.

Lockwood, Ben (2006), "The Political Economy of Decentralization", in Ehtisham

Ahmad and Giorgio Brosio (eds), *Handbook of Fiscal Federalism*, Cheltenham, UK and Northampton, MA, USA: Edward Elgar.

Ravallion, Martin (2007), *Geographic Inequity in a Decentralized Anti-poverty Program: A Case Study of China*, Washington DC: The World Bank.

Spahn, Bernd (2006), "Contract Federalism", in Ehtisham Ahmad and Giorgio Brosio (eds), *Handbook of Fiscal Federalism*, Cheltenham, UK and Northampton, MA, USA: Edward Elgar.

Svensson, Jakob (1999), "Aid, Growth and Democracy", *Economics and Politics*, **11** (3), 275–97.

Svensson, Jakob (2003), "Why Conditional Aid Does Not Work and What Can Be Done About it?", *Journal of Development Economics*, **LXX** (2003), 381–402.

Veras Soares, Fábio and Tatiana Britto (2007), "Confronting Capacity Constraints on Conditional Transfers in Latin America: The Cases of El Salvador and Paraguay", International Poverty Center, Working Paper No. 38, Brasilia: UNDP.

Von Braun, Joachim and Ulrike Grote (2002), "Does Decentralization Serve the Poor", in Ehtisham Ahmad and Vito Tanzi (eds), *Managing Fiscal Decentralization*, Washington, DC: Routledge.

World Bank (1990), *The World Development Report: Poverty*, Washington, DC: World Bank.

13. Subnational insolvency and governance: cross-country experiences and lessons

Lili Liu and Michael Waibel*

1 INTRODUCTION

The effectiveness of decentralization depends in part on the design and operation of subnational access to credit. Three factors have propelled the growth in subnational capital markets in developing countries since the 1990s and will continue to drive their future growth.[1] First, decentralization in many developing countries has given subnational governments significant spending responsibilities, taxation power and the capacity to incur debt. Second, large infrastructure financing needs in developing countries are increasingly seeking capital market financing to match the intertemporal nature of infrastructure. Infrastructure networks benefit future generations as well; thus sound public policy demands that the financing of infrastructure networks be shared by future generations through matching repayment of debt financing with maturity of assets. Third, liquidity and growing mobility of international capital across national borders have lowered the cost of borrowing and thereby strengthened financing opportunities for infrastructure. Although the current financial crisis has strained the subnational credit market, the mobility of capital is likely to resume over the medium term.[2]

This growth in subnational credit markets is characterized by two distinct features. First, subnational bonds have become an increasingly important source of funding due to diversification of financial instruments and increasing flow of international capital to developing countries. Second, although public institutions continue to dominate subnational lending in a number of countries such as Brazil and India, private capital has emerged to play an important role in subnational finance in countries such as Hungary, Mexico, Poland, Romania and South Africa and a dominant role in Russia.

Yet, growth in subnational bond markets in developing countries has not been steady. Annual volume gradually increased from US$5.7 billion in 1992 to US$22.2 billion in 1995, to be followed by a general downward trend to US$3.5 billion in 2001.[3] From 2001 until recently, growth in subnational bond markets picked up in emerging markets such as Russia, Mexico, Poland and Romania.[4] However, the recent worldwide tightening of liquidity has significantly reduced private credit available to subnational entities.

Even at the peak of the subnational bond market growth in developing countries, the availability of credits to subnational governments remains limited to top-tier subnational governments.[5] By developed country standards, the market was small even at its growth peak. In the United States, US$400 billion subnational bonds are issued per year on average.[6] In contrast, 19 Mexican subnationals issued US$1.44 billion bonds over the period 2001–05. In Colombia, only the capital Bogota accessed the capital market from 2003–06.

Several opposing forces explain the still thin subnational bond markets in emerging economies. As highlighted by the *World Development Report* (World Bank, 2000), subnational debt is "one of the thorniest issues for decentralization, with many potential pitfalls". These opposing forces range from incomplete decentralization, which limits a subnational's own-revenue capacity, to a lack of transparency in fiscal accounts, which makes it difficult to evaluate subnational creditworthiness. Furthermore, several emerging economies have tightened subnational borrowing restrictions after experiencing subnational or national debt crises.[7] Such tightening is part of broader ongoing efforts to develop a sound regulatory framework to tackle subnational insolvency.[8]

Subnational insolvency is a reoccurring event in development. In 1842, eight US states and the Territory of Florida were in default on their debt and three other states were in perilous financial condition (Wallis, 2004). Similarly, during the Great Depression, 4770 local governments defaulted on US$2.85 billion of debt between 1929 and 1933, and by 1933 over 16 percent of the US municipal market was in default.[9] As capital markets and their regulatory framework matured, defaults by US subnationals became less frequent. Yet crises continue to occur. Prominent examples include the fiscal crisis of New York City in 1975, the default on US$2.25 billion in bonds of the Washington Public Power Supply System in 1983 and the bankruptcy of Orange County in 1994 and the District of Columbia in 1995.[10] There have also been many cases of local government financial distress in Japan and Western European and the Nordic Countries.[11]

Several major emerging markets experienced subnational debt crises in the 1990s. Newly decentralized countries face similar risks. To many observers runaway provincial debt in the Provinces of Mendoza and

Buenos Aires was a major factor behind Argentina's sovereign debt default in 2001. Brazil experienced three subnational debt crises in the 1980s and 1990s. In India, many states experienced fiscal stress in the late 1990s to the early 2000s, with a rapid increase in fiscal deficits, debt and contingent liabilities. The 1995 Tequila Crisis in Mexico exposed the vulnerability of subnational debt to the peso devaluation and led many Mexican subnationals into default. In Russia at least 57 out of 89 regional governments defaulted over 1998–2001.

The perils of subnational insolvency are serious. At a minimum, provision of local public goods and services may be severely impaired. When New York City was in fiscal crisis in 1975, essential services such as fire protection, police patrols and schools were cut back. Maintenance on bridges and roads was postponed. Many capital projects were delayed or cancelled.[12] Beyond local service delivery, systemic subnational insolvency may impede the growth of subnational capital markets, curtail fiscal space for infrastructure financing and threaten macroeconomic and financial stability.

The ongoing global financial crisis has brought the nexus into sharper focus between borrowing constraints and the levels of public service delivery. States and municipalities in the United States are struggling financially and there are signs of stress threatening the fiscal sustainability of subnational governments in a growing number of developing countries. Slower economic growth and revenue shortfalls of national governments are likely to reduce fiscal transfers from the national government to subnational governments; and fiscal transfers account for a significant share of subnational finance in many developing countries. Service delivery is also likely to be impacted by shortfalls in subnational governments' own-source revenues.[13]

Given the impact of subnational insolvency on service delivery and macroeconomic stability, many developing countries have been searching for systemic frameworks for subnational borrowing and insolvency (Liu and Waibel, 2005; Webb, 2005).[14] Experience from developed economies suggests that ex ante subnational borrowing regulations need to be complemented by ex post mechanisms for insolvency resolution. More and more countries regard ex ante limits on subnational fiscal indicators (such as balanced budget rules, limits on the ratio of debt over gross subnational domestic product (GSDP) and debt service ratios) as insufficient.[15] The effectiveness of ex ante regulation is limited without an ex post mechanism for subnational insolvency to deter irresponsible borrowers and imprudent lenders.

Several arguments favor ex post subnational insolvency mechanisms. First, insolvent subnationals are put back on a sustainable fiscal path to guarantee public service delivery. Second, restoring subnational sustainability serves creditors collectively. Third, protecting creditor rights helps nurture embryonic capital markets. Fourth, clarity in default helps improve creditworthiness of subnational entities and enable subnational entities to re-enter the capital market for financing infrastructure. A well-designed workout procedure results in equitable debt collection for creditors, while lowering the costs of borrowing and creating fiscal space for infrastructure investment.

This chapter surveys mechanisms for the resolution of subnational financial insolvency in selected countries. It fleshes out basic concepts and highlights transferable features. Focusing on the experiences of Brazil, Bulgaria, Hungary, Romania, South Africa and the United States, we draw lessons for tailoring subnational insolvency mechanisms to country-specific circumstances. Although there are individual country case studies,[16] the literature lacks a cross-country survey. This chapter seeks to fill this gap. Comparison across country experiences helps draw out core principles of subnational insolvency mechanisms and demonstrate how the application of these principles varies by a country's unique context.

The chapter is structured as follows. The next section examines the events triggering the development of subnational insolvency mechanisms in various countries. This motivation is country-specific and shapes the design. We then explore the core principles of insolvency mechanisms, encapsulated in the trade-off between protecting creditors' contractual rights and maintaining minimum public services. We next discuss the central elements of mechanisms: triggering, filing, collective enforcement, fiscal adjustment and debt restructuring. In the concluding section we draw policy lessons for other developing countries. In the Appendix we outline the main elements of subnational insolvency procedures in Hungary, South Africa and the United States.

2 WHY REGULATE SUBNATIONAL INSOLVENCY?

Sustaining healthy growth in subnational credit markets requires a transparent framework for allocating risks and losses in default. The first purpose of the framework is to credibly signal to lenders that debt restructurings or potential discharges will be predictable and equitable. The second aim is to maintain minimum essential public services such as law and order, fire protection and water and sanitation during a subnational government's debt restructuring and fiscal adjustment.

While sharing these objectives, a country's political, economic, legal and historical context in combination with unique triggers results in a country-specific motivation. These differences affect the entry point for reform, the framework's design and its relation to subnational borrowing legislation. Despite important differences, individual experiences are valuable to other countries as they consider their policy options. This section summarizes experiences in the United States, South Africa, Hungary, Brazil and four Central and Eastern European Countries.

2.1 United States

In response to widespread municipal defaults during the Great Depression, the US Congress adopted a municipal insolvency law in 1937.[17] The primary aim of this legislation was to deal with the holdout problem. Individual creditors often demanded preferential treatment and threatened to derail debt restructurings voluntarily negotiated between a majority of creditors and the subnational debtor.

The enactment of the municipal bankruptcy statue in 1937 was one more step in a series of regulatory reforms on subnational borrowing since the first subnational debt crisis in the early 1840s. After the 1840s crisis, 12 states adopted new constitutions, and 11 of the 12 required that state legislatures adopt new procedures for authorizing state borrowing. Other reforms at the time included opening access for infrastructure finance and development and eliminating taxless finance.[18]

Following the reform in the 1840s and 1850s, various states also reformed their municipal borrowing regulations. One important concern was debt service in the event of default. In theory, the main remedy was one without analogue in private bankruptcy; the issuance of a writ of mandamus imposing new taxes. The 1870 Illinois Constitution, for example, obliged the general assembly to tax all property within the limits of municipal corporations for debt payment. In theory, creditors could thus use the mandamus to compel municipal officers to service debt obligations; in practice, this remedy was largely ineffective.[19]

The Great Depression, when subnational financial distress was prevalent, revealed the practical drawbacks of the mandamus. At the time, 4770 local governments defaulted on US$2.85 billion of debt. By 1933 over 16 percent of the US municipal market was in default.[20] In such circumstances, raising taxes is not likely to produce more revenue, as high taxes often lead to the flight of higher-income taxpayers and businesses. During the Great Depression, taxes were already at historical highs. Mandamus is useful for enforcing unpaid discrete obligations; it is ineffective if the subnational is unable to pay. Moreover, courts often regarded the mandamus as discretionary, and when it was ordered, municipal officers took various actions to escape the mandamus. In extreme cases, they resigned.

As an individual creditor action, the mandamus cannot solve the collective action problem. When widespread defaults occur, individual creditor enforcement is impracticable, costly and potentially harmful to the interests of a majority of creditors. The inability to compel holdouts to cooperate in a negotiated compromise motivated the passage of Chapter 9 of the US Bankruptcy Code.[21]

Chapter 9 is not the only subnational insolvency mechanism in the United States. Many states have adopted their own frameworks for dealing with municipal financial distress, for two reasons. First, municipalities are political subdivisions of the states, thus they are creatures of the states. Second, state consent is a precondition for municipalities to file for Chapter 9 in federal court. There is no uniform approach across states. Twenty-one of the 50 states give blanket consent, three states attach important conditions and 27 states grant permission on a case by case basis.[22]

When New York City went into financial crisis in 1975, then the largest municipal fiscal crisis since the Great Depression, the state of New York intervened directly. The state took over the city's financial management through the Municipal Assistance Corporation (MAC) in June 1975. MAC was a public benefit corporation of the state of New York to help the city restructure its glut of short-term debts.[23] Three months later the state established the even more powerful Emergency Financial Control Board (EFCB) for New York City.[24]

The EFCB took over fiscal management of the city, imposed difficult fiscal adjustment measures, restructured debt, curtailed borrowing, oversaw the creation and execution of a three-year fiscal adjustment imposed on the city that would result in balanced budgets, increased taxes and fees, dismissed 60000 public servants and enforced transparency in accounting, auditing and financial reporting.

As the EFCB was created by the state legislature, it had the legitimacy and broad authority to directly address the root cause of fiscal decline. Had New York City instead petitioned for bankruptcy protection under Chapter 9, the federal court, unlike the EFCB, could not have interfered so strongly in the fiscal affairs of the city. Unlike off-the-shelf bankruptcy protection, the state here decided to use an ad hoc approach tailored to the specific circumstances of the city. Among the few areas where the EFCB could not interfere were setting budget priorities, which remain the prerogative of elected city officials, and the right of employees to bargain collectively.[25]

2.2 South Africa

South Africa's motivation for enacting a municipal insolvency framework differed from that of the United States. After the fall of Apartheid, capital market lending to subnational governments had come to a virtual halt. The Treasury wanted to ensure municipal governments' continuous access to the capital market and to avoid future subnational financial crises. Investors were concerned whether their debt would be repaid. The Parliament's concern was how to protect a fledgling democracy, as addressing subnational insolvency touches on the role of the legislature, courts and local executives. These different interests came together to create a consensus for a municipal bankruptcy framework.[26]

During Apartheid, white communities, which were wealthier than black communities, could raise funds from the capital markets directly, based on their steady local revenues and even central guarantees. Defaults were absent, as were legal remedies. Black communities relied on central transfers and on-lending from a public financial parastatal that had the guarantee of central government.[27]

After the fall of Apartheid, the new decentralized constitution ended the guarantee of local debt. The democratic process requires the abolishing of racial jurisdictions. Municipal boundaries were redrawn in 1995 to combine poor black urban communities with wealthier white urban communities. The boundaries were redrawn again in 2000 to combine rural and urban communities in 2000.

These developments brought perceived uncertainty regarding the revenue strength of amalgamated municipal governments. Prolonged financial troubles of several municipalities without the prospect of resolution also dampened the confidence of lenders.[28] Among financial market participants, the view was widespread that the discretionary financial resolutions were insufficiently insulated from political pressure, entailing risks of lobbying federal government to bail out troubled municipalities. Also, enthusiasm for giving banks strong remedies against democratically elected local officials was low. These factors, combined with the lack of legislative and judicial procedures for dealing with subnational defaults, greatly increased the risks perceived by lenders, resulting in little capital market lending to local authorities.[29]

The South African case points to the impact of existing institutional structure on regulatory reform. Under the old Section 139 of the Constitution (1995–2002), few remedies existed to effect debt and fiscal adjustments for a financially troubled local government. Under the old Section 139, budgets, spending and taxes were under the purview of the local legislature. Intervention into local government affairs was limited to cases where an "executive obligation" was not fulfilled. The province could only issue "a directive to the council" and/or "assum[e]responsibility" for the obligation.

Two constitutional amendments paved the way for a municipal

insolvency mechanism.[30] The new Section 139 is entitled "intervention" in lieu of "supervision". Intervention is strong, with potential substantial loss of local political autonomy. The amendments also strengthened court independence. Only courts can stay debt payments and discharge debt obligations. The Municipal Finance Management Act, enacted in 2003, contains a new framework for municipal finance and borrowing. Chapter 13 of the Act spells out detailed criteria for interventions and recovery plans, specifies the role of higher-level governments and courts in the insolvency mechanism and outlines the fiscal and debt adjustment process.

Types of interventions include the issuance of directives, full loss of municipal autonomy in financial matters under a mandatory intervention, and dissolution of the Municipal Council in extreme circumstances. Primary responsibility lies with the provincial government, but the central government may intervene when the province is unable or unwilling to act. Compared with Hungary, where the court-appointed financial trustee takes the center stage, in South Africa the provincial executive branch plays an important role.

The South African case demonstrates the complexity of subnational borrowing and insolvency legislation and the path dependency of reforms. It also illustrates the importance of building political consensus among differing interest groups. It took the country two years to develop the basic policy framework (1998–2000), another year for the cabinet approval (2001), followed by two years of parliamentary debate on the constitutional amendments and on the Municipal Finance Management Act (2001–2003).

2.3 Hungary

If South Africa's motivation for developing a regulatory framework for subnational insolvency was to revive private lending to municipal governments, Hungary had two motivations in the mid-1990s.[31] The first was to discipline lenders. Lending by public banks was viewed as indiscriminate and imprudent, without proper evaluation of creditworthiness. The lack of credit differentiation was attributed to the assumed central government guarantee for subnational debt and potential problems associated with public sector lending. The second motivation rose from the deteriorating financial performances of local governments, which foreshadowed contingent state liabilities. In financial distress, borrowers and lenders were expected to lobby strongly for bailouts.

The 1990 Act on Local Government granted Hungary's local governments independence in financial management. Municipalities had unfettered freedom to manage their finances and started to borrow for commercial activities, thus increasing the risks of insolvency. The macroeconomic deterioration in 1995 exposed the seriousness of subnational financial distress. Furthermore, municipalities began to borrow long term to finance short-term operating deficits. Several local governments successfully lobbied for one-time grants from the central government.[32] This threatened to set a bailout precedent, raising concerns of adverse incentives for local governments and for creditors. Representatives of several commercial banks argued that these loans were for the public benefit and deserved bailout by the state.

Several options were debated at the time. The first option was for the central government to credibly adopt a no-bailout policy. The second option was to impose restrictions on borrowing and strengthen monitoring and enforcement. The third option was to rely on informal restructuring negotiations between major financial institutions and local governments.

Even though informal negotiations may lead to debt adjustment, they could not formalize debt restructuring procedures, the transparency and predictability of which are central to an effective subnational insolvency mechanism. In the end, maintaining essential public services, protecting debtors, creditors and the state budget, while clarifying what would happen in defaults, justified a debt adjustment law. The Law on Municipal Debt Adjustment (Law XXV) was approved by the Hungarian Parliament in March 1996 by an overwhelming majority. The Debt Adjustment Procedure consists of seven major phases: (1) initiation; (2) court review of the petition; (3) formation of a debt adjustment committee; (4) adoption of a crisis budget; (5) financial reorganization plan; (6) debt agreement negotiations and (7) asset liquidation if no agreement is reached.

Hungary differs from South Africa and the United States in one important way, namely the central role of courts in fiscal and debt adjustment for local governments in Hungary. In both South Africa and the United States, the courts' role is limited. They guide the parties in their negotiations and grant an eventual debt discharge, but provinces and the central government in South Africa and many states in the United States can directly effect fiscal and debt adjustments of financially troubled local governments. In Hungary, courts play the central role in the debt and fiscal adjustment.

2.4 Brazil

Brazil has opted for an administrative approach to subnational insolvency, in contrast to the United States, South Africa and Hungary where the role of the judiciary is more pronounced. Since the 1980s, Brazil has experienced three state debt crises (Ter-Minassian, 1997 and Dillinger, 2002).[33] The complex structure of fiscal federalism caused a lack of fiscal co-responsibility and the absence of hard budget constraints by lower levels of government. There was no control of subnational debt. On several occasions, the federal government bailed out states and municipalities. From the late 1980s to 1990s, the federal government restructured subnational debt three times.

In the two earlier subnational debt crises (1980s and the early 1990s), the central government bailed out insolvent subnational entities. And during the third subnational crisis (1997), the central government intervened directly, pushing difficult structural reforms to tackle the root causes of insolvency, instilling fiscal transparency and essentially imposing a fiscal and debt adjustment package based on reform conditions.

The first debt crisis was a legacy of the international debt crisis of the 1980s, when states, along with the federal government, ceased servicing their debt to foreign creditors. After the federal government reached agreement with the creditors, in 1989, the federal government transformed the accumulated state and municipal arrears and remaining principal into a single debt to the federal government. US$19 billion was rescheduled. The second crisis involved debt owed by the states to federal financial institutions. The federal government refinanced debt in 1993 amounting to US$28 billion. The third and largest debt crisis was resolved through the conditional bailout of the federal government in 1997. The federal government restructured the states' debt, equivalent to 11.5 percent of GDP.

Although with the first two debt workouts, the federal government made attempts to tighten the regulations on state borrowing, the efforts were insufficient. The 1997 debt workout was conditional upon each state's compliance with fiscal and structural reform programs. The motivation for the conditional bailout was to resolve the moral hazard associated with unconditional bailouts. In exchange for the rescue package, the federal government negotiated agreements with 25 states in 1997 and 1998.[34] These agreements were sanctioned by Law No. 9496 of September 1997.

Law No. 9496 established a comprehensive list of fiscal targets: a debt/revenue ratio, primary balance, limits on personnel spending, own-source revenue growth, investment ceilings and a list of state enterprises to be privatized or concessioned. Each state had to agree to such targets in exchange for financial relief. Crucially, the debt adjustment agreement collateralized resources for debt service and threatened withholding central government transfers in case of breach. Subsequent Senate Resolution No. 78, 1999 imposed fixed ceilings on new borrowing, debt servicing and the stock of debt. All these controls were strengthened by the 2000 Fiscal

Responsibility Law, which consolidated many restrictions and regulations into one unifying framework.[35]

2.5 Albania, Bulgaria, Macedonia and Romania

A group of Central and Eastern European Countries – Albania, Bulgaria, Macedonia and Romania – represents another set of interesting cases.[36] These countries see a subnational borrowing framework (including an insolvency mechanism) as a crucial element to underpin fiscal decentralization and their fledgling subnational debt markets. Aspiration to European Union membership provides added impetus for such reforms.[37]

In Bulgaria, only the capital Sofia has issued international bonds.[38] The near absence of a subnational borrowing market is commonly explained by an ambiguous borrowing framework, a lack of local budget and spending autonomy, weak local finances and a fragile banking system.[39] The inability to issue subnational bonds to finance infrastructure projects has also hampered the ability to draw on the European Union structural funds.

In June 2005, borrowing legislation was approved. A working group was then established to propose a mechanism for subnational financial distress. Insolvency is outside the group's term of reference. Bulgaria is the best example of a country looking at such a mechanism before signs of trouble appear. The lending community favors an insolvency mechanism. Bulgaria, by deciding to look into the merits of such a policy early, is able to start with a clean slate. However, the development of a regulatory framework for subnational borrowing needs to go hand in hand with improving the intergovernmental fiscal system, granting subnationals greater fiscal autonomy and reforming the financial markets.

Romania's capital market for subnational borrowing has been developing at a faster pace than Bulgaria's. Subnational debt is evenly divided between loans and bonds, with about 30 bond issues and 30 bank loans between 2002 and 2005. So far, lending has been limited to top-tier municipalities, small-scale projects and three- to five- year maturities for most offerings (recently maturities have been extended to up to 10 or 15 years for a few issues). To tap the European Union's accession financing, subnational borrowing needs to expand in size and spread to more municipalities.

One reason for limited growth of subnational credit in Romania is the case by case approach to financial distress. Due to a lack of predictable rules, lenders are unable to assess default risk. Lenders worry about political influence and unequal treatment of subnational governments. They want clarity on available remedies against defaulting municipalities. A high-level working group has been established to develop legislation for municipalities in financial distress and insolvency. The aim is to further capital market development and establish proper incentives for lenders and borrowers. In corporate bankruptcy, Romania has already accumulated substantial experience over the past three years.

A similar effort is under way in Albania where the subnational debt market is just starting to develop with consideration of a comprehensive legislative framework for borrowing. The government is interested in establishing a framework early on based on the experiences of Hungary and other countries. Adoption of Albania's subnational insolvency statute is imminent.

Today, Macedonian subnationals have no bank or bonded debt. The bulk of subnational debt consists of arrears to domestic construction companies. Legal disputes on the origin of debt as the result of merging and consolidating municipalities have raised uncertainty. The Macedonian case illustrates the tension between creditor rights and the need to maintain essential minimum services. Lenders went to court for overdue payments. The court judgments held that the lenders' repayment claim was subordinate to essential minimum services. Yet funds are not enough to cover essential minimum services, leaving little to pay creditors. The legal framework for local governments provides for a monitoring and surveillance regime for local governments in financial distress; however, it lacks the powers of intervention and legal remediation to deal effectively with the current situation.

A legal limit on debt issuance was introduced because of high municipal debt. Yet, for the current debt overhang, the absence of an insolvency mechanism prevents a debt restructuring. Efforts are ongoing to establish a debt restructuring law. Debt relief would be conditional on fiscal reform and consolidation. In the meantime, a game of hide and seek is taking place between creditors and municipalities, with municipalities moving their accounts frequently to escape attachment by creditors.

3 PRINCIPLES OF SUBNATIONAL INSOLVENCY

Notwithstanding different motivations, experiences from Brazil, Hungary, South Africa and the United States demonstrate certain principles that are inherent in a sound regulatory framework for insolvency. These principles are: balancing the tension between the contractual rights of creditors and the need for maintaining public services in the event of financial distress and default, a hard budget constraint for subnational entities and a credible no-bailout promise by the central government, clear and predictable rules to anchor expectations and burden-sharing between the subnational entity and creditors. Countries also face a choice between a judicial, administrative or a hybrid approach. Real-life mechanisms differ substantially, and the chosen design is in large part dependent on country-specific circumstances.

3.1 Comparing Public and Private Corporate Insolvency

Insolvency of subnationals is qualitatively different from private corporate entities. First, subnational governments provide public goods in fulfillment of mandated responsibilities. Second, compared with corporations, creditor remedies against defaulting subnationals are narrower. Third, while a corporation is able to self-dissolve, this route is barred for subnational governments. Fourth, the typical subnational has (or should have) some taxation power.

The core difference between the insolvency of private corporations and subnational governments is the public nature of the services provided by subnational governments. This core difference also explains the basic tension between protecting creditor rights and maintaining essential public services. Creditor rights are central to the development of capital markets; at the same time, providing essential public services such as police, drinking water and fire protection is the basic role of the government.[40] In this sense, the satisfaction of creditor claims is subject to an absolute functional limit: the protection of the core functions of the subnational entity.

In the event of private corporate bankruptcy, all assets of the corporation are potentially subject to attachment. By contrast, the ability of creditors to attach assets of subnational governments is greatly restrained in many countries. The reasons for granting subnationals immunity from attachment are concern over potential disruption of the government and the need to assure that essential services will continue to be provided to the people.

When Hungary deliberated its subnational insolvency mechanism, it was recognized that the country's corporate bankruptcy law, in force since the late 1980s, was not applicable to subnational borrowers. In the United States, a prominent judicial doctrine holds that only proprietary property is attachable. "Proprietary property", subject to debt foreclosure, was defined by the US Supreme Court as "held in (the municipality's) own right for profit or as a source of revenue not charged with any public trust or use".[41] Property dedicated to "public use" such as streets, hospitals or courthouses is exempt even in the absence of specific statutory protection, as are funds held in the local treasury for general use. As a result, the backstop of private creditor rights – the right to seize the property of the debtor – is often unavailable to the subnational debtors.[42]

Another key difference between subnational and corporate bankruptcy lies in the procedure's partial insurance function. This is the result of debt discharge when repayment would cause a sizeable decrease in the delivery of public services. The rationale is to protect the subnational entity and its population from long-term harm through a sharp decrease in public service delivery. Also, to allow a timely fresh start, one needs to balance incentives for the subnational entity to grow out of insolvency with repayment of creditors. As bankruptcy procedures lower the downside risk of borrowing, a higher bankruptcy exemption for essential public services will ceteris paribus lower the supply of financing (White, 2005). There is thus a trade-off. Where to draw this line is a crucial question in the design of such legislation.

Insolvency in the private sector is defined as a situation where a legal person or entity's liabilities exceed its assets. The insolvency procedure usually involves selling off assets to satisfy payment of liabilities. Those liabilities remaining unpaid are then de facto written off in liquidation. Reorganization procedures restructure liabilities in a legal procedure to allow a fresh start for viable entities.[43] In reorganization, courts are usually empowered to "discharge" debt (debt adjustment).[44]

In the design of such procedures for subnationals, one needs to think outside the box of liquidation. In contrast to corporations, subnational governments cannot be liquidated like commercial enterprises, unless another entity assumes their governmental responsibilities. Invariably, subnational insolvency mechanisms can only be of the reorganization type. The entity continues to exist and the government remains in control, keeping some of its assets to ensure continued public goods provision. A quick economic recovery of the entity concerned is also in the best long-term interest of creditors as a group, since it heightens the probability of repayment. The overarching aim of the procedure is thus financial rehabilitation of the debtor, and maximum recovery for creditors consistent with this objective.

In summary, the policy justification and legal procedures for private sector insolvency do not readily transfer to subnational entities. This results in a number of insolvency design features unique to subnationals. The usual way of defining "insolvent" as liabilities greater than assets is of little use. Liquidation of all assets is infeasible, as at least some public assets are critical to carrying out important governmental tasks.[45] These responsibilities are *independent* of the subnationals' financial condition. Municipalities are governed by elected officials. Interference in the subnational's sphere of responsibility is problematic,[46] because of the political nature of rights and obligations.[47] It may also run counter to constitutional protection and electoral choices.

3.2 Hard Budget Constraint for Subnational Entities

Unconditional bailouts of financially troubled subnational entities by the national government create moral hazard, encouraging fiscal irresponsibility with little concern for how debt will be serviced and imprudent lending without balancing risks and returns. A lax subnational budget constraint distorts the price signal guiding the allocation of credit, creates potential liabilities for the central government and endangers macroeconomic stability. The time will come for over-indebted entities to confront a difficult economic and political reality. Their policy choices will be between raising taxes, cutting spending, lobbying the central government for a bailout or seeking relief from creditors.

In the United States, the no-bailout principle was established during the first subnational defaults in the 1840s. In 1842, 11 States and the Territory of Florida were in serious financial trouble. States and investors lobbied the federal government for bailouts. The no-bailout principle had the upper hand, and eight states and the Territory of Florida defaulted their debt. The crisis prompted states to impose new limits on borrowing. Between 1842 and 1852, 12 states wrote new constitutions. Eleven adopted novel procedures for authorizing government borrowing.[48] The principle of no-bailouts has been upheld over various subnational default cycles.[49]

As illustrated by the Hungarian case, the motivation for establishing a regulatory framework for subnational insolvency was to reduce moral hazard, impose a hard budget constraint for municipalities and shrink contingent liabilities of the central government. After repeatedly bailing out subnational governments, Brazil followed a stricter approach, demanding subnational fiscal adjustment in return for fiscal relief. However, the mere existence of a hard budget constraint is not sufficient for nurturing the development of capital markets, as illustrated by the case of South Africa. The post-Apartheid decentralized constitution ended the guarantee of local debt. But the resumption of lending to municipal governments by the capital market did not start until the insolvency mechanism was put in place, with the clarity of rules as a central element of the mechanism.

3.3 Clarity of Rules

The twin aims of a subnational insolvency framework are to create a predictable and transparent framework for managing expectations about default and to coordinate competing interests on the subnational's financial recovery. The first enables accurate risk pricing and credit differentiation, and prevents moral hazard. The second helps the subnational to restore fiscal sustainability, which not only allows the subnational to carry out its governmental responsibilities while undergoing restructuring but also serves the collective interest of creditors.

Lack of clear rules for insolvency is likely to raise borrowing costs through higher interest rates, shorter maturity, or both, and thereby limits market access for creditworthy borrowers. The experience of Romania with municipal capital market shows this clearly: facing substantial uncertainty about available remedies upon default, private lenders are reluctant to supply credit to more municipalities, lower cost, or extend maturities. In the extreme cases, a lack of clear rules for insolvency can shut down the capital market altogether, as demonstrated by the experience of South Africa prior to the enactment of the Municipal Finance Management Act in 2003.

The insolvency framework aims to clarify rules on three key aspects of the insolvency process. The first aspect concerns orderly debt restructurings. The second aspect concerns the maintenance of essential public services. The third aspect concerns structural adjustment to restore subnational fiscal sustainability.

In the absence of a clearly-defined framework for insolvency, subnational governments may adjust debts in negotiations with creditors or repudiate their obligations. As the experiences of the United States, Hungary, South Africa and Macedonia show, ad hoc debt restructurings are complex. Interests of the subnational government, which is responsible for maintaining essential minimum services, and those of creditors, who insist on fulfillment of contractual promises, diverge. Oftentimes, reconciliation through a voluntary bargaining process proves elusive.

Clear creditor remedies allow collective enforcement and facilitate efficient debt adjustment. Creditor remedies in contract laws, instead of insolvency mechanisms, are effective to enforce discrete unpaid obligations. However, individual lawsuits or negotiations become ineffective if there is a general inability to pay. In systemic subnational insolvency, individual negotiations with each creditor are impractical, costly and potentially harmful to the interests of the majority of creditors. A small group of creditors may derail a debt restructuring agreement reached between the debtor and creditor majority. This holdout problem causes uncertainty and prolongs the debt restructuring process. Resolving the holdout problem was the primary motivation for the United States to enact the municipal bankruptcy legislation (Chapter 9) to clarify the rules for debt restructuring.[50]

On maintaining essential public services, there are three general approaches. In the first, the legislation specifies a closed list of essential services (assets) in detail.[51] In the second, a broad clause protects those assets used for public purposes (essential services). This later distinction between property for public use and property for private use is a principle of subnational insolvency procedures. Such protection is at times found in a specific municipal insolvency statute; in the absence of a specific protective clause for subnational entities in the laws on attachment. Court may also decide on a case by case basis, taking into account the fiscal and debt adjustment agreement reached between the debtor and creditors.[52] On fiscal adjustment, the insolvency mechanism, in combination with ex ante regulation, can define various stages of financial distress and insolvency, using clearly defined fiscal and financial indicators such as primary balance, debt service ratio, arrears and liquidity. It can also spell out judicial or administrative proceedings for restoring fiscal and financial health to the troubled subnational entity.

A well-designed insolvency procedure will have important ex ante effects anchoring the expectation of borrowers and creditors. For this reason, such a mechanism not only helps resolve financial distress ex post, but also deters irresponsible borrowing and imprudent lending ex ante. In the United States, Chapter 9 is rarely invoked. Chapter 9 is designed to carry a strong stigma for the borrowing municipality, to offset debtor moral hazard. Municipalities are thus wary that capital markets would interpret the filing for federal bankruptcy protection as a strong signal of financial mismanagement, to which lenders are likely to react by charging a risk premium.

In Hungary, four years after the 1996 Act on Municipal Bankruptcy, only a handful of municipalities (11 out of 3158) filed for bankruptcy protection. There is strong evidence that the legislation preempted more filings, because creditors and debtors were encouraged to seek redress outside the court system and to take other steps to ensure solvency and operational efficiency. Furthermore, financial institutions have been more prudent in lending to municipalities.[53] Although voluntary resolutions without insolvency procedures are unlikely, the mere existence of a legal framework that could impose solutions often induces voluntary agreements.

3.4 Equitable Burden Sharing

Clear rules ease the distributional struggle typical of insolvency. The basic tension between the need to maintain essential minimum services and the creditor's contractual rights implies that the pain of insolvency needs to be shared between lenders and creditors. The insolvency mechanism needs to balance competing interests. This distribution also matters ex ante, as it shapes the expectation and behavior of borrower and lender in the next cycle of borrowing.

In the aftermath of the Great Depression, Hillhouse described the situation in colorful words: "Every municipal default is like a drama in which there are many players. Bankers, lawyers, municipal bondholders, holders of the unfunded obligations and real estate mortgages, local officials, taxpayers, municipal employees and civic groups, all play some parts".[54] To this long list, one should also add the central government. For example, in resolving the Brazilian subnational debt crises, almost the entire burden was placed on the central government.

What should a rational framework for subnational insolvency look like? This chapter argued above that there are many benefits to clarifying the rules. One key component is establishing ex ante the repayment order in insolvency, which helps prevent moral hazard and encourage pricing of default risk by lenders.

The collision of interests, a clash between creditor rights and the subnational debtor's inability to pay, is here to stay. This clash is at its extreme when a debt discharge is needed, a major curtailment of creditor rights. Creditors will insist that all valid debts be honored and repaid. Ex ante, the subnational entity will pledge assets for financial resources; ex post, it will argue that many assets cannot be used for the satisfaction of creditors as they serve a public purpose. Can the public nature of the debtor justify curtailing creditors' valid private law claims?

In principle the answer is an equitable sharing of misery. Many corporate insolvency systems provide for equal creditor treatment of similarly situated creditors, including similarly situated foreign and domestic creditors. Without a strong reason to depart from this principle, like creditors should be satisfied ratably. This principle would call, for example, for treating all bondholders equally. A subnational insolvency framework also provides guidance on the priority of settling competing creditor claims.

The economic literature on bankruptcy asserts that the absolute priority rule (APR) is optimal, since it provides the right incentives for lending ex ante (White, 2005). If lenders are repaid in the exact order of their lending, implying that no lender can jump the queue, then costs of additional lending are fully internalized and reflected in pricing. In other words, there is no risk of debt dilution, since the effect of the marginal dollar lent on the debtor's payment capacity is fully incorporated in the costs of lending.

Yet in practice, no country has adopted a pure absolute priority rule. The reason is twofold. Although the APR rule might be efficient ex post, it need not be efficient ex ante. The rule may have a deterrent effect on new lending, *even* when such lending is desirable. Debtor-in-possession financing in US corporate bankruptcy law addresses this concern. Contrary to the APR rule, priority is given to new financing once the debtor is under bankruptcy protection. The convincing rationale is to allow refinancing in financial distress.

Second, distributing the pool of available assets in bankruptcy is never about efficiency alone. There are distributional impacts. The APR is only one possible policy choice. Many other configurations of priority are possible. Which one is most appropriate for the insolvency of subnational entities will depend, first, on the distributional judgment of the society concerned and, second, on the effect of a chosen priority structure on the capital market and its impact on new financing during a liquidity crunch. It is also important to allow sufficient flexibility within a general priority framework.

In the absence of a clear priority structure, the defaulting borrower may choose the order in which to satisfy creditors. A subnational insolvency framework eliminates this source of arbitrariness by providing guidance on the priority of creditor claims. Yet the devil is in the details of "equitable priority structure". This notion will differ across countries, reflecting society's distributional judgments over sharing the insolvent's dwindling pie of assets.[55] The US approach in Chapter 9 of the Bankruptcy Code gives first priority to secured creditors and second priority to unsecured creditors, after essential public services and costs of the bankruptcy proceedings are paid for. Hungary chose to give preference to subnational employees over creditors as a group.

The priority structure for settling competing claims expedites the resolution of debt restructuring and payments. It also eases the pain of sharing the reduced assets for distribution, because the losses suffered by different creditor groups are more predictable and more likely to be accepted, and moreover, the structure can keep the absolute size of losses in check, since the costs of protracted negotiations and litigation are high and often take priority over other claims. The shadow of priorities provides the backstop for voluntary restructuring negotiations, shaping bargaining power of creditors and debtor even outside bankruptcy. Clearly, the priority structure is a policy choice, with a variety of trade-offs. If the lending community perceives that financial distress is entirely or mostly resolved on its back, then desirable future lending will suffer.

A reason for introducing a subnational insolvency mechanism might be a desire to change leverage in the debtor–creditor relationship. Much will depend on shortcomings identified in the current subnational borrowing arrangements. If the analysis revealed that the current system is tilted in favor of borrowers, then the insolvency framework could be designed to shift bargaining power to the creditor. If, on the other hand, creditors enjoy too much leverage, then the insolvency system could provide more protection to a subnational entity in financial distress.

3.5 Judicial versus Administrative Approach

This section contrasts two alternative approaches to subnational insolvency: the judicial and the political-administrative approach. In addition, various hybrids exist. Judicial procedures place courts in the driver's seat. Courts make key decisions to guide along the restructuring process. Administrative interventions, by contrast, usually allow a higher level of government to intervene in the entity concerned, temporarily taking direct political responsibility for many aspects of financial management.

The judicial approach tends to target insolvency and is triggered by the filing of a petition. Under the administrative approach, a higher-level government typically intervenes earlier to prevent deterioration of subnational fiscal distress into insolvency. The judicial approach is rarely used in the United States, as Chapter 9 serves primarily as a deterrent.[56] The states in the United States have adopted various approaches to resolving local financial distress. New York and Ohio represent two broad intervention types: an early warning system to prevent local governments from slipping into fiscal distress (Ohio), and strong ex post intervention by the state to restore local government solvency (New York).

While Chapter 9 in the United States, and Hungary's legal insolvency mechanism deal with insolvency through the courts, South Africa's legal framework is a hybrid, blending administrative intervention followed by judicial intervention if the financial distress deteriorates into insolvency. There are three steps in South Africa in the event of municipal financial distress: an early warning system consisting of various indicators, intervention by provincial governments and then by the central government and intervention by the judicial system in debt restructuring. Brazil has chosen an administrative approach to dealing with subnational insolvency. The choice of procedure links in part back to the motivation. In Hungary, for example, a desire to neutralize political pressure during the restructuring favored the judicial approach.

The earliest documented attempt of introducing a municipal insolvency procedure occurred in Switzerland. In 1883, four municipalities were on the brink of insolvency after a guarantee for the benefit of the Swiss National Railway Corporation was triggered. Insolvency was only averted by a sizeable federal bailout. This crisis prompted a search for a legal framework for municipal insolvency.

Friedrich Meili (1885), a renowned Swiss law professor, undertook a comprehensive survey on municipal insolvency for the Swiss federal government, and put forward a detailed proposal for a law.[57] Meili regarded the crisis of the four municipalities as a welcome opportunity to introduce clarity into the relationship between municipalities and their creditors. In his view, like to so many who followed, the main benefit is legal certainty.[58]

The inherent political character of subnational entities is a key consideration in design. Many subnational governments are elected. Their removal by administrative fiat or by a judge might directly conflict with the democratic governance at the subnational level. This need to safeguard internal decision-making, which is peculiar to public bodies with elected officials, is referred to as "sovereignty concerns".

The United States displays an interesting variant of such sovereignty concerns. Chapter 9 vests jurisdiction in federal courts; this raises sovereignty concerns, since municipalities are creatures of the states. The solution adopted is the specific authorization requirement of Chapter 9.[59] As a result, the federal bankruptcy courts cannot interfere with a state's ability to control its municipalities.

Outside insolvency, sovereignty concerns are apparent in the limitations on seizure of subnational property, which are found in many jurisdictions. Under this rule, a private person cannot attach public property for satisfaction of a debt. In extreme cases, attachment could endanger the municipality's functions. Importantly, if a court were to order such attachment, it would put the judicial branch in direct conflict with the subnational-administrative branch. As courts lack the political legitimacy for deep interference in financial affairs, sovereignty concerns are more pronounced under the judicial approach.

A narrow scope of intervention is one way of safeguarding subnational autonomy. Under Section 904 of the United States Bankruptcy Code, the Federal Court's jurisdiction depends on the debtor's volition and cannot be extended beyond it. Financial management remains the responsibility of the municipality. The court may not interfere with the municipality's choice on services to citizens. It is the municipality's prerogative to prioritize spending, within the envelope established through the adjustment plan. Hence, the insolvency mechanism is separate from internal decision-making. Court-ordered replacements of politicians are ruled out.

4 SUBNATIONAL INSOLVENCY FRAMEWORK: KEY ELEMENTS

This section analyzes key elements of subnational insolvency frameworks based on the experiences of the United States, Hungary and South Africa. The focus is on central elements, to illustrate typical design choices a country faces when developing subnational insolvency mechanisms. The section does not discuss their full legal complexity. The section defines insolvency, which serves as trigger for the procedure, and discusses collective enforcement. The section then analyzes the dual adjustments during the insolvency proceeding. The first adjustment – fiscal adjustment by the debtor – is to bring spending in line with revenues and to bring borrowing in line with debt service capacity. The second adjustment is negotiations between creditors and the debtor to restructure debt obligations and potential debt relief.

4.1 Insolvency and Commencement of Bankruptcy

What is meant by "subnational financial distress" and "subnational insolvency"? While the economics literature defines insolvency in relation to the sustainability of fiscal policies,[60] a specific legal definition serves as "procedural trigger" for initiating insolvency proceedings. The typical administrative approach to subnational insolvency kicks in earlier than judicial procedures. The higher level of government may intervene in financial distress, before the subnational's financial situation deteriorates into insolvency.

In a legal sense, insolvency refers to the inability to pay debts as they fall due. Yet details vary across countries. In the United States, insolvency is defined as the debtor either: (1) currently not paying its debts as they become due, unless such debts are the subject of a bona fide dispute, or (2) not being able to pay its debts as they become due.[61] In Hungary, the two central triggers are: the debtor (1) has neither disputed nor paid an invoice sent by a creditor . . . within 60 days of receipt or of date due if the due date is later; (2) has not paid a recognized debt within 60 days of date due.[62]

South Africa, by contrast, chose one set of triggers for serious financial problems,[63] and another for persistent material breach of financial commitments.[64] If the first set of triggers is met,[65] the provincial government may intervene. Under the second set of triggers, intervention is mandatory. Unsuccessful provincial intervention calls for national government intervention. Independent of these interventions, the municipal government can apply to the High Court to stay all legal proceedings against the municipal government, and to relieve, suspend or discharge financial obligations.[66]

In all three countries, the bankruptcy code empowers the bankruptcy court to dismiss petitions not filed in "good faith", to prevent filing for bankruptcy despite ability to pay. Since bankruptcy procedures have the power to discharge debt, a subnational entity may be tempted to file purely for the purpose of evading debt obligations.

In the United States, the cash-flow definition of insolvency for municipalities differs from the balance sheet insolvency test used for corporations. For municipalities, the code looks to cash flow, while for other debtors, it looks to assets and liabilities. Even a municipality with many valuable assets can be insolvent. This reflects the common law view before the United States Bankruptcy Code, which treated the municipality as a debtor with few physical assets available for creditors and instead focused almost exclusively on the ability of the debtor to generate revenues through property tax.[67]

The insolvency standard in the United States serves as an effective gatekeeper, discouraging unnecessary municipal bankruptcy filings. The Bankruptcy Code erects obstacles to municipal filing beyond those faced by private debtors. Only municipalities face a statutory requirement of insolvency. Section 109(c) imposes a procedural bar that is unique to Chapter 9 debtors: it requires pre-filing efforts by the municipal debtor to work out its financial difficulties. The debtor must have reached agreement towards a plan, have failed to do so despite good faith negotiations or such negotiation must be "impracticable". And, municipalities need state authorization to file for bankruptcy [(109 (c) (2)].[68]

A subnational government can be financially distressed, yet solvent. Financial distress can be measured by various indicators, such as the ratio of current expenditure over revenues. The resulting operating deficit determines needed borrowing (a warning signal) and the ratio of debt service to total revenues, which measures the capacity to service debt. Each country's definition is different. For example, Brazil defines the debt service ratio as share of current revenue net of transfers (Brazil, 2001), Colombia defines it as share of operational savings (Colombia, 1997), Peru defines it as share of current income including transfers (Peru, 2003) and Russia defines it as share of total budgetary expenditures (Russia, 1998). Fiscal responsibility laws in various countries cap the ratio beyond which a subnational is deemed to experience debt distress.

Who can file for bankruptcy? The class of eligible filers differs across countries. In the United States, only the municipality can file for bankruptcy under Chapter 9, conditional on being insolvent, having worked or attempted to work out a plan to deal with its debts and having been authorized by the state to file for bankruptcy.[69] The more stringent requirement for filing under Chapter 9, as compared with filing under Chapter 11, is due to the constraint set by the US Constitution. A creditor cannot bring a municipality, against its will, into a federal court, based on the 11th amendment of the US Constitution. In South Africa, any creditor can file a claim against the municipality.[70] Similarly, in Hungary, a creditor can petition the court if a municipality is in arrears of more than 60 days.[71] Schwarcz's model law allows only municipalities to file.[72]

4.2 Collective Enforcement

An insolvency proceeding is the process by which a financially distressed subnational entity resolves its debts collectively, as opposed to various individual and uncoordinated attempts at enforcement. Central to this process is a collective framework for simultaneously resolving debt claims when eligible assets fall short of liabilities. Following the Great Depression, Hillhouse (1936) emphasized that the main aim of insolvency for public entities is to avoid unnecessary waste of time, money and energy by all parties that arise in countless unsuccessful attempts at individual enforcement.

The coordinating role of insolvency mechanisms is central. The implicit assumption is that the self-interest of creditors (as a group and taken individually) may at times diverge, at least over the medium term. This could result in a breakdown in voluntary restructuring negotiations. In such circumstances there is a need for a procedure able to bind in holdout creditors, who refuse to go along with a restructuring.

The holdout problem arises from heterogeneity of stakeholders. For this reason voluntary negotiations may run out of steam and fail to provide a long-term solution. The underlying premise is that majority acceptance of an adjustment plan indicates that – in the majority's judgment – the plan is in line with the entity's capacity to pay. A holdout creditor may obstruct restructuring negotiations by refusing to accept the agreement, bringing suit on the original contract and trying to execute against attachable property of subnational entity.

The collection options against subnational governments tend to be limited, compared with corporations or individuals. The race to the courthouse is therefore a less salient concern. The need for a stay to conserve the current situation remains strong. A stay provides breathing space to the subnational entity to negotiate in good faith with its creditors, unobstructed by lawsuits. Current subnational insolvency procedures all incorporate such a stay in one form or the other. A stay is an authorization by the bankruptcy authority freezing ongoing litigation and prohibiting further financial transactions. In the US the stay is automatic; in South Africa court approval is required.[73]

A well-designed system should provide strong incentives for collective action encouraging creditors and lenders to conduct restructuring negotiations early. Negotiated adjustments involving all stakeholders are the most cost-effective and efficient tool to resolve financial distress. If the shadow of insolvency is too remote and interests diverge, such voluntary bargaining will fail. This provides the rationale for off-the-shelf insolvency legislation for subnational entities. In systemic crises, there may be a need for interim framework enhancement measures tailored to the circumstances of the crisis at hand, without undermining the basic arrangements of the established insolvency framework.

4.3 Fiscal Adjustment

Fiscal adjustment and consolidation are preconditions for financial workouts and recovery. If the municipality and other stakeholders do not address the root causes of insolvency, and yet all debts were discharged through some insolvency mechanism, then the subnational government could jump onto another cycle of fiscal mismanagement and financial distress.

Financial distress and insolvency are often the result of fiscal mismanagement. The fiscal crisis of New York City in 1975 was the result of spending persistently exceeding revenues and an oversized public sector (Bailey, 1984). In South Africa, fiscal mismanagement and failure to raise revenue were major causes of subnational financial crises after the ending of Apartheid regime (Glasser, 2005). Borrowing for commercial activities and for operational deficits (both should be prohibited) and unchecked fiscal management prompted financial distress of many Hungarian local governments in the first part of the 1990s (Jokay et al., 2004). Fiscal deterioration of Indian states in the late 1990s was attributed to rapid increases in salaries, pensions and subsidies; and rising debt services as the result of rising borrowing cost and increases in borrowing to support growing operating deficits.

Contingent liabilities associated with fiscal support to the public sector units, cooperatives and the statutory boards heightened fiscal risks (Ianchovichina et al., 2006). Besides fiscal mismanagement, macroeconomic shocks also impact subnational insolvency. Macroeconomic crises – currency depreciation, inflation and rising interest rates – exacerbated the vulnerability of subnational fiscal positions and led to massive subnational defaults in countries such as Mexico (1994–95), Russia (1998–99) and Argentina (2000–01). However, macroeconomic crisis was not the sole cause of the subnational debt crisis in these countries; it only exposed and exacerbated the vulnerabilities already rooted in the subnational finances. Deficiencies in the intergovernmental fiscal system, expected guarantees by central governments for subnational debt and non-transparent fiscal accounting all contributed to the subnational debt crises in these countries.

Ianchovichina et al. (2006) present a framework for analyzing subnational fiscal adjustment. Subnational debt sustainability is influenced by economic growth of the subnational economy, real interest rates and the subnational's primary balance. They argue that subnational fiscal adjustment qualitatively differs from national fiscal adjustment. The former is complicated by the respective legislative mandates of central vis-à-vis subnational governments and the intergovernmental finance system. Unable to issue their own currency, subnationals cannot use seigniorage finance. Subnationals cannot freely adjust their primary balance due to legal constraints on raising own revenue, dependence on central government transfers and central government influences on key expenditure items such as wages and pensions. If public sector banks dominate lending, lending rates could be subsidized, bank lending to subnational entities could exceed the statutory requirements and credit risk concerns could be compromised. Many policies that affect the economic growth and the fiscal health of the subnational economy are designed largely or exclusively by the central government.

Even in a decentralized system such as in the United Sates where subnationals have broad freedom to control expenditures, raise revenues, affect the interest rate spread in a competitive capital market and influence growth environment, fiscal adjustment often requires difficult political choices of cutting expenditure and raising revenues. In the administrative approach to insolvency, the scope of intervention by higher levels of government in subnational fiscal adjustment is often extensive. Judicial interventions vary across countries, depending on the relationships among the judicial, executive and legislative branches. Since courts are to interpret law but not to legislate, and the courts in many countries are independent of the executive branch, courts' interventions into subnational fiscal adjustment are narrower than under the administrative approach.

In the United States, Chapter 9 of the Bankruptcy Codes explicitly protects the right of the state to control its political subdivisions and the right of the municipal debtor to manage its internal affairs. Section 904 provides that the court may not interfere with the "political or government powers of the debtor" the "properties or revenues of a debtor" or the "debtor's use of or enjoyment of any income-producing property". The effect is to preserve the power of political authorities to set their own spending priorities, without constraints imposed by the bankruptcy court. As part of fiscal adjustment the court can issue mandamus. This is not direct judicial interference in the political subdivision of the state, but enforcement of the power granted by the state to municipals to levy taxes for debt payment.[74]

In contrast to the narrow judicial role in fiscal adjustment of municipalities, state laws in the United States for distressed municipalities commonly provide for a transfer of control over municipal affairs. This confirms that in the United States non-interference is an artifact of federalism rather than an expression of inherent autonomy of municipalities.[75] The cases of New York City's fiscal crisis and the Ohio Fiscal Watch Program illustrate the state's direction of municipal fiscal adjustment. Court interventions, by contrast, tend to be less intrusive.

In Ohio, the Fiscal Watch Program is implemented by the Office of

Auditor of State. The program has a detailed list of indicators (such as wage arrears, deficits, payment arrears, cash shortages, and so on) to monitor the fiscal health of local governments. The Fiscal Emergency Law has three intervention modalities: fiscal caution, fiscal watch and fiscal emergency.[76] If a local government's fiscal deficit exceeds one-twelfth of its annual revenue, the State Auditor issues a fiscal watch warning. Local authorities then need to limit spending and build reserves. The Auditor of State provides advice, for example, on performance audits, outlining options for budget cuts and operational improvements.

Once a local government is declared in emergency, the state establishes a financial planning and supervisory commission. The municipality needs to submit a detailed fiscal adjustment plan to restore financial health. The commission has the power to review taxation, spending and borrowing policies to ensure consistency with the fiscal adjustment plan, to bring civil actions to enforce the Fiscal Watch Program and to ensure proper accounting and reporting.

Higher levels of government prescribe transparency in reporting and auditing. This is an unsurprising common feature of subnational fiscal adjustment across countries. As a key aim of fiscal adjustment, it helps a subnational government re-access capital markets. Without fiscal transparency, private creditors cannot accurately price credit risk. As part of the administrative intervention for the city of New York, the Office of Special Deputy Comptroller for New York City was created to improve the accounts jointly with the Financial Control Board. The purpose of the Financial Planning and Supervisory Commission in Ohio is to ensure that the accounts, accounting systems and financial procedures and reports comply with the rules established by the Auditor of State. By the same token, fiscal transparency in accounting and reporting is a key element of recent fiscal responsibility legislation in Brazil, Colombia and Peru.[77]

4.4 Debt Restructuring and Discharge

Debt restructuring lies at the heart of any insolvency framework – judicial or administrative. Without an insolvency framework, subnationals and their creditors can only resort to consensual and ad hoc restructuring negotiations. Success in such restructurings is often elusive, especially when debtor–creditor and within–creditor interests diverge. Collective action is a central challenge among creditors. Coordination is harder the larger and the more anonymous the group of lenders. These features are more pronounced for subnational bonds issued to different and numerous lenders. When a voluntary arrangement cannot be reached, the cram-down power given to an independent party becomes critical.[78]

In administrative interventions, the higher level of government often restructures the subnational's debt obligations into longer-term debt instruments. In the case of New York City, the Municipal Assistance Corporation was set up to issue longer-term bonds of the state to repay maturing short-term obligations of the city.[79] In Brazil, the federal government has routinely restructured the subnational debt. However, fiscal austerity or subnational fiscal adjustment needs to accompany debt restructuring, to minimize the moral hazard of debt restructuring. This was precisely what happened to New York City in 1975 and to Brazil in the 1997 debt restructuring agreement between the federal government and states.

While administrative approaches tend to focus on debt restructuring, independent courts are viewed as best equipped to discharge debt. Debt discharge is a major departure from the principle that contracts ought to be fulfilled.[80] Overriding contracts requires strong justification. A mature judicial mechanism is well placed to ensure that discharges are fair and equitable. As a result, discharges are typically limited to judicial mechanisms. In South Africa, for example, the municipality needs to go to the court for a discharge. Administrative procedures, on the other hand, tend to lack the power to discharge debt.

Ex post modification of contracts needs to be tightly circumscribed. If creditors feel treated unfairly, there is a substantial risk that they will stop lending. Perceptions of "equitable" are likely to differ across countries, as distributional judgments are involved. While the procedure could narrowly focus on debtor moral hazard, purely exogenous factors could have caused the subnational's inability to pay. Absent imprudent lending, this potentially still leaves an irreconcilable gap between binding contractual commitments and payment capacity.

Debt restructuring and debt discharge is a complex process. This chapter is interested in two basic questions: whether creditors and the debtor can reach an agreement on debt resolution; and who holds the cram-down power when both sides fail to reach an agreement, or when the agreement is rejected by class of creditors.

In US municipal bankruptcy law, the municipal debtor controls the debt adjustment plan and modifies the terms of existing debt instruments. The critical question is what the debtor can do over the objection of creditors. The standards for confirming a Chapter 9 plan are complex. Nonetheless, Chapter 9 incorporates basic Chapter 11 requirements: at least one impaired class of claims approves the plan; secured creditors to receive at least the value of the property securing the plan; unsecured creditors often lose out.[81]

In private insolvency, objecting unsecured creditors are entitled to be paid in full as long as stockholders receive any value on account of their stock. Subnationals have no stockholders. Their officials need not pay off unsecured creditors to remain in control. Therefore unsecured creditors would look for protection to Section 943 (b) (7) of Chapter 9, which requires the court to decide that the plan is in the "best interests of creditors and is feasible". The court would ensure that bondholders effectively receive what they would have received outside of bankruptcy if they were able to obtain mandamus relief requiring an increase in the taxes.[82]

In Hungary, the Debt Committee is chaired by a court-appointed financial trustee, who is completely independent of the local government under proceeding. The Committee is charged with preparing a reorganization plan and debt settlement proposal.[83] Fiscal and debt restructuring proposals are decided by a majority vote of the Committee and presented to creditors. A debt settlement is reached if at least half of creditors whose claims account for at least two-thirds of total undisputed claims agree to the proposal. Creditors within the same group must be treated equally.[84] The Act also stipulates the priority of asset distributions. If disagreements arise on distribution, the court makes the final decision, which cannot be appealed.[85]

South Africa's legislation stipulates that debt discharge and settlement of claims must be approved by the court. The settlement of claims follows the following order specified by the law: secured creditor provided that the security was given in good faith and at least six months before mandatory intervention by provinces; thereafter preferences provided by the 1936 Insolvency Act; and non-preferential claims be settled in proportion to the amount of different claims.[86]

The rescaling of debt obligations is a major intervention in contract rights. Insolvency law reconciles this clash of creditor rights and inability to pay. It formalizes the relationship between creditors and subnational debtor in financial distress. Insolvency law closes the legal order by curing previous contractual violations through a new legal act.[87] A procedure for subnational insolvency recognizes that resolving financial distress via mechanisms guided by law is to be preferred over muddling through repeated, costly and often unsuccessful negotiations.

5 LESSONS AND CONCLUSIONS

This final section draws out lessons for middle-income countries in Asia, Latin America and Eastern Europe. It highlights policy considerations and trade-offs in designing subnational insolvency procedures.

A good subnational insolvency mechanism encourages voluntary bargaining in the shadow of bankruptcy law, anchors risks and rewards of borrowing ex ante, is tailored to the specific country circumstances and is perceived as balanced ("equitable") by all stakeholders.

Subnational insolvency mechanisms are just one element in the broader subnational borrowing framework.[88] Ex ante borrowing regulation and ex post insolvency mechanisms complement each other. Insolvency mechanisms increase the pain of circumventing ex ante regulation for lenders and the subnational borrower and thereby enhance the effectiveness of preventive rules. Without an ex post insolvency mechanism, ex ante regulation can easily turn into excessive administrative control and game-playing between the central and subnational governments.

Furthermore, subnational insolvency mechanisms are embedded in contract and securities law and complemented by constitutional and administrative law on financial management (Maco, 2000). Improved decentralization frameworks and expanded subnational fiscal autonomy underpin a subnational's fiscal strength. Such strength is fundamental to the subnational's access to capital markets.

The mere existence of subnational insolvency mechanisms shapes incentives ex ante.[89] Aligning incentives of all players and establishing a predicable set of rules for allocating default risk are at the heart of insolvency mechanisms. These incentives encourage lenders and debtors to comply with rules voluntarily, because if they do not, they suffer the consequences. While the full financial implications of default cannot be spelled out ex ante, subnational insolvency procedures go a long way in anchoring restructuring and negotiations. For example, the principle of sharing the pain between lenders and borrowers tends to encourage careful lending decisions and accurate risk pricing. Lenders are aware of the circumstances under which they may have to take losses. This enhanced predictability on returns to capital is likely to lower the cost of lending to creditworthy subnationals.

Insolvency procedures strengthen the hard budget constraint. Pressure for political ad hoc intervention decreases, as restructuring becomes institutionalized. Enhanced credibility for the non-bailout promise better aligns incentives. By standing on their own feet subnationals become miniature sovereign borrowers. They know that over-borrowing particularly for operating deficits implies painful adjustment. Subnational insolvency procedures also serve several macroeconomic goals. First, effective insolvency and creditor rights systems allow better management of financial risk. Minimizing systemic risk in the banking sector enhances financial stability. Second, they ensure efficient access to credit and allocation of resources (World Bank, 2005).

One potential downside of judicial procedures is cost and duration. In the US, some Chapter 9 cases are complex and expensive. The most prominent example is Orange County's bankruptcy. For a small subnational entity the costs of such proceedings could be substantial compared with assets available for distribution to creditors. Furthermore, speed matters in debt renegotiations. Proceedings dragging on for years unnecessarily delay the entity's economic recovery. This concern is more pronounced in underdeveloped judicial systems. Yet collective enforcement via subnational insolvency mechanism, as opposed to individual creditor remedies, builds incentives for parties to reach agreement within a reasonable timeframe (Schwarzc, 2002). Finally, lending to less creditworthy subnationals could decrease. In some countries, this will raise considerable equity concerns over uniform public service provision across the national territory. A more effective policy alternative is to use the intergovernmental grant transfer system instead of capital markets to narrow interregional gaps in public goods provision.

Subnational insolvency procedures become more important as the subnational bond markets deepen. The competition between subnational bank lending and bond financing tends to lower lending costs and extend maturities. However, a large number of bondholders exacerbate the principal-agent problem, requiring an insolvency framework to reduce protracted and costly negotiations between the debtor and numerous creditors. If a country relies largely on relationship-based banking, the need for an insolvency framework is less pressing.

Subnational insolvency procedures also become more important as a country decentralizes expenditure, taxation and borrowing decisions to lower levels of government. The insolvency mechanisms can help neutralize political pressures for overborrowing and bailouts. The lack of a subnational insolvency procedure is a smaller concern where the higher levels of government exercise tight control over subnational borrowing and where there are few signs of over-borrowing.[90] If serious fiscal imbalances at the subnational level persist even with little borrowing, then a reform aligning the transfer system could go a large way toward resolving the underlying fiscal imbalances.

Competing considerations need to be balanced in designing subnational insolvency procedures. First, creditors need to be repaid enough such that the private sector provides future credit on reasonable terms. Second, continued provision of public goods requires that some assets of the subnational entity be exempt from bankruptcy. Third, it is important to resolve the tension with subnational autonomy, and potentially the government's electoral mandate. Fourth, the design needs to be consistent with the broader cultural, economic, legal and social context of the country. Many desirable design features, as apparent from different motivations of present subnational insolvency legislation, are country-specific.

Policy objectives of debt restructuring and the subnationals' circumstances influence design. For example, countries differ considerably in how they balance forgiveness against creditor recovery and the stigma attached to default. Furthermore, the constitutional setup affects (but does not determine) the choice of an administrative, judicial or hybrid approach.[91] In the United States, for example, municipalities possess no constitutional personality. Thus, theoretically, they can be created, destroyed and reorganized by their state.[92] In other countries, municipalities previously enjoyed (federal) constitutional protection. One example is South Africa, where the constitution was amended to permit provincial interventions.

Capacity and entry point matter. The maturity of the legal system influences the "optimal" choice of procedure. Implementation of insolvency procedures – in the corporate and the subnational context – rests on the shoulders of insolvency experts and on institutions (courts) resisting political influence and corruption. In many emerging economies, limited judicial and administrative capacity may be a binding constraint. The first focus should be on developing institutional ingredients and on training bankruptcy professionals. In countries where the judicial system is embryonic, formal procedural guidelines might be a stepping stone to a fully-developed mechanism. This interim solution can be used to build up institutional and professional capacity and restructuring expertise (Gitlin and Watkins, 1999).

Lack of comprehensive and timely information is another major constraint. Fiscal transparency and adequate reporting systems, in the lead up to financial distress, are preconditions for successful insolvency mechanisms. Corporate bankruptcy law relies on full disclosure of assets and liabilities. Similarly, subnational insolvency procedure would require public disclosure of comprehensive financial information, including hidden and contingent liabilities.

A commonly held belief asserts that default happens only where subnational entities and the central government are financially weak. The evidence belies this statement. Subnational financial distress is an increasingly common phenomenon in many middle-income countries. Subnational insolvency mechanisms ought to be on the reform agenda in a wide range of developed and developing countries.

NOTES

* The authors appreciate extensive discussions with Michael De Angelis, whose comments have been incorporated. We thank Matt Glasser on the case of South Africa and Mihaly Kopanyi on the case of Hungary. We also benefited from discussions with

Michel Noel, Christoph Paulus, Adolfo Rouillon and Steven Webb. This paper incorporates feedback from a Bankwide seminar. The findings and conclusions expressed herein are those of the authors. They do not necessarily reflect the views of the World Bank and, its affiliated organizations, or those of the Executive Directors of the World Bank or the governments they represent. The World Bank does not guarantee the accuracy of data included in this work.

1. The term subnational refers to those public entities in the tiers of government lower than the federal or central government. Subnational entities include states/provinces, counties, cities, towns, public utility companies, school districts and other special-purpose government entities that have the capacity to incur debt. The term subnational capital market refers to both the banking system and the bond markets.
2. See Eddy and Richter (2000, pp. 9–10), on international capital financing of subnationals.
3. Subnational bonds issued outside Canada, Europe and the United States were $5.7 billion in 1992, $9.4 billion in 1993, $12 billion in 1994, $22.2 billion in 1995, $12.7 billion in 1996, $4.3 billion in 1997, $4.4 billion in 1998, $1.5 billion in 1999, $6.4 billion in 2000, $3.5 billion in 2001. The 1990s therefore saw huge positive, but also strongly negative growth rates (source: Thompson Financial Securities Data).
4. The sub-sovereign bond market has grown vigorously, until recently, since its re-emergence in 2001 and became the largest sub-sovereign market among emerging economies with US$5.6 billion bonds outstanding as of June 2006 (Noel et al., 2006). As part of the fiscal stimulus package, China plans to issue US$30 billion subnational bonds in 2009 (China Ministry of Finance press conference, 17 March 2009).
5. Based on the findings of the Subnational Development Working Group of the World Bank, of which one of the authors for this chapter (Liu) has been a member.
6. In 1 January 2006, subnational bonds outstanding reached US$2.2559 trillion. This represents close to 10 percent of the US domestic bond market and 26 percent of all US public sector bonds (authors' calculation is based on World Bank, 2006). The figure of US$400 billion issues is from Petersen (2005).
7. For a survey of recent developments in controlling subnational borrowing in several emerging economies, see Liu and Waibel (2005).
8. This chapter uses insolvency and bankruptcy interchangeably. These two terms refer to the financial condition of a particular subnational entity. We add "mechanism" or "procedure" to refer to the legal framework.
9. Maco (2000).
10. Cf. District of Columbia Financial Responsibility and Management Assistance Act (Public Law 104-8), 17 April 1995.
11. For discussion on Japanese local debt, see Schwarcz (2002). Moody's (2002) eight subnational default studies covering France, Italy, Switzerland, the UK, Argentina, Brazil, Mexico and Russia provide quantitative and qualitative evidence of a limited number of documented defaults and numerous cases of non-payment and distressed exchanges. Sars (1999, pp. 1–2) provides evidence on Western Europe ("As illustrated by these cases, local governments sometimes do face financial distress despite the strength and stability of the underlying local government system"). Spiotto (1984) lists 6195 defaults on US municipal bonds from 1839 to 1969.
12. Bailey (1984).
13. The interaction of borrowing constraints and service delivery, though not the focus of this chapter, deserves further study.
14. Many countries lack robust mechanisms to resolve subnational financial distress efficiently and fairly. The UNCITRAL (United Nations Commission on International Trade Law) *Guide on Insolvency* (2004), which lays down recommended principles for corporate insolvency law, does not cover public entities (states and subnationals). The guide refrains from recommending the introduction of a separate procedure for municipalities.
15. Interestingly, Germany, whose subnationals have traditionally relied on bank financing,

is actively exploring a subnational workout procedure because of the difficult financial position of many municipalities. See Paulus (2003), and Wissenschaftlicher Beirat beim Bundesministerium für Finanzen (2005).
16. For example, McConnell and Picker on the United States (1993), Jókay et al. on Hungary (2004) and Glasser on South Africa (2005). Schwarcz (2002) compares the US and Japan.
17. This was the first legislation of its kind in the world, even though other countries have contemplated the introduction of similar mechanisms earlier (for example, Switzerland in the second half of the nineteenth century, see Meili, 1885). In 1934, the US Supreme Court had declared a previous version of this legislation unconstitutional, see *Ashton* v. *Cameron County Water Improvement District* No. 1, 298 U.S. 513.
18. See Wallis (2004).
19. For a more detailed and excellent account on the mandamus and its implications for the motivation for Chapter 9 of the US Bankruptcy Code, see McConnell and Picker (1993).
20. Maco (2000).
21. Chapter 9 of the US Bankruptcy Code applies to municipalities, Chapter 13 applies to private bankruptcy. See McConnell and Picker (1993) for a detailed discussion on the motivation for Chapter 9.
22. See Laughlin (2005). The three states with conditions are Pennsylvania, North Carolina and most prominently, New York.
23. The MAC was created by the State Municipal Assistance Corporation Act and other enabling legislation.
24. The state asserted its power by declaring an emergency in the Financial Emergency Act. The Act created the EFCB and adopted other financial emergency measures to prevent the city from defaulting on its bonds.
25. While the EFCB never explicitly violated these limits, the impacts of its policies did (Bailey, 1984).
26. We benefited from discussion with Michael De Angelis and Matthew Glasser.
27. Ahmad (2002).
28. For example, Butterworth, Noupoort, Ogies, Stilforntein, Tweeling, Viljoenskronn, and so on, Glasser (2005).
29. Based on Glasser (2005) and discussion with Michael De Angelis. Provinces in South Africa do not access capital markets as provinces do not have own-source taxes.
30. South Africa Act No. 34 of 2001 and Act No. 3 2003.
31. This section is largely based on Jokay et al. (2004).
32. For example, Bakonszeg, Nagocs, Batorliget and Paty (see Jokay et al., 2004).
33. Unless otherwise noted, the discussion on Brazil is mainly based on Ter-Minassian (1997) and Dillinger (2002).
34. Only two states (Tocantins and Amapá) did not have any bonded debt, and hence did not participate in the refinancing agreements.
35. For a detailed survey of legislations, see Liu and Waibel (2005).
36. Unless otherwise indicated, this section benefited from discussion with Michael De Angelis.
37. Council of Europe (1996): "The competent authorities should clearly state the consequences in the event of local authority insolvency".
38. The economic upheavals and fiscal pressures of the early 1990s led to widespread deferral and cancellation of capital projects and infrastructure in all Bulgarian cities. Since then, Sofia has managed its budget prudently. As a capital city, however, it has unique advantages. Relatively debt free, the city has successfully entered the international bond market. Sofia issued a 50 million euro bond on 12 May 1999 (Ellis and Ionkova, 2004).
39. Ellis and Ionkova (2004).
40. A narrow view would include only a limited range of public services such as police, drinking water and fire protection. The scope of protected essential services is likely to differ significantly across countries.

41. Variants of such limitations on attachment of subnational assets are found in many countries. An early example is a Swiss court judgment of 15 December 1881. Speaking to Winterthur's financial distress, the court held that taxation power and those buildings serving a public purpose were outside bankruptcy. Fasching (1983, p. 84) described the general principle of law that enforcement of private rights against public bodies is permitted as long as the existence and operation of the public entity is thereby not endangered.
42. For a more detailed discussion, see McConnell and Picker (1993).
43. Chapter 11 of the US Bankruptcy Code.
44. De Angelis (2006).
45. Chapter 9 of the US Bankruptcy Code contains a more appropriate definition of "insolvency" for municipalities, that is, "not paying its debts as they become due unless such debts are the subject of a bona fide dispute".
46. Certain local government powers may be constitutionally protected and hence no interference is possible in insolvency. In the case of South Africa, strong intervention powers with decisions of elected officials granted by Municipal Financial Emergency Act called for a constitutional amendment.
47. See Hillhouse (1936) and De Angelis (2006). The political nature of subnationals adds complexity to defaults. According to Hillhouse (1936), the average local government default is highly complicated, since the subnational entity is a large aggregate of economic and social groups.
48. For a detailed account of state debt crises in the 1840s and resulting regulatory reforms, see Wallis (2004). Also see Scott (1974) for a history of state debt crises and repudiation in the United States. An interesting question is why such repudiation, the most extreme form of violating creditor rights, did not present a greater setback for the development of subnational capital markets. One should be cautious in extrapolating from the US experience. In the typical middle-income country today, repudiation could have longer-term negative consequences for the development of the capital market.
49. The subnational defaults during the Great Depression were exceptional insofar as widespread defaults were associated with an economywide downturn. Subsequently, subnational defaults in the United States have been much less frequent. The hard budget constraint as practiced in the United States should not be misconceived as a complete hands-off approach by the states. As illustrated by the example of New York City, states in the US do help restructure local government debt in exchange for fiscal reforms. Thus the hard budget constraint placed by states on local governments is more accurately described as conditional bailout.
50. See McConnell and Picker (1993).
51. Hungary chose this approach. Cf. Annex to Law XXV (1996).
52. The United States does not have a standard list of essential services. The judge interprets the legal principles and rules accordingly.
53. Jokay et al. (2004). In addition to the deterrence impact of the Act, the deficit grant program handled 700-1000 applications out of 3200 municipalities annually, which also served as a tool for bankruptcy prevention. Local governments must cut back discretionary activities and rationalize their expenditures to qualify for the grant program, ibid.
54. Hillhouse (1936, p. 428)
55. In German corporate bankruptcy, for example, wages, taxes and arrears to suppliers are in the first class, with shareholders in the second. In Japan, it is administrative claim holders, taxes and workers' salary for three months prior to commencement of bankruptcy, other claim holders and finally shareholders. In China the order is, secured debt, bankruptcy expenses, staff wages and insurance, followed by taxes, unsecured debt and shareholders. The priority structure of US corporate bankruptcy places secured creditors first and unsecured creditors second. In the second class, the debt adjustment plan determines the order of repayment. Restructuring practice tends to give high priority to bondholders in the second class. We are grateful to Darshini Manraj from Doing Business, World Bank Group for sharing the information.

56. From January 1972 to June 1984, municipalities only filed 21 petitions under Chapter 9. Between 1938 and 1991, 452 municipal bankruptcy cases were filed; 343 of those were filed before 1952 (Spiotto, 1984; McConnell and Picker, 1993, p. 471).
57. *Entwurf zu einem Bundesgesetz betreffend die Schulbetreibung und den Konkurs gegen Gemeinden* (Meili, 1885, pp. 249–58).
58. Meili (1885).
59. Prior to the Bankruptcy Reform Act of 1994, only general authorization to file for bankruptcy was required. In the past, inference from general statutes was sufficient. After the 1994 amendment, a direct and specific enabling piece of legislation is required.
60. See for example, Burnside (2005) on defining insolvency in general and Ianchovichina et al. (2006) for its application to the subnational context.
61. Chapter 9 of the US Bankruptcy Code, 11 USC 101(32) (C).
62. Law on Municipal Debt Adjustment, Law XXV, 1996, Section 4.
63. South Africa, Municipal Finance and Management Act, 2003, Chapter 13, Section 138 (a), (b), (c), (d), (e), (f), (g), (h), including failure to make payments as and when due (a), defaulting due to financial reasons (b), current expenditure exceeding current revenues plus available surpluses for at least two consecutive years (c), and operating deficit to revenues greater than 5 percent (d).
64. South Africa, Municipal Finance and Management Act, 2003, Chapter 13, Section 140 (1), (2), (3), (4).
65. Any single indicator or a subset of indicators in the first set of trigger suffices.
66. South Africa, Municipal Finance and Management Act, 2003, Chapter 13, Sections 152, 153 and 154.
67. McConnell and Picker (1993).
68. Ibid.
69. United States, Chapter 9 (109 (C) (2).
70. South Africa, Municipal Finance and Management Act, 2003, Chapter 13, Section 151 (a).
71. Law on Municipal Debt Adjustment, Law XXV, 1996. Four years after the Act, neither vendors nor banks petitioned for bankruptcy. According to Jokay et al. (2004), these creditors probably assumed that the local governments had few negotiable assets available and that operational cutbacks could not produce a cash flow sufficient for fully satisfying claims.
72. Schwarcz (2002).
73. The stay on litigation is the most highly developed mechanism to prevent a rush to the courthouse. It is an authorization by the bankruptcy authority, freezing ongoing litigation and prohibiting future payments for some time. A more primitive instrument is the moratorium. The debtor unilaterally ceases to pay mature debt, while acknowledging the validity of the debt obligations. As a unilateral arbitrary act, the moratorium is at odds with a developed legal system. A standstill refers to a unilateral engagement by its creditors not to press their claims while the debt is restructuring, without intention to be legally bound, *given* that the subnational entity has suspended debt service payments.
74. McConnell and Picker (1993).
75. Ibid. Note that in other countries, non-interference could be the direct result of constitutional protection for municipalities' autonomy.
76. Ohio Code on Local Fiscal Emergencies (Title 1, Chapter 111): Financial emergency: (i) more than a 30-day default on a debt obligation, (ii) a failure to pay employees within 30 days, or (iii) a deficit or overdue amounts payable exceeding one-sixth of the previous year's revenue.
77. Brazil (2000), Colombia (2000) and Peru (2003).
78. Under the US Bankruptcy Code, the court has the power to "cram down" an agreement on a dissenting minority. The plan may still be confirmed if creditors in each class receive value under the plan equal to the amount of their claims, or if creditors whose claims are junior in priority receive nothing (Section 1129).
79. To make the MAC bonds more attractive, the state legislature declared the stock

transfer tax and the city sales tax to be state tax, and directed revenues from these be transferred to a fund under the MAC management and applied to the debt service and administration cost (Bailey, 1984).

80. In the United States, the Contracts Clause of the US Constitution (Article I. 10,1) puts the principle of pacta sunt servanda into constitutional form.
81. For more details and case histories, see McConnell and Picker (1993) and Kupetz (1995).
82. Ibid.
83. Law on Municipal Debt Adjustment, Law XXV, 1996, Chapter II, Section 9 (3) stipulates the financial trustee's independence.
84. Law on Municipal Debt Adjustment, Law XXV, 1996, Chapter III, Section 23.
85. Law on Municipal Debt Adjustment, Law XXV, 1996, Chapter IV, Section 31. Assets are distributed to creditors in the following order: (1) regular personnel benefits including severance pay; (2) securitized debt (securitized by mortgage and other lines); (3) due to the central government; (4) social insurance debts, taxes, public contributions as tax; (5) other claims and (6) interest and fees on debt obligations continued during the bankruptcy proceeding.
86. South Africa, Municipal Finance and Management Act, 2003, Chapter 13, Section 155 (4).
87. The US experience suggests that public entities in financial distress will resort to using every possible technicality to challenge the validity of their outstanding obligations in the absence of a bankruptcy framework. Widespread challenges in a default wave of the nineteenth century led to the development of the bond council opinion, which certifies that the obligation is "legal, valid and enforceable".
88. See Ter-Minassian and Craig (1997) for a summary of subnational borrowing control frameworks in over 50 countries, and how these control frameworks reflect "the individual country's history, the balance of power among the different levels of government, macroeconomic and fiscal conditions, and the state of development of financial markets" (p. 169).
89. Even if used only rarely, subnational insolvency mechanisms shape bargaining power in voluntary restructuring negotiations. In the US, for example, the mere presence of Chapter 9 (the shadow of bankruptcy law) prods parties to voluntary agreement.
90. Many continental European countries have elaborate administrative mechanisms for supervising the actions of subnational governments, including their financial management.
91. In countries where reforms are proceeding on multiple fronts, the constitution itself can be subject to change, as illustrated by the constitutional amendments in South Africa to pave the way for establishing an insolvency framework.
92. *Hunter v. City of Pittsburgh*, 207 U.S. 161, 178 (1907) (holding that localities are no more than "convenient agencies for exercising such governmental powers of the State as may be entrusted to them").

REFERENCES

Ahmad, Junaid (2002), "Creating Incentives for Fiscal Discipline in the New South Africa", in Jonathan Rodden, Gunnar Eskeland and Jennie Litvack (eds), *Fiscal Decentralization and the Challenge of Hard Budget Constraints*, Cambridge, MA: MIT Press.

Ashton v. *Cameron County Water Improvement District* No. 1, 298 U.S. 513.

Bailey, Robert W. (1984), *The Crisis Regime: The MAC, the EFCB, and the Political Impact of the New York City Financial Crisis*, Albany: State University of New York Press.

Brazil (1997), Law No. 9496.

Brazil (1999), *Senate Resolution* No. 78.
Brazil (2000), *Fiscal Responsibility Law*.
Brazil (2001), *Senate Resolutions* 41 and 43.
Burnside, Craig (2005), *Fiscal Sustainability in Theory and Practice: A Handbook*, Washington, DC: The World Bank.
Colombia (1997), *Ley 358 de 1997* (30 January) Diario Oficial No. 42.973, 4 February.
Colombia (2000), *Ley 617 de 2000* (6 October) Diario Oficial No. 44.188, 9 October.
Council of Europe (1996), "Recommendation No. R. (96) 3 of the Committee of Ministers to Member States on Local Authorities Budgetary Deficits and Excessive Indebtedness".
De Angelis, Michael (2006), "Municipal Insolvency Policy Notes", Mimeo.
Dillinger, William (2002), *Brazil, Issues in Fiscal Federalism*, Washington, DC: The World Bank.
District of Columbia (1995), *Financial Responsibility and Management Assistance Act* (Public Law 104–8), 17 April.
Eddy, Jane and Monica Richter (2000), "Local Government Ratings in Emerging Markets", *Standard and Poor's CreditWeek Municipal*, 14 February.
Ellis, Peter and Kremena Ionkova (2004), Chapter 27 on Bulgaria in Mila Freire and John Petersen (eds), *Subnational Capital Markets in Developing Countries*, Washington, DC: The World Bank.
Fasching, Hans W. (1983), *Konkurs, Ausgleich und Zwangsvollstreckung bei Gemeinden*, Vienna: Institut für Angewandte Sozial- und Wirtschaftsforschung; Signum.
Gitlin, Richard A. and Brian N. Watkins (1999), "Institutional Alternatives to Insolvency for Developing Countries", *Building Effective Insolvency Systems*, Washington, DC: The World Bank.
Glasser, Matthew (2005), "Legal Framework for Local Government Insolvency", presentation at a World Bank seminar.
Hillhouse, Albert Miller (1936), *Municipal Bonds: A Century of Experience*, New York: Prentice-Hall, Inc.
Hungary (1996), *Law on Municipal Debt Adjustment, Law XXV*.
Ianchovichina, Elena, Lili Liu and Mohan Nagarajan (2006), "Subnational Fiscal Sustainability Analysis: What Can We Learn from Tamil Nadu?", World Bank Policy Research Working Paper, No. 3947.
Jókay, Charles, Gábor Szepesi and György Szmetana (2004), "Municipal Bankruptcy Framework and Debt Management Experiences 1996–2000" in M. Kopanyi, D. Wetzel and S. El Daher (eds), *Intergovernmental Finance in Hungary – A Decade of Experience*, Washington, DC: The World Bank.
Kupetz, D.S. (1995), "Municipal Debt Adjustment Under the Bankruptcy Code", *Urban Lawyer*, **27** (Summer), 531.
Laughlin, Alexander (2005), "Municipal Insolvencies: A Primer on the Treatment of Municipalities under Chapter 9 of the US Bankruptcy Code", *Municipal Finance Journal*, **26** (2), 37–59.
Liu, Lili and Michael Waibel (2005), "Subnational Borrowing Notes on Middle-income Countries", Mimeo: The World Bank.
Liu, Lili and Michael Waibel (2008), "Subnational Borrowing, Insolvency and Regulation", in Anwar Shah (ed.), *Macro Federalism and Local Finance*, Washington, DC: World Bank.

Maco, Paul S. (2000), "Building a Strong Subnational Debt Market – a Regulator's Perspective", Mimeo.
McConnell, Michael and Randal Picker (1993), "When Cities Go Broke: A Conceptual Introduction to Municipal Bankruptcy", *University of Chicago Law Review*, **60** (1), 425–35.
Meili, Friedrich (1885), *Rechtsgutachten und Gesetzesvorschlag betr. die Schulexecution und den Concurs gegen Gemeinden*, Bern: Schmid Franke & Cie.
Moody's (2002), "Non-US Subsovereign Cases of Default", by Valerie Montmaur and Yves Lemay of Moody's and eight individual country studies on Argentina, Brazil, France, Italy, Mexico, Russia, Switzerland and the UK by Moody's staff.
Noel, Michel, Zeynep Kantur, Evgny Krasnov and Sue Rutledge (2006), "Development of Capital Markets and Institutional Investors in Russia: Recent Achievements and Policy Challenges Ahead", World Bank Working Paper, No. 87.
Paulus, Christoph G. (2003), "Überlegungen zur Insolvenzfähigkeit von Gemeinden", *Zeitschrift für das gesamte Insolvenzrecht*, 6, Herne: Verlag für die Rechts- und Anwaltspraxis, pp. 869–72.
Petersen, John (2005), "U.S. Municipal Bond Market: Model or Maverick?", presentation at the World Bank, 3 October .
Peru (2003), *Ley que modifica la Ley No. 27245 de Prudencia y Transparencia Fiscal* (No. 27958), 8 May.
Russia (1998), *Budget Code of the Russian Federation*, Law No. 145-FZ of 31 July.
Sars, Anders (1999), "Local Government in Distress: A European Experience", *Standard and Poor's Ratings Direct*, 28 June.
Schwarcz, S.L. (2002), "Global Decentralization and the Subnational Debt Problem", *Duke Law Journal*, **51** (2002), 1179.
Scott, William Amasa (1974), *The Repudiation of State Debts; A Study in the Financial History of Mississippi, Florida, Alabama, North Carolina, South Carolina, Georgia, Louisiana, Arkansas, Tennessee, Minnesota, Michigan, and Virginia*, New York: AMS Press.
South Africa (2003), *Municipal Financial Management Act*.
Spiotto, James E. (1984), "Municipal Bonds in the 1980s: Validity, Enforcement, Default and Bankruptcy", in American Bar Association, *Municipal Bonds in the 1980s: Validity, Enforceability, Default, and Bankruptcy*.
Ter-Minassian, Teresa (1997), Chapter 18 on Brazil in Teresa Ter-Minassian (ed.), *Fiscal Federalism in Theory and Practice*, Washington, DC: International Monetary Fund.
Ter-Minassian, Teresa and Jon Craig (1997), "Control of Subnational Government Borrowing" in Teresa Ter-Minassian (ed.), *Fiscal Federalism in Theory and Practice*, Washington, DC: International Monetary Fund.
UNCITRAL (2004), *Guide on Insolvency*, http://www.uncitral.org/uncitral/en/uncitral_texts/insolvency/2004Guide.html, accessed 5 April 2009.
United States, *Chapter 9 of the US Bankruptcy Code*.
Wallis, John Joseph (2004), "Constitutions, Corporations, and Corruption: American States and Constitutional Changes, 1842–1852", National Bureau of Economic Research, Working Paper Series, No. 10451.
Webb, Steven (2005), "Fiscal Responsibility Legislation in Latin American Countries", mimeo, The World Bank.

White, Michelle J. (2005), "Bankruptcy Law", in A. Polinsky and S. Shavell (eds), *Handbook of Law and Economics*, Amsterdam: Elsevier.
Wissenschaftlicher Beirat beim Bundesministerium für Finanzen (Scientific Council to the Federal Ministry of Finance in Germany) (2005), *Haushaltskrisen im Bundesstaat* (Budget in the Federal State).
World Bank (2000), *World Development Report: Entering the 21st Century*, New York: Oxford University Press.
World Bank (2005), *Creditor Rights and Insolvency Standard.*
World Bank (2006), *East Asia Financial Sector Flagship Study.*

APPENDIX

Table 13A.1 Main elements of subnational insolvency procedures

	Hungary	South Africa	United States[a]
Insolvency triggers	1. Invoice not disputed or paid within 60 days 2. Not paid a recognized debt within 60 days (Section 4 Law XXV (1996))	1. Serious financial problems or anticipation of such problems 2. Persistent material breach of financial obligations (Chapter 13, Sections 136, 137, 138, 139)	1. Debtor generally not paying due debts 2. Unable to pay debts as they become due
Covered entities	Local governments	Only municipalities, not provinces	Municipalities (all political subdivisions and public agencies of a state) (Section 921)
Eligible filings	Municipality or creditor through court petition	Provincial/ national executive decides based on insolvency triggers Municipality admits to existence of trigger with application for a stay Any creditor can file a claim	Only the municipality itself (no involuntary filings) (Section 921)
Role of courts	Reviews petition, appoints financial trustee, approves reorganization/ liquidation plan; broad role for financial trustee	Limited, elaboration and approval of plan in administrative branch; court approves stay and debt restructuring	Takes key procedural decisions, approves restructuring plan

Table 13A.1 (continued)

	Hungary	South Africa	United States[a]
Stay	No enforcement outside the Act after commencement (Section 11)	Municipality may apply if unable to meet commitments, not automatic (Section 152)	Automatic with bankruptcy petition (Section 362; Section 922)
Obtaining credit	Possible if necessary to conclude a compromise (Section 34)	No specific provision in statute	Possible, if municipality could borrow money outside Chapter 9 (Section 364)
Creditor majority	Two-thirds of amount and one-half of eligible claims	Plan elaborated by Administrator and approved by Municipal Financial Recovery Service, not creditors	Chapter 11 requirements: two-thirds of amount, one-half of eligible claims (Sections 1124, 1126).
Essential services	Annex A: Mandatory Municipal Tasks (27 items)	Suspension of financial obligations only after provision for basic municipal services; term not defined in the legislation (Section 154)	Not defined, courts tend to construe narrowly
Conditionality[b]	Substantial, in the hands of the receiver Approval by representative body generally required	Very strong, including dismissal of non-essential employees and liquidation of assets, determined by intervening authority	Limited, depends on bargaining outcome between creditors and municipality

Table 13A.1 (continued)

	Hungary	South Africa	United States[a]
Priority of claims	1. Wages 2. Secured claims; 3. CG crisis support 4. Social security claims 5. Other claims (Section 31)	1. Secured creditors 2. Unsecured creditors pro rata (Section 155)	1. Administrative claims 2. Secured creditors 3. Unsecured creditors
Subnational autonomy	Crisis budget plan elaborated under supervision of financial trustee, who determines necessary assets	Strong powers of the Administrator, constitution amended to allow such strong intervention	No interference with any political or policy choices (Section 904). Requirement of state consent (Section 903)
Dismissal	1. Filer not eligible 2. Council did not authorize (Section 8)	Not applicable, because within the purview of administration	"Bad faith" of debtor (Section 930): 1. Unreasonable delay prejudicial to creditors 2. Failure to propose plan 3. Plan not accepted/ denied 4. Material default on terms of plan
Experience	19 procedures, 100 out-of-court settlements	None (Chapter 13 entered into force in July 2006)	> 50 filings since 1945, substantial number of settlements and state procedures

Notes:

a. This table covers only Chapter 9 of the US Bankruptcy Code, not fiscal and debt adjustments for local governments by states outside Chapter 9.

b. Adjustment measures that may be prescribed in exchange for a restructuring/debt relief.

Index